Palgrave Studies in Economic History

Series Editor
Kent Deng
London School of Economics
London, UK

Palgrave Studies in Economic History is designed to illuminate and enrich our understanding of economies and economic phenomena of the past. The series covers a vast range of topics including financial history, labour history, development economics, commercialisation, urbanisation, industrialisation, modernisation, globalisation, and changes in world economic orders.

Gijs Dreijer

Private Entrepreneurship and European Imperialism

Dutch Entrepreneurs in the Scramble for Africa, 1830s–1910s

palgrave
macmillan

Gijs Dreijer
Erasmus University Rotterdam
Rotterdam, The Netherlands

ISSN 2662-6497 ISSN 2662-6500 (electronic)
Palgrave Studies in Economic History
ISBN 978-3-032-01085-8 ISBN 978-3-032-01086-5 (eBook)
https://doi.org/10.1007/978-3-032-01086-5

This work was supported by the Dutch Research Council (NWO), project VI.C.191.027 (*Exploiting the Empire of Others*) at Leiden University. NWO also provided an Open Access Grant under nr.36.201.139.

Cover illustration : BTEU / RKM / Alamy Stock Photo. Original from Rijksmuseum Amsterdam, Object number RP-F-F00971-3.

This Palgrave Macmillan imprint is published by the registered company Springer Nature Switzerland AG.
The registered company address is: Gewerbestrasse 11, 6330 Cham, Switzerland

Acknowledgements

This book is the result of a four-year postdoctoral project at Leiden University, The Netherlands, written in the framework of the Dutch NWO-funded project *Exploiting the Empire of Others* (Grant number VI.C.191.027). I am grateful to NWO for funding the project, and in particular to the project PI, Cátia Antunes, for bringing me back to Leiden to engage in this *Habilitation*-style project, which differed quite a lot from my PhD topic. I first met Cátia in the spring of 2011 as a first-year BA student, and have in the fourteen years since profited from her supportive, kind and critical support. I could probably write a chapter on those fourteen years, but here I just like to say: thank you, Cátia, for your support, as an academic but more importantly as a person. The larger project team, which took various shapes throughout the years, I would like to thank for patiently reading and commenting on my drafts in the past four years. Susana, Lewis, Erik, Luc and Noelle, as fellow postdocs inside or outside the project, thank you for the support. Tessa and Ramona, my office mates, for your humour and all the gossip about academic but, above all, non-academic matters. I have learned more about reality TV than I could have ever imagined!

I am grateful for the many people who have given feedback and advice regarding this book. I have thanked some of them in individual footnotes, and would like to thank workshop and conference audiences in Leiden, Rotterdam, Gran Canaria, Gothenburg, Porto, Singapore, York, Busan, Leuven and Boston/Cambridge MA for the thought-provoking questions and suggestions. My BA and MA students in the past four years have sharpened my thinking on Dutch imperialism, and I am grateful to them for teaching me as much as I taught them. Special thanks goes to the informal *Congo Werkgroep* at the Museum Volkenkunde in Leiden (now Wereldmuseum Leiden), who read every chapter: Annette Schmidt, Elsbeth Dekker, François Janse van Rensburg, Karolien Nédée and John Kegel. My fellow Leiden postdoc Márcia Gonçalves, also part of the *Congo Werkgroep*, has probably done more than anyone else in framing and improving this study through her ever-critical feedback, for which I am grateful. In Leiden, I also would like to thank my colleagues in the Economic & Social History department for support.

I was extremely lucky to be able to spend the Fall semester of 2024–2025 as the Alfred D. Chandler Jr. International Visiting Fellow in Business History at Harvard Business School. Not only did the people at the Business History Initiative sharpen my thinking on entrepreneurship and allow to profit from feedback in seminars, the welcoming atmosphere also allowed me to rewrite the sloppy draft chapters into a proper manuscript. Thanks in particular to Walter Friedman, Sophus Reinert, Dave Shorten, Molly Keane, and Marlous van Waijenburg. My fellow early career scholars there, Elise Berggren, Ellen Nye, Yuan Jia-Zhang and Marcel Anduiza, thank you for making the fellowship a rather fun time as well! At Palgrave Macmillan, I would like to thank Ellie Duncan for her excellent editorship and help that was always at hand, and the production team at Palgrave Macmillan for the efficient process.

Besides 'academic' support, I was extremely grateful to work with *Gedeeld Verleden Gezamenlijke Toekomst* (GVGT, 'Shared Past Common Future') in Rotterdam over the past four years, and the people I met there (especially in the *History Matters* team) have taught me about the impact of colonialism in the present day: thank you to all of you, and in particular to Wim Reijnierse. I dedicate the book to our beloved team member Giovanni Burke, who sadly passed away in November 2023, and who inspired the GVGT 'family' with his humour, enthusiasm and ability to connect people between cultures and generations.

Finally, I would like to thank again my family and friends, who have so patiently supported me over the past years and have prevented me from becoming a reclusive hermit. As always, my final and biggest thanks goes to Suzanne, on whose unwavering support I can always count, even if things look difficult or insurmountable.

Gijs Dreijer

The Hague, The Netherlands, April 2025

Competing Interests The author has no competing interests to declare that are relevant to the content of this manuscript.

Contents

1	**Introduction**	**1**
1.1	*Introduction*	1
1.2	*Imperialism and Entrepreneurship in the Empire of Others*	4
1.3	*Setting the Scene: Rotterdam as a Global Colonial Port City*	15
1.4	*Approach: Gentlemanly Capitalism, Entrepreneurship and Business History*	19
1.5	*A Note on Sources*	24
1.6	*Timeframe, Geography and Structure*	27
2	**The Scramble for and Partition of West (Central) Africa**	**31**
2.1	*Introduction*	31
2.2	*The Global Liberal Nineteenth Century, Imperialism and 'Legitimate Commerce'*	34
2.3	*The 'Prelude' to the Scramble: European Economic Interests 1830–1875*	40
2.4	*The Lead-up to the First Partition 1870–1884*	43
2.5	*The Berlin Conference of 1884–1885 and the First Partition*	50
2.6	*The Congo Free State 1885–1908*	61
2.7	*The Scramble for Africa: European Economic Interests 1875–1899*	79
2.8	*The Scramble and Partition Converge (1890–1914)*	85
2.9	*Conclusion*	94

3 Dutch Entrepreneurs in the Early Scramble for Africa (1830s–1870s) 97
3.1 Introduction 97
3.2 Dutch Trade on the Gold Coast (1630s–Early 1860s) 100
3.3 Dutch Dispersion Across the African Continent (1850s–1870s) 109
3.4 Dutch Entrepreneurship in West (Central) Africa 1830s–1870s 143
3.5 Conclusion 149

4 Dutch Entrepreneurs in the Partition of Africa (1880s–1890s) 151
4.1 Introduction 151
4.2 Muller & Co *and the OAC in West Africa* 152
4.3 Rising from the Ashes: The NAHV, 1879–1898 157
4.4 Dutch Entrepreneurship in West (Central) Africa, 1880–1898 180
4.5 Conclusion 187

5 Dutch Entrepreneurship in the Era of the Concession Companies (1899–1921) 191
5.1 Introduction 191
5.2 The OAC in Liberia (1899–1921) 192
5.3 The NAHV in Angola: Minor Activities in Plantation Economy (1899–1910) 194
5.4 The NAHV in the Congo Free State in the Era of Concessionary Companies 197
5.5 The NAHV in the French Congo: Chasing Natural Resources 200
5.6 Dutch Entrepreneurship in West (Central Africa), 1899–1921 215
5.7 Conclusion 223

6 Dutch Entrepreneurs in the *Compagnie du Kasaï*, 1885–1910 227
6.1 Introduction 227
6.2 The Kasaï Region 1885–1900: Entrepreneurs, Missionaries and African Agency 228
6.3 The Compagnie du Kasaï, *1900–1910* 234

6.4 The NAHV and the Ibanche Factory 248
6.5 Dutch Entrepreneurship in the Kasaï 1900–1921 253
6.6 Conclusion 255

7 Conclusion 259
7.1 Conclusion 259

8 Epilogue 271
8.1 Epilogue 271

Bibliography 277

Index 311

List of Images

Image 1.1	Statue of Lodewijk Pincoffs. (Source: Wikifrits via Wikimedia Commons, available at https://commons.wikimedia.org/wiki/File:Rotterdam_kunstwerk_lodewijk_pincoffs.jpg [Retrieved 20/09/2024])	3
Image 2.1	Routes of Henry Morton Stanley's expeditions to Central Africa. (Source: André Engels at Dutch Wikipedia, available at https://commons.wikimedia.org/wiki/File:Stanleyroutes.PNG [Retrieved 04/03/2024])	45
Image 2.2	Cartoon depicting Leopold II and other imperial powers at the 1884–1885 Berlin Conference. (Source: François Maréchal, Public domain, via Wikimedia Commons [Retrieved 18/10/2023])	51
Image 2.3	Cartoon about the Berlin Conference, 1884–1885. (Source: Zz1y, Draner, CC BY-SA 4.0, via Wikimedia Commons [Retrieved 18/10/2023])	52
Image 2.4	Map of the Congo Free State districts, 1888. (Source: Institut Royal Colonial Belge, available at https://commons.wikimedia.org/wiki/File:1888_districts_Congo_Free_State_cropped_from_1950_administration_map_Atlas_General_du_Congo_611.jpg [Retrieved 12/03/2024])	64
Image 2.5	Reception at the Brussels Anti-Slavery Conference 1889–1890. (Source: Revue L'Illustration Européenne N°31–31, Published July 1898, available at https://commons.wikimedia.org/wiki/File:Festival_at_the_Brussels_Stock_Exchange._Ovation_made_to_the_king_	

during_the_delivery_of_the_address_in_favor_of_the_Congo._L%27Illustration_europ%C3%A9enne_N_%C2%B031,_4_May_1890.jpg [Retrieved 12/03/2024]) 67

Image 2.6 Cartoon depicting King Leopold II and the "gate" to the Congo Free State, 1906. (Source: Francis Carruthers Gould. Public domain, available at https://commons.wikimedia.org/wiki/File:Cartoon_by_British_caricaturist_%27Francis_Carruthers_Gould%27_depicting_King_Leopold_2,_and_Congo_Free_State.jpg [Retrieved 13/03/2024]) 72

Image 2.7 Cartoon depicting Leopold II of Belgium surrounded by Congolese skulls, 1904. (Source: Anonymous/Unknown Author, Public domain, available at https://commons.wikimedia.org/wiki/File:Leopold_II_of_Belgium.jpg [Retrieved 13/03/2024]) 73

Image 2.8 Cartoon depicting King Leopold II as a snake attacking a Congolese rubber collector, 1906. (Source: Edward Linley Sambourne. Public domain, available at https://commons.wikimedia.org/wiki/File:Punch_congo_rubber_cartoon.jpg [Retrieved 13/03/2024]) 75

Image 2.9 Cartoon depicting Leopold II laying the first stone of the Basilica of Koekelberg, 1905. (Source: Ashavérus (Didier Dubucq). Public domain, available at https://commons.wikimedia.org/wiki/File:Cartoon_depicting_King_Leopold_2_of_the_Belgians_laying_the_first_stone_of_the_Basilica_of_Koekelberg.jpg [Retrieved 13/03/2024]) 76

Image 2.10 Map of concession companies in the Congo Free State. (Source: Dumelow–Own work by uploader, derivative of public domain, available at https://commons.wikimedia.org/w/index.php?curid=5896964 [Retrieved 03/03/2023]) 90

Image 2.11 Concessions in the French Congo, 1900. (Source: *Bibliothèque Nationale de France*. Public domain, available at https://upload.wikimedia.org/wikipedia/commons/2/23/Congo_fran%C3%A7ais._Carte_documentaire_des_concessions._L._Robelin_del_-_Service_g%C3%A9ographique_de_%22La_Dep%C3%AAche_coloniale%22_-_btv1b532042215.jpg [Retrieved 06/03/2023]) 93

Image 3.1 Portrait of Huibert van Rijckevorsel. (Source: Friedrich Boser (Llowa 1809–Düsseldorf 1881), CC BY-SA 3.0, via Wikimedia Commons, Museum Rotterdam [Retrieved 18/10/2023]) 106

Image 3.2 Photograph of Hendrik Muller Szn. (Source: Unknown photographer in 1862, Public domain, via Wikimedia Commons, Rotterdam Municipal Archives [Retrieved 18/10/2023]) 113

Image 3.3 Photograph of Lodewijk Pincoffs in the 1870s. (Source: Unknown photographer, Public domain, via Wikimedia Commons [Retrieved 18/10/2023]) 120

Image 3.4 Map of the Kingdom of Kongo, late eighteenth century. (Source: Kingdom of Kongo ca. 1711 via Wikimedia Commons, available at https://commons.wikimedia.org/wiki/File:KingdomKongo1711.png [Retrieved 10/10/2024]) 127

Image 3.5 Portrait of Mr Marten Mees. (Source: Maritime Museum Rotterdam, Pascal De Beucker, Public domain, via Wikimedia Commons [Retrieved 18/10/2023]) 138

Image 3.6 Cartoon on Lodewijk Pincoffs' Fraud, 1879. (Source: Rijksmuseum, inv. Nr. RP-P-OB-89.270, available via Wikimedia Commons, https://commons.wikimedia.org/wiki/File:Spotprent_op_de_fraude_van_Lodewijk_Pincoffs_te_Rotterdam,_1879_Vooruit_en_niet_terug_(titel_op_object),_RP-P-OB-89.270.jpg [Retrieved 10/04/2025]) 140

Image 3.7 Cartoon on Lodewijk Pincoffs, 1879. (Source: Rijksmuseum, inv. Nr. RP-P-OB-89.272, available via Wikimedia Commons, https://commons.wikimedia.org/wiki/File:Spotprent_op_Lodewijk_Pincoffs,_1879,_RP-P-OB-89.272.jpg [Retrieved 10/04/2025]) 141

Image 4.1 Proof of dividend of the NAHV, 1880. (Source: Francoisdjvr via Wikimedia Commons, available at https://commons.wikimedia.org/wiki/File:NAHV_Dividend.tif [Retrieved 10/04/2025]) 160

Image 4.2 Stock certificate of the NAHV, 1880. (Source: Francoisdjvr via Wikimedia Commons, available at https://commons.wikimedia.org/wiki/File:NAHV_Stock_Certificate_(front).tif [Retrieved 10/04/2025]) 161

Image 5.1 NAHV factory in Coquilhatville (Mbandaka), Congo Free State, 1910–1925. (Source: Collectie Wereldmuseum, inv. Nr. TM 60032119, available via https://commons.wikimedia.org/wiki/File:COLLECTIE_TROPENMUSEUM_Een_kleine_groep_mannen_gezeten_voor_het_gebouw_van_de_Nieuwe_Afrikaansche_Handels_Vereeniging_TMnr_60032119_(corrected).jpg [Retrieved 10/04/2025]) 198

Image 5.2	Building of the NAHV, 1910–1925. (Source: Collectie Wereldmuseum, inv. Nr. TM 60032123, available via https://commons.wikimedia.org/wiki/File:COLLECTIE_TROPENMUSEUM_Het_gebouw_van_de_Nieuw_Afrikaansche_Handelsvereeniging_TMnr_60032123.jpg [Retrieved 10/04/2025])	202
Image 5.3	Concession companies in the French Congo. (Source: Bibliothèque nationale de France, Public domain, via Wikimedia Commons, Available at https://commons.wikimedia.org/wiki/File:Congo_fran%C3%A7ais._Carte_documentaire_des_concessions._L._Robelin_del_-_Service_g%C3%A9ographique_de_%22La_Dep%C3%AAche_coloniale%22_-_btv1b532042215.jpg [Retrieved 19/11/2024])	204
Image 5.4	Share of the *Compagnie française de l'Ouhamé et de la Nana*, 1900. (Source: https://www.entreprises-coloniales.fr/afrique-equatoriale/Ouhame_et_Nana.pdf [Retrieved 25/04/2023])	208
Image 6.1	The Kasaï River (shown in red). (Source: By Kwamikagami–Own work, CC BY-SA 3.0, https://commons.wikimedia.org/w/index.php?curid=15723776 [Retrieved 04/04/2023])	229
Image 6.2	Kingdoms in the Kasaï area (late nineteenth century). (Source: By Library of Congress–*Zaire: a country study* (1994), Public Domain, https://commons.wikimedia.org/w/index.php?curid=37840534 [Retrieved 06/04/2023])	230
Image 6.3	The Kasaï region (location Ibanche underlined in red). (Source: Land and Peoples of the Kasaï, via Wikimedia Commons, available at https://commons.wikimedia.org/wiki/File:Land_and_peoples_of_the_Kasai;_being_a_narrative_of_a_two_years%27_journey_among_the_cannibals_of_the_equatorial_forest_and_other_savage_tribes_of_the_south-western_Congo_(1911)_(14770273764).jpg [Retrieved 29/10/2024])	249

List of Graphs

Graph 3.1	Rotterdam firms trading in Elmina and Liberia	98
Graph 3.2	Rotterdam firms trading in Congo Basin area	98
Graph 3.3	Rotterdam firms trading in Mozambique	98
Graph 3.4	Profits and Losses of Van Rijckevorsel & Zoonen, 1851–1867, in guilders. (Source: *NL-SAR, Archief Muller, nr. 154*)	111
Graph 3.5	Profits and losses of *Muller & Co*, 1863–1869, in guilders. (Source*: NL-SAR, Archief Muller, nr. 169*)	115
Graph 3.6	Profits and losses on the West Africa trade of *Muller & Co*, 1863–1879, in guilders. (Source: *NL-SAR, Archief Muller, nr. 168*)	116
Graph 3.7	Total imports of palm oil into the Netherlands (1857–1876), in guilders (1858–1859 & 1863–1864 Missing). (Source: *Statistiek van den handel en de scheepvaart (1847–1877)*)	145
Graph 3.8	Palm oil imports from West Africa into the Netherlands (1857–1876), in guilders (1858–1859 and 1863–1864 missing). (Source: *Statistiek van den handel en de scheepvaart (1847–1877)*)	146
Graph 3.9	Dutch-West (Central) Africa trade, imports and exports (1874–1879), in millions of guilders. (Source: Jaarcijfers *van het Koninkrijk der Nederlanden. Rijk in Europa (1882–1884)*)	146
Graph 4.1	Profits and losses on the Guinea Coast trade of Muller & Co, 1879–1891, in guilders. (Source: *NL-SAR, Archief Muller, inv. 41, nr. 168*. Note: *Profits in black, losses in red*)	153

Graph 4.2	Imports and exports from and to West Africa, 1879–1898, in millions of guilders. (Source: *Jaarcijfers van het Koninkrijk der Nederlanden. Rijk in Europa* (1882–1899))	180
Graph 4.3	Major commodities imported from West Africa, 1879–1898, in guilders. (Source: *Statistiek van den handel en de scheepvaart* (1847–1918), later *Statistiek van den in- uit- en doorvoer)*	181
Graph 4.4	Palm oil imports into the Netherlands 1878–1898, in guilders. (Source: *Statistiek van den handel en de scheepvaart* (1847–1918), later *Statistiek van den in- uit- en doorvoer*)	182
Graph 4.5	Peanut imports into the Netherlands 1878–1898, in guilders. (Source: *Statistiek van den handel en de scheepvaart* (1847–1918), later *Statistiek van den in- uit- en doorvoer*)	182
Graph 4.6	Palm nut kernel imports into the Netherlands 1878–1898, in guilders. (Source: *Statistiek van den handel en de scheepvaart* (1847–1918), later *Statistiek van den in- uit- en doorvoer*)	183
Graph 4.7	Exports from the Congo Free State (in fr.), 1888–1897. (Source: Wauters, *L'État Indépendant du Congo*, 484)	184
Graph 5.1	Simplified NAHV investment structure in the French Congo	205
Graph 5.2	Imports and exports from and to West Africa, 1899–1916 (in millions of guilders). (Source: *Jaarcijfers van het Koninkrijk der Nederlanden. Rijk in Europa* (1882–1922))	217
Graph 5.3	Imports and exports to and from West Africa, 1899–1916, 1910 left out (in millions of guilders). (Source: *Jaarcijfers van het Koninkrijk der Nederlanden. Rijk in Europa* (1882–1922))	218
Graph 5.4	Cotton and alcohol exports to West Africa, 1899–1915, in guilders. (Source: *Statistiek van den handel en de scheepvaart* (1847–1918), later *Statistiek van den in- uit- en doorvoer)*	218
Graph 5.5	Imports of four West African commodities, 1898–1921, in thousands of kilos. Source: *Jaarcijfers van het Koninkrijk der Nederlanden. Rijk in Europa* (1882–1922)	218
Graph 5.6	Imports of four West African commodities, 1899–1916, in guilders. (Source: *Statistiek van den handel en de scheepvaart* (1847–1918), later *Statistiek van den in- uit- en doorvoer*)	219
Graph 5.7	Palm oil imports, 1899–1916, in guilders. (Source: *Statistiek van den handel en de scheepvaart* (1847–1918), later *Statistiek van den in- uit- en doorvoer*)	219
Graph 5.8	Peanut imports, 1899–1916, in guilders. (Source: *Statistiek van den handel en de scheepvaart* (1847–1918), later *Statistiek van den in- uit- en doorvoer*)	220
Graph 5.9	Palm nut kernel imports, 1899–1916, in guilders. (Source: *Statistiek van den handel en de scheepvaart* (1847–1918), later *Statistiek van den in- uit- en doorvoer*)	220

List of Tables

Table 2.1	Foreign capital invested in Africa by colonial empire, 1870–1936	81
Table 2.2	British investments in Africa per sector, 1865–1914	83
Table 2.3	Investments in French Equatorial Africa, 1900–1913, in Francs	83
Table 2.4	Total returns per sector on Brussels Stock Exchange, Congo Free State and Belgian Congo, 1890–1914	83
Table 2.5	Twenty-four largest firms in Congo Free State by market capitalisation, 1913, in Francs	84
Table 3.1	Chronology of the Rotterdam-Africa trade	99
Table 3.2	Profits and losses on Guinea Coast Trade of *Van Rijckevorsel & Zoonen*, 1851–1861, in guilders	112
Table 3.3	Losses by the AHV (1869–1879), in guilders	142
Table 3.4	Balance of the AHV on 14 May 1879, according to the AHV Directors, in guilders	142
Table 3.5	Actual balance of the AHV on 14 May 1879, in guilders	143
Table 3.6	Palm oil imports and exports in the Netherlands (1847–1876), ten-year averages, x1000kg; 50 guilders per 100 kg	145
Table 3.7	West African palm oil imports as share of total palm oil imports into the Netherlands, 1857–1879 (1858–1859 & 1863–1864 missing), in guilders	147
Table 4.1	Profits and losses of Muller & Co, 1863–1900	153
Table 4.2	Exports of ivory and rubber from the Congo Free State, 1892–1900	177
Table 4.3	Congo Free State income from ivory and rubber taxation, 1892–1900	178

Table 4.4	Import of gum into Rotterdam, 1889–1894, in kilograms	184
Table 5.1	Import of rubber into Rotterdam, 1910–1913, in kilograms	221
Table 5.2	Imports of rubber into major ports, 1905–1913, in kilograms	222
Table 6.1	Shares in the *Compagnie du Kasaï* (1901)	236
Table 6.2	Gross profit margin and depreciations of the *Compagnie du Kasaï*, 1902–1911 (in fr., rounded)	242

CHAPTER 1

Introduction

1.1 Introduction

In 1872, a rhyme did the rounds in the Dutch city of Rotterdam:

"*Laat de Afrikaansche handel bloeien,*	"Let the African trade prosper
Zij toch, die zooveel schoons bevat,	She, who contains so much beauty,
En 't dividend het aandeel boeien,	And the dividend captivate the share,
Tot sieraad onzer nijvre stad.	To become the jewel of our industrious city.
Guinea's kust door u ontgonnen	Guinea's coast mined by you
Heil u! heeren Pincoffs en Kerdijk,	Hail! Gentlemen Pincoffs and Kerdijk
En 't goud getrokken uit haar bronnen,	And the gold mined from her sources
Opdat de Brit er niet meê strijk!"[1]	Lest the British take the credit"

The rhyme mentions the 'African' trade of two men, Lodewijk Pincoffs and Henry Kerdijk, who had apparently managed to set up a profitable trade on the African continent. This rhyme does not seem remarkable at first sight, but reconsider time and place: the rhyme was written at the very start of what historians call the Scramble for Africa, and it refers to Dutchmen being active (and apparently making significant profits) in the African-European trade. What did a bunch of men from Rotterdam, today

[1] *Middelburgsche Courant*, 28-05-1879. I thank François Janse van Rensburg (Wereldmuseum Leiden) for sending me the document. The rhyme itself dates from 1872; the English translation is mine.

G. Dreijer, *Private Entrepreneurship and European Imperialism*,
Palgrave Studies in Economic History,
https://doi.org/10.1007/978-3-032-01086-5_1

a major port city but around 1850 still a mid-sized town in the Netherlands (at this point not a major colonial actor in Africa), do in West Africa? *Why* were they there? And they even appeared to have been successful: *how*, then, did they do this?

These two questions stand at the core of this book. The book explains and analyses the involvement of Dutch entrepreneurs in the Scramble for Africa (starting in the 1830s, up to the 1910s), demonstrating how entrepreneurs from a state not engaged in claiming territory in Africa managed to exploit, and profit from, Africa's resources. All too often, the Scramble has been seen in terms of great power rivalry (between Britain, France, Germany, Portugal and the Belgian king Leopold II), neglecting the complexities and various actors beyond these states.[2] In reality, the Scramble for Africa was at least as much an act by private actors as by state actors.[3] Building and expanding on such recent insights in the historiography, this book emphasises the crucial yet overlooked role Dutch entrepreneurs played in building, establishing and expanding European empires in West and West Central Africa in the second half of the nineteenth century, while profiting from Africa's resources.

As Image 1.1 shows, Pincoffs (one of the men named in the poem) is for example still honoured for his work to build Rotterdam's port infrastructure by a statue, all but neglecting his involvement in the Congo basin through his firm, the *Afrikaansche Handels-Vereeniging* (AHV). Its successor, the *Nieuwe Afrikaansche Handels-Vennootschap* (NAHV), established in 1879 after Pincoffs was unmasked as a fraudster, became the largest firm operating in the Congo basin in the 1880s and would remain active across Africa until 1982, when it was taken over by a Pakistani investment company.[4] Less visible than the legacies of slavery and Dutch colonialism in, say, Suriname or Indonesia, this long-term involvement of private Dutch actors in the Scramble Africa is an important issue which should be discussed as well when it comes to thinking about the legacies of the Dutch colonial past. While not primarily *responsible*, these

[2] See e.g. popular literature on the Scramble like: T. Pakenham, *The Scramble for Africa* (London 1991). Older literature on the Congo is, for example: R.S. Thomson, *Fondation de L'état indépendant du Congo: un chapitre de l'histoire du partage de l'Afrique* (Brussels 1933). Some more recent literature is aiming to change this; see e.g. S. Press, *Rogue Empires: Contracts and Conmen in Europe's Scramble for Africa* (Cambridge MA 2017).

[3] Press, *Rogue Empires.*

[4] L. Van der Laan, 'Trading in the Congo: The NAHV from 1918 to 1955', *African Economic History*, 12 (1983), 241–259.

Image 1.1 Statue of Lodewijk Pincoffs. (Source: Wikifrits via Wikimedia Commons, available at https://commons.wikimedia.org/wiki/File:Rotterdam_kunstwerk_lodewijk_pincoffs.jpg [Retrieved 20/09/2024])

entrepreneurs were certainly *complicit* in the advent of European nineteenth-century imperialism. This book therefore tries to *deepen* as well as *complicate* our understanding of the Dutch, and broader European, colonial past, by moving beyond a focus on national empires only and shedding light on the role foreigners played in building, expanding and maintaining the 'empire of others'.[5]

[5] See for a similar argument: U. Jun, *Brokers of Empire: Japanese Settler Colonialism in Korea, 1876–1945* (Cambridge MA & London 2011).

The book thus sets two main goals: first, showing how Dutch entrepreneurs played a crucial role in the Scramble for Africa (a process different from the Partition of Africa); and second, demonstrating (what I call) the *colonial complicity* of these Dutch entrepreneurs in European nineteenth-century imperialism. The book therefore shows how business history and colonial history were firmly intertwined in the case of European imperialism in the Scramble for and Partition of Africa.

1.2 Imperialism and Entrepreneurship in the Empire of Others

The Partition of and Scramble for Africa did not occur in a historical or geographical vacuum: it was part of the so-called 'new imperialism' (as to distinguish it from early modern colonialism) that developed from the mid-nineteenth century onwards.[6] This 'new imperialism' is often connected to the process of industrialisation (and/or the Industrial Revolution), as capital accumulated in Europe following the Industrial Revolution sought an outlet in other continents.[7] Most historians of imperialism have taken European imperialism in Africa as one of their

[6] See for a long-term overview of European colonialism and imperialism: W. Reinhard, *Die Unterwerfung der Welt: Globalgeschichte der europäischen Expansion 1415–2015* (Munich 2016); U. Von Hirschhausen & J. Leonhard, *Empires: Eine globale Geschichte 1780–1920* (Munich 2023). The question of colonialism versus imperialism is also a much-considered topic in the literature. See for example: D.K. Fieldhouse, '"Imperialism": An Historiographical Revision', *The Economic History Review*, 14, 2 (1961), 187–209; D.S. Landes, 'Some Thoughts on the Nature of Economic Imperialism', *The Journal of Economic History*, 21, 4 (1961), 496–512; N. Etherington, 'Reconsidering Theories of Imperialism', *History and Theory*, 21, 1 (1982), 1–36; R. Robinson, 'Non-European Foundations of European Imperialism: Sketch for a Theory of Collaboration', in: W.M. Roger Louis (ed.), *Imperialism: The Robinson and Gallagher Controversy* (New York & London 1976), 128–151.

[7] The link between capitalist, financial expansion and territorial expansion has often been made (see also below), starting with John A. Hobson and Vladimir Lenin, among many others. See for example: J.A. Hobson, *Imperialism: A Study* (Cambridge 1902/2010); V.I. Lenin, *Imperialism, the Highest Stage of Capitalism: A Popular Outline* (Moscow 1963); A.M. Eckstein, 'Is There a "Hobson-Lenin Thesis" on Late Nineteenth-Century Colonial Expansion?', *The Economic History Review*, 44, 2 (1991), 297–318; T. Lloyd, 'Africa and Hobson's Imperialism', *Past & Present*, 55 (1972), 130–153. For an argument that declines economic factors were key to imperialism, see: Fieldhouse, *The Theory of Capitalist Imperialism* (Malta 1967); Idem, *Economics and Empire, 1830–1914* (London 1973). Many have taken issue with this idea, see e.g.: K. Rönnbäck & O. Broberg, *Capital and Colonialism: The Return on British Investments in Africa 1869–1969* (Cham 2019).

major case studies, or included Africa as a significant comparative element in their work.[8] In Africa, the period of the Scramble was preceded by the transition from the slave trade to the so-called 'legitimate commerce' during the first half of the nineteenth century, when Africa's economic structures transitioned from being largely based on the slave trade to a more commodity exports-based structure, for example in palm oil.[9] The presence of natural resources and cash crops was one reason for European imperialists to move into Africa and aim to gain control over the production and dispersion of these cash crops.[10]

Compared to the other continents, Europe's imperial conquest of Africa took place in a remarkably short timeframe of some twenty-five years. By 1870, European presence in Africa was largely limited to trade in coastal areas. In some areas, Europeans were better represented than in others, for example in the coastal area of West Africa, where they had long been involved in the slave trade, or in South Africa, where white Afrikaner

[8] See e.g.: H.L. Wesseling, *Verdeel en heers: de deling van Afrika 1880–1914* (Amsterdam 1999); Idem, *Europa's koloniale eeuw: de koloniale rijken in de negentiende eeuw, 1815–1919* (Amsterdam 2003); A. Anghie, *Imperialism, Sovereignty and the Making of International Law* (Cambridge 2004); L.E. Davis & R.A. Huttenback, *Mammon and the Pursuit of Empire: The Political Economy of British Imperialism, 1860–1912* (Cambridge 1986); P.J. Cain & A.G. Hopkins, 'The Political Economy of British Expansion Overseas, 1750–1914', *The Economic History Review*, 33, 4 (1980), 463–490; Idem, 'Gentlemanly Capitalism and British Expansion Overseas II: New Imperialism, 1850–1945', *The Economic History Review*, 40, 1 (1987), 1–26. However, there is also plenty of work on Latin America and Asia. See e.g. D.C.M. Platt, *Finance, Trade, and Politics in British Foreign Policy 1815–1914* (Oxford 1968); Idem, 'Further Objections to an "Imperialism of Free Trade", 1830–60', in: Roger Louis (ed.), *Imperialism*, 153–161. A recent addition to the field is: J. Pateman, 'The Centrality of Africa in Lenin's Theory of Imperialism', *Review of African Political Economy*, 49, 172 (2022), 287–302, https://doi.org/10.1080/03056244.2022.2026765.

[9] This literature has largely focused on West Africa but is taken to exist for other areas in Africa as well. See e.g.: A.E. Dalrymple-Smith, *Commercial Transitions and Abolition in West Africa 1630–1860* (Leiden & Boston 2020); R. Law (ed.), *From Slave Trade to 'Legitimate' Commerce: The Commercial Transition in Nineteenth-Century West Africa* (Cambridge 2009). For a recent book on the subject, see: R. Reid, *The African Revolution: A History of the Long Nineteenth Century* (Princeton NJ 2025).

[10] See for an overview: D. Sassoon, *The Anxious Triumph: A Global History of Capitalism, 1860–1914* (London 2020); E.J. Hobsbawm, *The Age of Empire (1875–1914)* (New York 1989), 35. For the impact in Africa: A. Deaton, 'Commodity Prices and Growth in Africa', *Journal of Economic Perspectives*, 13, 3 (1999), 23–40. For palm oil specifically: M. Lynn, *Commerce and Economic Change in West Africa: The Palm Oil Trade in the Nineteenth Century* (Cambridge 1997).

settlers had lived since the seventeenth century.[11] Only Portugal claimed sovereignty over significant territories in Africa (Angola, Mozambique and São Tomé & Principe).[12] In 1870, only 10% of Africa was claimed by Europeans, and often their sovereignty in practice was partial at best. By 1900, 90% of Africa was under European control: only Ethiopia (before the Second World War, eventually shortly under Italian colonial rule) and Liberia, a newish independent Republic formed by formerly enslaved Americans, were not under (formal) European rule.[13]

Whilst most historians would agree that there is something that we should call imperialism, several questions remain highly debated in the literature; for example, did it (and if yes, how) differ from the colonialism of the early modern period?[14] And did imperialism happen in similar ways on different continents? For a long time, however, the major question

[11] J.D. Hargreaves, *Prelude to the Partition of West Africa* (London 1963); R.T. Anstey, 'British Trade and Policy in West Africa between 1816 and the Early 1880s', *Transactions of the Historical Society of Ghana*, 3, 1 (1957), 47–71; Lynn, 'Change and Continuity in the British Palm Oil Trade with West Africa, 1830–55', *The Journal of African History*, 22, 3 (1981), 331–348; X. Damaulin, 'Commercial Presence, Colonial Penetration: Marseille Traders in West Africa in the Nineteenth Century', in: O. Pétré-Grenouilleau (ed.), *From Slave Trade to Empire: Europe and the Colonization of Black Africa 1750s-1880s* (London 2004), 209–230; Dalrymple-Smith, *Commercial Transitions*; Hopkins, *An Economic History of West Africa* (London 1973). For South Africa: E. Green, *Creating the Cape Colony: The Political Economy of Settler Colonization* (London 2022).

[12] For the Portuguese in Africa, see: R.J. Hammond, *Portugal and Africa 1815–1910: A Study in Uneconomic Imperialism* (Stanford CA 1966); M. Newitt, *Portugal in Africa: The Last Hundred Years* (London 1981); L. Da Veiga Pinto, *Le Portugal et le Congo au XIXe siècle: étude d'histoire des relations internationals* (Paris 1972); W.G. Clarence-Smith, 'The Portuguese and Spanish Roles in the Scramble for Africa: An Economic Explanation', in: S. Förster, W.J. Mommsen & R. Robinson (eds.), *Bismarck, Europe and Africa: The Berlin Africa Conference 1884–1885 and the Onset of Partition* (Oxford 1988), 215–227; Idem, *The Third Portuguese Empire 1825–1975: A Study in Economic Imperialism* (Manchester 1985); D.L. Wheeler, 'Portuguese Expansion in Angola since 1836: A Re-Examination', *The Central Africa Historical Association Local Series*, 20 (1967); G.R. Pirio, 'Commerce, Industry and Empire: The Making of Modern Portuguese Colonialism in Angola and Mozambique, 1890–1914', Unpublished PhD Dissertation University of California Los Angeles (Los Angeles CA 1982) [Retrieved 14/09/2021]; K. Alexopoulou, 'An Anatomy of Colonial States and Fiscal Regimes in Portuguese Africa: Long-Term Transformations in Angola and Mozambique, 1850s-1970s', Unpublished PhD Dissertation Wageningen University (Wageningen 2018).

[13] Pakenham, *The Scramble for Africa*, xv & 670.

[14] F. Cooper, *Colonialism in Question: Theory, Knowledge, History* (Berkeley CA 2005); see also L. Gardner & T. Roy, *The Economic History of Colonialism* (Bristol 2020), 1–42.

occupying historians concerned the forces that drove Europeans to enter into a renewed period of expansion outside their home continent in the nineteenth century. Was it fundamentally a process of economic expansion by capitalists seeking an outlet for capital, as for example John A. Hobson and Vladimir Lenin, as well as various other writers of a Marxist bend, have argued?[15] Or was it, as John Gallagher and John Robinson famously posited in their study on the British expansion during the Victorian period, more a strategic-political motive that drove the British political establishment to take formal control of Egypt and other parts of Africa to pre-empt French expansion?[16]

In essence, many theories of imperialism can be divided roughly into two major strands emphasising different motives for European imperial expansion: one focuses on economic factors, the other strand places the rationale primarily with (geo-)political factors. Within these two major strands, further 'schools' can be identified: within the economic factors strand, for example, there are Marxists (like Lenin, Rosa Luxemburg and others[17]) as well more liberal-oriented scholars who agree on the fact that economics trumped political concerns[18], but agree on little else in terms of the origins, goals and consequences of the economic factors. Within the 'political' school, the theorist of imperialism David Fieldhouse

[15] Hobson, *Imperialism*; Lenin, *Imperialism*. See also W. Rodney, *How Europe Underdeveloped Africa* (London 1972/2011).

[16] J. Gallagher & Robinson, 'The Imperialism of Free Trade', *The Economic History Review*, 6, 1 (1953), 1–15; Idem, *Africa and the Victorians: The Official Mind of Imperialism* (London 1961/1981). See also for debate about the Gallagher-Robinson thesis: Roger Louis (ed.), *Imperialism*.

[17] See for an overview: Fieldhouse, *The Theory of Capitalist Imperialism* (Malta 1967).

[18] See e.g. Hobson, *Imperialism*; Cain & Hopkins, 'Gentlemanly Capitalism'; Cain, *Economic Foundations of British Overseas Expansion 1815–1914* (London & Basingstoke 1980); Hopkins, 'Economic Imperialism in West Africa: Lagos, 1880–92', *The Economic History Review*, 21, 3 (1968), 580–606; Landes, 'Some Thoughts'; E. Reynolds, 'Economic Imperialism: The Case of the Gold Coast', *The Journal of Economic History*, 35, 1 (1975), 94–116; E. Stokes, 'Late Nineteenth-Century Colonial Expansion and the Attack on the Theory of Economic Imperialism: A Case of Mistaken Identity?', *The Historical Journal*, 12, 2 (1969), 285–301. For economic imperialism in the Portuguese case, see: Clarence-Smith, 'The Myth of Uneconomic Imperialism: The Portuguese in Angola, 1836–1926', *Journal of Southern African Studies*, 5, 2 (1979), 165–180; Platt, 'Introduction', in: Platt (ed.), *Business Imperialism 1840–1930: An Inquiry Based on British Experience in Latin America* (Oxford 1977), 1–14.

distinguished between three schools[19]: first, the 'high politics' explanation focusing on political competition in Europe itself between the Great Powers to explain imperial rivalry and expansion[20]; second, the 'imperialism of the masses' (or 'white men's burden') explanation, which focuses on the abolition of slavery and other moral concerns for imperial expansion[21]; and finally the non-Eurocentric explanations that bring internal political factors in Africa to the forefront as the main explanation for European expansion.[22] What united all theories is that they largely focused on the British case, thereby neglecting how imperialism from other European nations developed.[23]

Following increasing scholarly and societal debates over the legacies of the (Western) colonial past, scholars have increasingly developed new approaches and methodologies to look at the Western imperial past, also beyond the British case. In particular, the so-called 'New Imperial History' (NIH) has in this regard taken off among scholars of imperialism.[24] The NIH by and large followed the larger development of global history and

[19] Fieldhouse, *Economics and Empire*, 1–87. See also: S. Howe, 'David Fieldhouse and "Imperialism": Some Historiographical Revisions', *The Journal of Imperial and Commonwealth History*, 26, 2 (1998), 213–232, https://doi.org/10.1080/03086539808583033.

[20] Ibidem, 63–68; see e.g. H. Asby Turner jr., 'Bismarck's Imperialist Venture: Anti-British in Origin?', in: P. Gifford & Roger Louis (eds.), *Britain and Germany in Africa: Imperial Rivalry and Colonial Rule* (New Haven & London 1967), 47–82.

[21] Ibidem, 69–76.

[22] E.g. Gallagher & Robinson, *Africa and the Victorians*; Idem, 'The Partition of Africa', in: Roger Louis (ed.), *Imperialism*, 73–127; Robinson, 'Non-European Foundations of European Imperialism: Sketch for a Theory of Collaboration', in: Roger Louis (ed.), *Imperialism*, 128–151. For a recent intervention: Reid, *The African Revolution*.

[23] As Henk Wesseling remarked, British historians have a habit of writing about British imperialism only when they use the broader term 'imperialism'. See: Wesseling, 'The Giant that was a Dwarf, or the Strange History of Dutch Imperialism', *Journal of Imperial and Commonwealth History*, 16, 3 (1988), 58–70, there 58, https://doi.org/10.1080/03086538808582768.

[24] See e.g. Howe, 'Introduction: New Imperial Histories' in: Howe (ed.), *The New Imperial Histories Reader* (London & New York 2010), 1–20; Von Hirschhausen, 'Diskussionsforum: A New Imperial History?', *Geschichte und Gesellschaft*, 41 (2015), 718–757; B.C. Schär, 'Switzerland, Borneo and the Dutch Indies: Towards a New Imperial History of Europe, c. 1770–1850', *Past and Present*, Advance Articles, https://doi.org/10.1093/pastj/gtab045. For the Dutch case: R. Raben, 'A New Dutch Imperial History? Perambulations in a Prospective Field', *BMGN – Low Countries Historical Review*, 128, 1 (2013), 5–30. For an example in the Portuguese case, see: M. Bandeira Jerónimo, *The 'Civilising Mission' of Portuguese Colonialism, 1870–1930* (Basingstoke 2015).

emphasises connections, cooperation and competition between peoples, institutions and ideas across and between empires, rather than to focus on individual empires.[25] In short, while the twentieth-century debate largely focused on comparisons between (primarily) British, French and German imperial state expansion, historians have in the past decades sought to bring different perspectives and approaches to the study of imperialism, moving beyond historiographical and methodological boundaries. Often presented as new in the context of the modern (i.e. post-1800) period, this approach essentially follows what many early modern historians started doing in the 1990s already.[26]

[25] See e.g. S.J. Potter & J. Saha, 'Global History, Imperial History and Connected Histories of Empire', *Journal of Colonialism and Colonial History*, 16, 1 (2015), https://doi.org/10.1353/cch.2015.0009; D. Hedinger & N. Heé, 'Transimperial History – Connectivity, Cooperation and Competition', *Journal of Modern European History*, 16, 4 (2018), 429–452; J. Adelman, 'Mimesis and Rivalry: European Empires and Global Regimes', *Journal of Global History*, 10, 1 (2015), 77–98, https://doi.org/10.1017/S1740022814000291; U. Lindner, 'Colonialism as a European Project in Africa before 1914? British and German Concepts of Colonial Rule in Sub-Saharan Africa', *Comparativ*, 19, 1 (2009), 88–106; Idem, *Koloniale Begegnungen: Deutschland und Grossbritannien als Imperialmächte in Afrika 1880–1914* (Frankfürt am Main & New York 2011); V. Barth & R. Cvetkovski, 'Introduction – Encounter of Empires: Methodological Approaches', in: Barth & Cvetkovski (eds.), *Imperial Co-Operation and Transfer, 1870–1930: Empires and Encounters* (London & New York 2015), 3–34. For the Nordic Empires, see J.L. Hennessey & J. Lahti, 'Nordics in Motion: Transimperial Mobilities and Global Experiences of Nordic Colonialism', *The Journal of Imperial and Commonwealth History*, 51, 3 (2023), 409–240, https://doi.org/10.1080/03086534.2023.2205699. However, Hopkins already pointed towards a similar idea in 1999: Hopkins, 'Back to the Future: From National History to Imperial History', *Past & Present*, 164, 3 (1999), 198–243. See also for more general evidence of this trend: J. Burbank & Cooper, *Empires in World History: Power and the Politics of Difference* (Princeton NJ 2010), 305–306; Cooper, *Colonialism in Question*, 177–183; C.A. Bayly, *The Birth of the Modern World 1780–1914: Global Connections and Comparisons* (Malden MA, Oxford & Victoria 2004); J. Osterhammel, *The Transformation of the World: A Global History of the Nineteenth Century* (Princeton NJ & Oxford 2009); J. Darwin, *After Tamerlane: The Global History of Empire* (London 2007); Press, *Rogue Empires*; A. Porter, *Religion versus Empire? British Protestant Missionaries and Overseas Expansion, 1700–1914* (Manchester 2004).

[26] See for examples of the trend in modern history C.A. Bayly, *The Birth of the Modern World 1780–1914: Global Connections and Comparisons* (Malden MA, Oxford & Victoria 2004); J. Belich, *Replenishing the Earth: The Settler Revolution and the Rise of the Anglo-World, 1783–1939* (Oxford 2009); A. Phillips & J.C. Sharman, *Outsourcing Empire: How Company-States made the Modern World* (Princeton NJ & Oxford 2020); J. Osterhammel, *The Transformation of the World: A Global History of the Nineteenth Century* (Princeton NJ & Oxford 2009). See for an example from the early modern period: Z. Qian, 'The Rise of

For some of its shortfalls, the NIH approach, in the context of this book, brings four main advantages: first, it moves away from an exclusively state-centred view on the Scramble for Africa, also pointing out the role that other (private) actors played in the process;[27] second, it acknowledges the fact that besides the Great Powers such as Britain and France, there were many Europeans trying to grab a slice of the pie in the Scramble;[28] third, it allows to connect micro-perspectives with macro-economic and geopolitical perspectives, which gives us a fuller picture of how the Scramble worked out on the ground; and fourth, acknowledging that imperialism was a process of connections, cooperation and competition also allows us to move beyond binary questions whether something like a 'Dutch' imperialism existed. This was a much-debated issue in the 1980s and 1990s, looking at the nature of Dutch imperialism in the Dutch East Indies.[29] NIH approaches, however, allow us to look beyond this state-

the Shanxi Merchants: Empire, Institutions, and Social Change in Qing China, 1688–1850', Unpublished PhD Dissertation Stanford University (Stanford CA 2017), available at https://purl.stanford.edu/bg803zm7823 [Retrieved 23/09/2024]. See also for an acknowledgement of the 'debt' to the early modernists: M. Von Brescius, 'Empires of Opportunity: German Naturalists in British India and the Frictions of Transnational Science', *Modern Asian Studies*, 55: 6 (2021) 1926–1971, https://doi.org/10.1017/S0026749X19000428.

[27] For a state-centred view, see: Pakenham, *The Scramble for Africa*.

[28] See e.g. Press, *Rogue Empires*.

[29] An overview in: M. Kuitenbrouwer, 'Het imperialisme-debat in de Nederlandse geschiedschrijving', *BMGN-Low Countries Historical Review*, 113, 1 (1998), 56–73. More in: Idem, *Nederland en de opkomst van het moderne imperialisme: koloniën en buitenlandse politiek 1870–1902* (Amsterdam & Dieren 1985); Wesseling, 'Nederland en de Conferentie van Berlijn, 1884–1885', *Tijdschrift voor Geschiedenis*, 93 (1980), 559–576; Idem, 'The Netherlands and the Partition of Africa', *The Journal of African History*, 22, 4 (1981), 495–509; Idem, 'The Giant that was a Dwarf'; Idem, 'Nederland als koloniaal model', in: Idem, *Indië verloren, rampspoed geboren: En andere opstellen over de geschiedenis van de Europese expansie* (Amsterdam 1988), 140–176; Idem, 'Bestond er een Nederlands imperialisme?', in: Idem, *Indië verloren*, 177–194; J. Van Goor, 'Imperialisme in de marge?', in: Idem (ed.), *Imperialisme in de marge: De afronding van Nederlands-Indië* (Utrecht 1986), 9–18; J.T. Lindblad, 'Economic Aspects of the Dutch Expansion in Indonesia, 1870–1914', *Modern Asian Studies*, 23, 1 (1989), 1–24; E.B. Locher-Scholten, 'Dutch Expansion in the Indonesian Archipelago around 1900 and the Imperialism Debate', *Journal of Southeast Asian Studies*, 25, 1 (1994), 91–111; Idem, *Sumatraans Sultanaat en koloniale staat: de relatie Djambi-Batavia (1830–1907) en het Nederlands imperialisme* (Leiden 1994); J. À Campo, 'Orde, rust en welvaart. Over de Nederlandse expansie in de Indische archipel omstreeks 1900', *Acta Politica: Tijdschrift voor Politicologie*, 15, 2 (1980), 145–189. More general takes in: Raben, 'A New Dutch Imperial History?'; U. Bosma, 'The Economic Historiography of the Dutch Empire', *Tijdschrift voor Sociale en Economische Geschiedenis – Low Countries Journal of Social and Economic History*, 11, 2 (2014), 153–174.

based idea of imperialism and the idea that the Dutch colonial world was a singular and almost closed-off entity. Indeed, studying imperialism from a nominally 'Dutch' perspective also needs to take stock of participation in other imperial entities.

This is where the present study of Dutch entrepreneurial involvement in the Scramble for Africa comes in, adding crucial new knowledge about this part of Dutch imperial history. While groundbreaking in its approach and knowledge added, it would be unfair to say that the subject has been totally neglected in the Dutch and international historiography.[30] Various biographies of some of the entrepreneurs, like Pincoffs and Hendrik Muller Szn., have been written;[31] articles about aspects of the firms operating in Africa have been published, particularly in the late 1970s and early 1980s;[32] and in recent books about Rotterdam's colonial past, decent attention was paid to their role in Rotterdam's colonial ties.[33] Yet overall, it would also

[30] See for Pincoffs & Kerdijk and the AHV: K. Franssens, 'De vestiging van 'Kerdijk en Pincoffs' te Banana, 1857–1859', *Mededelingen der zittingen van de Koninklijke Akademie voor Overzeese Wetenschappen*, 22 (1976), 683–697; B. Oosterwijk, *Ik verlang geen dank: Lodewijk Pincoffs (1827–1911)* (Rotterdam 2011); H. Muller, *Muller: een Rotterdams zeehandelaar Hendrik Muller Szn (1819–1898)* (Schiedam 1977). For the NAHV: H. Obdeijn, 'The New Africa Trading Company and the Struggle for Import Duties in the Congo Free State, 1886–1894', *African Economic History*, 12 (1983), 195–212; Van der Laan, 'Trading in the Congo'; Idem, 'Selling Tropical Africa's Export Crops: The Experience of the Inter-War Period', in: C. Dewey (ed.), *The State and the Market: Studies in the Economic and Social History of the Third World* (New Delhi 1987), 238–261; F. Bontinck, 'Les archives de la Nieuwe Afrikaansche Handelsvennootschap conservees a Schaarsbergen (Pays-Bas)', *Bulletin des Seances de I'Academie Royale des Sciences d-Outre-Mer* (1970), 178–194. For the OAC: G. Van den Berg, 'Hendrik Pieter Nicolaas Muller en de Oost-Afrikaansche Compagnie', Unpublished MA Thesis VU Amsterdam (Amsterdam 1986); Muller, *Muller*; D. Van der Meulen, *Dr. Hendrik Muller: wereldreiziger voor het vaderland (1859–1941)* (Amsterdam 2020), 59–77 & 103–123. In general on the Dutch in West Africa in the nineteenth century: R. Baesjou & P.C. Emmer, 'The Dutch in West Africa: Shipping, Factories and Colonisation, 1800–1870', in: J. Everaert & J. Parmentier (eds.), *International Conference on Shipping, Factories and Colonization (Brussels, 24–26 November 1994)* (Brussels 1996), 191–213.

[31] Oosterwijk, *Ik verlang geen dank*; Muller, *Muller*.

[32] See e.g. Franssens, 'De vestiging'; Obdeijn, 'The New Africa Trading Company'; Van der Laan, 'Trading in the Congo'; Wesseling, 'Nederland en de Conferentie van Berlijn'.

[33] G.J. De Kok, 'De koloniale connectie: geschiedenis van de Rotterdamse koloniale scheepvaart en handel', in: G. Oostindie (ed.), *Het koloniale verleden van Rotterdam* (Amsterdam 2020), 35–89, there 60–68 & 70–73; Idem, 'De koloniale impact: industrie en financiële dienstverlening', in: Oostindie (ed.), *Het koloniale verleden van Rotterdam*, 91–143; H.J. Den Heijer, 'Rotterdamse ondernemers en bestuurders: een koloniale kruisbestuiving', in: Oostindie (ed.), *Het koloniale verleden van Rotterdam*, 145–193.

be fair to say that the Dutch involvement in the Scramble has largely been dealt with either as an exception that confirms the rules of Dutch imperialism, or looks only at a specific person, element or event. An analysis spanning the period between the 1830s (the 'start' of Dutch involvement in Africa) and the start of the First World War is thus still lacking, a major gap that needs to be addressed.

Four historiographical strands have indeed taken note of the Dutch entrepreneurial involvement across Africa, with each nevertheless suffering from its own problems. First, the aforementioned historiography on Dutch imperialism has for example largely focused on the Dutch East Indies. When attention was paid to Africa, it was about the Dutch presence on the Gold Coast up to 1872, the Dutch role at the Berlin Conference, or the so-called *stamverwantschap* (kinship) between the Dutch and the Afrikaners that rose to prominence again in the late nineteenth century.[34] Second, the historiography on Rotterdam's rise as a port city has either focused on the role the entrepreneurs played in Rotterdam itself, largely neglecting the on-the-ground dynamics in Africa, as well as the specific 'African' contribution to Rotterdam's rise as a global port city.[35] Third, the historiography on colonial empires (in Africa) by and large neglects the role that the Dutch entrepreneurs played.[36] In the case of the Congo Free State and the Belgian Congo, for example, Frans Buelens effectively denied that foreign entrepreneurs in the Congo Free State played much of a role.[37] Most of the literature on 'Belgian'

[34] Wesseling, 'Nederland en de Conferentie van Berlijn'; Kuitenbrouwer, *Nederland en de opkomst*, 205–206; Baesjou & Emmer, 'The Dutch in West Africa', for example limit their analysis to the pre-1870 period and to West Africa. For South Africa: See e.g. P.J. van Winter, *Onder Krugers Hollanders* (2 Vols.) (Amsterdam 1937–1938); Kuitenbrouwer, *Nederland en de opkomst*, 118–121, 173–175 & 189–190; See for a recent analysis: A. Burnett, *The Dutch Rediscover the Dutch-Africans (1847–1900)* (Leiden & Boston 2022).

[35] Oosterwijk, *Ik verlang geen dank*; Muller, *Muller*; P.T. Van de Laar, *Stad van formaat: geschiedenis van Rotterdam in de negentiende en twintigste eeuw* (Zwolle 2000).

[36] Recent overviews on new work in African economic history: T. Green, 'Africa and Capitalism: Repairing a History of Omission', *Capitalism: A Journal of History and Economics*, 3, 2 (2022), 301–332, https://doi.org/10.1353/cap.2022.0012; K. Frederick, D. Juif & F. Meier zu Selhausen, 'The Revival of African Economic History in the 21st Century: A Bibliometric Analysis', *Revista de Historia Industrial-Industrial History Review*, 33, 92 (2024), 11–48, https://doi.org/10.1344/rhiihr.47560; Hopkins, 'Fifty Years of African Economic History', *Economic History of Developing Regions*, 34, 1 (2019), 1–15.

[37] "De buitenlandse activiteiten in het land waren gering en beperkten zich hoofdzakelijk tot handelsactiviteiten aan de Atlantische oceaan": F. Buelens, *Congo 1885–1960: een financieel-economische geschiedenis* (Berchem 2007), 103.

imperialism in Africa implicitly endorses this view, instead privileging Belgian and to a lesser extent British investments in the region, with some notable exceptions.[38] In contrast, this book argues that the Dutch entrepreneurs were crucial in *establishing* and *expanding* European empires in Africa at its creation, as well as *sustaining* them during the 1890s and early 1900s, for example through their capitalisation of concession companies.[39] Fourth, contributions in business history have analysed some interesting aspects of Dutch entrepreneurship across Africa, but has offered no convincing explanation for the entrepreneurial *motives* and *actions*.[40]

As a result, we are still lacking a history that simultaneously analyses A) Dutch involvement in Africa for the period 1830s–1910s, B) historical Dutch entrepreneurship across Africa, C) the impact on the ground in Africa and D) the impact back in Rotterdam. This book aims to change this. In a nutshell, the book contributes two major arguments. First and foremost, it argues for the historiographical distinction between the *Partition* and *Scramble*, adding a new perspective to the voluminous literature on the topic. Second, it contributes to the literature on trans- and inter-imperial connections by examining the economic participation of Dutch entrepreneurs in other colonial empires, thereby both contributing to 'denationalising' imperial history and to laying out a new research agenda for how private actors participated in the 'empire of others'.[41]

[38] J. Marchal, *L'État Libre du Congo: paradis perdu: L'Histoire du Congo 1876–1900* (2 Vols.) (Borgloon 1996); B. De Roo, 'The Trouble with Tariffs. Customs Policies and the Shaky Balance between Colonial and Private Interests in the Congo (1886–1914)', *TSEG-Low Countries Journal of Social and Economic History*, 12, 3 (2015), 1–21, https://doi.org/10.5117/TSEG2015.3.DERO; C. Coquery-Vidrovitch, *Le Congo au temps des grandes compagnies concessionnaires 1898–1930* (Paris & The Hague 1972).

[39] See e.g. G.P. Dreijer, 'Exploiting Belgian Imperial Expansion? Dutch Entrepreneurs in the Congo Free State and the Belgian Congo, 1875–1908', forthcoming in *Bijdragen en Mededelingen betreffende de Geschiedenis der Nederlanden/Low Countries Historical Review* (hereafter BMGN-LCHR).

[40] Obdeijn, 'The New Africa Trading Company'; Van der Laan, 'Trading in the Congo'. See for the Dutch role in South Africa: G. Verhoef, 'Entrepreneurs in Africa—The Agenda for Business History in Africa: Complexity and Continuity', *Zeitschrift für Unternehmensgeschichte*, 69, 2 (2024), 187–211, https://doi.org/10.1515/zug-2023-0033.

[41] C.A.P. Antunes, S. Münch Miranda & J.P. Salvado, 'The Resources of Others: Dutch Exploitation of European Expansion and Empires, 1570–1800', *Tijdschrift voor Geschiedenis*, 131, 3 (2018), 501–522, https://doi.org/10.5117/TVGESCH2018.3.006.ANTU.

Next to these major contributions, the book adds crucial new knowledge in several domains. First, it does so on Rotterdam's colonial past, showing how the participation in West (Central) Africa contributed substantially to Rotterdam's rise as a global port city[42]; second and related, the book offers quantitative data on Dutch-African shipping and Dutch-African trade as supportive evidence for the first claim[43]; third, the book contributes to the literature on imperial business history and the relationship between colonial governments in firms, showing how the relationship between foreign firms and colonial governments developed in imperial Africa[44]; fourth, the book contributes to studies of the rise of 'multinational' enterprise, commonly studied in the context of nineteenth- and twentieth-century British or American expansion outside of their home markets, from the Dutch perspective[45]; and fifth, the book contributes to answering a recent call by Tony Hopkins to rediscover the importance of entrepreneurship and business history more broadly in African economic history.[46]

[42] Some hints in: De Kok, 'De koloniale connectie', 60–73; Idem, 'De koloniale impact', 118–125 & 131–133; also Van de Laar, *Stad van formaat*, 13–45.

[43] These data are available Open Access and therefore fully replicable, through the Dutch DANS Service (*Data Archiving and Network Services*). The shipping data are available: Dreijer, 'Dataset on Dutch-African Shipping (1830–1918)', DANS *(Data Archiving and Networked Services) Data Station Social Sciences and Humanities*, available at https://doi.org/10.17026/SS/JFI20J. The trade data are available at Dreijer, 'Dataset on Dutch-African Trade (1847–1918)', DANS *(Data Archiving and Networked Services) Data Station Social Sciences and Humanities*, available at https://doi.org/10.17026/SS/Z84SLW.

[44] See e.g. S. Mollan, *Imperialism and Economic Development in Sub-Saharan Africa: An Economic and Business History of Sudan* (Cham 2020) for such a study. For a study of the relationship between colonial government and firm, see: De Roo, 'The Trouble with Tariffs'.

[45] See e.g. G.G. Jones, *Merchants to Multinationals: British Trading Companies in the Nineteenth and Twentieth Centuries* (Oxford 2000); Idem, *Multinationals and Global Capitalism: From the Nineteenth to the Twenty-First Century* (Oxford 2005); Idem, *Entrepreneurship and Multinationals: Global Business and the Making of the Modern World* (Cheltenham & Northampton MA 2013); M. Wilkins, *The Emergence of Multinational Enterprise: American Business Abroad from the Colonial Era to 1914* (Cambridge MA 1970). In recent years, the new agenda of 'New History of Capitalism' has looked at the classic question of the links between slavery and capitalism, offering a critical perspective on the role that capitalism played in Europe's growth. This book does not engage in detail with this literature, for its focus on slavery does not fit this book, instead opting for more classical business history. However, this book adopts a critical approach towards the effects of imperialism.

[46] Hopkins, *Capitalism in the Colonies: African Merchants in Lagos, 1851–1931* (Princeton NJ 2024).

1.3 Setting the Scene: Rotterdam as a Global Colonial Port City

If one looks at Rotterdam today, it may be hard to imagine that the city was not always one of Europe's foremost global port cities. Only after the rise of China in the 1980s and 1990s, Rotterdam's port ceased to be the world's largest one. Rotterdam is however still Europe's largest port (with double the value of imports and exports of the number two, Antwerp), acting as a major transshipment port to the German hinterland.[47] Arguably, the city itself is today the most cosmopolitan city of the Netherlands, with over 170 nationalities living in the city. In this regard, Rotterdam is indicative of port cities across Europe that rose to prominence in the nineteenth century: much of what this book demonstrates could probably have happened in similar port cities such as Hamburg and Marseille. Indeed, it may be no coincidence that entrepreneurs from three cities were also actively engaged in activities across West and West Central Africa during the nineteenth century.[48] Similarly, the Rotterdam entrepreneurs had (family) links to British West African entrepreneurs from Manchester and Liverpool, as well as the London capital market.[49] In all those cities, similar questions about the colonial past have popped up in recent years.[50]

Long-standing societal pressure from activist groups in the Netherlands and Rotterdam itself resulted in 2020 in the publication of three books about Rotterdam's colonial past, its links to slavery and the slave trade and the emergence of Rotterdam as the Netherlands' main postcolonial or 'superdiverse' city.[51] Much of what followed in terms of societal debate focused on the links to (early modern) Atlantic slavery; however, as this book makes clear, much of Rotterdam's colonial 'responsibility' can be

[47] https://www.shipafreight.com/knowledge-series/largest-ports-in-europe/ [Retrieved 26/10/2022]. See also: H. Van Driel, 'Innovation and Integration in Mineral Bulk Handling in the Port of Rotterdam, 1886–1923', *Business History*, 44, 3 (2002), 63–90.

[48] For Hamburg, see: K.S. Todzi, *Unternehmen Weltaneignung: Der Woermann-konzern und der deutsche Kolonialismus 1837–1916* (Göttingen 2023). For Marseille: Damaulin, 'Commercial Presence'.

[49] Oosterwijk, *Ik verlang geen dank.*

[50] See e.g. '"Afrikahaus": Sitz des Woermann-Konzerns', in: J. Zimmerer & Todzi (eds.), *Hamburg: Tor zu kolonialen Welt: Errinerungsorte der (post-)kolonialen Globaliserung* (Göttingen 2021), 83–98

[51] Oostindie (ed.), *Het koloniale verleden van Rotterdam*; A. Van Stipriaan, *Rotterdam in slavernij* (Amsterdam 2020); F. Guadeloupe, P. Van de Laar & L. Van der Linden (eds.), *Rotterdam, een postkoloniale stad in beweging* (Amsterdam 2020).

pinpointed to the nineteenth century.[52] Although the city of Rotterdam did have colonial links in the early modern period and therefore profited from colonial investment (e.g. through slavery in Suriname), until 1850 Rotterdam in reality was a mid-sized hub in the Dutch (colonial) economy, and very much in Amsterdam's shadow.[53] Lacking a proper maritime infrastructure for a long time, Rotterdam's merchant elite gradually gained influence in colonial trade and developed a financial industry engaged in colonial trade (e.g. as bankers or insurers) during the eighteenth century. The city was however never able to match Amsterdam by any means.[54]

This only changed in the mid-nineteenth century. Under Liberal leadership in the City Council, the city after 1850 moved to create maritime, rail and road infrastructure and supported entrepreneurs in the city.[55] Both the development of railways to the coast and the opening of the so-called *Nieuwe Waterweg* ('New Waterway' or 'New Water Route') in 1872 allowed Rotterdam to create links to industrial cities in Belgium, like Antwerp.[56] Rotterdam thus developed as a global port hub in the second half of the 'global' liberal nineteenth century.[57] Improving its (maritime) infrastructure made Rotterdam significantly more attractive for trade. At the same time, the globalisation and liberalisation of nineteenth-century world trade, alongside the (renewed) European imperial expansion, made Rotterdam more important as a port city for European hinterlands (primarily Germany), importing significant amounts of colonial commodities.[58] With lucrative trade and production opportunities in the Dutch East Indies being monopolised by the old business elite from Amsterdam,

[52] De Kok, 'De koloniale connectie', 60–73; Idem, 'De koloniale impact', 118–125 & 131–133.

[53] Ibidem.

[54] De Kok, 'De koloniale impact', 125–133.

[55] P.T. Van de Laar, *Stad van formaat: geschiedenis van Rotterdam in de negentiende en twintigste eeuw* (Zwolle 2000), 13–45; M. Callahan, 'The Harbor Barons: Political and Commercial Elites and the Development of the Port of Rotterdam, 1824–1892', Unpublished PhD Dissertation Princeton University (2 Vols.) (Princeton NJ, 1981); J. Visser, 'Ondernemerselite 1850–1950', in: Visser, M. Van Jaarsveld & Van de Laar (eds.), *Rotterdamse ondernemers 1850–1950* (Rotterdam 2003), 10–19; J.L. Van Zanden & A. Van Riel, *Nederland 1780–1914: staat, instituties en economische ontwikkeling* (Amsterdam 2000), 389–390.

[56] Van de Laar, *Stad van formaat*, 65–70.

[57] Ibidem, 91–126. See for a comparable case in Hamburg: Todzi, *Unternehmen Weltaneignung*.

[58] Van de Laar, *Stad van formaat*, 65–70.

entry into the Dutch colonial market was however difficult.[59] Rotterdam's entrepreneurs were therefore reduced to running maritime transport to and from the Dutch East Indies, without access to the production of, and trade in, raw colonial commodities.[60]

A number of entrepreneurs from Rotterdam, unsatisfied with this situation, as a result started looking for new ways to take part in the scramble for colonial commodities. This (rather small) group included Huibert van Rijckevorsel, scion of a major aristocratic Rotterdam family, who pioneered the Rotterdam African trade by setting up shop in Elmina in 1846[61]; Hendrik Muller Szn., a German immigrant who married into the Van Rijckevorsel family and would go on to become the main player in the Rotterdam African trade[62]; Lodewijk Pincoffs, who initiated the trade in the Congo basin in 1857, before his downfall upon being exposed as a fraudulent conman in 1879[63]; and Marten Mees, a banker who funded

[59] See T. De Graaf, *Voor handel en maatschappij: geschiedenis van de Nederlandsche Handel-Maatschappij, 1824–1964* (Amsterdam 2012), 37–50.

[60] See e.g. Oosterwijk, *Reder in Rotterdam: Willem Ruys (1809–1889)* (Rotterdam 1989).

[61] J. Van Herwaarden, 'Rijckevorsel, Huibert van', in: in: Visser, Van Jaarsveld & Van de Laar (eds.), *Rotterdamse ondernemers*, 202–207; J.E. Van der Pot, 'Abram van Rijckevorsel HZN, 1790–1864', *Rotterdams Jaarboekje*, 5, 1 (1943), 111–152; Idem, 'Huibert van Rijckevorsel, 1813–1866', *Rotterdams Jaarboekje*, 5, 2 (1944), 10–24; H. Schmitz, 'Vragen rond Abram van Rijckevorsel (1790–1864)', *Rotterdams Jaarboekje*, 9, 5 (1987), 217–232; G.E. Van Walsum, 'Abram van Rijckevorsel Hzn., man van de vooruitgang', *Rotterdams Jaarboekje*, 7, 3 (1965), 148–174; 'A. (Abram) van Rijckevorsel Hzn.', Parlement.com, available at https://www.parlement.com/id/vg09ll6e63sv/a_abram_van_rijckevorsel [Retrieved 29/04/2022]; Muller, *Muller*, 25–168.

[62] Muller, *Muller*; P. Ingenbleek, 'Muller, Hendrik', in: Visser, Van Jaarsveld & Van de Laar (eds.), *Rotterdamse ondernemers*, 161–164.

[63] Oosterwijk, *Ik verlang geen dank*; P.J. Bouman, 'Lodewijk Pincoffs: een hoofdstuk uit de geschiedenis van Rotterdam', *Vragen des Tijds*, 53 (1927), 1–18; Franssens, 'De vestiging van "Kerdijk en Pincoffs"'; J. Hudig, 'In memoriam L. Pincoffs', *Rotterdams Jaarboekje*, 1, 10 (1912), 175–185; A.L. Pincoffs, 'Lodewijk Pincoffs', *Rotterdams Jaarboekje*, 3, 5 (1927), 68–74; L. Ottevanger, 'Pincoffs, Lodewijk', in: Visser, Van Jaarsveld & Van de Laar (eds.), *Rotterdamse ondernemers*, 185–188; 'L. Pincoffs', Parlement.com, available at https://www.parlement.com/id/vg09ll4m0mzy/l_pincoffs [Retrieved 05/08/2021]; 'Pincoffs, Lodewijk (1827–1911)', Resources Huygens KNAW, available at http://resources.huygens.knaw.nl/bwn1880-2000/lemmata/bwn1/pincoffs [Retrieved 05/08/2021]; A. Engelfriet, 'Mede dankzij de Rotterdammer Pincoffs kreeg Leopold II zijn privé-kolonie Kongo-Vrijstaat', available at http://www.engelfriet.net/Alie/Hans/congo.htm [Retrieved 09/08/2021]; Toen te zien, '1857–1868 Kerdijk & Pincoffs', available at http://www.toentezien.nl/musea/1857-1868-kerdijk-pincoffs/ [Retrieved 09/08/2021]; Quadackers, L., 'Pincoffs: van miljonair tot sigarenboer', *Accountant*, 3 (2015), 40–47, available at

most of the Rotterdam African trade.[64] Their international connections, in particular in Britain, were useful in obtaining foreign capitalisation and knowledge, as Rotterdam's own industrial and financial capacity was too limited to finance such ventures[65]: moreover, the Amsterdam capital market was unwilling to support their rival ventures.[66] Between the late 1840s and early 1860s, Rotterdam entrepreneurs started operating in various areas of West and West Central Africa with the help of German and British investors, demonstrating their international outlook and connections.[67]

The nineteenth century was therefore, this book contends, truly Rotterdam's 'colonial' century. Money earned in the colonial trade was to a significant extent also used to fund the development of Rotterdam's (maritime) infrastructure itself, as well as contributing to the city's architecture and museums (see Epilogue). The returns from the African trade played a substantial role in this, although this part of the colonial trade has only scarcely been addressed in the literature.[68] The African trade was one of the main outlets for capital from Rotterdam and one of the main sources of returns on investment.[69] This challenges the historiography and public perception of Rotterdam's colonial involvement, moving away from the somewhat narrow focus on Atlantic slavery links, and towards a more balanced assessment of the widespread Rotterdam colonial links in both the colonial and imperial era. This is not only relevant for Rotterdam, but also

https://www.accountant.nl/magazines/accountant-2015-q3/pincoffs-van-miljonair-tot-sigarenboer/# [Retrieved 09/08/2021]; Petram, L., 'De val van een fraudeur', *Historisch Nieuwsblad*, 4 (2021), 34–40; R. Janssen, *Grof geld: financiële schandalen en speculatie in Nederland* (Amsterdam 2013), Chapter 11.

64 R. Mees, *Gedenkschrift van de firma R. Mees & Zoonen ter gelegenheid van haar tweehonderd-jarig bestaan, 1720–1920* (Rotterdam 1920); P.A.J. Mees, 'R. Mees & Zoonen en de Pincoffscrisis', *Rotterdams Jaarboekje*, 9, 9 (1991), 323–330; E. Boonstoppel, 'Mees, familie', in: Visser, Van Jaarsveld & Van de Laar (eds.), *Rotterdamse ondernemers*, 142–149; W.C. Mees, *Man van de daad: Mr. Marten Mees en de opkomst van Rotterdam* (Rotterdam 1946).

65 Ibidem.

66 Van Zanden & Van Riel, *Nederland 1780–1914*, 246–248; Van Riel, *The Trials of Convergence: Prices, Markets and Industrialization in The Netherlands, 1800–1913* (Leiden & Boston 2021), 448 & 520–522; M. Wintle, *An Economic and Social History of the Netherlands, 1800–1920: Demographic, Economic and Social Transition* (Cambridge 2000), 192–199; De Kok, 'De koloniale impact', 130.

67 Oosterwijk, *Ik verlang geen dank*, 31–33; Muller, *Muller*, 45–46.

68 Exceptions are: De Kok, 'De koloniale connectie', 60–68 & 70–73; Idem, 'De koloniale impact', 118–125. See also: Den Heijer, 'Rotterdamse ondernemers en bestuurders'.

69 Ibidem.

contributes to the history of European port cities' global links more generally.

1.4 Approach: Gentlemanly Capitalism, Entrepreneurship and Business History

This book adopts Peter Cain and Antony Hopkins' concept of 'gentlemanly capitalism' as a general framework of reference.[70] This concept argues that imperialism was first and foremost an economic impulse, combining the idea of a necessity for capital outlet (as proposed by Hobson in the early 1900s) with an analysis of the complex interactions between people on the ground (e.g. entrepreneurs operating in Southern Africa like Cecil Rhodes), interest groups of financiers in the City of London and the British government.[71] In Cain and Hopkins' telling, trade and finance interests joined forces against Britain's ***industrial*** interests which lobbied for tariffs to protect industry.[72] Eventually, free trade (capital and mercantile) interests prevailed in Britain over industrial concerns. Various elements from the concept of 'gentlemanly capitalism' can also be observed in the case of Rotterdam, for example the cooperation between trade and finance interests against industrial interests, and the role that a 'new' class of entrepreneurs played in the process of imperial expansion: in contrast to Britain, the industrial interests were less formidable in the Dutch case, owing to its relatively late industrialisation. Therefore, the theory of Cain and Hopkins cannot be copied and applied to the case of Rotterdam without some important caveats, but the book nevertheless departs from the assumption that imperialism was first and foremost a process of 'economic' imperialism, preferring Cain and Hopkins' nuanced interpretation of gentlemanly imperialism over more simplistic theories of economic imperialism.

As the book analyses the entrepreneurial activities of Dutch entrepreneurs across West and West Central Africa, this means that the book

[70] Cain & Hopkins, 'Gentlemanly Capitalism (II)'. See also: R.E. Dummett, 'Introduction: Exploring the Cain/Hopkins Paradigm: Issues for Debate; Critique and Topics for New Research', in: Dummett (ed.), *Gentlemanly Capitalism and British Imperialism: The New Debate on Empire* (London & New York 1999), 1–43.

[71] Ibidem; Idem, *British Imperialism: Innovation and Expansion 1688–1914* (London & New York 1993); Idem, *British Imperialism: Crisis and Deconstruction 1914–1990* (London & New York 1993). See in particular the first volume of Cain & Hopkins' two-part *magnum opus*.

[72] Ibidem.

squarely falls within the discipline we would nowadays call business history. However, this book does not uncritically engage with business-historical scholarship. A number of special issues have in recent years been published that grapple with the future of business history.[73] Questions regarding methodology, focus, and links to other disciplines are among the most pressing. For example, to what extent should business history rely on case studies, and to what extent should it work towards testing theoretical frameworks drawn from economics and economic history?[74] In recent years, business historians have sought to bridge the gap to the more quantitively oriented economic historians and (re-)integrate the disciplines.[75]

From the perspective of this book, three interrelated problems of business history stand out. The first concerns the overarching focus on the twentieth-century history of the (managerial) firm, following the 'turn' inspired by the seminal work of Alfred Chandler jr.[76] As many historians of the early modern period have pointed out, however, such an approach neglects the fact that large-scale 'firms' or 'corporations' were not necessarily the choice of many entrepreneurs, who instead relied on a much wider array of instruments and legal forms to conduct business.[77] The second problem concerns the focus on the peculiarities of Anglo-American business, thus neglecting most other business traditions (not only in continental Europe, but also in other continents, notably Africa).[78] Both these

[73] See e.g. the special issues in *Business History*, 57, 1 (2015), https://www.tandfonline.com/toc/fbsh20/57/1; *Enterprise & Society*, 21, 3 (2020), https://www.cambridge.org/core/journals/enterprise-and-society/issue/8956F4A40F958D12C87D493920011784; *Business History Review*, 91, 3 (2017), https://www.cambridge.org/core/journals/business-history-review/issue/2068798EC4E7888CB71C80A9B8AC9411.

[74] See also for these issues also: Jones & J. Zeitlin (eds.), *The Oxford Handbook of Business History*.

[75] See for a historiographical explanation: O.C. Gelderblom & F. Trivellato, 'The Business History of the Pre-Industrial World: Towards a Comparative Historical Analysis', *Business History*, 61, 2 (2019), 225–259.

[76] See for these criticisms: R.D. Wadhwani & C. Lubinski, 'Reinventing Entrepreneurial History', *Business History Review*, 91, 4 (2017), 767–799, https://doi.org/10.1017/S0007680517001374. For examples, see e.g. A.D. Chandler jr., *Strategy and Structure: Chapters in the History of American Industrial Enterprise* (Cambridge MA 1962); Idem, *The Visible Hand: The Managerial Revolution in American Business* (Cambridge MA 1977).

[77] Gelderblom & Trivellato, 'The Business History'.

[78] A point made very well in: Hopkins, *Capitalism in the Colonies*, 15–20. See also: Verhoef, 'Entrepreneurs in Africa'; Idem, *The History of Business in Africa: Complex Discontinuity to Emerging Markets* (Cham 2017), https://doi.org/10.1007/978-3-319-62566-9;

problems do not preclude the fact that the Dutch firm(s) in West and West Central Africa moved from small-scale entrepreneurship within family firms towards large-scale enterprises in the space of some forty years, but they (for explainable reasons) never made the transition to the ideal type of the managerial enterprise, as described by Chandler and Mira Wilkins.[79] Third, business history is not necessarily doing a good job of connecting its results to other fields: the wish to contribute to major questions in economic history for example misses the important connections with colonial and global history, as businesses often played a crucial role in colonial and imperial endeavours.[80] A growing strand in business history has looked at imperial business and/or banking, but primarily so for the twentieth century.[81] This book explicitly aims to make these connections and draw out effect and impact of businesses in imperial ventures.

In line with the critique on the work of Chandler and others that focused on the firm, business historians have in recent years come to argue for a stronger historical focus on the entrepreneur, rather than on firms or corporations.[82] This essentially reiterates a focus that was common in business history 'before Chandler', in the works of business historians like N.S.B. Gras and Joseph Schumpeter.[83] This perspective of the

A. Akinyoade, T. Dietz & C. Uche, 'Introduction', in: Akinyoade, Dietz & Uche (eds.), *Entrepreneurship in Africa* (Leiden & Boston 2017), 1–21; M.E. Ochonu, 'Introduction: Toward African Entrepreneurship and Business History', in: Ochonu (ed.), *African Entrepreneurship: A Historical Approach* (Bloomington IN 2018), 1–27.

[79] Chandler jr., *Strategy and Structure*; Idem, *The Visible Hand*.

[80] See e.g. P.J. Stern, *Empire, Incorporated: The Corporations That Built British Colonialism* (Cambridge MA 2023). I am not uncritical of the book, as I have outlined in a book review for the *International Journal of Maritime History*, but the book makes a bold case for the importance of the role that entrepreneurs and firms play in colonial expansion. This is starting to change, however: see for example the forthcoming special issue in *Business History* on "Business History and Imperialism".

[81] See e.g. Hopkins, *Capitalism in the Colonies*, for a recent example of critique. See also: Jones, *Multinationals and Global Capitalism*; Wilkins, *The Emergence*. The work of Stephanie Decker, among others, is tackling this problem head on, also engaging with the issue of decolonisation in the 'cultural' sense of the word. See e.g.: S. Decker, *Postcolonial Transition and Global Business History: British Multinational Companies in Ghana and Nigeria* (New York 2022).

[82] See e.g. M. Casson & C. Casson, *The Entrepreneur in History: From Medieval Merchant to Modern Business Leader* (London 2013).

[83] Harvard Business School for example had a 'Centre for Entrepreneurial History' just after World War II. See: R. Crandall, *The Research Center in Entrepreneurial History at Harvard University, 1948–1959* (Cambridge MA 1960), and the work cited therein. See

entrepreneur allows both a temporal perspective that takes into account entrepreneurs across time, rather than only look at merchants in the early modern period or firms in the modern era, and also advances the field away from Eurocentric explanations that claim the rise of certain forms of business catapulted the West into economic growth.[84] Focusing on the entrepreneur allows us to compare between different areas in the world, for example between Europe, Africa and China: in short, it allows business historians to focus on comparative challenges entrepreneurs faced everywhere in the world.

Following the renewed interest in the historical entrepreneur, Daniel Wadhwani and Cristina Lubinski have called for the construction of a 'New Entrepreneurial History'.[85] Rather than to start from the actor or institutions, they argue that scholars should focus on "the study of the creative processes that propel economic change".[86] Following this, Wadhwani and Lubinski propose to focus on three entrepreneurial processes: first, envisioning and valuing opportunities (not unlike the definition as proposed by Mark and Catherine Casson[87]); second, allocating and reconfiguring resources (similar to how Howard Stevenson defines the entrepreneur[88]); and third, legitimising novelty (similar to Joseph Schumpeter's argument of creative destruction whereby entrepreneurs replace traditional industries[89]).[90] The advantage of Wadhwani and Lubinski's work is that they combine elements of the most common definitions of the entrepreneur, without losing focus on the core tasks of the entrepreneur. This book therefore largely follows their conceptualisation.

also: N.S.B. Gras, 'Why Study Business History?', *The Canadian Journal of Economics and Political Science*, 4, 3 (1939), 320–340; A. Cole, 'An Approach to the Study of Entrepreneurship: A Tribute to Edwin Gay', *Journal of Economic History*, 6, S1 (1946), 1–15, https://doi.org/10.1017/S0022050700052876.

[84] Casson & Casson, *The Entrepreneur in History*, 1–11.

[85] Wadhwani & Lubinski, 'Reinventing Entrepreneurial History'.

[86] Ibidem, 769.

[87] Casson & Casson, *The Entrepreneur in History*, 1–11.

[88] H.H. Stevenson & J.C. Jarillo, 'A Paradigm of Entrepreneurship: Entrepreneurial Management', *Strategic Management Journal*, 11, 4 (1990), 17–27. See also: Wadhwani & Lubinski, 'Reinventing Entrepreneurial History', 776.

[89] J.A. Schumpeter, *The Theory of Economic Development* (Cambridge MA 1934). Idem: 'Capitalism, Socialism, and Democracy: The Process of Creative Destruction', in: M. Becker (ed.), *Entrepreneurship: Classic Texts by Joseph Schumpeter* (Stanford CA 2011), 313–319. See also: Casson & Casson, *The Entrepreneur in History*, 53–58.

[90] Wadhwani & Lubinski, 'Reinventing Entrepreneurial History', 769.

While I endorse the idea of focusing on these entrepreneurial processes in theory, I still start my inquiry from the perspective of the Rotterdam *group of entrepreneurs*. The entrepreneurs under study after all formed, at the outset, a tight-knit group of four elite families from Rotterdam: the 'old money' of the Mees and Van Rijckevorsel families, combined with the immigrant background and entrepreneurship of Pincoffs and Muller Szn. Casson and Casson are rather explicit in pointing out that the entrepreneur cannot be seen outside of their social context, and this is particularly relevant to the case of the Rotterdam entrepreneurs central to this study.[91] They were embedded in the city of Rotterdam and were active members of many of the city's political and social organisations. Moreover, they were active agents in pushing Rotterdam onto the world stage, by taking the lead in developing its port infrastructure (Pincoffs), lobbying as members of the city's Chamber of Commerce (Abram van Rijckevorsel, father of Huibert), or in the Dutch Parliament (Pincoffs and Muller Szn.), besides being active philanthropists in the city. Moreover, they accumulated knowledge and capital within their tight-knit network, learning from one another, something that is not well addressed in the definition of the entrepreneurial processes.[92]

As such, the approach taken in this book starts from the socially embedded *group of entrepreneurs* that participated in the three entrepreneurial processes, and within the group *accumulated* knowledge and capital to do so. In short, the approach here combines a focus on the socially embedded entrepreneur with aspects of the proposed new entrepreneurial history.[93] While focused on the group of entrepreneurs and the entrepreneurial processes, the book does not deny that a development towards a multinational, 'managerial' firm can be detected in the analysis. Under the framework of 'colonial capitalism' (to use Hopkin's term), the initially

[91] Casson & Casson, *The Entrepreneur in History*, 120–134.

[92] I thank Cristina Lubinski for the discussion on this matter, and for help in bridging the gap between entrepreneurial processes and the network effects of this group of entrepreneurs.

[93] The book is therefore not unsimilar to the following books, which serve as an inspiration for structuring it: Press, *Rogue Empires*; Todzi, *Unternehmen Weltaneignung*; Möllan, *Imperialism and Economic Development*; C. Dejung, *Commodity Trading, Globalization and the Colonial World: Spinning the Web of the Global Market* (New York & Oxon 2018).

small family firms quickly developed to become large enterprises in the 1880s and 1890s, but this was no teleological or preordained matter.[94]

1.5 A Note on Sources

The book draws on a variety of sources from across European archives and a multitude of primary edited sources and data sets, as well as the significant secondary literature on imperial business history and the Partition of and Scramble for Africa. First, archives from the Netherlands are used primarily for the study of the Rotterdam entrepreneurs and their business networks. Of most early entrepreneurs (except Lodewijk Pincoffs), family and business archives are available in the Rotterdam municipal archives, as well as some additional information that is scattered in archives around the Netherlands.[95] The Dutch National Archives contain the business archives of the *Afrikaansche Handels-Vereeniging* (AHV) and *Nieuwe Afrikaansche Handels-Vennootschap* (NAHV), offering a wealth of information particularly for the post-1879 period.[96] Key information on for example the economic performance of the various firms can be found there, allowing us to reconstruct the profitability from imperial business. Moreover, letters between agents in Africa and the headquarters of the firm in Rotterdam, as well as letters between the firm and administrative and political representatives. Furthermore, additional legal, financial and economic documents regarding the legal establishment, stock emissions or the bankruptcy

[94] See for a similar analysis: Jones, *Merchants to Multinationals*. See also: Hopkins, *Capitalism in the Colonies*.

[95] See e.g.: Stadsarchief Rotterdam (hereafter NL-SAR), Handschriftenverzameling Gemeente Rotterdam (aanvullingen 1848–1987), inv. 33–01; Handschriftenverzameling Gemeente Rotterdam (aanvullingen 1988–1996), inv. 33–02; Archief Familie Mees privé, inv. 39; Archief Muller, inv. 41; Aanvulling Archief Muller, inv. 41a; Archief Familie van Rijckevorsel, inv. 42; Archief Mees & Zoonen, inv. 305; Archief Familie Dunlop, inv. 400. See also: NL-IISG-NEHA, Collectie Combinatie voor den Handel op de West en/of Zuidwestkust van Afrika, inv. ARCH03684; Collectie Huibert van Rijckevorsel (Rotterdam), inv. ARCH03896; Collectie Handelshuis Dunlop & Mees, Rotterdam, inv. ARCH04463; Archief ABN AMRO (hererafter NL-ABN), Archief Mees & Zoonen; Leiden University Library (hereafter NL-UBL-BC), Brieven aan Willem Geertrudus Cornelis Byvanck, inv. BPL2246a, Brieven L. Pincoffs, 2 stuks (1869–1870) & Brieven A.L. Pincoffs, 4 stuks (1869–1874), hierbij ook brief M.T. Goudsmit, 1 stuk (1869).

[96] NL-HaNA, Archief van de NAHV, (1854) 1880–1959 (1981), inv. 2.18.10.09.

of the firms are available in the Dutch National Archives and various private archival collections.[97]

The book furthermore draws on diplomatic, legal and political documents from the Dutch National Archives. In the so-called 'A-Dossiers' of the archives of the Ministry of Foreign Affairs, for example, fifteen boxes containing diplomatic correspondence on the geopolitical situation in the Congo basin (e.g. on the 1884–1885 Berlin Conference) can be found.[98] Moreover, additional documents from Parliament or certain diplomatic missions (e.g. in Lisbon) allow us to reconstruct the Dutch viewpoint regarding the complex geopolitical situation in the period 1875–1914.[99] Dutch archives thus form the core of the archival research carried out for this book. Additionally, various archival collections or documents from across Belgium have been consulted, and these sources highlight the importance of the Dutch entrepreneurs in the Congo Free State and offer a viewpoint into the (often difficult) relations between (N)AHV and Congo Free State.[100] In addition to the unpublished archival sources, the book (in particular for the early chapters) also draws on published primary sources, for example travelogues and pamphlets.[101] For Chap. 6 on the *Compagnie du Kasaï* (CdK), the memoirs of the NAHV employee Alfons Vermeulen are used extensively as well.[102] I have additionally drawn on

[97] Idem, Archief Hoge Raad der Nederlanden, inv. 2.09.28, nr. 534; Idem, Archief De Nederlandsche Bank NV, inv. 2.25.68, nrs. 16212–16217. See also: Stadsarchief Amsterdam (hereafter NL-SAA), Archief van de Commissiehandel Kerkhoven & Co, inv. 592, nr. 165; NL-ABN, Archief Mees en Zoonen, s.l., nrs. 390, 777 & 2284. See also: C.W. Vermeulen, *De Afrikaansche handels-vereeniging en haar werkkring: rapport aan den Hogen Raad der Nederlanden* (Rotterdam 1880).

[98] NL-HaNA, Archief Buitenlandse Zaken A-Dossiers, inv. 2.05.03, nrs. 141, 203–217 & 356–361.

[99] Idem, Archief van het Nederlandse Gezantschap in Portugal (1789) 1823–1889, inv. 2.05.10.12, nrs. 72 & 88–92 & Archief van de Tweede Kamer der Staten-Generaal, 1815–1945, inv. 2.02.22, nrs. 3273–3277.

[100] Archief Afrikamuseum Tervuren (hereafter BE-AMT), Stanley Archives, nrs. 42, 44, 76, 80, 641, 866, 1057–1103, 1326, 3739, 4355, 4366, 4437, 5216–5218, 5993–5995 & 6842; Archief Buitenlandse Zaken België (hereafter BE-BZ), Archives Africaines, Classement Provisoire, nr. 2571; Algemeen Rijksarchief Brussel, AGR-2, Depot Joseph Cuvelier (hereafter BE-AGR2-DJC), Archives Africaines, JUST, nr. 58.

[101] See e.g. H.M. Stanley, *The Congo and the Founding of its Free State: A Story of Work and Exploration* (New York 1885).

[102] F. Van den Hoek (ed.), A. Vermeulen (author), *De pioniersdagen van Chicongo: een verhaal uit het pioniersleven in den Congo* (Amsterdam 1934 / s.l. 2021); Ibidem, *De ingang der hel: episode uit het Afrikaansche pioniersleven* (Amsterdam 1938 / s.l. 2021); Van den Hoek m.m.v. J. Vansina (ed.), Vermeulen (author), *De memoires van Chicongo* (s.l. 2021).

contemporary statistical sources to quantify Dutch trade with West (Central).[103] As in particular the quantitative source material is incomplete and often unreliable, this material will act in the first place as supportive evidence for the book's main argument, rather than being used to demonstrate causal relationships. For the shipping business of the Rotterdam firms active in Africa, some data are also available which will be used to contextualise the transportation of the traded commodities.[104]

Various sources used in this book have been used by historians before. This applies in particular to the published primary sources, which have been criticised for the clear colonial mindset that underpinned their views. While this is indeed quite problematic, these sources still offer information, particularly regarding the economic and political circumstances of the time. None of the sources can (of course) be considered impartial or neutral in any sense, with most of the sources reflecting a strong colonial bias, for example concerning the position of the black population in the Congo basin. Where possible, I am guided by eminent Africanists like Jan Vansina to counter these biases.[105] Unfortunately, no African archives have

For critical examinations, see: Vansina, 'History in Novels and Memoirs: Alfons Vermeulen on Rural Congo (1899–1904), *History in Africa*, 39 (2012), 123–142, https://doi.org/10.1353/hia.2012.0006; K. van Walraven, 'European Memoirs and Colonialism in Equatorial Africa: Reflections on the Reminiscences of Alfons Vermeulen (1877–1965)', *ASC Working Paper*, nr. 151 (2021), available at https://www.ascleiden.nl/publications/european-memoirs-and-colonialism-equatorial-africa-reflections-reminiscences-alfons [Retrieved 05/08/2021].

[103] The full dataset is available open access via DANS: Dreijer, 'Dataset Dutch-African Trade (1847–1918)', *DANS*, available at https://doi.org/10.17026/SS/Z84SLW. This may be consulted in relation to the *African Commodity Trade Database*, see https://www.aehnetwork.org/data-research/african-commodity-trade-database/ [Retrieved 25/10/2022]. An introduction in: E. Frankema, P. Woltjer, Dalrymple-Smith & L. Bulambo, 'An Introduction to the African Commodity Trade Database, 1730–2010: Social and Economic History', *Research Data Journal for the Humanities and Social Sciences*, 3, 1 (2018), 1–12, https://doi.org/10.1163/24523666-01000009. For an application, see: Frankema, J. Williamson & Woltjer, 'An Economic Rationale for the West African Scramble?.

[104] See for a fuller analysis Dreijer, 'Handel en scheepvaart in de Nederlandse West-Afrikahandel 1830–1914', *Tijdschrift voor Zeegeschiedenis*, 43, 2 (2024), 38–55. The underlying data and methodological accounting can be found here: Dreijer, 'Dataset on Dutch-African Shipping (1830–1918)'.

[105] See e.g. Vansina, *Kingdoms of the Savanna* (Madison WI, Milwaukee WI & London 1968); Idem, *Paths in the Rainforest: Towards a History of Political Tradition in Equatorial Africa* (Madison WI 1990); Idem, 'Long-Distance Trade-Routes in Central Africa', *Journal of African History*, 3, 3 (1962), 375–390; and in particular Idem, *Being Colonized: The Kuba Experience in Rural Congo, 1880–1960* (Madison WI 2010).

been utilised in this study, either because there are none (as is the case in the DRC Congo) or because they are too poorly inventoried (as is the case in Congo-Brazzaville[106]). The book is therefore based mostly on the (very) biased European sources but is attentive to modern sensitivities around the subject.

1.6 Timeframe, Geography and Structure

The book analyses the period between the 1830s and the 1910s, more specifically the end of the First World War. The timeframe has been chosen for three reasons, two historical and one practical. First, as the First World War is generally considered the end of the Scramble for Africa, this is for all intents and purposes also a natural endpoint for the book. Second, as Laurens van der Laan has remarked, the Interwar period witnessed a totally new economic direction for the African continent, as circumstances changed a great deal.[107] Conquest gave way to empire-building and administrative consolidation; economically, meanwhile, the transition to the legitimate commerce ended and Africa's economic history entered a new phase in relation to the world market. Third, studying the 1830s–1910s period was manageable within the timeframe of a postdoc and the space that an academic book allows. Geographically, the book focuses on West and West Central Africa, roughly the region between present-day Liberia and Angola. This means that one particular aspect of the Rotterdam entrepreneurs in Africa, the firm operating in Mozambique first known as the *Handels-Compagnie Mozambique* (HCM) and later as the *Oost-Afrikaansche Compagnie* (OAC), will not be taken into account here, except where strictly necessary for understanding the situation in West and West Central Africa.[108]

[106] There may be some information on the concession companies in the French Congo in the *Affaires Economiques 1899–1959* section of the Colonial Archives in Congo-Brazzaville, but given the state of the archives as well as the limited information in the inventory, I have opted not to go there.

[107] Van der Laan, 'Selling Tropical Africa's Export Crops'.

[108] See Van den Berg, 'Hendrik Pieter Nicolaas Muller'; Muller, *Muller*. This, as well as the Dutch investments in the nearby Transvaal Republic, is the subject of a follow-up project with funding from the Gerda Henkel Stiftung, which should result in a sequel-annex-companion to this book. For the Transvaal, see: J-J. van Helten, 'German Capital, the Netherlands Railway Company and the Political Economy of the Transvaal 1886–1900', *The Journal of African History*, 19, 3 (1978), 369–390.

The book opens with a historiographical chapter (Chap. 2) explaining in greater detail the difference between the *Partition of* and *Scramble for* Africa. It covers the period from the gradual decline of the slave trade in Africa (early nineteenth century) up to the First World War, including the various phases of European imperialism in Africa in its various forms. Important events like the (in)famous Berlin Conference of 1884–1885 and the subsequent establishment of the Congo Free State are analysed in some detail, as these events in the *Partition of* Africa had a substantial impact on the private actors in the *Scramble for* Africa. The book subsequently charts the role of the Rotterdam entrepreneurs in the Scramble in three chapters corresponding to distinct periods. Chapter 3 analyses the first steps of the Rotterdam entrepreneurs in the West African trade from the late 1830s onwards, showing the volatility of the trade in these early years, culminating in the bankruptcy of the AHV in 1879.

Chapter 4 analyses the period of the 1880s and the majority of the 1890s, as European imperialism in Africa reached its zenith and the firms had to adapt to the reality of imperial states consolidating control over almost all territories in Africa. It analyses the (often difficult and fraught) relationships with the various European imperial states, but also how the successor to the AHV, the NAHV, expanded its business against the odds in the often rather challenging circumstances. Chapter 5 analyses the apex of power of the Rotterdam entrepreneurs and their firms in Africa, the period between 1899 and 1914. Having survived the 1880s and 1890s, they were able to manoeuvre their way to profitability by participating in various concession companies in various imperial entities, including Angola, the Congo Free State (after 1908: Belgian Congo) and French Congo. This chapter also contributes to the buoying literature on the (effects of) the concession companies, the public-private entities that were established by states and investors to further the goals of imperial states.

Chapter 6 offers a case study of the involvement of the NAHV in the *Compagnie du Kasaï* (CdK, established 1901), one of the Congo Free State's infamous 'red rubber' companies, engaged in the shocking atrocities by means of forced labour and harsh violence against the local population to secure wild rubber.[109] The NAHV was against its will forcefully incorporated into the CdK, but was a large shareholder and active participant (e.g. by appointing a director) during the first years of its existence.

[109] See for an overview D. Vangroenweghe, *Rood rubber: Leopold II en zijn Congo* (Brussels 1986/2010).

Given the abundance of archival material (see also previous section), this chapter analyses the involvement of the NAHV in the CdK in some detail, with special attention to the (forced) labour practices. Finally, the book concludes and contains an epilogue, briefly reflecting on how the story told here matters in the present day.

CHAPTER 2

The Scramble for and Partition of West (Central) Africa

2.1 Introduction

This chapter sets the scene for the following, more analytical chapters, arguing for a historiographical re-interpretation of the literature on imperialism in nineteenth-century Africa, with a particular focus on West and West Central Africa.[1] The literature on the Partition of and Scramble for Africa is voluminous, but suffers from one major problem: it often conflates the state-based *Partition of* Africa('s territory) with the actor-based *Scramble for* Africa('s resources).[2] Through a critical reading of the scholarly literature, this chapter will explain the key differences in timing, geographical focus and actors in the process. In a nutshell, this chapter argues

[1] See in general: Pakenham, *The Scramble for Africa*; Gallagher & Robinson, *Africa and the Victorians*. For East Africa: R. Coupland, *The Exploitation of East Africa 1856–1890: The Slave Trade and the Scramble* (London 1968); J.F. Gjersø, 'The Scramble for East Africa: British Motives Reconsidered, 1884–95', *The Journal of Imperial and Commonwealth History*, 43, 5 (1015), 831–860, https://doi.org/10.1080/03086534.2015.1026131. For South(ern) Africa: R.I. Lovell, *The Struggle for South Africa 1875–1899: A Study in Economic Imperialism* (New York 1934); J.S. Galbraith, *Crown and Charter: The Early Years of the British South Africa Company* (Berkeley CA 1974); R.V. Kubicek, *Economic Imperialism in Theory and Practice: The Case of South African Gold Mining Finance 1886–1914* (Durham NC 1979); M. Lukasiewicz, *Gold, Finance and Imperialism in South Africa, 1887–1902* (Cham 2024).

[2] See e.g. Hargreaves, 'Towards a History of the Partition of Africa', *The Journal of African History*, 1, 1 (1960), 97–109.

G. Dreijer, *Private Entrepreneurship and European Imperialism*, Palgrave Studies in Economic History,
https://doi.org/10.1007/978-3-032-01086-5_2

that the *Scramble for* Africa's resources was a long-term process already starting in the mid-nineteenth century, whereas the *Partition of* Africa happened in two short, distinct phases (the first between 1875 and 1885 and the second between 1890 and 1899). The conflation between the two terms is particularly glaring in the English-speaking literature.[3]

This may also have to do with the fact that the Partition and/or Scramble are often analysed in the framework of general theories of imperialism, meaning that the particularities and nuances of European nineteenth-century imperial expansion in Africa have sometimes been skated over for the sake of theoretical uniformity.[4] Discussions on 'informal' imperialism or about the specificities of British imperial control (e.g. through Protectorates) do moreover not always allow for the full picture of *European* imperial expansion across Africa, for example as Dutch, Swiss or Danish entrepreneurs also participated in extracting Africa's raw commodities without their state participating in Partitioning of Africa: the role of other 'Great Powers' like Germany and Portugal were different in other regards, with the former entering the race for colonies rather late, and the latter being the Western world's oldest colonial power asserting its claims from a position of relative weakness.

That, however, is not to say that no scholar (British or otherwise) has not picked up on the differences between state-based views of European nineteenth-century imperialism in Africa, and the role private actors played in this process. Antony Hopkins and Roland Oliver have for example argued that there were two Partitions (one in the 1880s and one in the 1890s, with Hopkins for example arguing for a 'Political Partition' and a 'Business Partition'), but neither has made the distinction between the Scramble and Partition as resolutely as is being done here.[5] The argument

[3] For example, Coquery-Vidrovitch, *Le Congo*, is more nuanced in this regard.

[4] Of course, many of these theories of British imperialism were developed based on evidence from Africa, like the theories of Hobson in the early twentieth century, as well as the theories of Cain & Hopkins. Perhaps unsurprisingly, the introduction has already outlined that I by and large agree with the assessment of Cain & Hopkins. See: Hobson, *Imperialism*; Cain & Hopkins, *British Imperialism* (Vol. 1).

[5] Hopkins, 'Imperial Business in Africa. Part II; Interpretation', *The Journal of African History*, 17, 2 (1976), 267–290, there 274; R. Oliver, 'The Partition of Africa: The European and African Interpretations', in: S.A. (ed.), *Bijdragen over de honderdste verjaring van de Onafhankelijke Kongostaat* (Brussels 1988), 41–50, there 41–45. See also for general takes on the role of business in Africa: Clarence-Smith, 'Business Empires in Equatorial Africa', *African Economic History*, 12 (1983), 3–11; Hopkins, 'Imperial Business in Africa. Part I: Sources', *The Journal of African History*, 17, 1 (1976), 29–48; Idem, 'Big Business in

made here nevertheless builds on their nuanced interpretations, emphasising differences in time and space that played out across the African continent: West Africa, in this regard, was for example different from East Africa in terms of timing and actors, and local circumstances naturally impacted the turn of events in different ways.[6]

In short, there is an urgent need to re-assess the historiographical narrative of the 'Scramble for Africa', going beyond simplistic ideas often perpetuated in popular and sometimes scientific literature.[7] Drawing on the booming literature of the so-called 'New Economic History of Africa' (NEHA), this chapter thus analyses the economic and political trajectory of the African continent between 1830 and the First World War, proposing that European economic and political interests in Africa developed at different moments and from different incentives.[8] Economically, a transition, first, from the slave trade to agricultural commodities and, second, a process of economic diversification from agricultural commodities to financial investments, mining, transport and infrastructure took place.[9] The economic and political interests could interact (as was the case around the 1884–1885 Berlin Conference) but could at other times as easily diverge (as was the case before 1875). Only in the late 1890s, the interests of the Scramble and Partition converged, joining forces to create the oppressive and extractive system that characterised European imperialism in Africa.

Where it is convenient and necessary, the participation of the Dutch state or by Dutch entrepreneurs in these dual processes are included here.

African History', *The Journal of African History*, 28, 1 (1987), 119–140. See also: L. Adele Jinadu, 'Conceptual and Theoretical Issues in the Scramble for Africa', in: O.C. Eze & C.A. Anigbo (eds.), *New Scramble for Africa* (Lagos 2010), 15–26.

[6] See for this also Reid, *The African Revolution*.

[7] Pakenham, *The Scramble for Africa*, is a good example in this regard.

[8] See for an overview Frankema & M. van Waijenburg, 'Bridging the Gap with the "New" Economic History of Africa', *The Journal of African History*, 64, 1 (2023), 38–61, https://doi.org/10.1017/S0021853722000792.

[9] See Frankema, Williamson & Woltjer, 'An Economic Rationale'; Law, 'Introduction', in: Law (ed.), *From Slave Trade to 'Legitimate' Commerce*, 1–31; Idem, 'The Historiography of the Commercial Transition in Nineteenth-Century Africa', in: T. Fayola (ed.), *African Historiography: Essays in Honour of Jacob Ade Ajayi* (Ikeja 1993), 91–115; Dalrymple-Smith, *Commercial Transitions*; A. Gwaindepi & K. Siebrits, 'How Mineral Discoveries Shaped the Fiscal System of South Africa', in: Frankema & A. Booth (eds.), *Fiscal Capacity and the Colonial State in Asia and Africa, c. 1850–1960* (Cambridge 2019), 264–298.

The chapter first considers the characteristics of the global, 'liberal' nineteenth century and the transition to 'legitimate commerce' that took place in West (Central) Africa. Subsequently, the chapter looks at the economic *Scramble for* West (Central) Africa between 1830 and 1914, which was interjected by two periods (temporally centred between 1875–1885 and 1890–1899) of European states *Partitioning* Africa. Special attention is on some of two (perhaps most famous) historical events that still haunt much of the historiography as well as popular memory of nineteenth-century European imperialism, and that were particular crucial for the region today known as West and West Central Africa: the Berlin Conference of November 1884-February 1885 and the subsequent establishment of the Congo Free State under the Belgian King Leopold II. Some well-informed academic readers may opt to skip various well-rehearsed parts here, as the chapter lays down the historiographical background for the chapters to come.

2.2 The Global Liberal Nineteenth Century, Imperialism and 'Legitimate Commerce'

The 'long' nineteenth century, often taken to run from 1815 (following Napoleon's defeat at Waterloo) to 1914 (outbreak of the First World War), is often known as the 'global', 'liberal' century.[10] As clichés go, this is at the same time generally true as well as a sweeping mischaracterisation of the complexities of the period. Economically, the nineteenth century was indeed largely 'liberal' in the classic, British sense of the word. In particular, the period 1870–1914 is remembered as a period of almost unlimited capital flows and foreign direct investment (FDI) across the globe: in short, a period of laissez-faire capitalism.[11] Politically, the nineteenth century witnessed the rise of the nation-state, in particular in Europe and South America (the latter also being at the receiving end of much of the FDI). Nation-states and national cultures developed under the guarantees of the Vienna Congress of 1815, which established a balance of powers and peace that held until at least 1870–1871, when the Franco-German War broke out.

[10] See e.g. Sassoon, *The Anxious Triumph*.

[11] Ibidem.

However, history tends to be more complex than this. The two developments outlined above suffer from some problems: first and foremost, they argue almost exclusively from a European and/or Western perspective; and second, the nineteenth century was arguably more an age of contradictory developments than of teleological moves towards liberal democracies and/or nation-states. Indeed, the nineteenth century was as much an age of protectionism (in particular in the non-Western world) as it was of liberalism; and it was as much an age of empire as an age of nationalism. Moreover, class formation and related labour activism (in opposition to the aforementioned capitalist system) was arguably as important as the development of laissez-faire capitalism.[12] Finally, imperialism (associated with violence and formal government control) stands in opposition to laissez-faire capitalism, which existed in financial centres like London but less so on the ground in Africa. British, American and Dutch (capital) markets were indeed 'free' in the nineteenth century, but this came at the cost of working-class people across the world.

In Africa, the nineteenth century was a century of substantial political and economic transformation.[13] Following the gradual abolition of the slave trade and slavery by European empires (e.g. Britain in 1807 resp. 1833, France in 1814 resp. 1848, and The Netherlands in 1814 resp. 1860/1863), Africa's economic focus gradually shifted from exports of people to the export of raw agricultural commodities, in particular in West Africa: this was the so-called 'transition to legitimate commerce'.[14] As Ewout Frankema, Jeffrey Williamson and Pieter Woltjer have demonstrated, there was a clear transition in African exports from the slave trade to commodities across Africa, with the latter taking primacy after 1850.[15]

At first, the trade in commodities primarily concerned products that had long been produced in Africa, such as palm oil, as well as peanuts and palm nut kernels; later, other commodities gained prominence, notably rubber in West Central Africa and cotton in East Africa.[16] Commodities

[12] See e.g. I. Wallerstein, *The World World-System, Volume IV: Centrist Liberalism Triumphant, 1789–1914* (Oakland CA 2011).

[13] See Reid, *The African Revolution*, which does not take the Scramble as the turning point in Africa's nineteenth century, but rather the long-term transitions in African societies.

[14] Dalrymple-Smith, *Commercial Transitions.*

[15] Frankema, Williamson & Woltjer, 'An Economic Rationale', 234, there Figure 1.

[16] See e.g. for rubber B. Linneweh, 'Global Trading Companies in the Commodity Chain of Rubber between 1890 and the 1920s', *Business History*, 65, 5 (2023), 863–879, https://doi.org/10.1080/00076791.20.

like palm oil gained prominence in the nineteenth century in the transition to the legitimate commerce, as for example palm oil changed from a luxury product to a common staple of Western imports.[17] From around 1885 onwards, minerals like diamonds (mostly in Southern Africa) also became major African exports to the world market. Economic historians have debated to what extent the transition from the slave trade to the so-called 'legitimate commerce' really constituted a new phase in African economic history:[18] the slave trade for example still existed in various places (primarily so in Angola, wherefrom enslaved people were transported to Brazil).[19] Others have argued that the *beneficiaries* remained largely the same (African) elites.[20] It is, however, clear that in general, (West) Africa's economy became more dependent on the export of raw commodities over the course of the nineteenth century.[21]

Africa's economic conjunctural ebbs and flows did not perfectly align with trends prevalent on the world market. Three concurrent forces pushed down the price of palm oil, West Africa's most important export commodity, after the mid-1860s, at a time when most Western economies were still experiencing an investment boom:[22] first, the introduction of the steamship, which lowered freight rates, as more supplies could be sold

[17] J. Robins, 'Primary Commodities and Industrial Consumers: The Case of Palm Oil', in: J. Curry-Machado, J. Stubbs, Clarence-Smith & J. Vos (eds.), *The Oxford Handbook of Commodity History* (Oxford 2024), 287–308, https://doi.org/10.1093/oxfordhb/9780197502679.013.16, there 289 & 297–299.

[18] Dalrymple-Smith, *Commercial Transitions*; Hopkins, 'The "New International Economic Order" in the Nineteenth Century: Britain's First Development Plan for Africa', in: Law (ed.), *From Slave Trade to 'Legitimate' Commerce*, 240–264; Law, 'The Historiography'; T. Falola, *A History of West Africa* (London & New York 2024), 247–277. More general: S. Broadberry & Gardner, 'Economic Growth in Sub-Saharan Africa, 1885–2008: Evidence from Eight Countries', *Explorations in Economic History*, 83, Article 101424, https://doi.org/10.1016/j.eeh.2021.101424;Gardner,'Slavery, Coercion, and Economic Development in Sub-Saharan Africa', *Business History Review*, 97, 3 (2023), 199–223, https://doi.org/10.1017/S0007680523000338.

[19] Vos, 'Work in Times of Slavery, Colonialism and Civil War: Labor Relations in Angola from 1800 to 2000', *History in Africa*, 41 (2014), 363–385, https://doi.org/10.1017/hia.2014.8, there 374–378.

[20] See for an overview of the historiographical positions Law, 'The Historiography'.

[21] Dalrymple-Smith, *Commercial Transitions.*

[22] Lynn, 'The West African Palm Oil Trade in the Nineteenth Century and the "Crisis of Adaption"', in: Law (ed.), *From Slave Trade to 'Legitimate' Commerce*, 57–77; Idem, *Commerce and Economic Change.*

quicker and in larger quantities on the European market;[23] second (and related), the opening of the Suez Canal, which also lowered freight rates substantially, in particular from places like the Dutch East Indies where palm oil plantations sprang up;[24] and third, the gradual replacement of palm oil as a lubricant in the Western world by other mineral oils.[25]

The world market was met with a prolonged economic crisis after 1873, the result of price drops in agricultural commodities in particular between 1873 and 1879. The period 1873–1896 has commonly been considered by economic historians as the so-called 'Great' or 'Long' Depression.[26] Most Western governments depreciated their currency, while the price of silver also dropped, leading to severe deflation and the Panic of 1873 on the US stock market, before spreading to Europe and the rest of the world.[27] Although some speculative investments like railroads did crash during the early Long Depression, most industrial product prices soon recovered: in contrast, prices of agricultural commodities remained low for a long time, with the price of grain falling by two-thirds between 1867 and 1894.[28] African agricultural commodities like palm oil were thus presented with a double whammy: the price slump of the mid-1860s and the general economic crisis of the 1870s. In the 1880s, most markets largely recovered from the turbulent 1870s, and so it was the case for the palm oil market to an extent: however, oversupply as a result of palm oil production in Asia (notably the Dutch East Indies) caused prices to drop again in the 1890s.[29] Palm oil remained in great demand, but its relative importance diminished: other products like rubber and cotton replaced it as Africa's main export commodities in the 1890s.[30] Attempts to produce

[23] Idem, 'From Sail to Steam: The Impact of the Steamship Services on the British Palm Oil Trade with West Africa, 1850–1890', *The Journal of African History*, 30, 2 (1989), 227–245.

[24] Ibidem, 228.

[25] Idem, *Commerce and Economic Change*, 186–187; Robins, 'Primary Commodities', 298.

[26] The term Great Depression nowadays being more common to describe the crisis following the U.S. stock market crash of 1929 and the general economic contraction of the 1930s: as a result, we will use the term 'Long' Depression here to indicate this period.

[27] S.B. Saul, *The Myth of the Great Depression, 1873–1896* (London & Basingstoke 1969), 35; R. Perren, *Agriculture in Depression, 1870–1940* (Cambridge 1995), 9–16; Sassoon, *The Anxious Triumph*, 478–490.

[28] Sassoon, *The Anxious Triumph*, 489; Perren, *Agriculture in Depression*, 9.

[29] Lynn, *Commerce and Change*, 103–150; Robins, 'Primary Commodities', 298.

[30] Frankema, Williamson & Woltjer, 'An Economic Rationale', 242.

palm oil on an industrial scale (i.e. on plantations) failed in Africa, whereas they were successful in Southeast Asia.[31]

In the wake of the Long Depression, protectionism became the default response of most Western countries, Great Britain being the main exception (e.g. following the abolition of the Corn Laws in 1846, or the abolition of import duties on palm oil in 1845).[32] The Netherlands and Belgium did have tariffs, but were among the few who did not raise them between 1875 and 1913, and could therefore be classified as more or less in Britain's camp.[33] Other major economies, including France and the United States, consistently raised tariffs between 1875 and 1913, even as foreign direct investment (FDI) from these countries also rose during this period.[34] This period thus saw two distinct, contradictory processes: one of raising tariffs to protect infant national industrial capacity (except in Great Britain), and the almost unlimited expansion of capital across the globe, particularly so in Latin America and Asia, and to a lesser extent also Africa. Under the impact of the technological advances, transport and communication facilities increased significantly, mostly through the introduction of the steam ship, as well as railways on land, capital could be invested.

For colonial powers, the development of infrastructure became more important after roughly 1890. Across Africa, infrastructure developed, often by imposing harsh labour requirements on the local populations. In particular in the coastal areas, railways were developed, for example in South Africa, Angola and West and East Africa.[35] The infrastructural improvements allowed further integration of former frontier areas into the world economy.[36] Next to the development of infrastructure, the political integration of colonial political entities also encouraged economic

[31] Robins, 'Primary Commodities', 298–299. This is also a reason why the production of palm oil cannot easily be classified as "commodity frontiers", as most production remained in centres that had produced palm oil for centuries.

[32] Sassoon, *The Anxious Triumph*, 491; Robins, 'Primary Commodities', 297.

[33] Ibidem, 492.

[34] Ibidem, 499–501.

[35] Van Helten, 'German Capital'; J-L. Vellut, 'Garenganze/Katanga—Bié—Benguela and Beyond: The Cycle of Rubber and Slaves at the Turn of the 20th Century', *Portuguese Studies Review*, 19, 1–2 (2011), 133–152; Davis & Huttenback, *Mammon and the Pursuit of Empire*, 81–82; Coquery-Vidrovitch, *Le Congo*, 281–287.

[36] Wallerstein, *Centrist Liberalism Triumphant*.

integration *within* these political entities.[37] Although common currencies and the abolition of tariffs only followed after the First World War, infrastructural developments and growing investments from the metropole meant greater market integration, for example in France. French capital was overwhelmingly directed towards its Empire before the First World War; parts of the capital also flowed to Great Britain's colonial empire.[38] Tariffs rose during the 1900s and 1910s, but this did not prohibit foreign capital from flowing into various empires.[39] Tariffs in the colonial world were generally lower than in Europe, as contrary to the European industries that were considered to need protection from competition, cheap supplies of raw material from the colonies were important to feed the industries in Europe. Moreover, a general resistance to the deployment of European taxpayer's money in the colonies meant that public money directed towards the colonies was quite small, with most taxes being raised through import and export duties on firms or through levying (harsh) taxes, such as a hut tax, on the local population.[40]

Africa, and in particular West Africa, thus developed to become a powerhouse of raw commodity exports in the nineteenth century, increasingly in the service of Western industrial development, going through a gradual period of transformation from the centuries-old slave trade. Economic integration into the world market made West Africa more vulnerable to economic shocks in the world economy as well, as was made evident by the Long Depression. Eventually, Africa's transition to the 'legitimate commerce' contributed to the advent of European imperialism.[41]

[37] See e.g. for the French Empire: S. Amin & Coquery-Vidrovitch, *Histoire économique du Congo 1880–1968: du Congo Français à l'union douanière et économique d'Afrique centrale* (Paris 1969), 27–30.

[38] J. Marseille, *Empire colonial et capitalisme français: Histoire d'un divorce* (Paris 1984), 150 & 190.

[39] Sassoon, *The Anxious Triumph*, 491–492.

[40] Gardner, 'New Colonies, Old Tools: Building Fiscal Systems in East and Central Africa', in: Frankema & Booth (eds.), *Fiscal Capacity*, 193–229, there 204–205; Gardner & Roy, *The Economic History of Colonialism*, 163.

[41] Cain & Hopkins, 'Gentlemanly Capitalism II', 1–26.

2.3 The 'Prelude' to the Scramble: European Economic Interests 1830–1875

Contacts between Africans and Europeans of course long predated the nineteenth century, with relations between the Northern African states in the Mediterranean being a constant throughout history. The early modern period (1400–1800) witnessed increasing contacts between Europeans and Africans, although these were largely limited to the *coastal* areas of the African continent: of course, the interaction between Europeans and Africans was dominated by the slave trade, first in the Western part of Africa and soon also in the Eastern part, which was integrated into the Indian Ocean economy.[42] Nineteenth-century economic interactions (from the European point of view) were subsequently largely concerned with the abolition of the slave trade and the subsequent transition to the legitimate commerce.[43]

It is, of course, common to date the starting point of the Partition and/or Scramble for Africa to the late 1870s or early 1880s.[44] However, various authors have argued that the intense race for Africa's resources and territories was not a one-off, but rather the culmination of a longer process. Studying the case of West Africa specifically, John Hargreaves for example called the period between 1850 and 1880 the 'prelude' to the Scramble, arguing that in this period the Europeans showed a diminished interest in the slave trade from Africa (abolitionist attention had turned to the abolition of slavery in the Americas), and increasingly new groups of European and African entrepreneurs started trading in West Africa by bartering guns, alcohol and other commodities for agricultural commodities like palm oil.[45] This was primarily the case for West Africa, as in East Africa

[42] See e.g. D. Richardson & F. Ribeiro da Silva (eds.), *Networks and Trans-Cultural Exchange: Slave Trading in the South Atlantic, 1590–1867* (Leiden & Boston 2015); S. Miers, *Britain and the Ending of the Slave Trade* (Bristol 1975); Vos, '"Without the Slave Trade, No Recruitment": From Slave Trading to "Migrant Recruitment" in the Lower Congo, 1830–90', in: B.N. Lawrance & R.L. Robert (eds.), *Trafficking in Slavery's Wake: Law and the Experience of Women and Children in Africa* (Athens OH 2012), 45–64.

[43] Dalrymple-Smith, *Commercial Transitions*; Law, 'The Historiography'; Lynn, *Commerce and Economic Change*.

[44] See e.g. Pakenham, *The Scramble for Africa*.

[45] Hargreaves, *Prelude*. See also: Reid, *The African Revolution*.

the slave trade remained a major issue under the influence of so-called 'Arab' traders.[46]

It is thus important to emphasise that these were not the Europeans active in the chartered companies as slave traders, but often a *new* group of entrepreneurs seeking opportunity in the market for raw commodities like palm oil. In Britain, these entrepreneurs largely hailed from Manchester and Liverpool, the two main industrial cities, forming a distinct group from the 'legacy merchants' from London. Similarly, in the Dutch case, these entrepreneurs came from Rotterdam and markedly not from Amsterdam: in Germany, they came from Hamburg.[47] *Economic* interests dominated their political worldview (and many of them were therefore liberals advocating for free trade): European interests in West Africa before 1875 were therefore dominated, by *economic* interests of a small group of entrepreneurs who slowly gathered political influence in their respective home countries.[48]

Europeans' claims of sovereignty across Africa were therefore rather limited before 1875. If European nations held territories, these were often small territories in coastal areas and often the result of claims made centuries earlier. The British for example slowly but steadily claimed possessions in West Africa, as well as in the Cape Colony (taking over the latter from the Dutch in 1795). In 1850, the Danes for example sold their possessions on the Gold Coast to the British, making it easier for the British to connect their territories across West Africa.[49] The Dutch followed in 1871–1872 by selling Elmina and other forts on the Gold Coast to the British, leaving the Dutch without any possessions in Africa.[50] In 1861,

[46] Coupland, *The Exploitation of East Africa*, 14–235. With 'Arab' traders, the group of mixed Arab-African descent from East Africa (primarily Zanzibar) are indicated in the literature. See e.g.: R.P. Ceulemans, *La question arabe et le Congo (1883–1892)* (Brussels 1959); F. Renault, *Tippo Tip: un potentat arabe en afrique centrale au XIXème siècle* (Paris 1987); P. Salmon, 'L'État Indépendant du Congo et la question arabe (1885–1892)', in: S.A. (ed.), *Bijdragen*, 437–460; P. Marechal, *De «Arabische» campagne in het Maniema-gebied (1892–1894): situering binnen het kolonisatieproces in de Onafhankelijke Congostaat* (Brussels 1992); J.C. Wilkinson, *The Arabs and the Scramble for Africa* (Sheffield 2015).

[47] De Kok, 'De koloniale connectie', 70–73; Todzi, *Unternehmen Weltaneignung*.

[48] Hargreaves, *Prelude to the Partition*.

[49] Reynolds, *Trade and Economic Change on the Gold Coast 1807–1874* (London 1974), 100.

[50] R. Storm, '1871: Kust van Guinea verdwijnt van de Nederlandse kaart', in: L. Heerma van Voss, N. Bouras, M. 't Hart, M. Van der Heijden & L. Lucassen (eds.), *Nog meer wereldgeschiedenis van Nederland* (Amsterdam 2022), 397–402; L.H.J. Sicking, *Frontières*

the British furthermore had proclaimed Lagos, one of West Africa's major port cities, to be a British Protectorate.[51] In response, the French also extended influence across some of its former strongholds, primarily in North and West Africa. The French had already invaded Algiers in 1827 and effectively annexed present-day Algeria in 1834, before incorporating it as French territory in 1865.[52] Moreover, it conquered present-day Senegal in 1854 and proclaimed sovereignty over some port cities, most importantly Porto Novo in present-day Benin in 1864.[53] The opening of the Suez Canal in 1869 (work having started in 1859) also provided a strategic and commercial rationale for European powers to get involved in Egypt (and to a lesser extent Sudan), in particular because it was largely financed by British capital.[54]

Until the late 1870s, no particular strategic value was however assigned to Africa by the European powers, except for some coastal areas that were considered economically important. To safeguard those interests, both France and Britain in limited episodes claimed sovereignty and consolidated jurisdiction over strategic port cities. Franco-British competition in West Africa was real in the period 1850–1875, but competition never reached a major breaking point until the late 1870s, particularly as the stakeholders in the economic conflicts were simply not powerful enough in their respective home countries to leverage their influence.[55] The French (slave) trading house *Régis* even explicitly relied on the protection of the Dahomey Kingdom (present-day Benin) rather than French power in the region.[56] This was not uncommon, as many strong African states still existed, such as the Fante and Asanti on the Gold Coast and the Dahomey Kingdom.[57] Elites in these states played major roles in supplying palm oil

d'Outre-Mer: La France et les Pays-Bas dans le monde atlantique au XIXe siècle (Paris 2006), 63–101 for the Gold Coast in general.

[51] I. Van Hulle, *Britain and International Law in West Africa: The Practice of Empire* (Oxford 2020), 121.

[52] D. Todd, *A Velvet Empire: French Informal Imperialism in the Nineteenth Century* (Princeton & Oxford 2021), 5 & 34.

[53] Daumalin, 'Commercial Presence', 220–221; Hargreaves, *Prelude*, 112–113.

[54] Rönnback & Broberg, *Capital and Colonialism*, 102.

[55] Hargreaves, *Prelude*, 140–142; C.W. Newbury & A.S. Kanya-Forster, 'French Policy and the Origins of the Scramble for Africa', *The Journal of African History*, 10, 2 (1969), 253–276, there 253 & 257.

[56] Newbury & Kanya-Forstner, 'French Policy', 254; Hargreaves, *Prelude*, 110–112.

[57] See Falola, *A History of West Africa*, 247–270.

and other commodities.[58] In 1847, Liberia declared independence and quickly also started exporting commodities such as palm oil, helped in part by the introduction of the steam ship.[59] Meanwhile, the erstwhile Iberian colonisers also retained some influence: the Portuguese for example still held nominal sovereignty over Angola and Mozambique (with *de facto* control being rather limited to coastal areas) as well as the islands of São Tomé and Principe, with the Spanish claiming *de jure* sovereignty over the island of Fernado Po (present-day Bioko in Equatorial Guinea), as well as conquering the territories of Ceuta and Melillia on the North African coast and the present-day Western Sahara.[60]

2.4 The Lead-up to the First Partition 1870–1884

In the early 1870s, the importance of Africa in European eyes rather suddenly changed. Politicians, scientists, soldiers and so-called 'explorers' showed a sudden interest in Africa's interior, away from the coast where a small number of Europeans were based.[61] Contrary to the Americas and large swathes of Asia, Africa's interior was considered 'unknown territory' by many of the Europeans, even if of course these places had been inhabited by people for a long time. The development of quinine as an effective medicine against malaria, historically a killer for over 50% of Europeans in Africa, helped Europeans to survive expeditions into the interior. Of these, the Scottish doctor David Livingstone is probably among the best-known among the public-at-large: he left London in 1840 for the Cape of Good Hope and explored Southern and Central Africa between 1851 and 1873. In 1871, an expedition was commissioned by the American newspaper *New York Herald* to look out for Livingstone. This expedition was led by Henry Morton Stanley, an American by birth who by adoption by a rich British family was catapulted into the upper layers of British society, who

[58] See e.g. G. Austin, 'Between Abolition and *Jihad*: The Asante Response to the Ending of the Atlantic Slave Trade, 1807–1896', in: Law (ed.), *From Slave Trade to 'Legitimate' Commerce*, 93–118; L.W. Yarak, *Asante and the Dutch 1744–1873* (Oxford 1990).

[59] Gardner, *Sovereignty Without Power: Liberia in the Age of Empires 1822–1980* (Cambridge 2022), 20–29; Lynn, 'From Sail to Steam'.

[60] Clarence-Smith, 'The Portuguese and Spanish Roles', 225.

[61] See for this perspective: Pakenham, *The Scramble for Africa*.

found Livingstone in November 1871 on the shores of Lake Tanganyika in the town of Ujiji.[62]

Despite their meeting having been mythologised in some histories since, European interest in the first instance remained muted among the broader public. Interests largely came from some upper-class entrepreneurs and academics, with politicians remaining largely indifferent until the mid-1870s. Various Colonial Associations were set up for so-called 'scientific' expeditions to various parts of Africa (for example in Germany[63]), but mostly these were the pursuit of a small group of rich people. Enthusiasm for colonial expansion was generally low in Europe in the 1860s and early 1870s, particularly when this colonial expansion was associated with taxpayers' money. Stanley was therefore disappointed to find that the British government was unwilling to pay him to go to Africa in their service. As a result, he started looking for other employers.

Between 1874 and 1877, the *New York Herald* and *Daily Telegraph* financed another of Stanley's expeditions, going from East Africa up to Boma on the Congo River in the present-day DR Congo. In April 1877, Stanley eventually reluctantly accepted an invitation from the Belgian King Leopold II for an expedition to Central Africa.[64] A first attempt by Leopold to send an expedition to Central Africa in 1877 had failed, as most members of the expedition passed away or resigned soon upon arriving. Leopold subsequently tried to lure Pierre Savorgnan de Brazza to his service, but he had already been contracted by the French.[65] Stanley's first expedition under Leopold's auspices consisted of a trip along the Congo river from 1879 onwards, officially under the so-called *Comité d'Études du Haut-Congo* (CEHC), one of Leopold's organisations that served as smokescreens for his own expansionist ambitions (Image 2.1). Stanley

[62] See for Stanley: T. Jeal, *Stanley: The Impossible Life of Africa's Greatest Explorer* (London 2007), in particular 91–132. The famous words "Dr. Livingstone, I presume?" supposed to have been spoken by Stanley may well have been an invention.

[63] B.D. Naranch, 'Beyond the Fatherland: Colonial Visions, Overseas Expansion, and German Nationalism, 1848–1885', Unpublished PhD Dissertation John Hopkins University (Baltimore MD 2006), 219–269.

[64] Jeal, *Stanley*, 234.

[65] See for De Brazza: I. Lanslot, 'Pierre Savorgnan de Brazza, le "Grand Chef Blanc": Le portrait contemporain d'un homme légendaire', in: D. Comberiati, P. Halen & R. Iounes-Vona (eds.), *Des Italiens au Congo aux Italiens du Congo: Aspects d'une glocalité* (Paris 2020), 43–54; Coquery-Vidrovitch, 'Les idées économiques de Brazza et les premières tentatives de companies de colonisation au Congo Français, 1885–1898', *Cahiers d'Études Africaines*, 5, 17 (1965), 57–82, there 59.

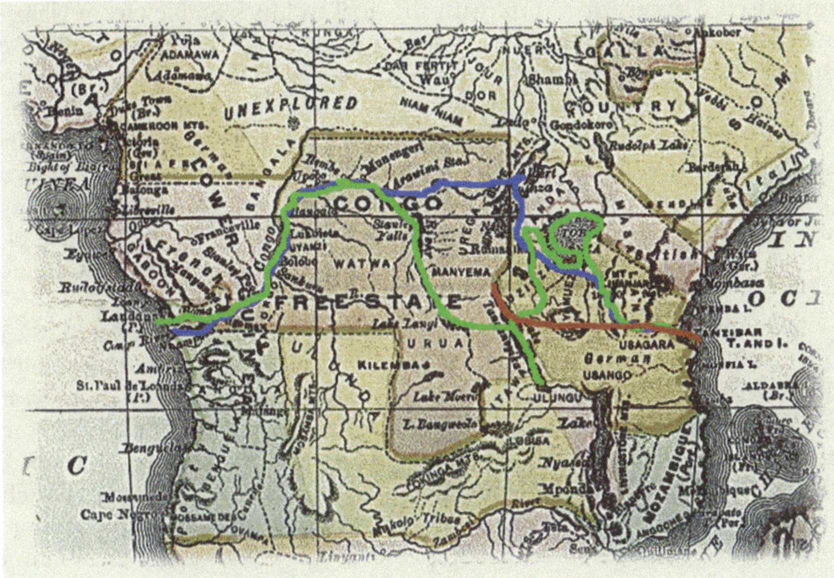

Image 2.1 Routes of Henry Morton Stanley's expeditions to Central Africa. (Source: André Engels at Dutch Wikipedia, available at https://commons.wikimedia.org/wiki/File:Stanleyroutes.PNG [Retrieved 04/03/2024])

remained in Central Africa until 1884 as Leopold's agent and subsequently wrote his *The Founding of the Congo Free State* upon returning to Europe[66].

Leopold's growing interest in Central Africa coincided with a surge of sudden interest in the continent by Europeans. Stanley's expeditions were soon followed by French, German and other British 'explorers' setting up expeditions into Africa's interior.[67] The aforementioned De Brazza, an Italian-born French naturalised citizen, could be counted among his main competitors.[68] De Brazza already visited Africa in the 1870s as part of anti-slavery missions, before setting up a small expedition between 1875 and 1878, formally for trading purposes.[69] In 1879, the French government

[66] Stanley, *The Congo and the Founding of its Free State*; see also N. Ascherson, *The King Incorporated: Leopold II in the Age of Trusts* (London 1963), 107–109.

[67] Jeal, *Stanley*; S. Cornelis *et al*, *H.M. Stanley: explorateur au service du Roi* (Tervuren 1991).

[68] See Lanslot, 'Pierre Savorgnan de Brazza'.

[69] Coquery-Vidrovitch, *Le Congo*, 45–50.

authorised a larger expedition with the goal to block Stanley from claiming (part of) the Congo Basin on behalf of Leopold II, and in 1880, De Brazza reached the Congo River. There, he signed the so-called Makoko treaty with King Makoko Iloo I of the Batéké, a people living on the Ogooué river in present-day Gabon, laying the first French claim to parts of the area that would later become the French Congo. It is with the two twin expeditions of Stanley and De Brazza to the Congo Basin that many historians have reckoned European imperialism in Africa really started, and changed the overwhelming economic interests to broader, strategic interests.[70]

It would be an understatement to say that the decade between 1875 and 1885 was rather consequential for the African continent. The role of the Belgian king Leopold II, who was among the first to show an interest in Central Africa, was crucial. Leopold had sought colonies for a long time in places as far-flung as China and South America.[71] Inspired by a book (J.W.B. Money's *Java; Or, How to Manage a Colony*) about the Dutch Cultivation System (*Cultuurstelsel*), which praised the system for the purpose of extracting resources from a colony, Leopold set out to obtain a colony by first contacting Stanley in 1875, and subsequently organising the so-called Geographical Conference in Brussels in 1876.[72]

[70] See e.g. Pakenham, *The Scramble for Africa*, 11–39.

[71] R.C. Alltmont, 'Belgian Overseas Expansion during the Nineteenth Century', Unpublished PhD Dissertation University of Delaware (Newark DE 1969), 269–275; J.A. Abbeloos, 'Belgium's Expansionist History between 1870 and 1930: Imperialism and the Globalisation of Belgian Business', in: C. Lévai (ed.), *Europe and Its Empires* (Pisa 2008), 105–127, there 113–114. See also: T. Vandamme, 'Beyond Belgium: The Business Empire of Edouard Empain in the First Global Economy (1880–1914)', Unpublished PhD Dissertation Ghent University (Ghent 2019), available at https://biblio.ugent.be/publication/8640740/file/8643749.pdf [Retrieved 23/10/2024], showing Belgium's global economic links.

[72] J. Stengers, 'Léopold II et le modèle colonial hollandais', *Tijdschrift voor Geschiedenis*, 90 (1977), 46–71; Wesseling, 'Nederland als koloniaal model'. The Cultivation System was a monopolistic system of forced labour with the goal to extract as many resources as possible from the Javanese peasantry. See: H.W. van den Doel, *Het Rijk van Insulinde: Opkomst en ondergang van een Nederlandse kolonie* (Amsterdam 1996), 91–124; Idem, *Zo ver de wereld strekt: de geschiedenis van Nederland overzee vanaf 1800* (Amsterdam 2011) 63–81. For Stanley and the Geographical Conference: Stengers, 'Léopold II entre l'Extrême-Orient et l'Afrique (1875–1876)', in: P. Staner & Stengers (eds.), *Bijdragen over de Aardrijkskundige Conferentie van 1876* (Brussels 1976), 303–374; J. Vandermissen, *Koningen van de wereld: Leopold II en de aardrijkskundige beweging* (Leuven 2009), 440; Jeal, *Stanley*, 234.

There were already Europeans active in the Congo Basin, including the Dutch AHV, the British firm *Hatton & Cookson*, the French firm *Régis* and various Portuguese firms, having set up shop in the coastal Congo basin in the 1850s in search of palm oil and other commodities.[73] After the 1876 Geographical Conference, Leopold established the so-called *Association Internationale Africaine* (AIA) as a vehicle for expansion.[74] In theory, this was an international association with member associations everywhere (including in the Netherlands):[75] in reality, this was a means for Leopold to organise support for his colonial ambitions. In 1878, the aforementioned CEHC was established by Leopold to finance expeditions to Central Africa: Stanley's expedition was the only one being made under the flag of the CEHC. The CEHC was partly financed by Lodewijk Pincoffs, as well as British and Belgian businessmen and investors who tried to use the expeditions to further their own commercial goals. The goals of the CEHC formally were manifold, including assessing navigability of the Congo River and the potential for trade.

Leopold had other plans, however. Privately, he had instructed Stanley to look for the possibilities to set up a colonial state there. The bankruptcy of the AHV in May-June 1879 (see Chaps. 3 and 4) presented him with the chance to take control and oust the foreign shareholders in the AIA and CEHC, who were, to Leopold's taste, too much focused on commercial matters rather than establishing a colonial state. He announced that he would disband both the AIA and the CEHC. The AIA was indeed dissolved, and the foreign shareholders received back their money: Stanley still believed until returning from the Congo Basin that he had been working under the flag of the CEHC.[76] Instead, Leopold in November 1879 announced the establishment of a third organisation: the *Association Internationale du Congo* (AIC), which was not really an association as it stood solely under Leopold's control.[77] With a small number of employees, the AIC was formed to realise Leopold's aim of colonising large swathes of the Congo Basin.

[73] Anstey, *Britain and the Congo in the Nineteenth Century* (Oxford 1962), 16–21; Marchal, *L'État Libre* (Vol. 1), 234–235.

[74] Stengers, 'Léopold II entre l'Extrême-Orient', 303–374; Vandermissen, *Koningen van de wereld*, 440; Jeal, *Stanley*, 234.

[75] Franssens, 'Nederland na de Aardrijkskundige Conferentie van Brussel (1877–1879)', in: Staner & Stengers (eds.), *Bijdragen*, 501–516, there 503–504.

[76] Stengers, 'Leopold II and the Association Internationale du Congo', 229.

[77] Ibidem, 230.

Of course, the interest of European states was not limited to the Congo basin area, even if Leopold's actions in the Congo Basin between 1875 and 1885 have, in the popular conscience, become one of the defining factors of European nineteenth-century imperialism in Africa. Following the 1876 Geographical Conference and Leopold's broader attempts to establish a colony in Africa, other European governments also were caught by a virus of (quite sudden) interest in the African continent that they had lacked for so long. Britain, France and Portugal, the three main colonial powers already established in small parts of Africa, suddenly rediscovered the importance of Africa as a place to project power and extract resources. Portugal for example reasserted her claims in areas adjacent to its main colonies in Angola and Mozambique, including the northern bank of the Congo River.[78] Next to Leopold's AIC, some countries (most notably Germany, see below) also developed an interest in colonising Africa. Although economic exploitation was certainly an important motivation behind the sudden interest, political-strategic motives were probably dominant in the period between 1875 and 1885.[79]

This was the period when the First Partition of Africa happened, and when the private economic motives for the Scramble were connected to the larger geopolitical concerns. In North Africa, for example, Franco-British competition heated up over Sudan and Egypt, with the French solidifying control over the Western belt of North Africa;[80] in East Africa, a rivalry between the British and Germans developed, eventually leading to the two powers consolidating northern East Africa (Britain) and southern East Africa (Germany);[81] and in Southern Africa, a complex set of rivalries between the Afrikaners, British, Germans and Portuguese developed, partly following the discovery of mineral deposits (gold and

[78] E. Axelson, *Portugal and the Scramble for Africa 1875–1891* (Johannesburg 1967), 38–83; Newitt, *Portugal in Africa*, 73–80; L. Da Veiga Pinto, *Le Portugal et le Congo au XIXe siècle: étude d'histoire des relations internationals* (Paris 1972), 191–194.

[79] Fieldhouse, *Economics and Empire*, 91–104.

[80] See e.g. Todd, *Velvet Empire*; Kanya-Forstner, 'French African Priorities and the Berlin West Africa Conference', in: Förster, Mommsen & Robinson (eds.), *Bismarck, Europe and Africa*, 171–187, there 171–173; Gallagher & Robinson, *Africa and the Victorians*, 76–121 & 210–273.

[81] See e.g. S. Conrad, *German Colonialism: A Short History* (Cambridge 2012), 23–54; E.R. Vere-Hodge, *Imperial British East Africa Company* (London 1960); Coupland, *The Exploitation of East Africa*; Pakenham, *The Scramble for Africa*, 336–357, 602–628 & 641–655.

diamonds) near what is today Johannesburg.[82] Eventually, the British consolidated South Africa, with the Germans settling in Namibia.[83]

Here the focus primarily is on the case of West Africa. In 1878–1879, the French moved to occupy parts of inland Senegal.[84] Britain tightened control over the Gold Coast and the production sites inland, as well as the Lagos coastline and the Niger delta as well as Sierra Leone.[85] In 1884, German forces arrived and quickly snapped up Togo and parts of present-day Cameroon.[86] After the Berlin Conference of 1884–1885, this process continued for a little while: in 1886, French forces for example reached the upper Niger from the Senegal river and occupied the area between Lagos and Togo, present-day Benin, after already having occupied the city of Porto Novo in 1854.[87] In response, the British proclaimed protectorates over most of the Lower Niger delta, as well as the Gambia River delta and the Gold Coast.

The decade between 1875 and 1884, therefore, saw a flurry of activity by European states aiming to claim parts of Africa. This differed from previous decades in the sense that *private, economic* interests were not in all cases the most important driver of European expansion in this decade. Although economic interests were certainly of great importance and private economic actors often actively lobbied for, participated in and profited from colonial expansion in this decade, political motives like geopolitical competition, national pride and ideas of contiguity and preemption were also part of the mix.[88] European encroachment almost

[82] Pakenham, *The Scramble for Africa*, 372–392; P. Slinn, 'Commercial Concessions and Politics during the Colonial Period: The Role of the British South Africa Company in Northern Rhodesia 1890–1964', *African Affairs*, 70, 281 (1971), 365–384, there 365–370; Gwaindepi & Siebrits, 'How Mineral Discoveries'; Rönnbäck & Broberg, 'From Defensive to Transformative Business Diplomacy: The British South Africa Company and the End of Chartered Company Rule in Rhodesia, 1910–1925', *Business History Review*, 96, 4 (2022), 777–903, https://doi.org/10.1017/S0007680522000022.

[83] Conrad, *German Colonialism*, 42; Pakenham, *The Scramble for Africa*, 602–615.

[84] Kanya-Forstner, 'French African Priorities', 184–185.

[85] J. Flint, 'Chartered Companies and the Transition from Informal Sway to Colonial Rule in Africa', in: Förster, Mommsen & Robinson (eds.), *Bismarck, Europe and Africa*, 69–83, there 72–77.

[86] Conrad, *German Colonialism*, 36–45.

[87] Kanya-Forstner, 'French African Priorities', 184–185.

[88] R.F. Betts, *The False Dawn: European Imperialism in the Nineteenth Century* (Minneapolis MN 1975), 121–149; Fieldhouse, *Economics and Empire*, 459–478; Mommsen, *Imperialismustheorien: Ein Überblick über die neueren Imperialismustheorien* (Göttingen 1977), 111–124; Wesseling, *Verdeel en heers*, 452–462; Idem, *Europa's koloniale*

always happened without the consent of Africans who lived on those territories, and their rulers were often made to sign unequal treaties which largely benefited Europeans.[89]

In Europe, meanwhile, the threat of war rose with colonial expansion: the 1882 take-over by Britain of Egypt had for example almost led to war between Britain and France. Attempting to solve the issue peacefully, the German Chancellor Otto von Bismarck proposed the convention of a conference on Africa. This so-called Berlin Conference, which took place between November 1884 and February 1885, succeeded in its stated goal of preventing war over the Partition of Africa, and did create a legal framework for the Partition between European states. On the other hand, the Berlin Conference has been seen as the high point of European imperial ambitions, and as a symbol of Western imperial decision-making without the involvement of Africans.[90] The next section seeks to untangle the conflicting views on the aims, causes and consequences of the Berlin Conference.

2.5 The Berlin Conference of 1884–1885 and the First Partition

The Berlin Conference haunts the historical memory of European imperialism, standing as the symbol of European arrogance, disdain for indigenous viewpoints and the cause of much of Africa's misfortune. Images 2.2 and 2.3 show this process well and stand as examples of the old cliché that Africa was partitioned in Berlin by white European men, which was true

eeuw, 171–203; R. Aldrich & A. Stucki, *The Colonial World: A History of European Empires, 1780s to the Present* (London 2023), 445–454.

[89] C.H. Alexandrowicz, *The European-African Confrontation. A Study in Treaty Making* (Leiden 1973); Van Hulle, 'The Blood Brotherhood and Colonial Treaties and Alliances: Between Myth and Reality', *Journal of the History of International Law*, 25 (2023), 471–498; Idem, *Britain and International Law*, 165–205.

[90] In the popular imagination, the Berlin Conference is taken to be the place where Africa was partitioned. Scholars have however long nuanced this point, as the Scramble started earlier and the Berlin Conference' aim was narrower than 'partitioning Africa'. See e.g.: Stengers, 'Les cinq legends de l'Acte de Berlin', in: Idem, *Congo, mythes et réalités: 100 ans d'histoire* (Paris & Louvain-La-Neuve 1989), 79–90; Wesseling, 'The Berlin Conference and the Expansion of Europe: A Conclusion', in: Förster, Mommsen & Robinson (eds.), *Bismarck, Europe and Africa*, 527–540, especially 531–532.

Image 2.2 Cartoon depicting Leopold II and other imperial powers at the 1884–1885 Berlin Conference. (Source: François Maréchal, Public domain, via Wikimedia Commons [Retrieved 18/10/2023])

Image 2.3 Cartoon about the Berlin Conference, 1884–1885. (Source: Zz1y, Draner, CC BY-SA 4.0, via Wikimedia Commons [Retrieved 18/10/2023])

to an extent, but at the same time presents an oversimplification of historical complexity.[91]

One scholarly issue concerns the different values historians and lawyers attach to the Berlin Conference. As Matthew Craven argued in a persuasive 2015 article, the Berlin Conference finds itself 'between law and

[91] See for example the work of Robinson, emphasising the African agency: Robinson, 'Non-European Foundations of European Imperialism: Sketch for a Theory of Collaboration', in: Roger Louis (ed.), *Imperialism*, 128–151; Idem, 'European Imperialism and Indigenous Reactions in British West Africa, 1880–1914)', in: Wesseling & F. Braudel (eds.), *Expansion and Reaction: Essays on European Expansion and Reaction in Asia and Africa* (Leiden 1978), 141–163.

history':[92] whereas historians nowadays largely play down the importance of the Berlin Conference, for most (international) lawyers the Berlin Conference still plays a significant role in the development of international law. According to Craven, historians downplayed the importance of the Berlin Conference both as a historical milestone in European imperial expansion and as the established *legal regime* in Berlin to govern imperial expansion.[93]

As the Belgian historian Jean Stengers wrote in a groundbreaking article, five myths about the Berlin Conference have persistently dogged the image of the event. These five myths are (1) Africa was partitioned only and solely in Berlin, (2) Africa was partitioned into spheres of influence in Berlin, (3) the Berlin Conference recognised the Congo Free State, (4) Berlin created the Congo Free State as an 'international colony' and (5) the decisions agreed upon at the Berlin Conference quickly became a 'dead letter'.[94] While some of his views have been modified since, in particular, his first point is widely accepted today in the scholarly historical literature.[95] In contrast, lawyers and legal historians argue that the general legal framework agreed upon in Berlin was crucial for the development of international law in the late nineteenth century. Anthony Anghie, for example, one of the foremost proponents of critical analysis of international law, argued that the Berlin Conference essentially codified and

[92] M. Craven, 'Between Law and History: The Berlin Conference of 1884–1884 and the Logic of Free Trade', *London Review of International Law*, 3, 1 (2015), 31–59, https://doi.org/10.1093/lril/lrv002.

[93] Ibidem.

[94] Stengers, 'Les cinq legends'. See for a similar argument: S. Katzenellenbogen, 'It Didn't Happen at Berlin: Politics, Economics and Ignorance in the Setting of Africa's Colonial Boundaries', in: P. Nugent & A.I. Asiwaju (eds.), *African Boundaries: Barriers, Conduits and Opportunities* (London & New York 1996), 21–34, there 21–22.

[95] Craven, 'Between Law and History', 32–36; Wesseling, 'The Berlin Conference', 527–540; G.N. Sanderson, 'The European Partition of Africa: Coincidence or Conjuncture?', *The Journal of Imperial and Commonwealth History*, 3, 1 (1974), 1–54, https://doi.org/10.1080/03086537408582421; A.D. Nzemeke, 'Free Trade and Territorial Partition in Nineteenth-Century West Africa: Course and Outcome', in: Förster, Mommsen & Robinson (eds.), *Bismarck, Europe and Africa*, 59–68; Robinson, 'The Conference in Berlin and the Future in Africa, 1884–1885', in: Förster, Mommsen & Robinson (eds.), *Bismarck, Europe and Africa*, 73–127; Robinson & Gallagher, 'The Partition of Africa', in: Roger Louis (ed.), *Imperialism* 73–127; Oliver, 'The Partition of Africa'.

legitimised Europe's racist legal order, a view widely shared among lawyers after the 'historical turn' in international law.[96]

These disciplinary parameters are indeed important in judging the Berlin Conference, with lawyers generally viewing the legal framework established in Berlin as pathbreaking. Some historians in the twentieth century tended to agree with this assessment.[97] Nowadays, most historians would however argue that the Berlin Conference was an important moment for negotiations, but also acknowledge that much of what was discussed in Berlin was essentially the codification and ratification of many bilateral or trilateral agreements, for example between Portugal and Britain, or between Germany and France.[98] Indeed, large parts of Africa were already claimed by Europeans between 1875 and 1884: the many treaties between Europeans and Africans, but also between Europeans, prove this.[99] Moreover, indigenous African elites often worked with Europeans to advance their own interests.[100]

Yet acknowledging the importance of the *legal framework* for the development of international law agreed upon in Berlin does not necessarily mean agreeing with the *historical view* that the Berlin Conference was a crucial turning point in the nineteenth-century European imperial expansion in Africa: in short, the revisionist views of Stengers on one side and Anghie on the other can exist next to each other (with the legal implications being more far-reaching than the actual historical implications on the ground).[101]

[96] Anghie, *Imperialism*, 73 & 90. See e.g. I. Geiss, Free Trade, Internationalization of the Congo Basin, and the Principle of Effective Occupation', in: Förster, Mommsen & Robinson (eds.), *Bismarck, Europe and Africa*, 263–280; J. Fisch, 'Africa as *terra nullius*: The Berlin Conference and International Law', in: Förster, Mommsen & Robinson (eds.), *Bismarck, Europe and Africa*, 347–375; Van Hulle, *Britain and International Law*, 237–254; Craven, 'Between Law and History', 32–33; M. Koskenniemi, *The Gentle Civilizer of Nations: The Rise and Fall of International Law 1870–1960)* (Cambridge 2004), 121–127; M. Van der Linden, *The Acquisition of Africa (1870–1914): The Nature of International Law* (Leiden & Boston 2017).

[97] See e.g. M.E. Chamberlain, *The Scramble for Africa* (London 1974); Pakenham, *The Scramble for Africa*.

[98] Stengers, 'Les cinq legends'.

[99] Alexandrowicz, *The European-African Confrontation*.

[100] Robinson, 'Non-European Foundations'; Idem, 'European Imperialism and Indigenous Reactions'.

[101] Stengers, 'Les cinq legendes'; Anghie, *Imperialism*; see also Hopkins, 'Imperial Business in Africa', 274; Oliver, 'The Partition of Africa', 41–45.

The convention of the Berlin Conference cannot be explained without a look at two important developments: first, the newly assertive Portuguese claims over the Congo Basin, and second, the curious 'colonial conversion' of Von Bismarck. Up to the early 1880s, three main powers were involved in claim-making over the African territory: France, Britain and Portugal. Portugal's claims did not only include Angola and Mozambique, but also surrounding territories, including parts north of the Congo River. Portuguese claims over the northern parts of the Congo River were weak, but the entrance of two new major players (Leopold II and Von Bismarck), led Portugal to assert its claims over the region of the Congo basin more forcefully. This already led to the (later abandoned) Anglo-Portuguese Treaty of 1884, which was meant to solidify Portuguese claims over the Congo Basin with British support to prevent France from claiming sovereignty there. Opposition to this Treaty came from many sides, including from France and from the Manchester Chamber of Commerce, eventually leading the British to abandon the Treaty.[102]

In the late 1870s, Germany entered the race for African territory. Von Bismarck had long been opposed to German colonial expansion, judging it too expensive. Private actors, primarily entrepreneurs and geographical 'explorers', had since the late 1830s taken to operate in colonial environments. Notwithstanding Von Bismarck's opposition, general public opinion was largely favourable to colonial expansion, and some efforts to claim some possessions were made by the Prussians (e.g. in 1859 with a failed attempt to claim Formosa, present-day Taiwan). Moreover, some naval and trading stations were set up, for example in the Pacific Ocean and China.[103] Under public pressure and as part of his political strategy, Von Bismarck eventually consented to formal colonisation efforts under the German flag in 1884, including in Africa.[104] Upon doing so, he allowed the German army to invade and claim various territories both in Asia and

[102] See e.g. Axelson, *Portugal*, 55–83; Da Veiga Pinto, *Le Portugal*, 123–210; Newitt, *Portugal in Africa*, 25–32; Hammond, *Portugal and Africa*, 77–132; Clarence-Smith, 'The Myth'; Idem, 'The Portuguese and Spanish Roles'; Idem, *The Third Portuguese Empire*, 81–84.

[103] Naranch, 'Beyond the Fatherland', 270–324; Conrad, *German Colonialism*, 54–65.

[104] Conrad, *German Colonialism*, 36; Roger Louis, 'Great Britain and German Expansion in Africa, 1884–1919', in: P. Gifford & Roger Louis (eds.), *Britain and Germany in Africa*, 3–46, there 7–8; Ashby Turner jr., 'Bismarck's Imperalist Venture', 47–50.

the Pacific as well as Africa.[105] In Asia, claims were laid on a series of islands to be known as German New Guinea (largely present-day Papua New Guinea); in Africa, on German East Africa (present-day Burundi, Rwanda and mainland Tanzania), German South West-Africa (present-day Namibia), German Cameroon (comprising parts of present-day Cameroon, but also Gabon, Congo-Brazzaville, the Central African Republic, Chad and Nigeria) and Togoland (largely present-day Togo with parts of present-day Ghana).

Von Bismarck's much-discussed volte-face raised the geopolitical temperature across Europe, as rather suddenly a new, heavily militarised European power entered the scramble for colonial territories.[106] Taken alongside Leopold's increasingly clear aims to establish a colony in the Congo Basin, Portugal's renewed assertiveness in claiming territories in the region and Franco-British competition over various territories in the region (notably Egypt, but also various places in West Africa); this was a cocktail of events and interests that could have easily led to war.[107] Partly on the initiative of the Portuguese and with the support of Great Britain, Von Bismarck invited everyone to Berlin to solve the 'African issue' via negotiations rather than violence. Historians generally credit Bismarck with peacefully solving the issue in Europe.[108] While the Berlin Conference indeed managed to avoid war in Europe, the perspectives of Africans were not at all incorporated into these discussions.

The Berlin Conference essentially consisted of a series of negotiations starting on 15 November 1884. The final acts of the conference were agreed on 26 February 1885. Fourteen countries were invited and present: Germany, Austria-Hungary, Belgium, Spain, Denmark, the United States, France, the United Kingdom, Italy, the Netherlands, Portugal, Russia, Sweden-Norway and the Ottoman Empire. Next to the obvious

[105] Conrad, *German Colonialism*, 36–45; H.R. Rudin, *Germans in the Cameroons 1884–1914: A Case Study in Modern Imperialism* (Oxford 1938/1968), 35.

[106] See for a recent re-interpretation of Germany's colonial efforts; Press, 'Buying Sovereignty: German "Weltpolitik" and Private Enterprise, 1884–1914', *Central European History*, 55, 1 (2022), 15–33, https://doi.org/10.1017/S0008938921001746.

[107] See e.g. Axelson, *Portugal*, 55–83; Da Veiga Pinto, *Le Portugal*, 123–210; Newitt, *Portugal in Africa*, 25–32; R.J. Hammond, *Portugal and Africa*, 77–132; Clarence-Smith, 'The Myth of Uneconomic Imperialism'; Idem, 'The Portuguese and Spanish Roles'; Idem, *The Third Portuguese Empire 1825–1975: A Study in Economic Imperialism* (Manchester 1985), 81–84.

[108] Wesseling, 'The Berlin Conference'.

large colonial powers interested in acquiring territory in Africa, various other countries were also present in Berlin: The Netherlands, having transferred its remaining colonies on the Gold Coast to British control in 1872, was for example present partly for its commercial interests in Africa, but primarily as the world's third-largest colonial power. The Ottoman Empire, meanwhile, was invited as the still-formal suzerain ruler over Egypt, and Russia was a major European country. The invited countries had strongly different interests and reasons to be present in Berlin.

The most important topics at the Berlin Conference were free trade and the prerequisites for occupying territories in Africa. For public opinion purposes, the Conference also agreed to abolish slavery and the slave trade.[109] The Conference introduced the 'Principle of Effective Occupation', which held that there had to be a form of effective presence and actual government on the ground before a European country could claim an African territory as its own.[110] Upon claiming possession or establishing a Protectorate, a European country had to notify the other participants of the Berlin Conference, even if a compromise between the British and the Germans effectively limited this to the coastal areas, contrary to the common perception that this concerned the whole continent.[111] According to legal historians, the Acts of the Berlin Conference did often not conform to standards of international law: for example, Africa was legally conceptualised as *terra nullius* and thus declared vacant, but on the other hand, treaties made by Europeans with local rulers were used to prove the 'effective occupation'.[112] From a legal point of view, several incompatible principles were thus combined in the Acts of the Berlin Conference.[113]

Free trade was another major issue. As most countries agreed that Africa would be partitioned among the European countries, guarantees for free

[109] Anghie, *Imperialism*, 90.

[110] Craven, 'Between Law and History'; Katzenellenbogen, 'It Didn't Happen at Berlin', 22.

[111] Katzenellenbogen, 'It Didn't Happen at Berlin', 22.

[112] Geiss, 'Free Trade'; Craven, 'Between Law and History', 54; Fisch, 'Africa as *terra nullius*', 353–354; Anghie, *Imperialism*, 90; Van Hulle, *Britain and International Law*, 237–248; Koskenniemi, *The Gentle Civilizer*, 126–127.

[113] This point was made especially clear by Inge van Hulle at a workshop held at the World Museum in Leiden on 7–8 December 2022. While no written text is available from this presentation (yet), I'd like to make clear that this point is explicitly drawing on Van Hulle's work.

trade were of importance, particularly for the British (the Dutch also pushed hard for this).[114] Next to the Congo basin, the Lake Malawi area was proclaimed as a free trade area. In addition, the Niger and Congo rivers were declared free shipping areas, regardless of flag that the ship flew.[115] The Lower Congo area was thus both a free trade and free shipping area; the Niger River was free for shipping, but free trade was not guaranteed in areas occupied by British or French forces. In the final Act of the Berlin Conference, an International Commission was established to supervise the free navigation (Article 17).[116]

In essence, the Berlin Conference thus largely codified existing arrangements, with two major shifts involving Portuguese claims.[117] Portugal's claim on the Lower Congo area, in the 1883 Anglo-Portuguese Treaty accepted by the British (though never ratified due to public opposition by anti-slavery campaigners and free traders in Britain), was set aside in favour of the sovereignty of the *Association Internationale du Congo* (AIC), Leopold's vehicle. In contrast, all parties bar the United Kingdom agreed upon Portuguese sovereignty over the area linking Angola and Mozambique.[118] In 1890, the British would eventually present Portugal with an ultimatum and take possession of those areas themselves, such as present-day Zambia.[119]

Here, we also take a closer look at the Dutch position during the Berlin Conference, where the Dutch had to reckon with two paradoxical goals.[120] On the one hand, the Dutch argued for free trade in Africa; on the other hand, the Dutch were reluctant to agree to anything on political matters as it risked being also applied outside of Africa. Most importantly for the

[114] Stengers, 'Leopold II and the Association Internationale du Congo', 239–242; Geiss, 'Free Trade'.

[115] Craven, 'Between Law and History', 54–57.

[116] Ibidem, 37–39.

[117] Clarence-Smith, 'The Portuguese and Spanish Roles', 217–224.

[118] Ibidem.

[119] Idem, *The Third Portuguese Empire*, 82–85.

[120] See e.g.: Wesseling, 'Les Pays-Bas et la creation du Congo', in: S.A. (ed.), *Bijdragen*, 467–476; Idem, 'Nederland en de Conferentie van Berlijn'; Idem, 'The Netherlands and the Partition of Africa'; Idem, 'Bestond er een Nederlands imperialisme?'; Kuitenbrouwer, 'Het imperialisme-debat'; Idem, *Nederland en de opkomst*, 50–54, 59–79, 99–118 & 133–173. For the main focus on the Dutch East Indies, see: Van Goor, 'Imperialisme in de marge?'; Lindblad, 'Economische aspecten'; Van den Doel, *Het Rijk van Insulinde*.

Dutch, the legal principle of 'effective occupation' presented a problem.[121] Following this principle, Dutch imperial claims over most of present-day Indonesia would have been either very questionable or non-existent, as the Dutch effective occupation was largely confined to Java and parts of Sumatra.[122] As Wesseling succinctly stated about the Dutch, "they spoke about Africa, but were thinking about the Dutch East Indies".[123] Dutch sovereign claims over Sumatra had become stronger since 1871–1872, when, as part of the Anglo-Dutch Treaty, Britain took over the remaining fortifications on the Dutch Gold Coast from the Dutch, and the British acknowledged Dutch sovereignty over Sumatra.[124] Outside Java and several other smaller islands, however, Dutch control was limited.

At the same time, the Dutch argued for the importance of free trade at the Conference, and found the United Kingdom at its side. The NAHV, among the largest firms active in the Congo Basin, pushed hard with the Dutch government to lobby for the establishment of a free trade area in the region.[125] Although recognition of the AIC was not formally among the negotiated topics, informally this was very much the case. Although Leopold and his AIC promised a free trade area, many were sceptical of his promises (rightly so, it would turn out).[126] The eventual compromise between France, Germany and Britain eventually tilted the balance towards Leopold's AIC, who was seen as the lesser evil for all the major colonial powers bar Portugal: as a result, Britain abandoned the free trade position in favour of this compromise, leading the Dutch to reluctantly abandon their position against the AIC and supporting the compromise, with some reservations.[127] The NAHV's interests were thus partly abandoned by the Dutch when faced with the new British position; moreover, the political importance of the agreements not being made applicable to the Dutch

[121] Craven, 'Between Law and History'; Koskenniemi, *The Gentle Civilizer of Nations*, 121–127.

[122] Van Goor, 'Imperialisme in de marge?'.

[123] Wesseling, 'Nederland en de Conferentie van Berlijn', 571: "men sprak over Afrika, maar dacht aan Nederlands-Indië".

[124] Kuitenbrouwer, *Nederland en de opkomst*, 43–47.

[125] Muller, *Muller*, 371–372; Wesseling, *De Mullers, Nederland en Afrika* (The Hague 2009), 13; Idem, 'Nederland en de Conferentie van Berlijn', 570; Kuitenbrouwer, *Nederland en de opkomst*, 90.

[126] Marchal, *L'État Libre* (Vol. 1), 115–124.

[127] Wesseling, 'Nederland en de Conferentie van Berlijn', 571–576.

East Indies was considered more prescient than holding out support against the AIC for the Dutch state, sacrificing the NAHV.[128]

The Berlin Conference's aim was therefore more limited in scope than often presented: Africa was not 'partitioned' there, although various, previously concluded, bilateral agreements were ratified in Berlin (e.g. French claims in West Africa). A legal framework was established for *future* claims to sovereignty over African territory by Europeans, and guarantees for free trade and navigation over parts of Africa (the Niger and Congo rivers) were made by all parties involved. Importantly, the agreements were not applicable to other areas than Africa. The Berlin Conference was thus an important moment in European imperial expansion in nineteenth-century Africa but was certainly not a catch-all moment. The principle of effective occupation did lead to a flurry of claim-making by European nations, which were however largely solved without conflict (e.g. by treaty-making). Moreover, the Conference *legitimised* Leopold's claims to territory in the Congo Basin, which would only *after* the Conference would be formally accepted by most negotiating powers.

The Acts of the Berlin Conference did not include an article about Leopold, the AIC or about the Congo Free State, even if Belgium was among the signatories: this is why Stengers has been so adamant in his claim that the Berlin Conference did not put in place the Congo Free State.[129] Indeed, some countries already had acknowledged the AIC's flag even before the Berlin Conference, most notably the United States on 10 April 1884.[130] Although many parties at the Berlin Conference had agreed (or were forced to accept) to allow the AIC sovereignty over the northern bank of the Congo Basin, this did not mean the Congo Free State was established in Berlin.[131] What it did do was to speed up the individual ratification by states to acknowledge the AIC's sovereignty. Germany soon followed the United States by first recognising the AIC's flag in May 1884, and the sovereignty of the AIC over the Congo Basin in November 1884.[132] The United States followed on 28 November; on 13 December, the United Kingdom also did so, both during the Berlin Conference. The

[128] Ibidem.

[129] Stengers, 'Les cinq legends'.

[130] A.P. Mohun, *American Imperialist: Cruelty and Consequence in the Scramble for Africa* (Chicago 2023), 40–41.

[131] Stengers, 'Les cinq legends'.

[132] Idem, 'Léopold II et l'Association Internationale du Congo' in: S.A. (ed.), *Bijdragen*, 51–76, there 52.

Netherlands felt forced to recognise the AIC on 28 December 1884. Portugal and France were among the holdouts. In February 1885, the Portuguese even sent warships to Cabinda to strengthen their claim militarily, but they had to retreat in the face of international pressure.[133]

Only in May 1885, after another failed military intervention by the Portuguese and the French compromising, could Leopold negotiate the final details of the AIC's take-over (which in particular had to do with tariff regulations). The French were satisfied with Leopold's promise that if the AIC would pull out at some point, the French had the first right to claim the territory; for the British and Germans, preventing the French from claiming the territory in the first place was the maximum they could bargain for. Portugal was left empty-handed.[134] In August 1885, Leopold finally proclaimed the 'annexation' of the huge Congo basin by the AIC, and immediately announced that the name would change to the Congo Free State. After the lengthy negotiations in Berlin, most countries quickly recognised the Congo Free State and its sovereign Leopold: the Dutch for example did so on 3 August 1885, and appointed Baron Gericke van Herwijnen as their ambassador in Brussels (where officially the 'state' that became the Congo Free State was headquartered).[135]

2.6 The Congo Free State 1885–1908

Leopold got what he wanted: a colony with the potential for economic exploitation, backed by the major European powers.[136] In marked contrast to (for example) some areas in West Africa, colonisation was not done with

[133] Axelson, *Portugal*, 60–61; Da Veiga Pinto, *Le Portugal*, 285–291; Clarence-Smith, *The Third Portuguese Empire*, 83. See also: NL-HaNA, Buitenlandse Zaken A-Dossiers, nr. 216, Letters Gericke van Herwijnen to Ministry of Foreign Affairs, 18-02-1885 & 14-04-1885.

[134] Stengers, 'The Congo Free State', 262; Idem, 'Leopold II and the Association Internationale du Congo', 52–53.

[135] NL-HaNA, Buitenlandse Zaken A-Dossiers, nr. 216, Letter Gericke van Herwijnen to Ministry of Foreign Affairs, 28-12-1884. With the letter, Gericke van Herwijnen sent a concept agreement with Strauch, the unofficial PM of the Congo Free State in the making, about the recognition. On 08-05-1885, the Dutch King William III officially signed the recognition into law. Copies of the agreement and the proclamation by William III can be found in the same map.

[136] Of course, Marxist historians have also incorporated the Congo Free State into its analysis. See for example: B. Jewsiewicki, 'Notes sur l'Histoire socio-économique du Congo (1880–1960)', *Etudes d'Histoire Africaine*, 3 (1972), 209–241; Idem, 'Raison d'Etat ou raison du capital: l'accumulation primitive au Congo belge', *African Economic History*, 12

the (tacit) support of local elites.[137] Moreover, Leopold did not have any experience in running a colonial effort.[138] The Congo Free State was promoted by Leopold as an 'international colony' where all Europeans were welcome. In theory, there were no links to Belgium except for the fact that Leopold was the sovereign head of the two states: in practice, the links to Belgium were plentiful as the Congo Free State administration was based in Brussels, and many of its high-ranking officials were Belgian.[139] In discussions in Belgium itself, a majority in Parliament had argued against a Belgian role in colonisation, judging it too expensive.[140] As a result, the Congo Free State was recognised by the Belgians as a state but was explicitly not entitled to Belgian financial support. Both Chambers of the Parliament did, however, agree to make an exception for Leopold to become the Congo Free State head of state.[141] This led to a personal union under Leopold: Leopold was bound as a constitutional monarch in Belgium, while he had the almost absolute freedom to do as he pleased in the Congo Free State.

The government of the Congo Free State was formed by Leopold and a small number of his confidants, who often already had long been in Leopold's private service or worked for the Belgian government. In Brussels, the triumvirate of Edmond van Eetvelde (Foreign Affairs), Hubert van Neuss (Treasury) and Maximilien Strauch (Home Office) was put in charge of the daily government business of the Congo Free State.[142]

(1983), 157–182; Idem, 'Zaire Enters the World System: Its Colonial Incorporation as the Belgian Congo, 1885–1960', in: G. Gran (ed.), *Zaire: The Political Economy of Underdevelopment* (New York 1979); J-L. Peemans, 'Capital Accumulation in the Congo under Colonialism: The Role of the State', in: P. Duignan & L.H. Gann (eds.), *Colonialism in Africa 1870–1960. Volume 4: The Economics of Colonialism* (Cambridge 1975), 165–212.

137 See e.g. Vos, *Kongo in the Age of Empire, 1860–1913: The Breakdown of a Moral Order* (Madison WI, Milwaukee WI & London 2015).

138 Van den Doel, *Het Rijk van Insulinde*, 91–97.

139 Stengers & Vansina, 'King Leopold's Congo, 1886–1908', in: Oliver & Sanderson (eds.), *The Cambridge History of Africa. Volume 6: Western Equatorial Africa* (Cambridge 1985), 315–358, https://doi.org/10.1017/CHOL9780521228039.009, there 323.

140 V. Viaene, 'King Leopold's Imperialism and the Origins of the Belgian Colonial Party, 1860–1905', *The Journal of Modern History*, 80, 4 (2008), 741–790, there 760–764; G. Vanthemsche, *Belgium and the Congo, 1885–1980* (Cambridge 2012), 14–100. See also: M.G. Stanard, *Selling the Congo: A History of European Pro-Empire Propaganda and the Making of Belgian Imperialism* (Lincoln NE 2012) 2–4.

141 Viaene, 'King Leopold's Imperialism', 770–771; Vanthemsche, *Belgium and the Congo*, 36–38.

142 Gann & Duignan, *The Rulers of Belgian Africa, 1884–1914* (Princeton NJ 1979), 85–87.

They were supported by only a rather small administrative support staff. Leopold appointed Francis de Winton as the first Governor-General in the Congo Free State, although he was soon replaced by Camille Janssens. The Governor-General first resided in the newly established town of Vivi, and from 1 May 1886 onwards in Boma, which was designated as the capital of the Congo Free State. In Boma, a High Court of Justice was therefore also established as the superior court, as were many other governmental organisations.[143] Leopold had already founded an army in 1877, the so-called *Force Publique*: although there were many Belgian officers in the *Force Publique*, many of its rank-and-file members were mercenaries or former soldiers and officers from other European countries, who were paid well to move to the Congo Free State.[144] Its (formal) status as an international colony meant that while many of the upper layers of governmental institutions like courts, tax authorities and the army were Belgian, among the lower layers there were numerous Europeans, including Dutchmen, Italians, Germans, Swiss and even Luxembourgers.[145]

Some historians have argued that the Congo Free State was, due to its hybrid nature, different from most other European colonies in Africa.[146] As Bas de Roo has however argued, the Congo Free State was fairly comparable to its peers in many regards, including because (1) of the push to "rule and exploit his colony at the lowest possible cost", (2) the basic characteristic of the extractive system did not change, as the Congo Free State surplus was transferred to Brussels, (3) the extractive system of outsourcing exploitation to private colonies was found elsewhere and (4) the Congo Free State was by the Acts of the Berlin Conference allowed to levy tariffs, contrary to received wisdom, and could therefore be considered as

[143] Ibidem, 89–90; Gann, 'Belgian Administration in the Congo: An Overview', in: Gann & Duignan (eds.), *African Proconsuls: European Governors in Africa* (New York, London & Stanford CA 1978), 367–373, there 368.

[144] D.M. Gordon, 'Precursors to Red Rubber: Violence in the Congo Free State, 1885–1895', *Past and Present*, 236, 3 (2017), 133–168, https://doi.org/10.1093/pastj/gtx018, there 161–166; A. Roes, 'Towards a History of Mass Violence in the Etat Indépendant du Congo, 1885–1908', *South African Historical Journal*, 62, 4 (2010), 634–670, https://doi.org/10.1080/02582473.2010.519937, there 637–638.

[145] See e.g. M. Broeckaert, 'Het blank personeel van de Kongo-staat 1885–1908: Recrutering—profiel—carrières?', Unpublished PhD Dissertation Ghent University (Ghent 1988), 9–25; Gann & Duignan, *The Rulers of Belgian Africa*, 100.

[146] See e.g. Press, *Rogue Empires*.

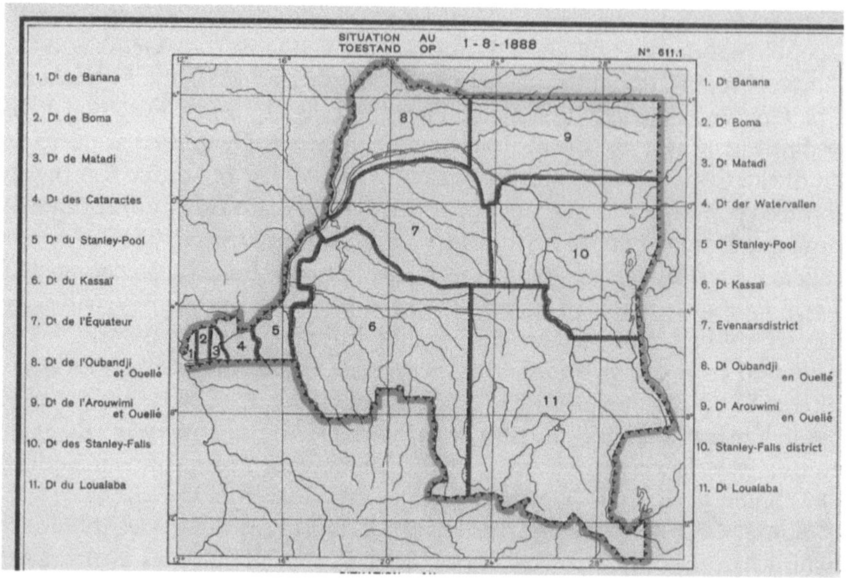

Image 2.4 Map of the Congo Free State districts, 1888. (Source: Institut Royal Colonial Belge, available at https://commons.wikimedia.org/wiki/File:1888_districts_Congo_Free_State_cropped_from_1950_administration_map_Atlas_General_du_Congo_611.jpg [Retrieved 12/03/2024])

a fairly 'normal' colonial state.[147] Leopold had been given *de jure* power over a huge territory, in which (like so many places in Africa) different peoples who would normally have never been united in one state. *De facto*, his power at the start however remained confined to the coastal inland area along the Congo River, roughly the area starting at Banana (at the mouth of the Congo River at the Atlantic Ocean) to Stanley Pool, nowadays Pool Malebo, where Leopoldville (later Kinsasha) and Brazzaville were established. This corresponded to the five districts of Banana, Boma, Matadi, the (Stanley) Falls and Stanley Pool, which, as Image 2.4 shows, only covered a small part of the area of the state's territory. Slowly but steadily

[147] De Roo, 'The Trouble with Tariffs', 6–9. Similarly, see P-L. Plasman, 'L'État independent du Congo et Léopold II (1876–1906): étude sur le paradoxe de la gouvernance léopoldienne', Unpublished PhD Dissertation UC Louvain (Louvain-la-Neuve 2015), available at https://dial.uclouvain.be/pr/boreal/object/boreal:159323 [Retrieved 23/10/2024], there 584–585.

and with the help of the *Force Publique*, the Congo Free State claimed power and control over the interior.[148]

The support of Tippu Tip (also Tippo Tip, real name Hamid bin Mohammed el Moerjebi, 1837–1905) was instrumental at the start as well. Tippu Tip was born on the island of Zanzibar but was of mixed Arab-African descent.[149] Tippu Tip was the largest slave and ivory trader in the Eastern part of Congo, a huge area that ran from Zanzibar through the Great Lakes region to the Stanley Falls district. Giacomo Macola has classified Tippu Tip as a warlord who extracted taxes in a huge area through his rule by fear and violence.[150] Tippu Tip had already been in touch with Stanley and other European expedition leaders when they had visited Zanzibar for some of their expeditions, and therefore was experienced in negotiating with the Europeans.[151] His power made him an indispensable ally for Leopold to control the Eastern part of the Congo Free State, in particular as Tippu Tip had claimed effective control over the Eastern part between 1884 and 1887, defeating his long-time local enemies. In 1887, Tippu Tip was appointed Governor of the Stanley Falls District by Leopold, in effect cementing his power in the region.[152]

With the help of the *Force Publique* and Tippu Tip, Leopold managed to expand his *de facto* power in the Congo Free State beyond Stanley Pool. However, Tippu Tip's position as the region's largest slave trader stood at odds with the commitment Leopold had shown to abolish the slave trade and slavery, as agreed in Berlin.[153] Back in Europe, Leopold came under increasing pressure to make an end for good to the slave trade and slavery.[154] This largely happened under public pressure of various missionaries, who were among the first to move inland, often alongside entrepreneurs and before states. Cardinal Charles Lavigerie, who established the

[148] Gordon, 'Precursors to Red Rubber' 161–166; Roes, 'Towards a History of Mass Violence' 637–638.

[149] Ceulemans, *La question arabe*, 86–121; Renault, *Tippo Tip*, 7–12; Salmon, 'L'État Indépendant'; Marechal, *De «Arabische» campagne*, 5–31.

[150] G. Macola, 'Warlordism in the Congo Basin between the Nineteenth and Twentieth Centuries', *International Journal of African Historical Studies*, 56, 1 (2023), 1–19, there 7–10.

[151] Renault, *Tippo Tip*, 103–124.

[152] Ibidem, 159–174.

[153] See L. Chatelet, 'Het humanitaire optreden van Leopold II in Kongo-Vrijstaat. De anti-slavernijconferentie van Brussel (1889–1890)', *Afrika Focus*, 4, 1–2 (1988), 5–47.

[154] Ibidem. See also e.g. Marchal, *E.D. Morel tegen Leopold II en de Kongostaat* (Antwerp 1985); Pakenham, *The Scramble for Africa*, 656–667.

Missionaries of Africa organisation in 1868, was particularly instrumental in bringing the issue back on the agenda, by starting a public campaign for awareness on the Arab slave trade in Eastern Congo and the Great Lakes District in 1888.[155] He pushed Leopold II to do more to bring this to an end.[156] Seeking to shore up international support, Leopold decided to call an Anti-Slavery Conference in Brussels to drum up support for the cause of anti-slavery.[157] This alienated him from Tippu Tip who subsequently turned against Leopold, but at least guaranteed Leopold of continuing support of the European powers who had agreed to back Leopold up in Berlin.[158]

Seen with the benefit of hindsight and the knowledge of Leopold's later use of slavery-like forced labour to extract rubber, Leopold's zeal in seeking support for the anti-slavery cause is rather surprising.[159] Another motive however lay behind the organisation of the Conference: Leopold claimed to have no financial space to battle slavery and the slave trade in the Congo Free State, and thus sought financial support for this.[160] Leopold proposed to levy import duties on firms to pay for this, which would clash with the agreements made at the Berlin Conference about the free trade area. The Brussels Anti-Slavery Conference eventually took place between 18 November 1889 and 2 July 1890, with many of the participants being the same as at the Berlin Conference. The Congo Free State was allowed to take part besides Belgium, and furthermore, Iran was also invited to join. Despite opposition by many private firms, the agreements of the Berlin Conference were torn up, and Leopold was allowed to levy import duties on firms active in the Congo Free State, up to 10% *ad valorem*.[161] The Netherlands and the United States initially opposed the idea of import duties, but eventually gave way to British and Belgian pressure, saving face so as not to be seen as hindering anti-slavery measures.[162] (Image 2.5)

[155] Marchal, *E.D. Morel*, 20–35.

[156] R.W. Harms, *Land of Tears: The Exploration and Exploitation of Equatorial Africa* (New York 2019), 320–321; Vansina, *Kingdoms of the Savanna*, 235–241.

[157] A. Hochschild, *King Leopold's Ghost: A Story of Greed, Terror, and Heroism in Colonial Africa* (New York 1998), 92–95.

[158] Harms, *Land of Tears*, 42–48.

[159] Ibidem.

[160] De Roo, 'The Trouble with Tariffs', 10–14; Idem, 'Customs in the Two Congos: A Connected History of Colonial Taxation in Africa (1885–1914), *Journal of Colonialism and Colonial History*, 19, 1 (2018), https://doi.org/10.1353/cch.2018.0005, before note 50.

[161] De Roo, 'The Trouble with Tariffs', 10–14.

[162] Ibidem, 13–14.

Image 2.5 Reception at the Brussels Anti-Slavery Conference 1889–1890. (Source: Revue L'Illustration Européenne N°31–31, Published July 1898, available at https://commons.wikimedia.org/wiki/File:Festival_at_the_Brussels_Stock_Exchange._Ovation_made_to_the_king_during_the_delivery_of_the_address_in_favor_of_the_Congo._L%27Illustration_europ%C3%A9enne_N_%C2%B031,_4_May_1890.jpg [Retrieved 12/03/2024])

Next to measures combatting the slave trade, the Acts of the Brussels Conference also agreed that the sale of alcohol and arms to Africans should be stopped, getting there by first substantially raising tariffs on those commodities.[163] This posed another major problem for many European firms, for whom spirits and arms were a major export product. The Act was not only declared applicable to the Congo Free State, but to all areas of Africa and thus also had significant repercussions outside the Congo Free State. Other countries, like Portugal, used the Act to levy higher import duties on the import of arms and alcohol as well. In the end, only the slave trade was targeted by the Conference, not the institution of slavery as such.

With Leopold and Tippu Tip on collision course, foreign firms hit by the import tariffs agreed upon in Brussels also looked for ways to push back against Leopold's power. As a result, several of the foreign firms, including the Dutch NAHV, allied with Tippu Tip against Leopold in an effort to control the ivory trade and claw back the initiative from Leopold and his administration.[164] Unsurprisingly, this led to disputes. After a number of skirmishes between Tippu Tip's army and the *Force Publique* in 1890, a full-scale war broke out in 1892 (commonly known as the Congo-Arab War of 1892–1894).[165] In 1894, the Congo Free State's *Force Publique* proclaimed victory, allowing Leopold to strengthen his grip on the inner regions of the Congo Free State and restrict the opportunities for foreign firms to monopolise the ivory trade while at the same time claiming to combat the slave trade in the region. After the victory in the Congo-Arab War, Leopold also struck a deal with the British to take over the Lado Enclave in present-day South Sudan, which connected the Congo River to the Nile and was therefore of some strategic significance to Leopold.[166] What the preceding shows is that next to the strategic-political and economic motives, the moral argument also became a major imperative for European imperialism in Africa, largely as an *ex post* rationalisation of colonisation:[167] even if economic exploitation may still have

[163] Ibidem.

[164] Marchal, *L'État Libre* (Vol. 1), 319–332.

[165] Marechal, *De «Arabische» campagne*, 92–230, for the chronological development of the Congo-Arab War. See for an overview of the relations in general: Wilkinson, *The Arabs and the Scramble for Africa*.

[166] Pakenham, *The Scramble for Africa*, 525–527; Stengers & Vansina, 'King Leopold's Congo', 331. The Lado Enclave was about the remain part of the Belgian Congo until 1910.

[167] See for the Congo Free State for example: D. Pavlakis, *British Humanitarianism and the Congo Reform Movement, 1896–1913* (Abingdon 2015); Marchal, *E.D. Morel*;

been the goal, the *language* of imperial expansion also became clothed in moral concerns as well, partly under pressure of public opinion.[168]

In his quest for absolute power, Leopold increasingly sanctioned the use of violence against everyone standing in his way. In 1895, the Irish ivory trader (and former missionary) Charles Stokes was arrested for (supposedly) illegally trading ivory for guns in the Eastern Congo, where a power vacuum had opened up after Tippu Tip's defeat.[169] Stokes was hanged without a proper trial by the *Force Publique* captain Hubert Lothaire on 15 January 1895.[170] Although the execution did initially not attract much attention, press attention from August onwards turned the tables against Leopold and Lothaire. Lothaire was eventually put on trial after British and German pressure but was acquitted in Boma and (on appeal) in Brussels.[171] The Stokes Affair, as the incident became known, essentially marked the start of the campaigns against Leopold's rulership of the Congo Free State, particularly in Britain.[172]

At the time Leopold faced increasing international pressure for his policies, the Congo Free State also faced increasing economic problems. In 1892, Leopold declared the Crown Domain (by and large District 7 in Image 2.4) his personal domain, where no one except his agents could trade: other European entrepreneurs were thus barred from entering these areas, and private traders were confined to the so-called Free Trading

R. Burroughs, *African Testimony in the Movement for Congo Reform: The Burden of Proof* (Abingdon 2019).

168 Chatelet, 'Het humanitaire optreden'.

169 Macola, 'Warlordism', 13–15; Marchal, *L'État Libre* (Vol. 1), 104–109 & 319–332.

170 See for the Stokes Affair: Vangroenweghe, *Voor rubber en ivoor: Leopold II en de ophanging van Stokes* (Leuven 2005); Roger Louis, 'The Stokes Affair and the Origins of the Anti-Congo Campaign, 1895–1896', *Revue belge de philologie et d'histoire*, 43, 2 (1965), 572–584.

171 Vangroenweghe, *Voor rubber en ivoor*, 201–268.

172 As argued in: Roger Louis, 'The Stokes Affair'. Similarly, in 1901, the so-called Rabinek affair, when a Czechian trader called Rabinek was tried and executed, aroused sentiments in the West. See: H.W. MacMillan, 'The Origins and Development of the African Lakes Company: 1878–1908', Unpublished PhD Dissertation University of Edinburgh (Edinburgh 1970), available at https://era.ed.ac.uk/bitstream/handle/1842/24105/MacMillanHW_1970redux.pdf?sequence=1&isAllowed=y [Retrieved 21/07/2022], there 397; Vanthemsche, 'Free Trade and Fair Justice in the Congo Free State? The Origins of the Rabinek Case (1901)', in: P. van Schuylenbergh & M. Leduc-Grimaldi (eds.), *The Congo Free State: What Could Archives Tell Us? New Lights and Research Perspectives* (Brussels 2022), 291–336.

Zone, which covered a much smaller part than before.[173] This most obviously violated almost every clause in the Acts of the Berlin Conference, and many in the Brussels Anti-Slavery Conference Acts as well, as free trade and free navigation were essentially abolished. In 1892, Leopold's could still count on support among the British, French and German governments, meaning no actions were taken against him. Next to the Crown Domain, substantial plots of land were therefore given to private companies. These so-called concession companies were given monopolies over land and labour in exchange for a payment to the colonial state, and also performed state-like tasks such as maintaining 'order' and exercising justice, making them quasi-sovereigns in the areas they ruled.[174]

In the Congo Free State, most of these concessions had been handed out in 1892, when Leopold also declared the existence of the Crown Domain. Several concessions were handed out, including two in the northern Congo to companies that would later attract much public attention: *Anversoise* and the *Anglo-Belgian Indian Rubber* (ABIR).[175] Both focused on rubber extraction, a commodity that became important in the global market from the late 1880s and early 1890s onwards.[176] Rubber was found in abundance in various parts of the Congo Free State, but was found largely in its forests which in turn was rather labour-intensive. These concession companies thus devised a harsh system of forced labour for rubber collection, which came to be known as the 'red rubber' system. This system became eventually profitable (to a terrible human cost) but was not so in the first years of its existence: in 1895, Leopold therefore requested the take-over of colony by the Belgian state in an aim to offload his huge debts.[177] Belgian opposition in Parliament eventually prevented

[173] S.H. Nelson, *Colonialism in the Congo Basin 1880–1940* (Athens OH 1994), 89; Anstey, 'The Congo Rubber Atrocities—A Case Study', *African Historical Studies*, 4, 1 (1971), 59–76, there 61.

[174] See section 1.8 for a discussion on the concession companies across Africa and in the Congo Free State.

[175] Harms, 'The End of Red Rubber: A Reassessment', *The Journal of African History*, 16, 1 (1975), 73–88; Idem, 'The World ABIR Made: The Margina-Lopori Basin, 1885–1903', *African Economic History*, 12 (1983), 125–139; Idem, *Land of Tears*, 361–403, in particular 368–389.

[176] Ibidem.

[177] Stengers & Vansina, 'King Leopold's Congo', 318–323.

this, even if the Belgian state was eventually coerced to pay for huge loan to prop up Leopold's colonial fever dream.[178]

The combination of the Stokes Affair, the violation of various agreements of the Berlin and Brussels Conferences, and increasing evidence that slavery, the slave trade and other forms of forced labour were still common in the Congo Free State eventually diminished support for Leopold. Leopold always denied claims that slavery and the slave trade were still commonplace, and even presented himself as an anti-slavery crusader.[179] Supported by influential people like Henry Morton Stanley, no significant actions were taken against these abuses despite the fact that many people credibly accused Leopold of atrocities including forced labour and child slavery.[180] The Stokes Affair marked a change in public opinion in the United Kingdom, paving the way for a PR campaign against Leopold's rule over the Congo Free State.[181] In 1900–1901, the journalist Edmund Dene Morel famously published accusations against Leopold II by detailing trade imbalances between Antwerp and Boma, obtained during his work for the *Elder Dempster* shipping line.[182] Morel, based on the statistics of the shipping line, inferred that while many commodities came from the Congo Free State, the ships exported almost nothing from Europe to Africa, while the concession companies at the same time announced record profits. This led Morel to conclude that forced labour was still widespread, as this system could only be profitable when labour costs were extremely low.[183]

To put up the pressure, Morel founded a newspaper in 1903 (*West African Mail*) to pressure the British government into a more hawkish stance against the Congo Free State.[184] Morel inaugurated one of the first modern public-relations campaigns and attacked Leopold harshly (to great success): among other things, the cartoons printed in Images 2.6

[178] Ibidem; Stengers, 'The Congo Free State and the Belgian Congo before 1914', in: Gann & Duignan (eds.), *Colonialism in Africa 1870–1960. Volume 1: The History and Politics of Colonialism 1870–1914* (Cambridge 1969), 261–292, there 272–275.

[179] Chatelet, 'Het humanitaire optreden'.

[180] Marchal, *L'État Libre*, 116–131; Idem, *E.D. Morel tegen Leopold II* (Vol. 1), 28. See also: R. Wiggers, 'De "Federation pour la defense des interets belges à l'étranger' en de Congo', Unpublished MA Thesis Katholieke Universiteit Nijmegen (Nijmegen 1986).

[181] Roger Louis, 'The Stokes Affair'.

[182] E.D. Morel, *King Leopold's Rule in Africa* (London 1904); Marchal, *E.D. Morel tegen Leopold II*, 23–60.

[183] Morel, *King Leopold's Rule*, ix-xi; Marchal, *E.D. Morel tegen Leopold II*, 23–28.

[184] Marchal, *E.D. Morel tegen Leopold II*, 193.

Image 2.6 Cartoon depicting King Leopold II and the "gate" to the Congo Free State, 1906. (Source: Francis Carruthers Gould. Public domain, available at https://commons.wikimedia.org/wiki/File:Cartoon_by_British_caricaturist_%27Francis_Carruthers_Gould%27_depicting_King_Leopold_2,_and_Congo_Free_State.jpg [Retrieved 13/03/2024])

and 2.7 to a large extent determined the image the larger public had of Leopold's Congo. Alarmed by the allegations, the British Foreign Office sent the British Consul in French Congo, Roger Casement, to the affected areas from June 1903 onwards to check the allegations. The so-called Casement report, published in June 1904, detailed further accusations of forced labour and other abuses by including extensive testimonies of local labourers, leading the British government to start pushing for reform with American help.[185]

[185] Ibidem, 185–204; Anstey, 'The Congo Rubber Atrocities'. For mild criticism of Casement's report, for example when it comes to including African voices, see: Pavlakis, *British Humanitarianism*, 69; Burroughs, *African Testimony*.

Image 2.7 Cartoon depicting Leopold II of Belgium surrounded by Congolese skulls, 1904. (Source: Anonymous/Unknown Author, Public domain, available at https://commons.wikimedia.org/wiki/File:Leopold_II_of_Belgium.jpg [Retrieved 13/03/2024])

Morel subsequently established the *Congo Reform Association* (CRA) in 1904, which pushed for political reforms of the Congo Free State.[186] Morel published subsequent accusations against Leopold based on the Casement Report. These scandals subsequently became known as the so-called 'red rubber' scandals.[187] In 1905, the Belgian Commission of Enquiry confirmed most of the accusations made, even if some of the harshest accusations against Leopold were swept under the carpet by the commission[188] (Image 2.8).

Broader Western public opinion turned against Leopold in the wake of the red rubber scandals. The American writer Mark Twain for example published the excruciating *King Leopold's Soliloquy: A Satire*, in which a fictional Leopold defended himself.[189] Such satires had devastating consequences for Leopold's public image (Image 2.9).

Both Britain and the United States increasingly came to support the 'Belgian Solution' to the 'Congo Question', which meant the Belgian take-over, became largely inevitable under public international pressure.[190] France and Germany also tacitly supported such proposals. Even if Leopold resisted, he eventually bowed to the pressure as well, with the Belgians taking over the colony on 15 November 1908.[191] This happened against the initial wishes of most of the Belgian Parliament, as the Belgians had agreed to Leopold forming the Congo Free State under the agreement

[186] Pavlakis, *British Humanitarianism*, 102.

[187] See e.g. Vangroenweghe, *Rood rubber.*

[188] Vellut, 'Garenganze/Katanga—Bié—Benguela and Beyond', 152; B. Bevernage, 'The Making of the Congo Question: Truth-Telling, Denial and "Colonial Science" in King Leopold's Commission of Inquiry on the Rubber Atrocities in the Congo Free State (1904–1905)', Rethinking History, 22, 2 (2018), 203–238, https://doi.org/10.1080/13642529.2018.1451078.

[189] M. Twain, *King Leopold's Soliloquy: A Satire* (London 1907).

[190] See for a legal history of this take-over: J. Blocher & M. Gulati, 'Transferable Sovereignty: Lessons from the History of the Congo Free State', *Duke Law Journal*, 69, 6 (2020), 1219–1274.

[191] Ibidem; Gardner, 'Fiscal Policy in the Belgian Congo in Comparative Perspective', in: Frankema & Buelens (eds.), *Colonial Exploitation and Economic Development: The Belgian Congo and the Netherlands Indies compared* (London & New York 2013), 130–152, there 131–135; Stengers & Vansina, 'King Leopold's Congo', 322–323. In general, see: Anstey, *King Leopold's Legacy: The Congo under Belgian Rule 1908–1960* (Oxford, London, New York & Ibadan 1962).

IN THE RUBBER COILS.

SCENE—*The Congo "Free" State.*

Image 2.8 Cartoon depicting King Leopold II as a snake attacking a Congolese rubber collector, 1906. (Source: Edward Linley Sambourne. Public domain, available at https://commons.wikimedia.org/wiki/File:Punch_congo_rubber_cartoon.jpg [Retrieved 13/03/2024])

Image 2.9 Cartoon depicting Leopold II laying the first stone of the Basilica of Koekelberg, 1905. (Source: Ashavérus (Didier Dubucq). Public domain, available at https://commons.wikimedia.org/wiki/File:Cartoon_depicting_King_Leopold_2_of_the_Belgians_laying_the_first_stone_of_the_Basilica_of_Koekelberg.jpg [Retrieved 13/03/2024])

that no Belgian taxpayer money would go to the Congo Free State.[192] Yet, Leopold squeezed out large sums of money in negotiations with the Belgian state: he was for example allowed to keep much of the money he privately made from the Congo Free State. Leopold partly did so by transferring many of his assets in 1907 to the *Niederfüllbacher Stiftung*, a trust based in Germany, to keep it beyond the reach of the Belgian state.[193] Even worse, the Belgian state agreed (for reasons scholars still find puzzling) to take over the 'odious' debts of the Congo Free State, leaving Belgium with plenty of debt it did not want to pay for.[194]

In the Congo Basin itself, the new Belgian administration retracted many of Leopold's harshest policy measures, and many of the concession companies were reformed or taken away their monopoly between 1908 and 1910. Moreover, a legal purge of the agents of concession companies and members of the *Force Publique* was set up by the Belgian public prosecutor.[195] And so came an end to the experiment that was known as the Congo Free State, which resulted in the end in hundreds of thousands of deaths, substantial violence and problems in the economic, social and political structure of the country that are still visible to this day.[196] The Congo Free State still haunts the public memory as one of the most

[192] Stengers, 'The Congo Free State', 272–275; De Roo, 'Taxation in the Congo Free State, an Exceptional Case? (1885–1908)', *Economic History of Developing Regions*, 32, 2 (2017), 97–126, https://doi.org/10.1080/20780389.2017.1327807, there 98; Idem, 'Colonial Taxation in Africa. A Fiscal History of the Congo through the Lens of Customs (1886–1914)', *Afrika Focus*, 30, 2 (2017), 61–65.

[193] Ibidem; Idem & Vansina, 'King Leopold's Congo', 323–327.

[194] See e.g. Blocher, Gulati & K. Oosterlinck, 'King Leopold's Bonds and the Odious Debt Mystery', *Virginia Journal of International Law*, 60, 3 (2020), 489–530; Oosterlinck, Blocher & Gulati, 'Why Did Belgium Pay Leopold's Bonds?', *Law and Contemporary Problems*, 83, 2 (2020), 49–70. See also: Harms, 'King Leopold's Bonds', in: W.N. Goetzmann & G.K. Rouwenhorst (eds.), *The Origins of Value: The Financial Innovations that Created Modern Capital Markets* (Oxford 2005), 343–357.

[195] See for a recent survey of the archives: B. Henriet, A. Lauro & R. Juste, 'Archives of Military Courts in Colonial Congo: New Sources for the History of Violence and Agency in Central Africa', *History in Africa*, 50 (2023), 259–274, https://doi.org/10.1017/hia.2023.9. The archives can be found: BE-AGR2-DJC, Archives Africaines, JUST, nr. 58.

[196] See for popular books on the matter: Hochschild, *King Leopold's Ghost*; D. van Reybrouck, *Congo: een geschiedenis* (Amsterdam 2013).

extractive colonial systems that existed.[197] Although the Congo Free State was indeed unique in some ways and extremely extractive, in many other ways it was simply the worst among comparable cases in Africa. Indeed, under Belgian rulership, things initially got better, but soon reversed: the Belgian colonial authorities soon resorted back to policies of forced labour and land expropriation after the First World War.[198]

The history of the Congo Free State still leads to regular debate in today's Belgium, as well as outside of it. As many of the cartoons shown in the previous sections demonstrate, the idea that the Congo Free State was, even by the standards of European imperialism in Africa, extremely harsh is still common.[199] In this regard, some authors have claimed that the population decline in the Congo Free State can be called a 'genocide' by modern standards.[200] Adam Hochschild, who published perhaps the most famous popular-scientific book about the Congo Free State in 1998, does not mention the word genocide, but taking the Holocaust explicitly as a framework of reference made the point clear. Hochschild's work was attacked from many sides, including by Jean Stengers, Barbara Emerson and Jan Vansina, all eminent scholars of Leopold and the Congo Free

[197] There is for example some literature on the effects of present-day institutions. See e.g.: A. Exenberger & S. Hartmann, 'Extractive Institutions in the Congo: Checks and Balances in the *longue durée*', in: Frankema & Buelens (eds.), *Colonial Exploitation and Economic Development,* 18–40; S. Lowes & E. Montero, 'Concessions, Violence, and Indirect Rule: Evidence from the Congo Free State', *The Quarterly Journal of Economics*, 136, 4 (2021), 2047–2091, https://doi.org/10.1093/qje/qjab021; Ibidem, 'King Leopold's Ghost: The Legacy of Labour Coercion in the DRC', in: S. Michalopoulos & E. Papaioannou (eds.), *The Long Economic and Political Shadows of History—Volume 2: Africa and Asia* (London 2017), 75–86.

[198] J. Seibert, 'More Continuity than Change? New Forms of Unfree Labor in the Belgian Congo, 1908–1930', in: M. Van der Linden (ed.), *Humanitarian Intervention and Changing Labor Relations: The Long-Term Consequences of the Abolition of the Slave Trade* (Leiden & Boston 2010), 369–386, https://doi.org/10.1163/ej.9789004188532.i-556.88, there 373–382; Idem, *In die globale Wirtschaft gezwungen: Arbeit und kolonialer Kapitalismus im Kongo (1885–1960)* (Frankfürt am Main 2016), 161.

[199] Recently, research commissioned by the Belgian government produced a report on the country's colonial past. See for a critical reflection of two of the committee members: G. Mathys & S. van Beurden, 'History by Commission? The Belgian Colonial Past and the Limits of History in the Public Eye', *The Journal of African History*, 64, 3 (2023), 334–343, https://doi.org/10.1017/S0021853723000683.

[200] See e.g. Hochschild, *King Leopold's Ghosts*; Pavlakis, 'The Crime of the Congo: A Question of Genocide in the Congo Free State, 1885–1908', in: N. Blackhawk, B. Kiernan, B. Madley & R. Taylor (eds.), *The Cambridge World History of Genocide* (Vol. 4: Premonitions) (Cambridge 2023), 585–608, https://doi.org/10.1017/9781108765480.025.

State, for overstating the case.[201] More recently, however, scholars like Dean Pavlakis have however again made the case that the Congo Free State could qualify as genocide.[202] This debate primarily centres on the death toll, which ranges from 3 to 13 million, leading to much debate, including Hochschild's (unverified) claim that up to 10 million people perished.[203] However, scholars essentially do not know much about the demographic history of the Congo Free State, making definitive claims hard.[204]

2.7 The Scramble for Africa: European Economic Interests 1875–1899

The Partition of Africa significantly changed the attitudes, position and freedom of actions for entrepreneurs, and in its wake more generally the relationship between governments and businesses. Having left off around 1875 to describe the state-based Partition of Africa, this paragraph returns to the perspective of the entrepreneur in the Scramble for Africa. Most entrepreneurs were of two minds when it came to stately intervention and the Partition of Africa: on the one hand, they spotted opportunities in newly established states, as it gave entrepreneurs the opportunity to expand their business from coastal areas further inland or by seeking

[201] Stengers, *Mythes et réalites*; B. Emerson, *Leopold II of the Belgians: King of Colonialism* (London 1979). See also: M. Dumoulin, *Léopold II un roi genocidaire?* (Brussels 2005); Anstey, 'The Congo Rubber Atrocities', 69–70; De Roo, 'De Onafhankelijke Congostaat: plundermachine in dienst van een meedogenloze Leopold II?', in: I. Goddeeris, Lauro & Vanthemsche (eds.), *Koloniaal Congo: een geschiedenis in vragen* (Kalmthout 2020), 31–46, there 32; M.Z. Etambala, *Veroverd, bezet, gekoloniseerd: Congo 1876–1914* (Gorredijk 2020), 40; M. Ewans, *European Atrocity, African Catastrophe: Leopold II, the Congo Free State and its Aftermath* (London & New York 2002), 236–241; Vansina, *Being Colonized*, 127–149. Some have even offered more politically charged interventions. See e.g. G. De Weerd, *The Congo Free State: In Search of Historical Truth* (Brussels 2017), 474–475. De Weerd, however, goes on to claim the concession companies alone were responsible for the violence, neglecting the fact that the Congo Free State was a large (and most influential) shareholder, as well as responsible for aiding the concession companies in every way possible. See also: Plasman, 'L'État indépendant', 593.

[202] Pavlakis, 'The Crime of the Congo', 585.

[203] Ibidem.

[204] Only from 1920 onwards there are some reliable data. See: L. De St. Moulin, 'What is Known of the Demographic History of Zaire Since 1885?', in: B. Fetter (ed.), *Demography from Scanty Evidence: Central Africa in the Colonial Era* (Boulder CO 1990), 299–326, https://doi.org/10.1515/9781685851521-024.

government contracts for transport services or infrastructure development.[205] On the other hand, many entrepreneurs also perceived risks, as property rights became less secure and many feared free trade would be endangered across Africa. This general trade-off was true for entrepreneurs operating in their 'own' colonial empire as well as for firms operating in the 'empire of others'.

The 1880s and 1890s also witnessed a proliferation of European economic activities across Africa. With the advent of modern imperialism, different economic and financial activities developed in a relatively quick time.[206] Most important perhaps were financial services both to the public and private sectors (e.g. in the form of loans or investments), exemplified by people like Cecil Rhodes. Having figured prominently in Marxist theories of imperialism, their entrance often happened only relatively late—that is, only in the late 1870s or 1880s. Next to 'old-fashioned' commodity trading and banking, a transport sector developed (catapulted by the development of the steamship) for the purposes of both trade and military activities.[207] Finally, as Ewout Frankema has argued, the African economy went through a second transition at the end of the nineteenth and early twentieth century after the transition from the slave trade to the legitimate commerce, this time from agricultural commodities to mining (broadly defined, including diamonds and oil).[208] This was primarily the case in Southern Africa as well as Angola and Mozambique, but could also be observed in the Congo Free State, where Katanga was particularly mineral-rich.[209]

The development of these sectors of course also impacted the export sector of agricultural commodities. Faced with falling prices and stiff competition from Asia, the organisation of the agricultural sector changed and

[205] See e.g. Porter, *Victorian Shipping, Business and Imperial Policy: Donald Currie, the Castle Line and Southern Africa* (Woodbridge 1986).

[206] See e.g. J. Forbes Munro, 'Monopolists and Speculators: British Investment in West African Rubber, 1905–1914', *The Journal of African History*, 22, 2 (1981), 263–278.

[207] See the forthcoming Dreijer & Antunes, 'Transimperial Financing between 1720 and 1914', in: C. Schayegh *et al* (eds.), *The Oxford Handbook of Modern Transimperial History* (New York & Oxford 2026).

[208] Frankema, 'African Economic Development: Growth, Reversals, and Deep Transitions', in: Broadberry & K. Fukao (eds.), *The Cambridge Economic History of the Modern World. Volume II: 1870 to the Present* (Cambridge 276–305, https://doi.org/10.1017/9781316671603.011.

[209] See e.g. Gwaindepi & Siebrits, 'How Mineral Discoveries'; R. Derksen, 'Forminière in the Kasai, 1906–1939', *African Economic History*, 12 (1983), 49–65.

Table 2.1 Foreign capital invested in Africa by colonial empire, 1870–1936

Territory	*Capital investments (in pounds)*
British Africa	941,307,000
French Africa	70,310,000
Portuguese Africa	66,732,000
Belgian Africa	143,337,000
Total non-British	280,379,000
Total	1,221,686,000
British Share of Total	77%

Source: Frankel, *Capital Investment in Africa*, Table 28, 158–159

became, in many places in West and West Central Africa, more industrialised and large-scale, with plantations for palm oil and other commodities developing.[210] In general, however, investments in Africa remained subdued compared to other continents, even during the high point of European imperial expansion in Africa: Asia, the United States, Latin America and Oceania, for example, received substantially more capital investments from Great Britain. Mining in the Southern part of Africa was the exception in this regard, which was largely funded by British and, to a lesser extent, German capital.[211] As Table 2.1 shows, British capital on its own was more important than most other foreign capital combined; moreover, British territories received substantially more investment between 1870 and 1936, although these numbers exclude German Africa.

As Klas Rönnbäck and Oscar Broberg have argued, British capital invested in Africa was low compared to other continents like South America or Asia, with the possible exception of mining and railway capital in Southern Africa.[212] Indeed, as Irving Stone has documented, South Africa received 6.4% of British capital exports between 1865 and 1914, making it the sixth-placed destination of British capital exports after the

[210] Frankema, Williamson & Woltjer, 'An Economic Rationale'.

[211] I. Stone, *The Global Export of Capital from Great Britain, 1865–1914: A Statistical Survey* (New York 1999), 441. See also: H. Frankel, *Capital Investment in Africa: Its Course and Effects* (Oxford 1938).

[212] Rönnback & Broberg, *Capital and Colonialism*, 27; Stone, *The Global Export*, 411. See also: Buelens & Frankema, 'Colonial Adventures in Tropical Agriculture: New Estimates of Returns to Investment in The Netherlands Indies, 1919–1938', *Cliometrica*, 10, 2 (2016), 197–224, https://doi.org/10.1007/s11698-015-0128-z.

United States, Canada, Argentina, Australia and India.[213] Next to South Africa (here defined as the independent states of Cape of Good Hope, Natal, the Orange River Colony, Transvaal and the Orange Free State), only Egypt (1.6%) and the Rhodesias (1.1%) made the list, indicating the relative unimportance of Africa for British capital exports. Places in West and West Central Africa are not in the top 25.[214] Rönnbäck and Broberg, taking a longer timeframe (1869–1969), have in the same vein come to the conclusion that the real returns on capital investment were not specifically large, and even negative for selected British companies before the 1930s: for the period 1869–1900, the real return on capital invested in West Africa was -4%, and for the period 1901–1929, -6.2%.[215] According to Stone's estimates, the significant majority of British capital exports were in the colonial government finances or in raw materials (with over 70% of the capital exports), with finance and railways taking a relative back seat. These data do indicate that at least up to the First World War, the Scramble for Africa's raw resources did attract British capital; although this was indeed minor compared to other territories, it did have a major impact in parts of Africa itself (Table 2.2).

Capital flows in other empires probably paled in comparison, even if the impact on the ground was rather substantial. Catherine Coquery-Vidrovitch, for example, estimated French capital investments for French Equatorial Africa, as shown in Table 2.3. This shows that while private investments even in the early twentieth century in French Equatorial Africa (the time of the concession companies) were by no means insignificant, they were indeed much less significant than British capital investments. Data for Portuguese Africa are unavailable besides the general data provided by Frankel (shown in Table 2.1).

Data for the Congo Free State and the Belgian Congo are patchy, with most data available for the period 1918–1960. Nevertheless, Frans Buelens and Stefaan Marysse's numbers on the real returns on the Brussels Stock Exchange for the 1890–1914 period do allow us some insights.[216]

Table 2.4 shows how the period between 1890 and 1914 was generally profitable, but how between 1900 and 1914 was less so. This probably reflected an initial enthusiasm that waned when the red rubber scandals

[213] Stone, *The Global Export*, 411.

[214] Ibidem.

[215] Rönnback & Broberg, *Capital and Colonialism*, Table 9.1, 182.

[216] See: Buelens & S. Marysse, 'Returns on Investments during the Colonial Era: The Case of the Belgian Congo', *The Economic History Review*, 62, 1 (2009), 135–166.

Table 2.2 British investments in Africa per sector, 1865–1914

Sector	*Absolute (in pounds)*	*Relative (in %)*
Government	170,310,000	39.57%
Railways	23,598,000	5.48%
Public utilities	15,148,000	3.52%
Financial	59,799,000	13.88%
Raw materials	136,013,000	31.58%
Industrial and miscellaneous	21,383,000	4.96%
Shipping	4,354,000	1.01%
Grand total	430,738,000	100%

Source: Stone, *The Global Export*, Table 29, 322–331

Table 2.3 Investments in French Equatorial Africa, 1900–1913, in Francs

Date	*Public investments*	*Public guarantees*	*Private investments*
1900–1913	11,900,000	23,000,000	69,500,000

Source: Coquery-Vidrovitch, *Le Congo*, 520

Table 2.4 Total returns per sector on Brussels Stock Exchange, Congo Free State and Belgian Congo, 1890–1914

Sector	*Year*	*Geometric mean*	*Arithmetic mean*
Banking, colonial holdings and trading companies	1890–1914	2.07	9.65
	1900–1914	−2.80	1.70
Agriculture and tropical products	1896–1914	3.94	9.40
	1900–1914	−6.42	−3.72
Transport	1889–1914	6.43	9.29
	1900–1914	−0.88	0.80

Source: Buelens & Marysse, 'Return on Investments', Table 3, 154

became known. In times of uncertainty over the Congo Free State's future, stock market returns fell (as is for example evident in 1896, when Leopold had to request a huge loan from the Belgian Parliament to keep the Congo Free State afloat). After a peak in 1900, there is also a sharp drop in returns, probably as a result of the red rubber scandals that made their impact known in the economic realm as well. Perhaps surprisingly,

Table 2.4 moreover shows that the transport sector would have been the most profitable sector, even if the arithmetic mean, allowing statisticians to deal with outliers better, does indicate that this was probably the result of a few companies making large profits under the flag of the Congo Free State.[217]

As Table 2.5 shows, in 1913 most of the large companies in the Congo Free State were indeed companies categorisable as banking, trading companies, agricultural and mining companies, or transport companies.[218]

Table 2.5 Twenty-four largest firms in Congo Free State by market capitalisation, 1913, in Francs

Number	*Name*	*Market capitalisation*	*%*
1	Union Minière du Haut-Katanga	175,000,000	32.18%
2	CFL	96,300,000	17.71%
3	Chemin de Fer du Congo	90,836,418	16.70%
4	Compagnie du Katanga	53,250,000	9.79%
5	Compagnie du Kasaï	33,948,900	6.24%
6	Simkat	14,730,000	2.71%
7	Compagnie Belge Maritime du Congo	14,040,000	2.58%
8	CCCI	11,400,000	2.10%
9	SAB	11,252,000	2.07%
10	Coloniale Anversoise	9,307,500	1.71%
11	Plantations Lacourt	6,800,000	1.25%
12	Belgo-Katanga	6,443,750	1.18%
13	Société Commerciale et Financière Africaine	4,075,000	0.75%
14	Compagnie du Lomami	2,892,500	0.53%
15	Cominière	2,345,000	0.43%
16	Compagnie du Belge Congo	2,210,000	0.41%
17	Citas	2,120,000	0.39%
18	Intertropical Anglo-Belgian Trading Company	1,755,000	0.32%
19	Comptoir Belgika	1,385,200	0.25%
20	Produits du Congo	1,164,000	0.21%
21	Produits Végétaux du Haut-Kassaï	1,152,500	0.21%
22	Comptoir Commercial Congolais	693,280	0.13%
23	Plantations de la Luki	575,000	0.11%
24	Plantations de la Lukula	150,000	0.03%
	Total	543,826,048	100%

Source: Buelens, *Congo 1880–1960*, Table 2, 103

[217] See for the transport sector in the Congo Free State and Belgian Congo: L. Delmotte, *De Belgische koloniale holdings* (Leuven 1946), 56–120.

[218] Drawing on: Buelens, *Congo 1885–1960.*

Considering that these data are from 1913, the Dutch NAHV was no longer part of the largest companies for reasons explained in Chaps. 4 and 5. However, as the largest private shareholder alongside SAB (number 9 in this 1913 list) of the *Compagnie du Kasaï*, one of the large concession companies in the Congo Free State, the Dutch entrepreneurs were still contributors to the peculiar system of political economy devised in the Congo Free State.[219]

European economic interests in the period after 1875 thus changed, as the trade in cheap agricultural commodities ceased to be the sole reason to be present in Africa for Europeans: capitalist financial investments, and in its wake mining and infrastructure, became more important. In other words, economic concerns also became financial concerns, in line with the ideas put forward by the 'economic' school to explain imperialism. This was, in the words of Hopkins, truly a time of 'colonial capitalism'.[220]

2.8 The Scramble and Partition Converge (1890–1914)

With no change but to adapt to the new circumstances, private entrepreneurs changed their initial positions gradually during the 1890s to work with the colonial states, and lobbied for the most favourable monopolies within the colonial empires. Therefore, the *interests* of the parties in the Scramble and the Partition converged after roughly 1890, a development that sped up after the establishment of concession companies in the late 1890s and early 1900s. First, however, the second wave of the Partition took place. It was much smaller than the initial Partition around 1885, and was the result of European colonial administrators trying to strengthen their grip on the conquered territories or aimed to link the disparate territories into larger political entities.[221] Italy, present at the Berlin Conference but not a large imperial player around that time, set off the 'Second Partition' by taking possession first of present-day Eritrea in 1882 (following the establishment of Italian private-company rule in 1869) and in

[219] See Chaps. 5 and 6. See also: Dreijer, 'Exploiting Belgian Imperial Expansion?'.
[220] Hopkins, *Capitalism in the Colonies.*
[221] Pakenham, *The Scramble for Africa*, 452–582; Oliver, 'The Partition of Africa', 42–48.

1889–1890 conquering parts of present-day Somaliland in Somalia.[222] In 1895, a war with Ethiopia followed, which Italy famously lost.

The second wave of Partition was characterised mostly by administrative consolidation and scaling up territorial claims.[223] France for example joined most of its colonies under larger administrative units, such as French West Africa (comprised of Mauritania, parts of Gambia, Mali, Guinea, Senegal, Ivory Coast, Niger, Burkina Faso and Benin, as well as various other territories).[224] Britain actively enlarged its territorial scope as well, either by 1) incorporating a territory as a colony such as the Gold Coast 2) by proclaiming a territory as a Protectorate, such as Bechuanaland (Botswana), or 3) by giving the land to a concession company to manage it, like happened in the Rhodesias (named after Cecil Rhodes) under the British South Africa Company.[225] Both France and Britain continued to incorporate adjacent areas to already existing colonies throughout the 1890s, which eventually culminated in the so-called 1898 Fashoda Incident.[226]

The British, particularly under the influence of Cecil Rhodes, dreamed of connecting the British colonial territories in Africa south to north, the so-called Cape-Cairo Axis; the French, at the same time, tried to connect their territories throughout western and northern Africa as well with the territories in the Sahara and Sahel.[227] In an effort to complete these respective axes, British and French troops met at Fashoda (present-day Kodok in South Sudan) on 19 September 1898, narrowly avoiding military confrontation between the two powers after tumultuous diplomatic and political negotiations back in Europe. The Fashoda Incident is thus often seen as both the closure and the climax of European imperialism in Africa, as after 1898 no major changes in the geographical constellation of

[222] Ibidem, 470–486; M. Jerven, D. Strangio & J. Weisdorf, 'A Case of Its Own? A Review of Italy's Colonisation on Eritrea, 1890–1941', *The Journal of European Economic History*, 50, 1 (2021), 99–132.

[223] Ibidem, 504–523.

[224] Frankema & Van Waijenburg, 'From Coast to Hinterland: Fiscal Capacity Building in British and French West Africa, c. 1880–1960', in: Frankema & Booth (eds.), *Fiscal Capacity and the Colonial State*, 161–192, there 162 & 178.

[225] See Rönnbäck & Broberg, 'From Defensive to Transformative Business Diplomacy'; Slinn, 'Commercial Concessions'; Galbraith, *Crown and Charter*.

[226] Pakenham, *The Scramble for Africa*, 504–523 & 539–556; Gallagher & Robinson, *Africa and the Victorians*, 339–378.

[227] Pakenham, *The Scramble for Africa*, 641–655.

Partitioned Africa took place.[228] However, some exceptions remained, of course: in 1899, the Second South African War for example broke out following new Anglo-Boer tensions during the Second Partition. By 1902, the British declared victory and later, in 1910, merged all the independent republics into the Union of South Africa.[229] Another point of tension was Morocco, claimed by both France and Germany, leading to two 'Moroccan Crises' of 1905–1906 and 1911.[230] Moreover, uprisings by colonised people were common, and in the first decade of the twentieth century, uprisings took place in Somaliland, Aro (present-day Nigeria), Angola, Namibia, Tanganyika, the Zulu Empire, Chad and Western Sudan.[231] The Europeans often put these uprisings down with severe violence, the most horrendous example being the Herero and Nama Genocide of 1904–1907, where some 100,000 Herero and 10,000 Namaqua perished.[232]

Economically, the early twentieth century was the era of the concession companies.[233] Leopold's Congo Free State to a large extent pioneered this process, starting to close off areas for private exploitation already in 1892. Almost all colonial powers in Africa swung towards the use of so-called concession companies to spur economic development in the late nineteenth and early twentieth centuries.[234] Some scholars have interpreted

[228] There were some exceptions, of course: for example the Franco-German Treaty of 1911–1912 allowed Germany to take control over parts of Cameroon. See: Pakenham, *The Scramble for Africa*, 694.

[229] Ibidem, 641–655.

[230] Conrad, *German Colonialism*, 137.

[231] See e.g. for Mozambique: A. Isaacman & B. Isaacman, *The Tradition of Resistance in Mozambique: Anti-Colonial Activity in the Zambezi Valley 1850–1921* (London 1976), 104, for a list of revolts and uprisings against the colonial regime. In general: Isaacman & Vansina, 'African Initiatives and Resistance in Central Africa, 1880–1914', in: A.A. Boahen (ed.), *General History of Africa. VII: Africa under Colonial Domination 1880–1935* (Paris 1985), 169–193; Reid, 'Africa's Revolutionary Nineteenth Century and the Idea of the "Scramble"', *American Historical Review*, 126, 4 (2021), 1424–1447, https://doi.org/10.1093/ahr/rhab539; Reid, *The African Revolution*.

[232] Conrad, *German Colonialism*, 160–161; Press, *Blood and Diamonds: Germany's Imperial Ambitions in Africa* (Cambridge MA 2021), 113–117, 124–126 & 244–246.

[233] See e.g. for the British: P.J. Griffiths, *A Licence to Trade: The History of English Chartered Companies* (London 1974).

[234] See e.g.: E. Allina, *Slavery by Any Other Name: African Life under Company Rule in Colonial Mozambique* (Charlotsville VA & London 2012); Henriet, *Colonial Impotence: Virtue and Violence in a Congolese Concession (1911–1940)* (Berlin & Boston 2021); Lowes & Montero, 'Concessions, Violence, and Indirect Rule'; Coquery-Vidrovitch, *Le Congo*; Slinn, 'Commercial Concessions'. One of the few comparative studies is: Vangroenweghe,

this as a return to the chartered companies of the seventeenth and eighteenth centuries like the Dutch and English East India Companies,[235] but in fact, there were some important differences, legally and practically. Legally speaking, the East India Companies were allowed to monopolise trade between Asia and the Dutch Republic or England on a certain number of commodities, whereas the concession companies of the nineteenth century were given a land monopoly which included trade and production only *in that very area*.[236] Moreover, whereas the East India Companies were to a significant extent also maritime-based, the nineteenth-century concession companies were landlocked. Besides the fact that the two types received *a form of* monopoly in a colonial setting from a Western state government, not many similarities can however be observed between the two types of companies in terms of their shareholder make-up, limited liability or capital investment.[237]

Concessions came in various forms and sizes. For example, some concessions were explicitly focused towards the exploitation of natural resources (e.g. mining), others were more focused on agricultural development or about the management of land (e.g. the management of forests).[238] In total, some 1500 concession companies may have existed across Africa for the period 1880–1960.[239] Particularly in the British colonies, the concession companies were often still trading companies with a monopoly, although some (such as the *Royal Niger Company*) would eventually also start producing commodities (or controlling production). The concession companies, in general, often relied on forced labour, although the extent of this also varied across time and space. Particularly

'The "Leopold II" Concession System Exported to French Congo with as Example the Mpoko Company', *Journal of Belgian History*, 36 (2006), 323–372. This section draws on the ideas in the forthcoming work of, as well as personal discussions with, John Kegel, at the moment of writing at the Dutch Military Academy.

[235] Phillips & Sharman, *Outsourcing Empire*, 153–198.

[236] For a legal analysis of the concession as a *Rechtsfigur*: D.L.M.T. Danker-Hagenaars, *Op het spoor van de concessie: Een onderzoek naar het rechtskarakter van de concessie in Nederland en in Frankrijk* (The Hague 2000).

[237] Although Phillips & Sharman, *Outsourcing Empire*, argue otherwise.

[238] See e.g. H. Waltz, *Das Konzessionswesen im Belgischen Kongo* (2 Vols.) (Jena 1917); T. Heyse & H. Leonard, *Régime des cessions et concessions de terre et de mines au Congo Belge* (Brussels 1932), for the various types of concessions in the Congo Free State and the Belgian Congo.

[239] I thank John Kegel for discussing the general numbers with me [Personal Communication 04-03-2023].

in the Portuguese colonies, forced labour would long remain an issue even after the establishment of the *International Labour Organisation* (ILO) in the 1920s.[240]

The concession companies were thus a key factor in the European colonial endeavour in Africa, moving from a situation of trade at the coast to moving inland to control the factors of production. The concession companies were instrumental in speeding up the transition to the development of agricultural commodities, and during the twentieth century also the transition from agricultural commodities to mineral resources.[241] Theoretically speaking, the concession companies allowed the colonial states to move from bartering to controlling the three factors of production, being land, labour and capital. Land was by law expropriated from the local population, by declaring property rights over the fictional *terra nullius* that Africa was supposed to be.[242] Labour was through means of violence and force supplied: often, the colonial authorities introduced a tax *in natura*, for example by expecting a certain quantity of agricultural commodities everywhere to be delivered to the colonial state. In the Congo Free State, this was famously rubber, leading to the red rubber scandals under *Anversoise* and ABIR.[243] However, a study of the Mozambique *Nyassa Company* also shows that abuses were widespread.[244]

The origins of the concession company system lay in the Congo Free State, where Leopold II came up with the idea in 1892, when he decreed that the so-called vacant lands (which included almost all of the Congo Free State, drawing on colonial-era, European ideas of property rights that did not fit with the more communal land rights drawn from customary law in the region) were now the property of the state.[245]

[240] Allina, *Slavery by Any Other Name*, 82.

[241] Frankema & Van Waijenburg, 'Bridging the Gap', 49–50.

[242] See e.g. P. Clement, 'The Land Tenure System in the Congo, 1885–1960: Actors, Motivations, and Consequences', in: Frankema & Buelens (eds.), *Colonial Exploitation and Economic Development*, 88–108, there 89. For the legal principle: Craven, 'Between Law and History', Fisch, 'Africa as *terra nullius*'.

[243] Seibert, 'More Continuity than Change?', 373–382; Idem, *In die globale Wirtschaft gezwungen*, 161; Harms, 'The World ABIR Made'; Harms, *Land of Tears*, 420–430.

[244] Allina, *Slavery by Any Other Name*.

[245] Clement, 'The Land Tenure System in the Congo', 89; Vangroenweghe, *Rood rubber*, 32; Henriet, 'Colonial Law in the Making: Sovereignty and Property in the Congo Free State (1876–1908)', *Tijdschrift voor Rechtsgeschiedenis*, 83 (2015), 202–225, https://doi.org/10.1163/15718190-08312p10.

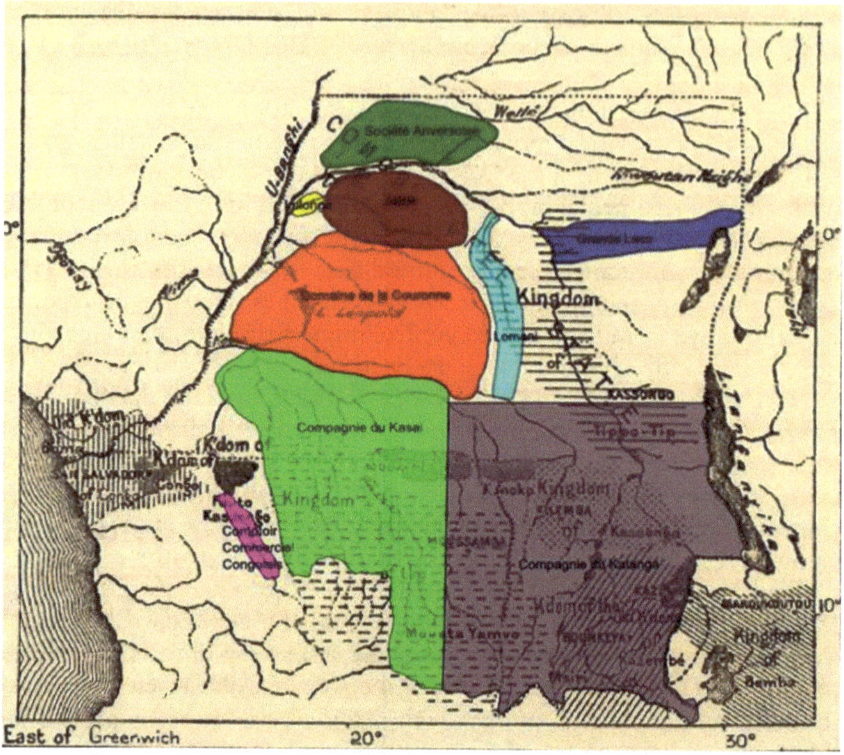

Image 2.10 Map of concession companies in the Congo Free State. (Source: Dumelow–Own work by uploader, derivative of public domain, available at https://commons.wikimedia.org/w/index.php?curid=5896964 [Retrieved 03/03/2023])

Image 2.10 shows the various concession companies across the Congo Free State. Next to the aforementioned Crown Domain where only eight of Leopold's agents could trade legally,[246] Leopold started also enclosing other areas and gave concessions to investor consortia, mostly comprised of British and Belgian investors. ABIR for example was set up in 1892 with Belgian and British private capital, although the Congo Free State itself was also a major shareholder.[247] In the words of Robert Harms, ABIR was

[246] Marchal, *L'État Libre*, 200–214; Vangroenweghe, *Rood rubber*, 271–304.
[247] Harms, 'The World ABIR Made', 128.

a "plundering and tribute-collecting empire of the crudest sort", which ruthlessly exploited the labour of the locals by violently enforcing them to work on their behalf.[248] After numerous revolts and significant losses, ABIR returned the concession to the Congo Free State in 1907 and disbanded.[249] *Anversoise*, an adjacent concession with many of the same shareholders, was nationalised after fifteen years in the wake of the red rubber scandals.[250]

Besides various smaller concessions close to the Crown Domain, two other important concession companies were the *Compagnie du Katanga* and the *Compagnie du Kasaï* (CdK).[251] The former was already formed in 1891 to exploit the Katanga region, rich in minerals (Katanga was not originally part of the Congo Free State territory and thus fell outside of the free trading agreement concluded in Berlin). Cecil Rhodes also aimed to control the Katanga region, but Leopold was allowed to take control over the area after lenghty negotiations.[252] In 1899, the *Compagnie du Katanga* and the Congo Free State formed the *Comité Special du Katanga* to further speed up the exploitation of minerals like diamonds in the areas, in 1906 allowing two concession companies to take over operations (*Union Minière du Haut-Katanga* and *Forminière*).[253]

The *Compagnie du Kasaï*, meanwhile, was the latest concession company to be established. The CdK was a quasi-monopoly, holding the rights to trade preferentially with the Congo Free State and holding land rights over a huge area, but it was not the sole company allowed to be active in the area.[254] The CdK was formed in 1900–1901 on the instigation of Leopold, who aimed to limit competition in the Kasaï area (sparsely populated, but rich in natural resources including rubber and ivory). As the Kasaï area was close to the Angolese border, the Kasaï was also a main outlet for smuggling, something Leopold aimed to stop. Leopold forced

[248] Ibidem, 125.

[249] Ibidem, 136; Idem, 'The End of Red Rubber', 87.

[250] Ibidem; Marchal, *E.D. Morel tegen Leopold II* (Vol. 2), 237–262.

[251] D. Martens, 'A History of European Penetration and African Reaction in the Kasai Region of Zaira, 1880–1908', Unpublished PhD Dissertation Simon Fraser University (Burnaby 1980), available at http://summit.sfu.ca/item/3231 [Retrieved 05/08/2021], 233–302; Galbraith, *Crown and Charter*, 104; Etambala, *Veroverd, bezet, gekoloniseerd*, 35–46.

[252] Galbraith, *Crown and Charter*, 104.

[253] Derksen, 'Forminière in the Kasai', 49–52.

[254] Martens, 'A History of European Penetration', 233–302; Etambala, *Veroverd, bezet, gekoloniseerd*, 37.

all the existing firms to work together in the monopolistic CdK, with the Congo Free State holding 50% of the shares.[255] The Dutch NAHV was, alongside the SAB, the largest private shareholder, and grudgingly had to accept the new set-up.

In French Africa, the concession companies were formed under Governor De Brazza.[256] De Brazza took significant inspiration from Leopold's system.[257] In 1900, forty-two concession areas were set up across the French Congo (see Image 2.11). Despite goals to favour French capital investment, much of the investment came from across Western Europe, often in tandem with a French front company or French capital.[258] This was also the case for Dutch capital investment in the French concessions.[259] Most concession companies were then formally established in French cities like Paris or Roubaix, but were run by international investment consortia (French combined with, mostly, British, Belgian or Dutch capital). In 1910, the concessions in the French Congo were redistricted and re-allocated.[260] A year later, the area in which, among other concessions, the 'Dutch' concessions were located was partly given to Germany under the Franco-German Treaty of 1911–1912, meaning part of the French concessions were again redrawn and the areas put under German control.[261]

Portugal also established concession companies, both in Angola and Mozambique, to speed up economic development. In Mozambique, concession companies were formed in the late 1890s;[262] in Angola, diamond

[255] Ibidem. See Chap. 6 for a case study.

[256] For a general overview of French imperialism: H. Brunschwig, *Mythes et réalités de l'impérialisme colonial français 1871–1914* (Paris 1960). Specifically in Africa: Coquery-Vidrovitch, 'French Colonization in Africa to 1920: Administration and Economic Development', in: Gann & Duignan (eds.), *Colonialism in Africa 1870–1960. Volume 1: The History and Politics of Colonialism 1870–1914* (Cambridge 1969), 165–198.

[257] Vangroenweghe, 'The "Leopold II" Concession System'.

[258] Coquery-Vidrovitch, *Le Congo*, 58–64; Idem, 'Investissements prives, investissements publics en AEF, 1900–1940', *African Economic History*, 12 (1983), 13–31, there 13–18.

[259] The Dutch bank *Mees & Zoonen* for example provided capital. See: Coquery-Vidrovitch, *Le Congo*, 59–60 and 60*n*2; see also NL-HaNA, Archief NAHV, nr. 671, Letter Mees to Directie NAHV, 01-06-1898.

[260] Coquery-Vidrovitch, *Le Congo*, 257–261.

[261] See Chap. 5 for the consequences for the Dutch entrepreneurs.

[262] L. Vail & L. White, *Capitalism and Colonialism in Mozambique: A Study of Quelimane District* (London, Nairobi & Ibadan 1980), 154; Vail, 'Mozambique's Chartered Companies: The Rule of the Feeble', *Journal of African History*, 17, 3 (1976), 389–416, there 391–392; B. Neil-Tomlinson, 'The Nyassa Chartered Company: 1891–1929', *The Journal of African*

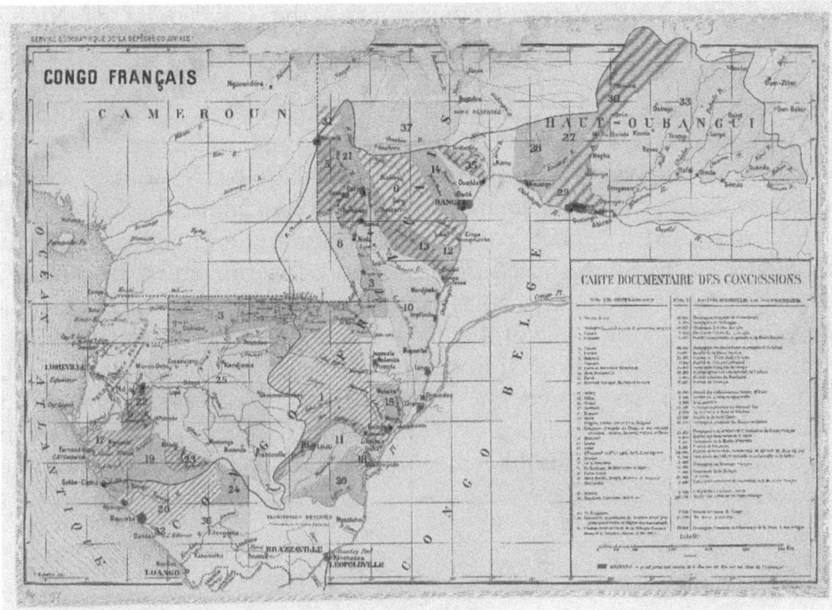

Image 2.11 Concessions in the French Congo, 1900. (Source: *Bibliothèque Nationale de France*. Public domain, available at https://upload.wikimedia.org/wikipedia/commons/2/23/Congo_fran%C3%A7ais._Carte_documentaire_des_concessions._L._Robelin_del_-_Service_g%C3%A9ographique_de_%22La_Dep%C3%AAche_coloniale%22_-_btv1b532042215.jpg [Retrieved 06/03/2023])

concessions were only formed in the late 1910s.[263] According to Álvaro Ferreira Da Silva and Pedro Neves, Angola should be characterised as more of a settler-capitalist state with a large plantation complex, whereas Mozambique held extensive concessions (such as the *Companhia de*

History, 18, 1 (1977), 109–128; Idem, 'The Mozambique Chartered Company: 1892 to 1910', Unpublished PhD Dissertation The School of Oriental and African Studies University of London (London 1982); B.P.T. Direito, 'Políticas coloniais de terras em Moçambique: o case de manica e sofala sub a Companhia de Moçambique, 1892–1942', Unpublished PhD Dissertation University of Lisbon (Lisbon 2013).

[263] A.F. Da Silva & P. Neves, 'The Paradox of Nationality: Foreign Investment in Portuguese Africa (1890–1974), *Business History*, 64, 9 (2022), 1623–1649, https://doi.org/10.1080/00076791.2020.1797683, there 1625.

Moçambique (Mozambique Company) and the *Companhia do Niassa* (Nyassa Company).[264] The concession companies in Mozambique were partly also established to battle the influence of the so-called *prazos*, the semi-feudal large land grants given to wealthy settlers and colonists in Portuguese Africa who often developed as personal fiefdoms.[265]

Foreigners actively aimed to participate in these concessions by means of front and/or shell companies. In Angola, for example, Belgian capitalists actively tried to obtain concessions for mining and rubber, but this process was actively frustrated by the Lisbon government.[266] In the end, the *Société Générale* bank was able to invest in the *Companhia de Diamantes de Angola* (Diamang), one of the major mining firms, through shell companies, and later also invested in oil and textile production.[267] In general, as Yonah Seleti has argued, the record of the concession companies in terms of their performance was rather mixed, as in particular in Mozambique concessions like the Nyassa Company failed to become profitable.[268]

2.9 Conclusion

This chapter has argued that the conflation of the Partition of and Scramble for Africa in the English-language literature is problematic, as in reality there were two distinct processes that played out on different geographical and temporal scales. This distinction has barely been made in much of the literature, bar the attempts by Hopkins and Oliver to distinguish between various phases in the Partition.[269] First there was the Scramble for Africa, a process whereby multiple private actors (Europeans and Africans) strove to exploit Africa's natural (and later mineral) resources) from the 1840s onwards, which itself followed from the slow and uneven transition from

[264] Ibidem.

[265] Vail & White, *Capitalism and Colonialism*, 113 & 120.

[266] Clarence-Smith, *The Third Portuguese Empire*, 103 & 129.

[267] Idem, 'Les investissements belges en Angola, 1912–1961', in: Coquery-Vidrovitch & A. Forest (eds.), *Entreprises et entrepreneurs en Afrique (XIXe et XXe siècles* (Vol. 1) (Paris 1983), 423–442, there 433–436.

[268] Y.N. Seleti, 'The Development of Dependent Capitalism in Portuguese Africa', in: Z.A. Konczacki, J.L. Parpart & T.M. Shaw (eds.), *Studies in the Economic History of Southern Africa. Volume one: The Front-Line States* (London 1990), 30–74, there 41.

[269] Hopkins, 'Imperial Business in Africa. Part II', 274; Oliver, 'The Partition of Africa', 41–45.

the slave trade to the so-called 'legitimate commerce'. These economic interests were long dominant in Europe's interaction with Africa. The rather sudden race that would become the Partition of Africa, a state-based process that took place in two waves, changed this: the first, most significant one between 1875 and 1885 (ending with the Berlin Conference), and a second smaller wave in the 1890s.

Economic interests had to adapt to the new situation where empires quickly expanded, but by and large the economic interests behind the Scramble for Africa were not necessarily happy with the political interests behind the Partition of Africa. Only in the late 1880s and 1890s, the capitalist investors slowly came round to the idea of the empires ruling large swathes of Africa and realised that this could also be beneficial. In the case of the Congo Free State, investors piled in money, until the red rubber scandals exposed by Morel and others became such a taint in their reputation that they retracted themselves largely from the Congo Free State, which was subsequently taken over by Belgium in 1908 under international pressure.

The violence of red rubber scandals were largely perpetrated by so-called concession companies, a privatisation of colonial government pioneered by Leopold but soon copied by many other colonial governments across Africa in a desperate attempt to spur economic development. The concession companies show how the interests of the Scramble (that is, economic exploitation of resources) and the Partition (that is, projecting state power in colonial competition) aligned with one another. This arrangement took off in the Congo Free State after 1892, and in most other colonies from 1898 to 1899 onwards, with the French Congo being the prime example. Forced labour and abuses were common in the concession companies, with the red rubber scandals in the Congo Free State as the most famous examples.

The Dutch entrepreneurs have not figured much in this chapter, as the chapter's purpose was primarily to sketch the main historiographical outlines based on the available secondary literature. The Dutch entrepreneurs were connected primarily to the Scramble, as the Dutch state retreated from the African continent after 1871–1872 (even if they were present at the Berlin and Brussels Conferences). The involvement of the Dutch entrepreneurs therefore illustrates the main historiographical claim outlined in this chapter: that the conflation of the Scramble for and Partition of Africa obscures much of what is going on in Africa in the nineteenth century, and who profited.

CHAPTER 3

Dutch Entrepreneurs in the Early Scramble for Africa (1830s–1870s)

3.1 Introduction

On 6 April 1872, almost two-and-a-half centuries of Dutch state presence in Africa came to an end. For a sum just short of 47,000 guilders, the Dutch state sold its fortifications on the Gold Coast, including the (in) famous slave trade fort in Elmina, to the Brits.[1] In return, the British state acknowledged Dutch sovereignty over Aceh, the westernmost part of the island of Sumatra in present-day Indonesia. The Dutch thus transferred its colonial remnants of the early modern period to the British, even if the fortifications on the 'Dutch Gold Coast' had long been an afterthought at best in Dutch colonial policy after 1815, when the Dutch formally abolished the slave trade. Yet for all the neglect from both the Dutch state and the (Amsterdam-based) powerful merchant community, the end of Dutch formal colonial sovereignty over Africa only sped up the interest and involvement of the Rotterdam-based entrepreneurs in West and West Central Africa, a process that started in the 1840s.

This chapter charts the involvement of the Rotterdam-based entrepreneurs in West and West Central Africa from the late 1830s onwards, against the background of the withdrawing Dutch colonial administration on the Gold Coast, the shifting balance in opportunities within the

[1] Storm, '1871'.

G. Dreijer, *Private Entrepreneurship and European Imperialism*,
Palgrave Studies in Economic History,
https://doi.org/10.1007/978-3-032-01086-5_3

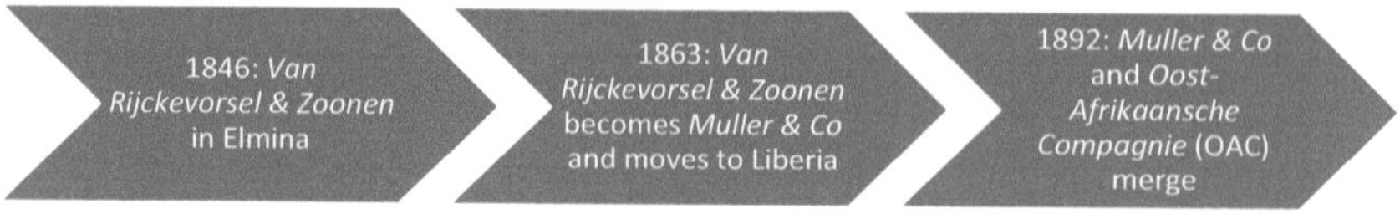

Graph 3.1 Rotterdam firms trading in Elmina and Liberia

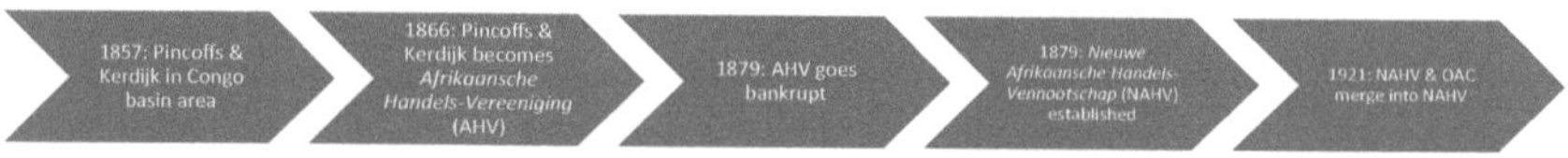

Graph 3.2 Rotterdam firms trading in Congo Basin area

Graph 3.3 Rotterdam firms trading in Mozambique

Netherlands to engage in colonial trade, production and investment, for example, through the *Nederlandsche Handel-Maatschappij* (NHM), the successor to the Dutch East India Company (*Vereenigde Oost-Indische Compagnie* or VOC), as well as the transition in Africa to the 'legitimate commerce'. The chapter explains *why* the Rotterdam-based entrepreneurs started trading on the Dutch-governed Gold Coast in the 1840s, before they branched out to other areas in West and West Central Africa, including Liberia and the coastal areas of the Congo basin in the period up to the late 1870s (see also Graphs 3.1, 3.2 and 3.3 and Table 3.1 for a visual overview of the Dutch entrepreneurs across West (Central) Africa).[2]

The focus here is therefore on the various Rotterdam firms operating across this large region, including *Van Rijckevorsel & Zoonen* (operating on the Gold Coast and run by Huibert van Rijckevorsel), *Muller & Co* (operating on the Gold Coast and in Liberia, and run by Hendrik Muller Szn.) and *Kerdijk & Pincoffs*, later the *Afrikaansche Handels-Vereeniging*

[2] This also includes the operations in Mozambique. As noted in the introduction, that part of the story is left out of the book for various reasons, but for the chronology and completeness, I include some basic information here.

Table 3.1 Chronology of the Rotterdam-Africa trade

Year	*Activity*
1846	Huibert van Rijckevorsel sends ships to Elmina
1851	Hendrik Muller Szn. joins firm *Van Rijckevorsel & Zoonen*
1857	Pincoffs & Kerdijk send first ships to Congo Basin area
1863	Muller takes control of *Van Rijckevorsel & Zoonen* and changes the name to *Muller & Co*, focusing on Liberia
1866	Pincoffs & Kerdijk becomes *Afrikaansche Handels-Vereeniging* (AHV)
1871	*Handels-Compagnie Mozambique* (HCM) established
1879	AHV goes bankrupt, *Nieuwe Afrikaansche Handels-Vennootschap* (NAHV) established under Muller's leadership
1883	Floundering HCM replaced by *Oost-Afrikaansche Compagnie* (OAC)
1892	*Muller & Co* and OAC merge as OAC
1905	OAC leaves Mozambique and focuses on Liberia only
1921	NAHV & OAC merge into NAHV

(AHV, operating in the Congo basin and run by Lodewijk Pincoffs), and the entrepreneurial choices made by these men. While the Rotterdam entrepreneurs started operating in Dutch-held regions on the Gold Coast, most of their trade eventually took place in non-imperial spaces (or at least non-imperial spaces until the late 1870s), *in casu* Liberia and the Congo basin. Some issues regarding labour and violence, presented by the advent of European imperialism in the 1880s, were much less pronounced during this period, even if the chapter will show evidence of some dubious labour practices, including slavery and child labour, by the AHV during this period.

The chapter starts with a survey of Dutch involvement in Africa before the 1840s, first looking at the early modern period under the Dutch West India Company (WIC) and subsequently at the 1815–1845 period, when various Dutch firms tried to revive trade to and from Elmina. After a more elaborate introduction of the main Rotterdam entrepreneurs than offered in the introduction, subsequent paragraphs explain the entrepreneurial choices of the Rotterdammers in the 1840s and 1850s to disperse from Elmina to other places in West and West Central Africa, look into the dynamics of Dutch-African trade between the 1840s and 1870s, and look at the three Dutch firms operating across the region during this period in their specific regional context. A conclusion follows.

3.2 Dutch Trade on the Gold Coast (1630s–Early 1860s)

Dutch involvement with the African continent, and West Africa in particular, went back to the early seventeenth century.[3] The Dutch West India Company (*West-Indische Compagnie* or WIC), as part of the Dutch plan to conquer present-day Brazil for the purposes of setting up a plantation economy there, also tried to make inroads into West Africa with an eye on the trans-Atlantic slave trade. To do so, the WIC attempted to attack Portuguese fortifications in Elmina (known by the Portuguese as São Jorge da Mina) in 1637 and Luanda in 1640, conquering both after several attempts. In Angola, Dutch rule only lasted eight years (1640–1648), and Dutch Brazil was also lost to the Portuguese in 1654. However, Dutch presence in Elmina, in present-day Ghana, lasted much longer (1637–1872). Elmina functioned as the centre of the Dutch trans-Atlantic slave trade in the early modern period, with the Dutch transporting over 550,000 people across the Atlantic in the early modern period.

Elmina was the most important Dutch fortification on the so-called Gold Coast (roughly the area that today covers Ghana), but by no means the only one. Until 1872, several others were under Dutch sovereignty, including Apollonia, Axim, Dixcove, Boutry, Saccondee and Chama: before 1867, the Dutch possessed even more fortifications.[4] No substantial economic activities were employed besides the slave trade. In 1792 the WIC was officially disbanded, with the Dutch Gold Coast being transferred to the sovereignty of the Dutch state. The Gold Coast fortifications were not brought under British sovereignty during the French occupation of the Netherlands (1794–1814), in contrast to most other colonial possessions (including the Cape Colony and parts of the Dutch East Indies).

After the Age of Revolutions, Dutch colonial involvement in Africa changed. Under English pressure, the Dutch *de jure* abolished the slave trade in 1814, although it would take until 1827 before the slave trade was *de facto* abolished as well, as many Dutch traders found loopholes to participate in the slave trade in any case (slavery itself remained legal in the Dutch Atlantic colonies until 1863, with an obligatory ten-year transition

[3] This section is mostly based on: H.J. Den Heijer, *Geschiedenis van de WIC* (Zutphen 2013).

[4] C. Jeekel, *Onze bezittingen op de kust van Guinea* (Amsterdam 1869), 5–15.

period that followed until 1873).[5] The decline of the slave trade, already apparent in the late eighteenth century, also significantly diminished the importance of Elmina for the Dutch. Whilst the Dutch state kept formal control over various fortifications on the Gold Coast, *de facto* the Dutch state largely neglected its possessions there.[6]

This was part of a bigger shift within Dutch colonial policy. After the abolition of the slave trade, the Dutch state focused its colonial policies on the Dutch East Indies and (to a lesser extent) Suriname and the Caribbean islands. The NHM concentrated its efforts on the Dutch East Indies as well. Some investments were made by the NHM in Africa after the 1880s, for example in banking and railways in Southern Africa (in particular in the Afrikaner Republics), cotton production in Egypt and, to a smaller extent, infrastructure development in Mozambique, which connected to the investments in the Afrikaner Republics in the north-east of what is today South Africa.[7] The NHM however never invested in other parts of the African continent, even in regions considered to be key in the Scramble for Africa, such as the coast of West Africa or the Congo basin.

This crucial detail demands an explanation. Even if firm evidence is lacking, a likely hypothesis is a combination of the Amsterdam-based domination of the NHM and therefore a focus on its investments in the Dutch East Indies, as well as the position of Hendrik Muller Szn. as commissioner within the NHM.[8] Muller Szn. soon after his appointment turned into an NHM critic and, in 1880, published a note arguing for a shift from the trade in commodities to financial services, exactly at the time the NAHV was (re-)established to focus on the commodity trade in West Central Africa.[9] Muller Szn.'s influence in the NHM may indicate that he was partly responsible for keeping out the NHM from the African continent.[10]

[5] Emmer, *Engeland, Nederland, Afrika en de slavenhandel in negentiende eeuw* (Leiden 1974).

[6] Ibidem, 80–81; Jeekel, *Onze bezittingen*, 5–15. Before 1867, the Dutch still controlled fifteen fortifications in the region: C.J.M. Nagtglas, *Een woord aangaande de vraag: "Wat moet Nederland doen met zijne bezittingen ter kuste van Guinea?"* (The Hague 1863), 4.

[7] De Graaf, *Voor handel en maatschappij*, 96–98.

[8] Ibidem, 79.

[9] Ibidem.

[10] Ibidem, 20 & 78–83.

After 1815, the Dutch state tried to revive the economic fortunes of the Gold Coast. Yet the Governors of the Dutch Gold Coast were presented with a dispersed colonial presence of the Dutch colonial state in Africa, a missing economic and political rationale for the Dutch presence, and a substantial lack of interest from the metropole. It may therefore be no surprise that many Governors did not last long, acted in a temporary capacity or were appointed as Governor of the Dutch Gold Coast to demote them from more prestigious positions, as was the case for the former Dutch East Indies Governor Herman Willem Daendels. One of the longer-lasting governors, Cornelis Nagtglas, in a pamphlet essentially agreed that the Dutch Gold Coast had no real value for the Dutch state.[11] Nagtglas was, alongside Anthony van der Eb, one of the few Governors who lasted longer than a few years and returned frequently when Dutch Governors of the Gold Coast opted for a job elsewhere.

The first Governor to take office after Napoleon's defeat at Waterloo and the Vienna Congress was Daendels, who was demoted from his Governorship and military commandership in the Dutch East Indies to the Gold Coast because of his opposition to various Dutch government policies. To prevent him from returning to the Netherlands, he was made Governor of the Dutch Gold Coast. As a result of the abolition of the slave trade, Daendels tried to set up a plantation colony in Elmina, modelled on his experience in the Dutch East Indies.[12] Moreover, Daendels initiated various infrastructure projects, including road development from and to Elmina.[13] The efforts never came to much, as Daendels passed away on 8 May 1818 because of malaria. After Daendels' death, the Dutch Gold Coast was essentially neglected by the Dutch state: various Dutch Governors tried to employ economically viable initiatives in Daendels' wake, but efforts to set up plantations, grow tobacco or mine gold in the region came to nothing.[14]

[11] Nagtglas, *Een woord aangaande*, 14.

[12] D.A. Hoogendijk, 'Mr. Herman Willem Daendels als Gouverneur ter kuste van Guinea', *Nieuwe West-Indische Gids*, 25, 1 (1943), 257–266 & 289–302; W.J. Koppius, 'Herman Willem Daendels, Gouv. Gen. Ter kuste van Guinea 1816–1818, *De Indische Gids*, 52, 2 (1930), 892–904 & 979–997; D. Van der Meer, 'De Goudkust na de slavenhandel: plannen om de Nederlandse bezittingen ter Kuste van Guinea rendabel te maken', Unpublished MA thesis Utrecht University (Utrecht 1990), available at https://meergeschiedenis.nl/goudkust/de-goudkust-na-de-slavenhandel.pdf [Retrieved 10/10/2022].

[13] Ibidem.

[14] Nagtglas, *Een woord aangaande*, 6–9.

The Dutch Gold Coast only retained some importance (from the Dutch viewpoint) as recruiting ground for African soldiers to fight in the many colonial wars in the Dutch East Indies, a project that started in 1831 in the wake of Belgium's secession and the colonial Java War of 1825–1830, which stretched Dutch military capabilities thin.[15] Dutch recruitment of black soldiers in West Africa (so-called *Belanda Hitam*, 'Black Dutchmen') remained common in the nineteenth century, with some 3000 West Africans being recruited to serve in the Dutch colonial army in the Dutch East Indies (*Koninklijk Nederlands Indisch Leger* or KNIL) during the century. New recruitment drives were made in 1836, 1855, 1872 and 1890, with mixed success.[16]

Notwithstanding the lack of interest from the metropole and the failed initiatives from the Governors to kickstart economic activities that would replace the slave trade, some private entrepreneurs from the Netherlands set up business activities on the Gold Coast from the 1830s onwards. Lured by the transition to the 'legitimate commerce', family firms from both Amsterdam and Rotterdam tried their luck on the Gold Coast. The Amsterdam-based *Johannes Boelen & Co* for example set up a line service between Elmina and the Netherlands, with its agents buying palm oil to sell this on the Dutch market.[17] *Boelen & Co* sent its first ships to West Africa in 1838, before appointing Jan Hendrik Barends as its agent in Elmina in January 1839.[18] This may not have been a great success, as in August 1843, *Boelen & Co* appointed Governor Anthony van der Eb as their agent.[19] Several years later (it is unclear exactly when), *Boelen & Co* stopped doing business on the Gold Coast, complaining about the bad behaviour of the Dutch colonial officials on the Gold Coast, which

[15] I. Van Kessel, *Zwarte Hollanders: Afrikaanse soldaten in Nederlands-Indië* (Amsterdam 2013), 166–180; Yarak, *Asante and the Dutch*, 104–113.

[16] Van Kessel, *Zwarte Hollanders*.

[17] See for example H.F. Tengbergen, *Verhaal van den reistogt en expeditie naar de Nederlandsche bezittingen ter West kust van Afrika* (The Hague 1839), 33; Emmer & Baesjou, 'The Dutch in West Africa', 197; J.F. Koopman, *Verslag van eene reize naar de westkust van Africa* (s.l. 1861), 49–50; Muller, *Muller*, 28–31, 62–63, 72, 78 & 103.

[18] See https://gcdb.doortmontweb.org/showmedia.php?mediaID=243 & https://gcdb.doortmontweb.org/showmedia.php?mediaID=247 [Retrieved 02/10/2024]. Based on: NL-HaNA, Archief Nederlandse Bezittingen ter Kuste van Guinea (1658–1872) (hereafter Archief Guinea), inv. 1.05.114, nr. 987, Notariële Archieven 1839–1856, nrs. 1 & 2. Today, they are digitised and can be found here: https://www.nationaalarchief.nl/onderzoeken/archief/1.05.14/invnr/%40B~IV~I~981A-988~987 [Retrieved 02/10/2024].

[19] http://www.engelfriet.net/Alie/Aad/elmina1.htm [Retrieved 01/10/2024].

included extorting bribes and using force against the local population to force them to hand over commodities.[20] Van der Eb, well-known for his private trade, may have contributed to this.

While most of these firms did not last long, the scale was not unsubstantial either: *Boelen & Co* for example bought six ships between 1840 and 1842, by the name of *Acra* (2x), *Afrika*, *Axim*, *Bij* and *Elmina*, clearly indicating they were to be used for the line service to the Gold Coast.[21] Similarly, the Amsterdam-based *Trakanen & Co* bought six ships in the late 1830s and early 1840s, albeit with names less clearly geared towards the West African line service.[22] *Trakanen & Co* also operated a line service to Old Calabar in present-day Nigeria.[23] Two other firms set up business with the Gold Coast in the late 1830s as well, one from Amsterdam and one from Rotterdam. According to the Dutch naval officer F.H. Tengbergen, who visited the Gold Coast in the 1830s, both *De Vries & Co* (from Amsterdam) and *Hoboken & Co* (from Rotterdam) operated in Elmina and employed agents there, who traded in (mostly) palm oil and ivory.[24]

Hoboken & Co was formed by Anthony van Hoboken, Rotterdam's largest ship-builder and -owner in the first half of the nineteenth century.[25] His firm was mainly focused on transport to and from the Dutch East Indies, but by 1841, Hoboken also secured the monopoly on the transport of the aforementioned West African black soldiers to the Dutch East Indies.[26] The decision to set up a liner service to Elmina (four ships in total) and employ an agent on the Gold Coast for the palm oil trade was therefore probably a by-product of the transport monopoly.[27] In the end, none of these four firms appeared to have operated longer than a couple of years on the Gold Coast in the late 1830s and early 1840s, indicating it

[20] Nagtglas, *Een word*, 12. This was not uncommon, as similar complaints were made in an 1864 letter to the *Dagblad van Zuid-Holland en 's-Gravenhage* (nr. 206), 28-12-1864. See https://gcdb.doortmontweb.org/showmedia.php?mediaID=547 [Retrieved 02/10/2024].

[21] See the shipping data of the Dutch firms trading on West Africa: Dreijer, 'Dutch-African Shipping Dataset (1830–1918)'; Idem, 'Handel en scheepvaart', 46–50.

[22] Ibidem.

[23] Koopman, *Verslag*, 49–50.

[24] Tengbergen, *Expeditie*, 33.

[25] See Oosterwijk, *Koning van de koopvaart: Anthony van Hoboken (1756–1850)* (Amsterdam 1996).

[26] Ibidem, 204–218; Van Kessel, *Zwarte Hollanders*, 40–41.

[27] Oosterwijk, *Koning van de koopvaart*, 219–220.

was hard to make money on either running transport facilities or operating a profitable palm oil trade between the Netherlands and the Gold Coast during this period.[28]

In 1846, the Rotterdam entrepreneur Huibert van Rijckevorsel (1813–1860) sent a ship to the Gold Coast.[29] With the exception of Van Hoboken (for whom trade was largely a side show to the recruitment of soldiers), Van Rijckevorsel was the first entrepreneur from Rotterdam to set up business in West Africa, thereby essentially offering a pathway for the Rotterdam group of entrepreneurs to move into the West African trade in raw commodities. Huibert van Rijckevorsel (Image 3.1) was the scion of a prominent Rotterdam family, with the Van Rijckevorsels' lineage going back to at least the sixteenth century. The family was knighted in 1829 and therefore can be taken to be counted among Rotterdam's 'old' aristocracy.

Huibert's father, Abram van Rijckevorsel (1790–1864) was among Rotterdam's most prominent businessmen. Abram van Rijckevorsel combined his entrepreneurship with a political career, something not uncommon in the nineteenth century. He was, for example, a member of the Liberal Party of the Rotterdam municipal council (1839–1849), the Dutch Parliament (1841–1844 & 1845–1850), the Provincial Estates (1850) and the Senate (1850–1862), thereby charting the path for many other Liberal entrepreneur-politicians to combine entrepreneurship with a political career. Van Rijckevorsel was instrumental in improving Rotterdam's maritime infrastructure. His primary contribution to Rotterdam's rise, however, was his chairmanship of the local Chamber of Commerce from 1838 to 1864, where he tirelessly lobbied for improving the position of the city's entrepreneurs.

Van Rijckevorsel's entrepreneurship in the early nineteenth century primarily focused on the trade in colonial products from the Dutch East Indies. Through the NHM, where he was a board member, Van Rijckevorsel actively participated in the trade with the Dutch East Indies, selling colonial commodities that arrived in Rotterdam's port to the hinterland. His son, Huibert van Rijckevorsel (1813–1866), already entered the family firm at a young age, receiving his entrepreneurial education within the firm. It was Huibert's decision, in 1846, to diversify the trade

[28] Emmer & Baesjou, 'The Dutch in West Africa', 197.

[29] Ibidem; De Kok, 'De koloniale connectie', 71; Muller, *Muller*, 25–152. The next section is primarily based on the literature cited in footnote 61 of the introduction.

Image 3.1 Portrait of Huibert van Rijckevorsel. (Source: Friedrich Boser (Llowa 1809–Düsseldorf 1881), CC BY-SA 3.0, via Wikimedia Commons, Museum Rotterdam [Retrieved 18/10/2023])

of the firm to West Africa.[30] His bridgehead to set up business in Elmina was the aforementioned Anthony van der Eb, Governor of the Dutch Gold Coast.[31] On his way back to Elmina in 1847 after a leave of absence in the Netherlands, Van der Eb sailed on the *Gouverneur Van der Eb* brigantine, which was owned by a firm under the name of *Anthony van der Eb en Huibert van Rijckevorsel.*[32] This indicates that Abram van Rijckevorsel, still head of the family firm, did not fully agree with this diversification, necessitating Huibert van Rijckevorsel to associate himself with Van der Eb in 1846–1847.

It appears that the first trip of the *Gouverneur Van der Eb* went well, as the ship was back in Hellevloetsluis (a port town near Rotterdam) in early 1848.[33] Van der Eb thereafter was appointed the agent for *Van Rijckevorsel & Zoonen* in Elmina, something that was allowed under Dutch law, and which had been the case before under *Boelen & Co* as well.[34] Van der Eb would remain the Dutch agent of *Van Rijckevorsel & Zoonen* in Elmina until his death in 1852.[35] This system, allowing Dutch colonial officials to privately trade, was formally abolished in 1858.[36] After the successful trip of the *Gouverneur Van der Eb* in 1847–1848, Huibert van Rijckevorsel acquired more ships for the trade to West Africa.[37] As most ships of *Van Rijckevorsel & Zoonen* were given names that clearly marked their destination, we can for example be reasonably sure that the *St. George de la Mina* (brig, 1849), *Goudkust* (schooner, 1852), *Gouverneur Schomerus* (schooner, 1853, named after Van der Eb's successor) and the *Guinea* (brig,

[30] Baesjou & Emmer, 'The Dutch in West Africa', 197; De Kok, 'De koloniale connectie', 70–73; Muller, *Muller*, 25–36.

[31] Emmer & Baesjou, 'The Dutch in West Africa', 197.

[32] See Dreijer, 'Dutch-African Shipping Dataset'.

[33] See http://www.engelfriet.net/Alie/Aad/elmina1.htm [Retrieved 01/10/2024].

[34] According to the "Instructies en Bestuursreglementen nopens het Beleid der Regering ter Kuste van Guinee" of 1838, Van der Eb was allowed to trade privately next to receiving 1200 guilders as an annual wage. See http://www.engelfriet.net/Alie/Aad/elmina1.htm [Retrieved 01/10/2024].

[35] Ibidem. See for the death of Van der Eb: https://gcdb.doortmontweb.org/showmedia.php?mediaID=646 [Retrieved 02/10/2024]. Interestingly, debts with Van der Eb could be claimed at Van Rijckevorsel's office in Rotterdam before 31-12-1852, according to the announcement upon his death.

[36] Ibidem.

[37] See NL-SAR, Archief Muller, nr. 157, Profits and Losses on Ships to the Coast of Guinea, showing the rather mixed results of the ventures. See also: Dreijer, 'Handel en scheepvaart', 42 & 49.

1856) were acquired with the explicit goal to expand the trade to Elmina.[38] In 1850, Huibert van Rijckevorsel argued against the implementation of import tariffs on the Gold Coast, in particular for alcoholic beverages like rum and gin.[39] Van Rijckevorsel appears to have been successful in this lobby, as none were established.[40]

In 1852, *Van Rijckevorsel & Zoonen*'s trade on the Gold Coast took two hits. First, in May 1852, the *Gouverneur van der Eb* shipwrecked before the coast of Elmina, even if much of the cargo was saved.[41] Second, Van der Eb passed away in 1852, depriving *Van Rijckevorsel & Zoonen* of a committed agent on the Gold Coast with decent contacts, for example with local Asante elites, to source palm oil.[42] On the balance of 31 December 1851, Van der Eb was for example mentioned for almost 200,118 guilders, the sum *Van Rijckevorsel & Zoonen* still owned to Van der Eb.[43] Van der Eb was succeeded by Hero Schomerus as Governor. Schomerus also acted as agent of *Van Rijckevorsel & Zoonen*, and had the *Gouverneur Schomerus* named after him shortly after he took office, yet appears to have been less strongly attached to the trade as Van der Eb had been.[44] Schomerus himself passed away in 1856, and no future Governor of the Dutch Gold Coast would act as agent of *Van Rijckevorsel & Zoonen* anymore.

Huibert van Rijckevorsel had nevertheless successfully managed to diversify the trade of his family from the trade in the Dutch East Indies (and to a lesser extent Suriname) in ten years, acting entrepreneurially in a number of ways.[45] Van Rijckevorsel took a risk in diversifying to the Gold Coast, but managed to both envision and value this opportunity, and allocate and reconfigure resources relatively efficiently to the trade. Moreover, Van Rijckevorsel legitimised novelty to an extent, even though he was not

[38] See https://www.marhisdata.nl/eigenaar&id=12519 [Retrieved 01/01/2024].

[39] See http://www.engelfriet.net/Alie/Aad/elmina1.htm [Retrieved 01/10/2024].

[40] Ibidem.

[41] Ibidem. See also NL-SAR, Archief Muller, nr. 158, Profits and Losses 1851–1859, Return Voyages from the Guinea Coast 1852, showing a substantial loss for that year of 15.359 guilders.

[42] Yarak, *Asante and the Dutch*.

[43] See http://www.engelfriet.net/Alie/Aad/elmina1.htm [Retrieved 01/10/2024]; for the original source see NL-SAR, Archief Muller, nr. 153, Balance 31 December 1851–1 Januari 1852, line 125.

[44] Ibidem.

[45] Muller, *Muller*, 25–152; see also NL-SAR, Archief Muller, inv. 155, for the activities on the Guinea coast.

the first Dutchman to move into Elmina. The support of the Dutch colonial state, in the form of Van der Eb as the agent, was crucial for Van Rijckevorsel. As René Baesjou and Piet Emmer have argued, the lack of state support for many of the other firms may have made it hard to make a profit for Dutch firms in West Africa in the 1830s to the early 1860s.[46] Indeed, another Amsterdam firm called *Herklots & Bouman* also set up shop in Elmina in 1858, the same year the Dutch state prohibited the private trade of its colonial officers.[47] By 1862, however, *Herklots & Bouman* had already stopped operating under that name, lacking support from the Dutch Governor to trade profitably.[48]

State support in the area around Elmina was thus crucial to turn a profit, as economic activity in the region had dropped after the abolition of the slave trade. Whereas some palm oil was produced around Elmina, this was by far not enough to be profitable, with other areas in West Africa producing more and better-quality palm oil.[49] For example, most British firms active across West Africa moved towards other places, most notably the region near the Niger river (present-day Nigeria and Niger).[50] For Dutch entrepreneurs, moving beyond Elmina thus also became imperative in the race for African commodities.

3.3 Dutch Dispersion Across the African Continent (1850s–1870s)

Despite the fact that trouble appeared on the horizon as a result of declining Dutch state support, *Van Rijckevorsel & Zoonen* remained the preeminent Dutch trading house in Elmina in the 1860s.[51] With *Herklots & Bouman* folding in 1862, Bouman associated himself with an Amsterdam-based entrepreneur called Van Rijckevorsel (no family of the Rotterdam-based Van Rijckevorsels) under the name *Bouman & Van Rijckevorsel* and

[46] Baesjou & Emmer, 'The Dutch in West Africa'.

[47] Ibidem, 197–198; Muller, *Muller*, 59–152; De Kok, 'De koloniale connectie', 70–73; J.S.G. Gramberg, *Schetsen van Afrika's Westkust* (Amsterdam 1861), 110 & 299; Van der Pot, 'Huibert van Rijckevorsel'.

[48] Baesjou & Emmer, 'The Dutch in West Africa', 199; Muller, *Muller*, 72.

[49] Ibidem. See also Lynn, *Commerce and Economic Change*.

[50] G.L. Baker, *Trade Winds on the Niger: The Sage of the Royal Niger Company* (London 1996), 89; Newbury, 'On the Margins of Empire: The Trade of Western Africa, 1875–1890', in: Förster, Mommsen & Robinson (eds.), *Bismarck, Europe and Africa*, 35–58, there 51.

[51] Muller, *Muller*, 139–144.

continued operating on the Gold Coast over the course of the 1860s, apparently to limited success (notwithstanding the fact that the firm acquired no less than ten ships between 1862 and 1867).[52][53] One shipping journal of this Amsterdam-based firm has survived, in this case that of the brig *Gouverneur Nagtglas* (bought in 1861 and named after the Dutch Governor) between September 1864 and October 1865.[54] Even if the crew, led by captain J. van Streyen, was able to buy palm oil in Elmina, Axim and Accra between January and July 1865, the journal indicates the difficulties for the firm to buy the commodity: only after suggestions from an American ship in Elmina and the Rotterdam-based Van Rijckevorsel firm, Van Streyen was able to buy decent amounts of palm oil.[55] Yet overall, the journal indicates the difficulties for the Amsterdam-based firm to make a profit on the Gold Coast.

Already in 1856, Huibert van Rijkevorsel hinted that profits from the trade to Elmina were declining, primarily as demand for Dutch arms, alcohol and cloth declined on the Gold Coast as a result of declining warfare.[56] Van Rijckevorsel around this time pondered moving into the Congo Basin area, but eventually decided against it for unknown reasons.[57] Having pivoted part of the family firm's attention to the Gold Coast in 1846–1848, the declining profits led Van Rijckevorsel to refocus the attention of the

[52] See https://www.marhisdata.nl/eigenaar&id=31656 [Retrieved 01/01/2024].

[53] Baesjou & Emmer, 'The Dutch in West Africa', 198; Muller, *Muller*, 72 and *n*67. Even more confusingly, the firm continued operating as *Van Rijckevorsel & Co* in the late 1860s and 1870s. One 1868 notarial contract has been left of the Amsterdam-based *Van Rijckevorsel & Co*, with the local merchant Tekyi Mensah, concerning the repayment of a debt. The notarial agreement on payment replaced a previous judicial agreement. See https://gcdb.doortmontweb.org/showmedia.php?mediaID=46 [Retrieved 02/10/2024], based on: NL-HaNA, Archief Guinea, nr. 988, Notariële Archieven 1857–1871, nr. 114. Today, they are digitised and can be found here: https://www.nationaalarchief.nl/onderzoeken/archief/1.05.14/invnr/988/file/NL-HaNA_1.05.14_988_0726?eadID=1.05.14&unitID=988&query=Nederlandse%20bezittingen [Retrieved 02/10/2024].

[54] See Scheepvaartmuseum Amsterdam (hereafter NL-SMA), Handschriften, inv.nr. I285, Logboek/Journaal Schoenerschip "Gouverneur Nagtglas" 1864–1865. The title indicates that the ship was a schooner, but most other sources indicate, in contrast, that the ship was a brig. Other documentation kept for 1861–1864 confirms that the trade was generally loss-making. See NL-IISG-NEHA, Collectie Combinatie voor den Handel op de West en/of Zuidwestkust van Afrika, inv. ARCH03684.

[55] Ibidem, Entries 06-04-1865, 07-04-1865, 14-04-1865, 15-04-1865 & 16-04-1865.

[56] Muller, *Muller*, 43–47.

[57] Ibidem.

Graph 3.4 Profits and Losses of Van Rijckevorsel & Zoonen, 1851–1867, in guilders. (Source: *NL-SAR, Archief Muller, nr. 154*)

firm to the Dutch East Indies in the early 1860s.[58] As Graph 3.4 shows, losses of the firm became rather common from 1856 onwards, with 1860 and 1862 being the only years turning up a profit. In particular, shipping in West Africa became loss-inducing (Table 3.2), which led Van Rijckevorsel to invest more in shipping to Padang (Sumatra), where he operated a plantation.[59]

This 'pivot' to the Dutch East Indies did however not save the firm. Besides the problems of the firm, tragedy struck the family in the private sphere as well. In 1862, Huibert van Rijckevorsel, since long having experienced mental health problems, collapsed and was subsequently sent to a hospital and faded from the scene. Abram van Rijckevorsel, the father, was in his sixties as well, and declined to take over the firm. The family firm, however, was saved by an Amsterdam-born son of a German immigrant by the name of Hendrik Muller (born Müller, 1819–1898), often denoted as Hendrik Muller Szn. (Samuelszoon), to distinguish him from his son and namesake.[60] Hendrik Muller Szn. was educated in business before moving to Rotterdam, where he married Marie Cornelie van Rijckevorsel, daughter of Abram and sister of Huibert, in 1851 (Image 3.2).

[58] Ibidem, 177–193.
[59] NL-SAR, Archief Muller, nr. 153, Balance 1860.
[60] This section is primarily based on: Muller, *Muller* & Ingenbleek, 'Muller, Hendrik'.

Table 3.2 Profits and losses on Guinea Coast Trade of *Van Rijckevorsel & Zoonen*, 1851–1861, in guilders

Year	Direct exports	Exports via Brazil	Imports	Shipping	Remainder
1851	15,115	824,63	10,744	-	5,196
1852	5,456	4,441	15,359	4,694	768
1853	3,419	8,383	27,191	10,467	42,622
1854	100,664	2,569	87,609	12,653	178,190
1855	138,141	-	78,638	40,196	176,583
1856	14,582	54,660	23,067	32,606	23,575
1857	30,603	7,105	38,168	53,824	22,052
1858	116,539	5,632	3,347	60,201	58,623
1859	39,410	2,712	59,370	89,645	11,848
1860	30,793	-	47,005	29,077	48,721
1861	17,016	-	14,728	38,253	6,509
Total	493,737	32,214	375,776	15,161	543,835
Loss	18,001	-	29,450	356,454	30,852
Profit	475,735	32,214	346,326	341,293	512,983

Source: *NL-SAR, Archief Muller, nr. 155.* Note: *Profits in black, losses in red*

Similar to Abram van Rijckevorsel and many of the other Rotterdam entrepreneurs in this story, Muller Szn. was an entrepreneur-cum-politician of liberal bent. From 1873 until 1885, Muller Szn. was a member of the Rotterdam municipal council. Moreover, Muller Szn. was a member of the Provincial Estates between 1877 and 1881 and in 1881 became a Senator, which he remained a member until his death in 1898. Muller Szn. was well-known for his fierce advocacy for free trade, following the position of the British Liberals: he for example co-edited *De Economist*, the Dutch equivalent of *The Economist*, and actively published opinion pieces in various news outlets to further his goals. Yet Muller Szn. was no anti-colonial activist, setting up a major press campaign in the early 1870s to oppose the Dutch-British agreements of 1871–1872 that transferred Dutch sovereignty over Elmina and other fortifications in present-day Ghana to the British.[61]

[61] See e.g. H. Muller Szn., *De afstand der kust van Guinea aan Engeland* (Rotterdam 1871).

Image 3.2 Photograph of Hendrik Muller Szn. (Source: Unknown photographer in 1862, Public domain, via Wikimedia Commons, Rotterdam Municipal Archives [Retrieved 18/10/2023])

Although Africa was the main continent of investment and interest for Muller Szn., he also invested in the Dutch East Indies. Moreover, Muller Szn. was co-editor of the *Tijdschrift voor Nederlands-Indië* (*Journal of the Dutch East Indies*) and co-founder of the *Maatschappij tot Nut van den Javaan* ('Society for the Use of the Javan'), a paternalistic society with the goal to improve the lives of the colonised people on the island of Java. In 1884–1885, Muller Szn. was one of the few Dutch delegates at the Berlin Conference,[62] where he advocated for free trade. Muller Szn. remained for some thirty years the key player in the Rotterdam network trading with Africa by steering Dutch trade in Africa away from Elmina.

Muller Szn. officially took over the firm from his brother-in-law Huibert van Rijckevorsel in 1862.[63] Muller Szn. moved fast from there: in 1863, Muller Szn. liquidated the firm *Van Rijckevorsel & Zoonen* and established a new one under the name *Muller & Co*, although it took over all the assets of Van *Rijckevorsel & Zoonen* and continued trading with the same agents and partners.[64] Soon after taking over, Muller Szn. decided to start operating in other areas in West Africa beyond Elmina, in particular Liberia, judging it to be profitable based on data on the African trade he compiled himself for the years 1851–1863.[65] Muller Szn. retained existing trading links of Van *Rijckevorsel & Zoonen* with the Dutch East Indies, as well as Japan and Macao, for most of the 1860s, even if slowly but steadily Muller Szn. pursued a narrower geographic focus and increasing specialisation in terms of commodities.[66] *Muller & Co* retained a presence in Elmina as well by keeping an agent employed there, but the majority of the firm's business focused on Liberia after 1863.[67] Using links already established in the late 1850s upon Liberia's independence, Muller Szn. quickly moved to expand in Liberia: in 1862, he, for example, became consul of Liberia in the Netherlands, also offering additional political

[62] Wesseling, 'Nederland en de Conferentie van Berlijn', 570.

[63] Muller, *Muller*, 169–176.

[64] NL-SAR, Archief Muller, nr. 153, Balance Van Rijckevorsel in Liquidation, 31-12-1863 & 01-01-1864; Idem, nr. 167, Profits and Losses 1863–1887.

[65] Idem, nr. 156, Profits on Guinea Coast Trade. Muller estimated the gross profits for this period had been 378,247 guilders.

[66] Muller, *Muller*, 169–176; NL-SAR, Archief Muller, nr. 167, Profits and Losses 1863–1887.

[67] Muller's financial administration only records the "Guinea coast" up to 1884, which included both Liberia and Elmina. In 1884, a distinction was made, showing that in Liberia Muller traded for 10,539,284 guilders compared to 764,75 guilders in Elmina. See: NL-SAR, Archief Muller, nr. 167, Profits and Losses 1863–1887. Moreover, an anonymous letter alleged that Van Rijckevorsel's business in Elmina had partly gone wrong for the bad Dutch governance on the Gold Coast: "Hoedanig dat handel drijven is afgelopen, daarvan zal het voormalige huis H. van Rijckevorsel, te Rotterdam, betere inlichting kunnen geven. Zouden dezen wel gunstig zijn?" See: *Dagblad van Zuid-Holland en 's-Gravenhage* (nr. 206), 28-12-1864, https://gcdb.doortmontweb.org/showmedia.php?mediaID=547 [Retrieved 02/10/2024].

Graph 3.5 Profits and losses of *Muller & Co*, 1863–1869, in guilders. (Source: *NL-SAR, Archief Muller, nr. 169*)

opportunities to press his case.[68] With Abram van Rijckevorsel passing away in 1864, Muller Szn. was left free to pursue opportunities as he saw fit on the basis of what *Van Rijckevorsel & Zoonen* had built in the eighteen prior years.

Judging from the business accounts of the firm (Graphs 3.5 and 3.6), *Muller* & Co was more successful than its predecessor.[69] Only in 1869, the firm made a loss, which was primarily due to the shipping in the Dutch East Indies.[70] As Graph 3.6 shows, *Muller & Co* successfully turned around the ailing business of *Van Rijckevorsel & Zoonen* in the West African palm oil trade, indicating the move to Liberia was successful. In 1879, another (this time substantial) loss was made, which was likely the result of the Pincoffs fraud of 1879 (see below). *Muller & Co* made a profit of almost 300,000 guilders on the West Guinea trade during the

[68] Muller, *Muller*, 170.

[69] Ibidem, 43–45; NL-SAR, Archief Muller, nr. 167, Profits and Losses 1863–1867.

[70] NL-SAR, Archief Muller, nr. 169, Statistics on Profits and Losses 1863–1869.

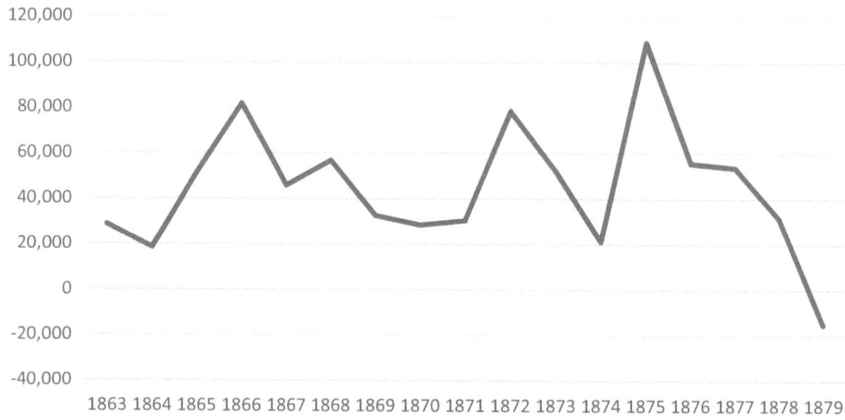

Graph 3.6 Profits and losses on the West Africa trade of *Muller & Co*, 1863–1879, in guilders. (Source: *NL-SAR, Archief Muller, nr. 168*)

period 1863–1869.[71] For the period 1863–1891, the West Africa trade netted *Muller & Co* a profit of roughly 866,000 guilders.[72]

Gradually, Muller Szn. focused on his firm on Liberia and, to a lesser extent, on parts of the Dutch East Indies where the production was not under control of the Amsterdam-based entrepreneurial elite.[73] The West African trade did however form the significant majority of the firm's business: in 1869, for example, trade with West Africa amounted to 41,714 guilders, compared with 144 for Java and 152 for Macassar.[74] In 1871, similar figures can be deducted from the account books (West Africa 44,900 guilders vs. Java 2499 guilders).[75] Except for the one-off of 1869 and the fateful year of 1879, *Muller & Co* turned a profit every year between 1863 and 1884.[76]

[71] Ibidem.

[72] Idem, nr. 168, Statistics on Profits and Losses 1863–1891 & 1892–1901, Profits and Losses 1863–1891.

[73] De Graaf, *Voor handel en maatschappij*, 96–98.

[74] NL-SAR, Archief Muller, nr. 167, Profits and Losses 1863–1887, Profits and Losses 1869.

[75] Idem, nr. 165, Balances 1864–1887, Balance 1871.

[76] Idem, nr. 168, Statistics on Profits and Losses 1863–1891 & 1892–1901, Profits and Losses 1863–1891.

Unfortunately, the archival documents do not allow us to track the shift from Elmina to Liberia specifically, even if we know from qualitative evidence that this was the case.[77] The Dutch Gold Coast, in any case, dwindled in both economic and political importance in the 1860s. The Dutch state signed the Anglo-Dutch Gold Coast Treaty in 1867, allowing the British to take over all Dutch fortifications east of Elmina, leaving the Dutch with eight fortifications (including Elmina).[78] The British had already taken over the Danish fortifications on the Gold Coast in 1850, and the former Governor Nagtglas in his 1863 pamphlet on the future of the Dutch Gold Coast seriously argued for the sale of the Dutch fortifications on the Gold Coast to the British as well, citing the high costs and limited value for the Dutch state.[79]

Following his advice and other opposition to keeping the Dutch Gold Coast, the Dutch state negotiated a trade of forts, with the Dutch state receiving all fortifications west of Elmina, and the British taking over all forts east of Elmina. The Treaty signed in 1867 led to protests by the Asante, who had long been allied with the Dutch against the British.[80] The people around Fort Komenda (Fante, who had long been allied with the British against the Dutch) refused to hoist the Dutch flag, taking Dutch naval officers hostage.[81] Even if the British negotiated a ransom sum, the Dutch instead opted for a punitive expedition, leading to the destruction of Komenda and several surrounding villages, and widespread displacement of the Fante population.[82] This, of course, did not help the Dutch case.

The Dutch state subsequently acknowledged the futility of keeping on the Gold Coast, and started negotiating with the British state for the transfer of sovereignty over its remaining fortifications. Between September 1870 and November 1871, the Dutch and British negotiated three

[77] Muller, *Muller*.

[78] A.M.P. Mollema, 'De afstand der Nederlandse bezittingen ter kuste van Guinea aan Engeland in 1872', in: S.A. (ed.), *Varia Historica: Aangeboden aan Professor Doctor A.W. Byvanck ter gelegenheid van zijn zeventigste verjaardag door de Historische Kring te Leiden* (Assen 1954), 215–242, there 223; D. Coombs, *The Gold Coast, Britain and The Netherlands 1850–1874* (London 1963), 41–49.

[79] Nagtglas, *Een woord aangaande*.

[80] Yarak, *Asante and the Dutch*, 239–240; Coombs, *The Gold Coast*, 50–56; Mollema, 'De afstand', 223.

[81] Yarak, *Asanta and the Dutch*, 239–240; Coombs, *The Gold Coast*, 50–56; Mollema, 'De afstand', 224–226.

[82] Ibidem.

treaties, one on the transfer of Dutch sovereignty to the British of the Gold Coast fortifications, one on the British acknowledging Dutch sovereignty over Sumatra and one concerning the immigration of contract labourers from British India to Suriname.[83] After some political hassling, the Dutch state ratified the treaties on 17 February 1872, and the Dutch Gold Coast came to an end on 6 April 1872 when sovereignty was transferred to the British.

While there was no great enthusiasm for the transfer of sovereignty in the Netherlands, neither did it arouse great upheaval. Even Governor Nagtglas was in favour and advised the Dutch government to finish the deal as soon as possible.[84] There was one exception, in the form of Muller Szn. Even if his trading interests mostly had moved to Liberia, Muller Szn. firmly opposed the transfer of sovereignty of Elmina and the other fortifications to the British. In May 1871, Muller Szn. published a pamphlet drawn from a speech he had held in the Dutch Senate months earlier.[85] He argued against the agreements concluded, arguing that as an entrepreneur he would suffer from the agreement. Even if the Dutch government argued equal treatment would apply to Dutch trade in the British-held Gold Coast, Muller Szn. argued that the British would claim jurisdiction and favour British entrepreneurs one way or the other.[86] Moreover, Muller Szn. argued that the Dutch government had acted disingenuously by using the 1869–1870 skirmishes as an excuse to get rid of the Dutch Gold Coast, but did not consider all the (commercial) arguments.[87] Muller Szn. expected that eventually things would settle down under British rule, but still preferred Dutch rule over the Gold Coast.[88] His very public protests, in the end, did obviously not result in much: even many of his Liberal colleagues voted for the transfer of sovereignty over the Dutch Gold Coast.[89] *Muller & Co* would remain in Elmina and trade on largely as before, essentially confirming his own prediction that things would settle down under British rule: indeed, this happened much sooner than Muller Szn. himself perhaps had expected.

[83] Mollema, 'De afstand'. 229–242.
[84] Ibidem, 237–240.
[85] Muller, *De afstand der Kust van Guinea.*
[86] Ibidem, 6–11.
[87] Ibidem, 12.
[88] Ibidem, 14–16.
[89] Muller, *Muller*, 204–205.

Van Rijckevorsel & Zoonen and *Muller & Co* were for all intents and purposes family affairs. Their moderate success and the transition to the legitimate commerce did attract other Rotterdammers aiming to participate in the exploitation of resources like palm oil. With the exception of the Amsterdam-based *Van Rijckevorsel & Co*, after 1850 Dutch interest in trading across Africa was limited to entrepreneurs from Rotterdam. Among the group of entrepreneurs, the efforts by Lodewijk Pincoffs and Henry Kerdijk (first called *Kerdijk & Pincoffs*) were particularly important.

Lodewijk Pincoffs (1827–1911) was a Jewish businessman and politician from the city of Rotterdam (the Netherlands).[90] In 1851, Pincoffs married Esther Raphael, the daughter of a Jewish banker from Amsterdam. Pincoffs' star quickly rose and in 1856 he became a member for the Liberal party in Rotterdam's municipal council, before moving on to memberships of the Provincial Estates (*Provinciale Staten*) of Zuid-Holland (1858) and the Senate (*Eerste Kamer*) of the Dutch Parliament in 1872, in the latter capacity the first Jew to hold a seat. In this, he was very similar to both Abram van Rijckevorsel and Hendrik Muller Szn. As a politician, Pincoffs tirelessly campaigned for the development of Rotterdam's maritime infrastructure and was instrumental in improving the city's port facilities. Through his Jewish heritage, Pincoffs brought in Jewish capital into Rotterdam investment vehicles, primarily so from Germany and Manchester, where small groups of Jewish merchants were also based.

Besides his political activities, Pincoffs developed various trading activities. In 1849, he set up a firm trading in indigo with his brother-in-law Henry Kerdijk (under the name *Kerdijk & Pincoffs*), before the firm sent ships in 1857 to the Congo river. In 1868 the two business partners retired the name *Kerdijk & Pincoffs* and formed the *Afrikaansche Handels-Vereeniging* (AHV). While the two men were nominally equal partners, in reality Pincoffs was by far the more dominant. Next to the AHV, Pincoffs also invested in the so-called *Nederlands-Indische Gasmaatschappij* to exploit the gas network in Batavia, the capital of the Dutch East Indies.[91] In 1872, Pincoffs moreover established the *Rotterdamsche Handels-Vereeniging* (RHV), which held the concession to improve Rotterdam's maritime infrastructure on the south bank of the river (present-day

[90] This section is largely based on the literature cited in footnote 63 of the introduction.

[91] C. Boele, 'Een erfenis van Pincoffs: de familie Enthoven en hun actions de jouissance van de N.V. Nederlandsch-Indische Gas-Maatschappij', *Rotterdams Jaarboekje*, 9, 9 (1991), 310–321.

Feijenoord), a plan linked to his political efforts to improve the city's maritime infrastructure. Pincoffs was thus among the main proponents of the development of Rotterdam's maritime infrastructure. Both the 'New Waterway' and the railway connection to Hoek van Holland were (at least partly) his idea, and Pincoffs was moreover instrumental in the development of the south bank of the Meuse River. Through the RHV, a public-private partnership initiated and set up by Pincoffs, Rotterdam's development as a port city gained significant clout (Image 3.3).

Image 3.3 Photograph of Lodewijk Pincoffs in the 1870s. (Source: Unknown photographer, Public domain, via Wikimedia Commons [Retrieved 18/10/2023])

All this came to an end in 1879. On 15 May, it came to light that Pincoffs had used money from the RHV to cover losses of the AHV, leaving both firms (and their main investors) with huge losses. *Mees & Zoonen* for example lost as much as one million guilders from the Pincoffs affair.[92] Pincoffs miraculously managed to flee to New York, via Brussels, Liverpool and Ireland. The United States and the Netherlands at the time had no extradition treaty, and despite various attempts by the Dutch government and Consulate in Washington Pincoffs never returned to the Netherlands to face justice.[93] Attempts by Pincoffs to regain standing by setting up new businesses in the United States failed and he died in relative poverty in 1911, ending his life as a cigar dealer. Pincoffs' fraud had significant national and international (financial) repercussions, even if Rotterdam eventually fairly quickly managed to recover from the financial hit.[94] To this day, the Pincoffs affair continues to inspire books, novels, plays, television series and other publications on the impact of the fraud, indicating the impact Pincoffs and his fraud have had on Rotterdam.[95]

Henry Kerdijk, born Henry Polak (later changed to Polak Kerdijk and subsequently only Kerdijk), was another Jewish entrepreneur from Rotterdam, from a family also having migrated from present-day Eastern Germany.[96] Kerdijk was the brother-in-law and co-director of Pincoffs, not unlike the set-up of the *Van Rijckevorsel & Zoonen*. Within the firm,

[92] Mees, 'R. Mees & Zoonen en de Pincoffscrisis'.

[93] See NL-HaNA, Archief van het Gezantschap Verenigde Staten / Legatie Washington (hereafter Archief Gezantschap Verenigde Staten), inv. 2.05.13, nr. 161, for details and correspondence surrounding Pincoffs' arrival in the US.

[94] Van de Laar, *Stad van formaat*, 81–88.

[95] See for example the biography of Pincoffs; Oosterwijk, *Ik verlang geen dank*. See also for uses in popular culture: R. Haasnoot, *Langzame wals* (Breda 2008); Petram, 'De val van een fraudeur'; Quadakers, 'Pincoffs'; *De IJzeren eeuw*, 'Het geheim van Rotterdam', season 1 episode 6, aired 12-07-2016, available at https://www.npostart.nl/de-ijzeren-eeuw/12-07-2016/VPWON_1262797 [Retrieved 09/08/2021]; W.J. De Leur & F.A.M. Schoone, *Tentoonstelling: Pincoffs en de Rotterdamse havens* (Rotterdam 1979).

[96] The information on (Polak) Kerdijk is primarily based on: E. Dorhout Mees, 'Kerdijk, Henri Polak', in: Visser, Van Jaarsveld & Van de Laar (eds.), *Rotterdamse ondernemers*, 119–121; A.F. Schepel, *Polak, Polak Kerdijk, Kerdijk: een familiegeschiedenis sedert 1779* (The Hague 1977).

Kerdijk largely played second fiddle to Pincoffs, and claimed not to know about the fraud perpetrated by Pincoffs. After the fraud came to light, an arrest warrant was issued against him. Kerdijk, upon having heard the news, fled to Antwerp and attempted suicide in a hotel there, which failed. Subsequently, Kerdijk was arrested, extradited, and brought before the Dutch High Court, which sentenced him to a lengthy prison time.[97] Henry Kerdijk had one brother, Lodewijk (Polak) Kerdijk, who was the main agent for the AHV in the early years of its existence in Portuguese Angola and north of the Congo River.[98] For a short time, Lodewijk Kerdijk also acted as the Dutch Consul to the Portuguese possessions in South-West Africa, offering the firm a useful position to use Dutch diplomatic channels to cement the firm's position in the area.[99] In 1861, Lodewijk Kerdijk died in Brazzaville and was buried there, his grave still to this day visible on the small Dutch cemetery there.[100]

The start of *Kerdijk & Pincoffs* in West Central Africa had been seen as an entrepreneurial masterstroke in Rotterdam in the late 1850s. After an inconspicuous start trading in indigo in 1849, *Kerdijk & Pincoffs* sent their agent Lodewijk Kerdijk to the West African coast in late 1857, seemingly advised to do so by Leopold Samsom. Samsom, a Manchester-based entrepreneur, was a family member of Kerdijk, and appears to have associated himself with *Kerdijk & Pincoffs* in late 1856 or early 1857 in anticipation of Lodewijk Kerdijk's trip to West Africa.[101] This allowed *Kerdijk &*

[97] The court case can be found in: H. Kerdijk & L. Pincoffs, *Stenografisch verslag van het getuigenverhoor en de pleidooien, gehouden voor den Hoogen Raad der Nederlanden* (Utrecht 1880).

[98] See Oosterwijk, *Ik verlang geen dank*, 33–34. Kerdijk wrote a travel report, which offers valuable information on the early Dutch trade in the Congo basin area. See: Schepel (ed.), L. Kerdijk (author), *Reisjournaal van Lodewijk Kerdijk: West-Africa 1857/1858* (Schiedam 1978).

[99] Oosterwijk, *Ik verlang geen dank*, 48–49; NL-HaNA, Legatie Portugal, nr. 88, Nomination Letter Lodewijk Kerdijk, 10-03-1859 & Letter of Appointment Lodewijk Kerdijk, 05-10-1859; NL-HaNA, Ministerie van Buitenlandse Zaken 1813–1870, nr. 2358, Agenda 25-09-1860 & Agenda 26-09-1860: Ibid., nr. 2359, Agenda 01-10-1860.

[100] See Van Walraven, 'Spirits and Love under the Mango Trees: Dutch-Congolese Heritage at a Cemetery in Brazzaville', available at https://www.ascleiden.nl/content/ascl-blogs/klaas-van-walraven/spirits-and-love-under-mango-trees-dutch-congolese-heritage [Retrieved 09/08/2021].

[101] Oosterwijk, *Ik verlang geen dank*, 31–33.

Pincoffs to profit from the knowledge and capital of British West Africa traders. The link to the Jewish network in Manchester was the way in for *Kerdijk & Pincoffs*.

Kerdijk & Pincoffs considered various places in West Africa, sending Lodewijk Kerdijk on the *Gitana*, a Samsom-owned schooner that sailed under the British flag.[102] *Kerdijk & Pincoffs* rented the *Gitana* for this journey (buying it from Samsom in 1858 alongside a factory in Ambriz after the journey).[103] The other ship, the *Adolf Martinus*, was already owned by the firm.[104] Lodewijk Kerdijk was employed as the chief agent of the firm. The two ships set sail for the Congo basin, but this was not necessarily the only destination *Kerdijk & Pincoffs* had in mind. Lodewijk Kerdijk for example made a stop in Elmina, meeting Doyer, an agent for *Van Rijckevorsel & Zoonen*, and buying alcohol to sell in the Congo basin from *Van Rijckevorsel & Zoonen*.[105] Lodewijk Kerdijk however decided against setting up a factory in Elmina. *Kerdijk & Pincoffs* also appears to have bought a factory in the Niger delta in 1857 after Lodewijk Kerdijk's trip, indicating that the Niger delta was also visited. For unknown reasons, this factory was quickly abandoned, and the focus of the firm shifted solely to the Congo basin.[106]

Much of what we know from the early years of *Kerdijk & Pincoffs* in the region comes from only a small number of sources: the travel log of Lodewijk Kerdijk about his trip to the Congo basin in 1857–1858 (published as a source edition in 1978), the logbooks of the *Gitana* and the *Biaffra*, and a more recently discovered manuscript of a mid-level

[102] Franssens, 'De vestiging', 690. See for the shipping: S. Hofstra, 'Eenige gegevens over het schip "Lodewijk en over den handel van Rotterdam op West Afrika in de negentiende eeuw', *Rotterdams Jaarboekje*, 4, 6 (1938), 179–195. The shipping data for the firm can be found in: Dreijer, 'Dutch-African Shipping Dataset (1830–1918)'. A further analysis of the maritime aspects of the trade in: Dreijer, 'Nederlandse handel en scheepvaart'.

[103] See Oosterwijk, *Ik verlang geen dank*, 33–34.

[104] Ibidem: see also Dreijer, 'Dutch-African Shipping Dataset (1830–1918)'.

[105] Muller, *Muller*, 116; Schepel (ed.), *Reisjournaal*, 51 & 143–144.

[106] N. Joosse, 'Afrikaanse droom: de handel van Henry P. Kerdijk en Lodewijk Pincoffs in Afrika, 1857–1879', Unpublished MA Thesis Erasmus University Rotterdam (Rotterdam 2016), available at https://thesis.eur.nl/pub/34933 [Retrieved 05/08/2021], there 24.

employee called Willem Aarts.[107] Kerdijk was the firm's main agent in the area, whereas Aarts was a low-level employee. The two men apparently were not on good terms, as Kerdijk for example complained about Aarts in letters to Pincoffs, but nevertheless left Aarts in charge of the Quisembo factory, the second factory the firm owned.[108] Kerdijk in any case complained about most other employees as well, most notably the British shipmaster John Cheeseman, calling him 'vermin' after Cheeseman (without consulting Kerdijk) tried to buy slaves on the Loango coast.[109] Cheeseman, in the logbook of the *Gitana*, painted a more positive picture of himself, writing that he used his British contacts to buy palm oil in Banana in August 1857 before sailing on to Luanda.[110] In October 1857, Kerdijk fired Cheeseman for supposedly lying to him, although it is unclear what had happened.[111] The *Gitana* returned in May 1858 from St. Paul de Loanda under captain Lewis, selling among other things orchil, coral and ivory.[112] The *Gitana* would make two more trips to Quisembo in northern Angola in 1859, this time also bringing palm oil and peanuts as cargo, before it perished before Rotterdam's coast in 1862, on its way back from another trip to northern Angola.[113]

For all the problems that these sources present, it is clear that the jump to the Congo Basin was moderately successful, as palm oil was easier to obtain and perhaps cheaper than on the Gold Coast or in the Niger delta.[114] Lodewijk Kerdijk set up various factories as well to operate year-round. The first factory was bought from Leopold Samsom and located in Ambriz (northern Angola), soon followed by the aforementioned factory in Quisembo (also known as Kinsembo), where other European firms were operating as well.[115] Already in 1858, Kerdijk added factories in

[107] Schepel (ed.), *Reisjournaal*; Maritiem Museum Rotterdam (hereafter NL-MM), Handschriften, nrs. H472, H508 & H753.

[108] NL-MM, Handschriften, nr. H753, p. 54 *n* 19.

[109] Schepel (ed.), *Reisjournaal*, 98–105.

[110] NL-MM, Handschriften, nr. H508, p. 47.

[111] Schepel (ed.), *Reisjournaal*, 98–105.

[112] See https://mmr.adlibhosting.com/ais6V50/Details/collect/102359 [Retrieved 10/10/2024].

[113] Ibidem; Oosterwijk, *Ik verlang geen dank*, 53; Hofstra, 'Eenige gegevens', 185.

[114] As for example becomes clear from the *Biaffra* logbook, which sailed for the Congo basin in 1859–1860. See: NL-MM, Handschriften, nr. H472, Logbook Biaffra.

[115] Oosterwijk, *Ik verlang geen dank*, 38–40. For the importance of Ambriz: R. Fereirra, 'The Conquest of Ambriz: Colonial Expansion and Imperial Competition in Central Africa', *Mulemba*, 5, 9 (2015), 1–16, https://doi.org/10.4000/mulemba.439. In Ambriz, several

Banana and Ponta da Lenha on the northern bank of the Congo River, an area where despite Portuguese claims *de facto* European sovereignty was non-existent. European firms like the French slave trading firm *Régis* and the British trading house *Hatton & Cookson* were based there as well.[116] Soon, *Kerdijk & Pincoffs* moved the majority of its activities to the northern bank, following the announcement of new tariffs on foreign firms operating in Angola by the Portuguese colonial administration.[117]

Early in 1860, Kerdijk took over a second factory from the French slave trading firm *Régis* in Banana: fittingly, one of the factories was called *Rotterdam*, the other one *Holland*.[118] Besides the factories of *Régis*, the firm also took over the Portuguese slave trading firm *Companhia dos Mercantes del Norte* in the early 1870s.[119] During the 1860s, the firm quickly expanded further, and by 1875 may have owned twenty-seven factories across the area.[120] The AHV owned a factory in São Paulo de Loanda (present-day Luanda) as well, but otherwise operated largely in non-urban areas. In comparison, *Hatton & Cookson*, the main British firm in the area, owned eight factories, and *Daumas Béraud & Cie*, the main French firm active in the area after the exit of *Régis*, six.[121] Next to these firms, there were primarily Portuguese trading firms, either partnerships or private traders.[122]

Kerdijk & Pincoffs (from 1866 onwards known as the *Afrikaansche Handels-Vereeniging* or AHV), as was the case for other European firms, operated in an area that was politically was going through turbulent times. The region in northern Angola and around Banana had largely been in the sphere of influence of the Kingdom of Kongo, one of Africa's longest-existing and powerful states.[123] The Kongo Kingdom was among the first

British firms were already operating by 1845, including *Tobin & Co*, *Horsfall & Son* and *Hatton & Cookson*. See: Anstey, 'British Trade and Policy'; Idem, *Britain and the Congo*, 21.

116 Oosterwijk, *Ik verlang geen dank*, 42–53.

117 Joosse, 'Afrikaanse droom', 24–6.

118 Ibidem; Franssens, 'De vestiging', 694.

119 A. Bastian, *Die deutsche Expedition an der Loango-Küste, nebst älteren Nachrichten über die die zu erforschende Länder* (2 Vols.) (Jena 1874–1875) (Vol. 1), 35.

120 E. Pechuel-Loesche, *Kongoland* (2 Vols.) (Jena 1887) (Vol. 1), 224.

121 Ibidem.

122 Ibidem.

123 See for literature on Kongo in the nineteenth century: H. Vanhee & Vos, 'Kongo in the Age of Empire', in: S. Cooksey, R. Poynor & Vanhee (eds.), *Kongo across the Waters* (Gainesville FL 2013), 78–87; Vos, *Kongo in the Age of Empire*. A more general history in: A. Hilton, *The Kingdom of Kongo* (Oxford 1985).

to be contacted by the Portuguese, converted to Catholicism already in the sixteenth century, and had traded with the Europeans in slaves, palm oil and other commodities for centuries.[124] It continued to exist as an independent Kingdom well into the nineteenth century, even if it became under Portuguese vassalage after 1859.[125] Many of the Kongolese acted as middlemen, producers and merchants, often speaking Portuguese which was the *de facto lingua franҫa* in the region. In this period of transition from independent kingdom to European vassalage (and later colonialism), many Kongolese and mixed-descent Africans (often creolised as a result of centuries-long intermingling between the Portuguese and local ethnic groups) operated as well-armed, crucial go-betweens for Europeans trading on the coast for palm and ivory (Image 3.4).

In return for support, knowledge and protection by these middlemen (called *corradores* or *capitas* in Portuguese), the European entrepreneurs often delivered European weapons to them.[126] The AHV was no exception in this regard: without the *corradores*, no trade would have been possible for the Europeans until the mid-1880s.[127] The Dutch naturally sought opportunity by trading with this group and drawing upon their knowledge of the local market.[128] This was particularly important as relations with the Portuguese colonial officials in Angola were often tense: in June 1860, for example, Lodewijk Kerdijk already asked (to no avail) for a Dutch navy ship to be deployed to protect Dutch trade in the area and the local population, who according to Kerdijk suffered under the harsh Portuguese regime.[129] To protect the Dutch factories in Angola, the formerly Dutch, naturalised entrepreneur Albert Schut was put in charge of the factories.[130]

[124] Ibidem.

[125] S.H. Broadhead, 'Beyond Decline: The Kingdom of the Kingo in the Eighteenth and Nineteenth Centuries', *The International Journal of African Historical Studies*, 12, 4 (1979), 615–650.

[126] For the *corradores*; E. Destrain, 'Bassin du Quilou Niadi: Le District de Stéphanieville', *Bulletin de Société Royale belge de Géographie*, 15 (1891), 485–513, there 504–506.

[127] J. Chavanne, *Reisen und Forschungen im alten und neuen Kongostaate in den Jarhen 1884 und 1885* (Jena 1887), 440.

[128] Vansina, *Kingdoms of the Savannas*, 208–42.

[129] NL-HaNA, Archief Buitenlandse Zaken 1813–1870, nr. 2349, Letter Kerdijk to Ministry of Foreign Affairs, 23-06-1860; Idem, Archief Buitenlandse Zaken A-Dossiers, inv. 2.05.03, nr. 203, Letter Kerdijk to Ministry of Foreign Affairs, *sine dato* 1860.

[130] Franssens, 'De vestiging', 692.

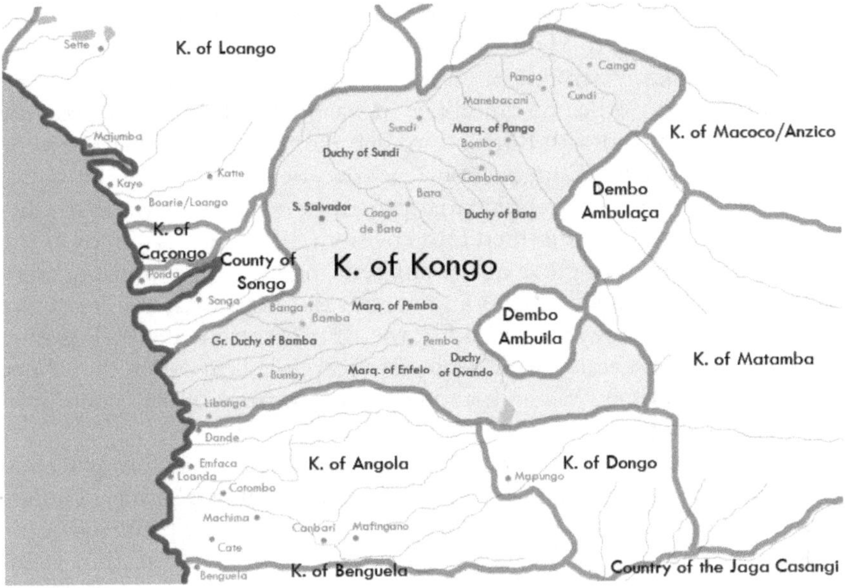

Image 3.4 Map of the Kingdom of Kongo, late eighteenth century. (Source: Kingdom of Kongo ca. 1711 via Wikimedia Commons, available at https://commons.wikimedia.org/wiki/File:KingdomKongo1711.png [Retrieved 10/10/2024])

The exploitation of cash crops like palm oil, palm nut kernels and peanuts was the main reason for operating in the Congo Basin, bartering those commodities for arms, alcohol and tobacco. The AHV employed various other activities as well, however: the firm for example supplied gunpowder to the British navy.[131] In exchange, the AHV promised not to engage in the slave trade, although it is unclear whether the AHV did indeed fully adhere to this promise: for example, the firm supplied goods to slave-trading firms and kept close links with the French and (in particular) Portuguese entrepreneurs active in the slave trade in the area.[132]

[131] Oosterwijk, *Ik verlang geen dank*, 41.

[132] De Kok, 'De koloniale connectie', 72. For the Portuguese slave trade in the region, see e.g. M.P. Candido, *An African Slaving Port and the Atlantic World: Benguela and Its Hinterland* (Cambridge 2013); Idem, 'Merchants and the Business of the Slave Trade at Benguela, 1750–1850', *African Economic History*, 35 (2007), 1–30.

Back in Europe, most of the palm oil was sent to Rotterdam and subsequently re-exported to Manchester or Liverpool, through the connections that, in particular, Pincoffs kept there.[133] In the Dutch market, the demand for palm oil and other commodities in particular was limited, and the AHV thus competed with British firms like *Hatton & Cookson* in the same supply market (the Congo Basin) as the demand market (Britain). Following the three entrepreneurial processes outlined in the introduction, Pincoffs and Kerdijk therefore envisioned an opportunity by being the first Dutchmen to move into a different market for palm oil and allocated significant resources to doing so, but did not necessarily legitimise novelty, largely following the lead of the British entrepreneurs. Focusing on the British market, however, seemed to serve the firm well in the 1860s, as demand in Britain was high and competition from other Dutch firms was non-existent.

The AHV appeared to have relied on various forms of free as well as unfree labour to operate in the Congo basin, including slavery. Despite promises to the contrary, the AHV appears to have participated indirectly in local slave trading. The Dutch slave trade had been abolished in 1814: shortly after the first ventures to the Congo basin, slavery in the Dutch Eastern (1860) and Western (1863) colonies was abolished as well. Much is unclear about the firm's role in the slave trade and slave labour on the West African coast, largely due to lack of source material. The AHV (unsurprisingly) largely relied on local labour in its coastal factories, as Europeans were few on the coast. Whilst there is no clear evidence that the firm ever engaged in the (illegal) slave trade itself, the AHV did in fact supply commodities to the French slave trading firm *Régis* before taking over its factories.[134] The extent to which the firm was engaged in the flourishing illegal slave trade in northern Angola during the 1860s is unknown.

In contrast, it is clear that enslaved labour was employed in the factories. At minimum, dozens of enslaved Africans (so-called *krumanos*) worked in bad circumstances at the factories in Banana, a fact that appears to have been an open secret to travellers in the area.[135] The firm therefore

[133] Oosterwijk, *Ik verlang geen dank*, 67.

[134] O. Zwier van Sandinck, *Herinneringen van de Zuid-Westkust van Afrika: eenige bladzijden uit mijn dagboek* (Deventer 1881), 95.

[135] See e.g. Bastian, *Die deutsche Expedition* (Vol. 1), 21–22; R.F. Burton, *Two Trips to Gorillaland and the Cataracts of the Congo* (2 Vols.) (London 1876) (Vol. 1), 170. The AHV was not the only firm using *krumannos*; the British firm Hatton & Cookson for example also used slave labour. See: Chavanne, *Reisen und Forschungen*, 446.

held, to put it mildly, an ambivalent position regarding the slave trade and slavery.[136] This was noted by contemporary observers, including AHV employees, as well: both Lodewijk Kerdijk and Otto Zwier van Sandinck (the latter an AHV employee writing in Banana in 1879) described *krumanos* working at the factory in Banana in some detail.[137] Kerdijk even wrote that "I have changed opinion on this matter and more and more I can reconcile myself with the slave trade", whereas Zwier van Sandinck wrote that during his time in Banana some hundred to hundred-fifty *krumanos* were bought to work on the factories.[138]

Three types of labourers are known to have worked on the factories, next to (Afro-)European employees such as translators (who were often Portuguese):[139] first, the so-called *kruboys*, highly specialised wage labourers specialising in maritime labour from present-day Sierra Leone and Liberia (called after the Kru people, and therefore also often called just *kru* in the sources);[140] second, so-called *cabindas*, wage labourers named after the Portuguese-controlled town north of the Congo River, who primarily did heavy work at the factories;[141] and third, so-called *krumanos* (not to be confused with *kruboys*), enslaved Africans from the Congo basin area, who were for example enslaved as prisoners of war or by slave raiding.[142] This tripartite distinction indicates a fairly high degree of labour specialisation and efficiency within the factories, with the *kruboys* specialising in certain tasks such as shipping and navigation, largely leaving the hard labour on the factories (e.g. unloading the ships and building the factories) to the

[136] Burton, *Two Trips* (Vol. 1), 170; Zwier van Sandinck, *Herinneringen*, 95; Toen te zien, "ca. 1880 Kru and 'Krumanos'", available at http://www.toentezien.nl/musea/ca-1880-kru-and-krumanos/ [Retrieved 09/08/2021].

[137] Schepel (ed.), *Reisjournaal*, 106; see also Zwier van Sandinck, *Herinneringen*, 95–96.

[138] Schepel (ed.), *Reisjournaal*, 106: "Ik ben dan ook op dit punt geheel en al van opinie veranderd en verzoen mij meer en meer met de slavenhandel." Zwier van Sandinck, *Herinneringen*, 96: "Er werden niet veel negers door de A.H.V. gekocht; in mijn tijd 100 à 150 stuks, waarvan enkele vrouwen."

[139] K. Friedman, *Catastrophe and Creation: The Transformation of an African Culture* (Chur 1991), 24–26.

[140] D. Frost, 'British Imperial Trade and West African Kru Seamen', in: Everaert & Parmentier (eds.), *International Conference*, 215–219. See also: J. Gunn, *Outsourcing African Labor: Kru Migratory Workers in Global Ports, Estates and Battlefields until the End of the 19th Century* (Berlin & Boston 2021).

[141] Friedman, *Catastrophe and Creation*, 28.

[142] Ibidem. See also H.H. Johnston, *The River Congo from its Mouth to Bolobu* (London 1895), 25–27.

cabindas and *krumanos*.[143] A clear hierarchy on the factories between the *kruboys* and others existed, with the *cabindas* having a higher status than the *krumanos*.[144] Of course, the term *kruboys* and *krumanos* give the false impression of being connected, which, however, is not the case: most Europeans even simply called everyone *kruboys*, even if they were not Kru themselves.

Contrary to what Pincoffs told everyone in Europe, not all was as well as it seemed. Already in 1859–1860, Lodewijk Kerdijk reported a lack of ships for the trade, as various ships were shipwrecked *en route* to or from the Congo River Basin.[145] Moreover, Kerdijk noted that there were sharp fluctuations in demand and supply on the coast, making it difficult for the AHV to guarantee a steady stream of profits.[146] For most of its transport, the AHV depended on English line shipping, which was expensive. For the period between 1857 and 1875, information on the trade of the AHV is scarce and comes largely from European eyewitness accounts, which are not necessarily the most reliable sources. These travelogues do note the presence of the factories of the firm in Banana and other places, often explaining that it was the most important firm trading on the banks of the Congo River.[147] Henry Morton Stanley, for example, wrote about the 'great Dutch house' in Banana, praising Lodewijk Kerdijk for opening factories in the area around Banana.[148] These contemporary texts thus offer the impression of a highly successful enterprise, an impression largely confirmed by the quick expansion of the factory system between 1857 and 1875.

Yet, as various scholars have rightly argued, the 1879 fraud so surprising to its contemporaries was perhaps not so surprising after all. Most of the older literature on the AHV essentially followed the 1871 claims of the

[143] See also Global Collaboratory on the History of Labour Relations, 1500–2000, 'Taxonomy of Labour Relations', available at https://datasets.iisg.amsterdam/file.xhtml?fileId=2078&version=2.0 [Retrieved 13/06/2022].

[144] Johnston, *The River Congo*, 25–27; B. Heintze, *Afrikanische Pioniere: Trägerkarawanen im westlichen Zentralafrika (ca. 1850–1890)* (Frankfürt am Main 2002), 172.

[145] Hofstra, 'Eenige gegevens'. For example, both the *Lodewijk* and *Gitana* were shipwrecked.

[146] Joosse, 'Afrikaanse droom', 43–50; Schepel (ed.), *Reisjournaal Lodewijk Kerdijk*, 43–5.

[147] See e.g.: Stanley, *Congo*, ix; Bastian, *Die deutsche expedition*, 21–22; W.H. Bentley, *Pioneering on the Congo* (2 Vols.) (London 1900) (Vol. 1), 74; Burton, *Two Trips* (Vol. 1), 64–65; Chavanne, *Reisen und Forschungen*, 81; Koopman, *Verslag*, 71–75; J.J. Monteiro, *Angola and the River Congo* (London 1875) (Vol. 1), 81; Peschuel-Loesche, *Kongoland*, 224.

[148] Stanley, *Congo*, ix.

Dutch geographer Pierre Robidé van der Aa that the firm was highly profitable and successful.[149] Robidé van der Aa, however, relied on numbers provided by Pincoffs himself.[150] Given Pincoffs' actions in the 1870s, it indeed appears likely that the financial troubles started earlier, although many of the numbers provided in the primary sources are unreliable. Well-known are Pincoffs' speculative activities in the 1870s (e.g. in Peruvian government bonds in 1875), but both Niek Joosse and Kamiel Franssens also have pointed to structural problems within the firm that may have already existed in the (early) 1860s.[151] Among the problems the AHV encountered, economic problems, political headwinds (both in the Netherlands and abroad) and the legal and organisational structure of the firm stood out.

The first problem had to do with a slump in the price of palm oil after 1860, which was partly the result of the transition from sail to steam and the oversupply that came with it.[152] The AHV still used sailing ships rather than steamers, leading to higher freight rates and slower transport opportunities, whilst at the same time having to deal with the lower prices on the world market.[153] As many of the firms bartered with local producers, they were dependent largely on the profit margins selling palm oil in Europe, with lower prices therefore leading to lower profits.[154]

The second problem concerned political headwinds the AHV encountered in the Netherlands and in the Congo Basin. In contrast to many of the British firms such as *Hatton & Cookson*, which could count on government support (such as subsidies and diplomatic support for negotiations over tariffs) and had also diversified its business,[155] support by the Dutch government for Dutch firms in West (Central) Africa was virtually non-existent, as has also been clear from the analysis of the Dutch entrepreneurs on the Gold Coast.[156] The Dutch historian Henk Wesseling has

[149] Joosse, 'Afrikaanse droom', 5; P.J.B.C. Robidé van der Aa, *Afrikaansche studiën: koloniaal bezit en partikuliere handel op Afrika's westkust* (The Hague 1871), 76–83.

[150] Ibidem; see also Robidé van der Aa requesting the numbers from Pincoffs in NL-KB, Stukken Robidé van der Aa, inv. KW 128 F 9, 4d, nr. 46 & Brieven aan de familie Van der Aa, inv. KW 132 G 17, nrs. E 3 & E 4.

[151] Joosse, 'Afrikaanse droom', 5–7 & 43–50; Franssens, 'De vestiging', 690–695.

[152] Lynn, *Commerce and Economic Change*, 111; Idem, 'From Sail to Steam'.

[153] Dreijer, 'Handel en scheepvaart', 47–48.

[154] Lynn, *Commerce and Economic Change*, 111; Idem, 'From Sail to Steam'.

[155] Lynn, *Commerce and Economic Change*, 147.

[156] Baesjou & Emmer, 'The Dutch in West Africa'.

therefore characterised the involvement of the Dutch in discussions over Africa's future as reluctant at best, and also noted the difficulties of Pincoffs to muster support back home.[157] According to Wesseling, the Dutch had mostly entrepreneurial interests in the Congo basin, whereas the British had broader concerns, including economic interests, but also combatting the slave trade and missionary interests.[158]

While Wesseling statement is largely right (and his viewpoint is largely backed up by scholars like Baesjou and Emmer as well),[159] the truth appears to have been a bit more nuanced, as it would be fair to say that there was a shift from cautious support to non-interest during the 1860s, and some isolated outbursts of interest in Africa during the 1880s and 1890s. In the early 1860s, Van Rijckevorsel for example was still able to muster support to block new customs arrangement on the Gold Coast: by 1869, Muller Szn. was unable to find support to keep the Gold Coast.[160] Notwithstanding their positions in Parliament, these Rotterdam entrepreneurs possessed insufficient political bargaining power, even as the Dutch government was dominated by the Liberals.[161] Even the Dutch Liberals focused, as a result of (either real or imagined) lack of colonial capacity, primarily on the Dutch East Indies, leaving arguments for free trade in West and West Central Africa to a very small interest group.[162]

It is in this context that the strategy of Pincoffs to engage with foreign states and empires should be seen, showing how private actors such as Pincoffs looked beyond their respective home state when support was lacking. Most historians have noted the efforts of Pincoffs to engage with Leopold II from late 1876 onwards to aid him in gaining sovereignty over what would become the Congo Free State.[163] Two (complementary) explanations for this move by Pincoffs are suggested by the present literature. First, there is the argument claiming that Pincoffs was aware of his

[157] Wesseling, 'Nederland en de Conferentie van Berlijn'; Idem, 'The Netherlands and the Partition of Africa'.

[158] Wesseling, 'Nederland en de Conferentie van Berlijn', 568. See also: Anstey, *Britain and the Congo*, 16.

[159] Baesjou & Emmer, 'The Dutch in West Africa'.

[160] Mollema, 'De afstand', 227–228.

[161] Van Zanden & Van Riel, *Nederland 1780–1914*, 209–236.

[162] Ibidem, 398.

[163] Franssens, 'Nederland en de Aardrijkskundige Conferentie', especially 502–509; Wesseling, 'Nederland en de Conferentie van Berlijn', 564–566; Idem, 'The Netherlands and the Partition of Africa', 498–502; Oosterwijk, *Ik verlang geen dank*, 145–150; Kuitenbrouwer, *Nederland en de opkomst*, 54–55; Van den Doel, *Zo ver de wereld strekt*, 112.

firms' financial difficulties and tried to sell his firm to Leopold, so as to walk away without losses.[164] The second argument emphasises that Pincoffs sought new opportunities in the northern Congo, particularly as many expected Leopold to open up new opportunities for trade in the Congo Basin's interior, which had hitherto been largely unexploited by European entrepreneurs for a lack of resources.[165]

In short, most historians assume that there was a 'pull' argument for Pincoffs to align his goals with Leopold. Opening up the hinterland of course offered new opportunities to exploit its resources, in particular considering the reliance on the aforementioned *corradores*.[166] Yet a hitherto unnoticed incident may also have contributed to the move northwards by the AHV, which we could well classify as a 'push' factor next to the 'pull' factor of the nascent Congo Free State. This shows both how keenly aware Pincoffs was of the geopolitical situation concerning the Congo Basin area, but also how difficult it was to execute such a strategy as a firm lacking much state support at a time when European interest in the African continent was at its peak.

In September 1876, a small ship (*kotter*) of the AHV, the *Maria*, was arrested in the Angolan port of Ambriz upon entering port.[167] According to letters from the AHV agent Andries Pape to the Portuguese colonial administration, the shipmaster had all the right papers to enter ports in Angola, but the colonial officials decided otherwise and forced the *Maria* to remain in port for months. Part of the ostensible problem was that the *Maria* flew the Dutch flag, whereas newish regulations stipulated that only Portuguese ships were allowed to enter Portuguese colonial ports. The *Maria* was supposed to sail to several factories of the AHV to drop off and load commodities as well as to bring letters between the various factories, severely disrupting the transport and communication networks of the firm. The AHV agents in the area immediately requested Dutch support, and in addition Pincoffs started lobbying the Dutch government for

[164] Wesseling, 'Nederland en de Conferentie van Berlijn', 565; Oosterwijk, *Ik verlang geen dank*, 145.

[165] Oosterwijk, *Ik verlang geen dank*, 145–146; Kuitenbrouwer, *Nederland en de opkomst*, 54–55.

[166] Lynn, *Commerce and Economic Change*, 103–187.

[167] See for the incident: NL-HaNA, Buitenlandse Zaken A-Dossiers, nr. 203, Letter Pape to Dutch Minister of Foreign Affair, 20-09-1876 & Letter Pape to Portuguese Governor-General in Angola, 05-09-1876; Idem, Legatie Portugal, nr. 89, Letter Pape to Dutch Minister of Foreign Affairs, 20-09-1876; Ibidem, Letter Pasteur to Pape, 22-09-1876.

aid.[168] Pincoffs attached various letters from 1860 as well, as the firm had at the time also been at loggerheads with the Portuguese colonial administration in Angola about tariffs.[169]

Pincoffs, and AHV agents on the ground like Andries Pape, saw the new actions of the Portuguese colonial administration in Angola as an infringement on free trade in the area.[170] Only several years before, the Dutch and the Portuguese had tried to negotiate a treaty on trade and shipping, but this had left many questions unanswered, including those on import and export tariffs in the Portuguese colonies.[171] Moreover, the relationship between the metropole and the Portuguese colonial governors in the colonies was ambivalent at best.[172] Whilst the Portuguese government sought better trading relations with the Netherlands and other European countries (at least in Europe itself), in the African Portuguese colonies the situation was more difficult.

The Portuguese Governor-General in Angola, for example, regularly established new restrictions on foreign firms operating in Angola, and similar restrictions came into place in Mozambique and São Tomé and Principe.[173] As a result, British and Dutch firms, whose governments often loudly insisted on free trade, were hit. In contrast, the French government quickly signed a treaty with the Portuguese government to secure access to the Portuguese colonies in Africa, allowing French firms to continue largely as they had before.[174] This obviously irritated Pincoffs, who hence urged the government to act and start negotiations over similar treatment

[168] NL-HaNA, Buitenlandse Zaken A-Dossiers, nr. 203, Letter Pincoffs to Dutch Minister of Foreign Affairs, 17-11-1876.

[169] NL-HaNA, Buitenlandse Zaken A-Dossiers, nr. 203, Letter Lodewijk Kerdijk to Dutch Minister of Foreign Affairs, 02-05-1860; NL-HaNA, Legatie Portugal, nr. 88, Letter Henry Kerdijk & Pincoffs to Dutch Minister of Foreign Affairs, 22-06-1860; NL-HaNA, Ministerie van Buitenlandse Zaken 1813–1870, nr. 2350, Agenda 30-06-1860.

[170] Other information indicates there was indeed some trouble with the Portuguese administration, as well as with the agents on the ground. See e.g. for the problems with the German-born Otto Lindner, who was the chief of the Ponta da Lenha factory between 1876–1880: M. Luwel, *Otto Lindner 1852–1945: Een weinig bekend medewerker van Leopold II in Afrika* (Brussels 1959), 20–21 & 119–126.

[171] NL-HaNA, Legatie Portugal, nr. 72, Letter Gericke van Herwijnen (Minister of Foreign Affairs) to Ministry of Finance, 20-12-1873. The Treaty was eventually concluded on 09-01-1875.

[172] Clarence-Smith, *The Third Portuguese Empire*, 22.

[173] Ibidem.

[174] NL-HaNA, Legatie Portugal, nr. 89, Letter Pape to Portuguese Governor-General of Angola, 16-09-1876.

for Dutch firms. When the Dutch government did not act upon these suggestions, Pincoffs sought support of his friends at the influential Manchester Chamber of Commerce.[175]

The Dutch only jumped into action as the British took action under pressure from the powerful Manchester Chamber of Commerce. The Dutch may well opted have solved the issue peacefully, but appeared to have acted undiplomatically by threatening to send a navy ship to the Portuguese coast.[176] The Portuguese called the Dutch bluff and the ship was never sent.[177] It appears that the Dutch government wanted to show its strength to the Portuguese colonial officials, but did also not want to hurt relations with the metropolitan government in Lisbon, essentially ending up with no strategy. The empty threat by the Dutch did not calm down things. Soon after, tensions flared up again when a Portuguese man only named as Oliveira killed thirty enslaved Africans near the AHV factory of Ponta de Lenha in March 1877, presumably with the help of a Dutchman, after supposedly having uncovered a plot to attack European factories.[178] Pincoffs subsequently sought support from the British government, as *Hatton & Cookson* transferred the news to London.[179] How this ended is however not recorded in the archival sources.

Next to the pull factors, there was thus certainly also a push factor at play in Pincoffs' decision to turn to Leopold II for protection and business opportunities. In 1876, following the Brussels Geographical Conference organised by Leopold, Pincoffs reached out to Leopold to discuss cooperation, in particular as no Dutchman (public official or in a private capacity) had been present at the Conference.[180] Following the Conference, Leopold set up his *Association Internationale Africaine* (AIA) to muster support for his colonisation plans in Central Africa, in part inspired by the Dutch Cultivation System in Java.[181] On 27 April 1877, Pincoffs set up

[175] Idem, Letter Van Bijlandt to Dutch Minister of Foreign Affairs, 25-12-1876.

[176] Wesseling, 'Nederland en de Conferentie van Berlijn'; Idem, 'The Netherlands and the Partition of Africa'; Baesjou & Emmer, 'The Dutch in West Africa'; NL-HaNA, Buitenlandse Zaken A-Dossiers, nr. 203, Letter Pincoffs to Dutch Minister of Foreign Affairs, 12-12-1876.

[177] NL-HaNA, Legatie Portugal, nr. 89, Letter Van Bijlandt to Dutch Minister of Foreign Affairs, 25-12-1876.

[178] NL-HaNA, Buitenlandse Zaken A-Dossiers, nr. 203, Letter Pasteur to Dutch Minister of Foreign Affairs, 28-06-1877.

[179] Ibidem.

[180] Franssens, 'Nederland na de Aardrijkskundige Conferentie', 505–509.

[181] See e.g. Wesseling, 'Nederland als koloniaal model'; Stengers, 'Léopold II et le modèle colonial hollandais'.

the Dutch department of the AIA, the *Nederlands Afrikaans Comité* (Dutch-African Committee), under the chairmanship of the Dutch Prince Henry.[182] The AIA, chaired by Leopold, ostensibly aimed to further European humanitarian motives in West Central Africa, but in reality mostly functioned as a vehicle for Leopold to further his goal to gain support for his idea to colonise the area under his leadership. Under the banner of the AIA, the *Comité d'Études du Haut-Congo* (CEHC) was formed with financial backing from Belgian and foreign investors (including Pincoffs).[183] The CEHC appointed Henry Morton Stanley to lead its 'explorations' in West Central Africa, with the goal to assess opportunities for trade and the navigability of the Congo River.[184]

The AHV promised to pay 145.000 guilders to the funds of the CEHC, a substantial sum of money from which the AHV hoped to profit sometime, in particular regarding trade upstream the Congo River.[185] Pincoffs was invited to dinner with Leopold to discuss their plans to expand trade on the mouth of the Congo river in January 1879, and it appears that the two men agreed on the mutual benefits: for Pincoffs, it meant an exploration of the trading opportunities upstream the Congo River (a dire necessity given the financial situation of his firm), and for Leopold it meant financial backing for his scheme and knowledge.[186] In other words, the two needed each other, and had an interest in aiding the other.[187] Soon, however, Pincoffs clashed with Stanley over motives and strategy. Stanley largely had non-economic motives for his expeditions, whereas Pincoffs viewed Leopold's plans as a way to save his firm from financial ruin. The relationship between the two men was tense, yet never broke into the open as Stanley left for the Congo basin in early 1879. Soon after, Pincoffs' fraud came to light in May 1879. Leopold made the most of the opportunity and kicked out the AHV by forming a new organisation, the *Association Internationale du Congo* (AIC). Pincoffs' vision of a free trading area in

[182] Franssens, 'Nederland na de Aardrijkskundige Conferentie', 505–509.

[183] Stengers, 'Leopold II and the Association Internationale du Congo'.

[184] Ascherson, *The King Incorporated*, 107–109; Cornelis, 'Stanley', 42–50; Stengers, 'Leopold II and the Association Internationale du Congo', 238–239; Jeal, *Stanley*, 233–240.

[185] Oosterwijk, *Ik verlang geen dank*, 147; Franssens, 'Nederland na de Aardrijkskundige Conferentie', 505–508.

[186] NL-SAR, Handschriftenverzameling Gemeente Rotterdam, aanvullingen 1988–1996, inv. 33–02, nr. 9552, Letter Strauch to Pincoffs, 21-01-1879. A duplicate of the letter can be found in: NL-HaNA, Archief NAHV, nr. 655, Letter Strauch to Pincoffs, 21-01-1879.

[187] Oosterwijk, *Ik verlang geen dank*, 145–150.

the Congo basin increasingly threatened Leopold's idea of a political entity.[188]

Returning to our main story, the third problem of the AHV concerned the structure of the firm, which changed several times over the years. Examples include the change to a so-called *Commanditaire Vennootschap* (CV) in 1862, coinciding with a round of capital injections.[189] This saw the firm through the next seven years, when the firm again changed structure to a so-called *Naamloze Vennootschap* (NV), starting an exchange listing.[190] In the meantime, the firm changed its name from Pincoffs & Kerdijk to the AHV as well in 1866. All these legal and organisational changes guaranteed a steady stream of investments, but as proper financial oversight was lacking, this did not make much of a change in terms of how the firm was run in practice: even as a supervisory board was established, they did not have the means to see through the numbers.[191]

The 1862 and 1869 requests for capital injections were accompanied by (false) rosy outlooks about the financial health of the firm, but in reality even the loans and frequent capital injections could not save the firm from ruin.[192] Crucial among those supporting Pincoffs was Marten Mees, a Rotterdam banker and investor in the AHV. The Mees family was another significant aristocratic Rotterdam family.[193] The Mees family came from Aken (present-day Germany) to Rotterdam in the late sixteenth century and over the course of the centuries developed as the major banking family in the city. Rudolph Mees (1665–1702) was the first to set up a *kassier*

[188] See for the AIC: Stengers, 'Leopold II and the Association Internationale du Congo'. See also: Ascherson, *The King Incorporated*, 116–117.

[189] See for these legal changes: NL-SAR, Archief Mees & Zoonen, nr. 623, Stukken betreffende het eerste commanditaire contract, 1863–1866. Here Pincoffs and Mees both already speak of the opportunity to obtain an exchange listing, which would indeed happen (see below).

[190] Oosterwijk, *Ik verlang geen dank*, 73–74.

[191] Ibidem.

[192] See NL-SAA, Archief Commissiehandel Kerkhoven & Co, nr. 165, Ingekomen stukken over inschrijving AHV, which shows that the firm also retrieved money from the Amsterdam capital market in 1871. See also NL-SAR, Archief Chabot, Kassiers en Makelaars in Assurantie, nr. 1195, Circulaire van de AHV, for a similar request on the Rotterdam capital market from 1877.

[193] This section is primarily based on the literature cited in footnote 58. See for the importance of Mees' financial support: NL-SAR, Archief Familie Mees Privé, nr. 3263, Afschrift van een schuldbekentenis van 450,000 gulden, 1862. This shows that *Kerdijk & Pincoffs* were 450,000 guilders in debt in 1862 after the capital injection of that year, including 50,000 guilders to Marten Mees himself.

(financial intermediary) business in Rotterdam, and his sons continued to act as financial brokers after his death under the name *R. Mees & Zoonen* and later simply *Mees & Zoonen*. Willem Cornelis (W.C.) Mees was among the founders of *De Nederlandsche Bank* (DNB), the Dutch central bank, and also one of its first presidents. For our purposes, the focus will primarily be on Marten Mees, who ran the *Mees & Zoonen* family firm from the 1870s onwards and was among the major financiers of Rotterdam's nineteenth-century rise (Image 3.5).

Image 3.5 Portrait of Mr Marten Mees. (Source: Maritime Museum Rotterdam, Pascal De Beucker, Public domain, via Wikimedia Commons [Retrieved 18/10/2023])

Marten Mees (1828–1917) was one of Rotterdam's main bankers and so-called *kassiers*.[194] He was for example instrumental in setting up the *Rotterdamsche Bank* in 1863. The *Rotterdamsche Bank* was instrumental in financing infrastructural developments of Rotterdam's port. Mees moreover was co-founder of the famous *Holland-Amerika Lijn* (Holland America Line) in 1871. Mees was also the main investor in the Rotterdam-African trade, but also acted as board members of the various Rotterdam firms active in the African trade. Marten Mees was in essence the financial glue of the small network, acting as commissioner of many of the firms, while simultaneously acting as a major investor and financial broker and/or intermediary for financing purposes. Financial backing for the Rotterdam investments in Africa would thus have been impossible, were it not for Marten Mees.

Mees also turned out to be crucial in discovering Pincoffs' malversations. The Pincoffs' fraud was only discovered when Mees, as president of the board, heard via his financial contacts in London that the AHV requested short-term, high-interest loans on the British market: despite the fact that Mees and Pincoffs were well-acquainted, neither Mees nor anyone else on the oversight board had any clue about the problems.[195] Upon confronting Pincoffs with the rumours, Pincoffs quickly confessed.[196] Two days later, he fled Rotterdam and spent the rest of his days in New York until he died there in 1911. Despite attempts by the Dutch state to return him to the Netherlands, the lack of an extradition treaty prevented this.[197] As Images 3.6 and 3.7 show, the affair aroused a good deal of turmoil across Rotterdam.

The lawyer Cornelis W. Vermeulen was asked, following the bankruptcy proceedings of the AHV, to investigate the financial administration of the firm and submit his report to the Dutch High Council. He noted in his report that the AHV had likely lost almost 8 million guilders in the period between 1869 and 1879 (see also Tables 3.3 and 3.5, with Table 3.4 showing the numbers as recorded by Pincoffs).[198] Henry Kerdijk had

[194] This section is based on: Mees, *Man van de daad*, especially 400–467.
[195] Ibidem, 1–4.
[196] Oosterwijk, *Ik verlang geen dank*, 151–158.
[197] Ibidem; see also NL-HaNA, Archief Gezantschap Verenigde Staten, nr. 161.
[198] Vermeulen, *De Afrikaansche Handels-Vereeniging*, 27.

Image 3.6 Cartoon on Lodewijk Pincoffs' Fraud, 1879. (Source: Rijksmuseum, inv. Nr. RP-P-OB-89.270, available via Wikimedia Commons, https://commons.wikimedia.org/wiki/File:Spotprent_op_de_fraude_van_Lodewijk_Pincoffs_te_Rotterdam,_1879_Vooruit_en_niet_terug_(titel_op_object),_RP-P-OB-89.270.jpg [Retrieved 10/04/2025])

already warned in 1872 about the dearth of money to pay employees, but Pincoffs had silenced his main business partner, according to Vermeulen.[199] Kerdijk had for example pointed to the high costs for insurance and payment of interests as sources of concern. Vermeulen showed how Pincoffs had hid these problems: many of the loans from either Brussels or London were shown on the balance as 'transfers' rather than loans with interest.[200] Much of the money to make up for the shortfall came from the *Rotterdamsche Handels-Vennootschap* (RHV) (Pincoffs' other firm that was focused on establishing Rotterdam's maritime infrastructure) which in turn lent more money on the Dutch and international capital markets,

[199] Ibidem, 22.
[200] Ibidem, 27.

Image 3.7 Cartoon on Lodewijk Pincoffs, 1879. (Source: Rijksmuseum, inv. Nr. RP-P-OB-89.272, available via Wikimedia Commons, https://commons.wikimedia.org/wiki/File:Spotprent_op_Lodewijk_Pincoffs,_1879,_RP-P-OB-89.272.jpg [Retrieved 10/04/2025])

purportedly to fund new investment in Rotterdam's maritime infrastructure. In several letters, Pincoffs apologised to the shareholders but argued this was an honest mistake, even if he had fled Rotterdam soon after the fraud having come to light (Tables 3.3, 3.4 and 3.5).[201]

A combination of economic and political headwinds, combined with the organisational malpractices by Pincoffs, thus ruined the AHV. Moreover, the strategy of the Rotterdam entrepreneurs to bet on extracting commodities from regions outside of European state control became an increasingly difficult proposition. Pincoffs therefore jumped to seek rescue from other European states than the Dutch, perhaps more as a necessity than as a well-thought-out strategy. While this act to salvage the firm did

[201] Pincoffs, *Open brief aan de redactie van "De Maasbode"* (Rotterdam 1871); Idem, *Open brief aan de aandeelhouders der Ned. Ind. Gasmaatschappy* (New York 1879).

Table 3.3 Losses by the AHV (1869–1879), in guilders

Year	*Distribution of profits to directors*	*True loss*	*Total*
1869	139,578	402,922	542,500
1870	227,333	136,367	363,700
1871	280,759	536,571	817,330
1872	278,846	128,505	407,351
1873	278,846	854,586	1,133,432
1874	201,923	976,077	1,178,000
1875	144,235	1,240,778	1,385,012
1876	221,154	1,927,308	2,148,462
1877	182,693	1,337,939	1,520,632
1878/1879	–	318,000	318,000
Total	1,955,366	7,859,053	9,814,419,05

Source: *Vermeulen, De Afrikaansche Handels-Vereeniging, 27.* Note: *Numbers rounded to full numbers*

Table 3.4 Balance of the AHV on 14 May 1879, according to the AHV Directors, in guilders

Debit		*Credit*	
Head agent north	10,072,652	Capital	5,745,000
Head agent south	1,999,541	Priority loan	1,870,000
Steamships and ships	428,147	Obligation loan	1,430,693
Furniture and tools	11,683	Insurance fund	265,000
Cash and remittances	53,448	Loans	1,403,000
Other debtors	8,822	Employees on the coast	170,517
Rotterdamsche Handels-Vereeniging	35,521	Various creditors	716,876
Kerdijk & Pincoffs	1,201,291	Balance due to credit paper	2,226,320
Debitors on the coast	178,381	Current money in transfer	2,467,253
Founding costs—Priority loan	175,453		
Founding costs—Obligation loan	17,990		
Goods—imports	319,883		
Goods—exports	328,987		
Goods—consignation	60,000		
Goods—total	708,870		
Loss in 1878/1879	1,402,861		
Total	16,294,669		16,294,669

Source: *Vermeulen, De Afrikaansche Handels-Vereeniging, 30.* Note: *Numbers rounded to full numbers*

Table 3.5 Actual balance of the AHV on 14 May 1879, in guilders

Debit		*Credit*	
Head agent north	5,114,403	Capital	5,745,000
Head agent south	912,317	Priority loan	1,870,000
Steamships and ships	386,657	Obligation loan	1,430,693
Furniture and tools	11,683	Loans	1,403,000
Cash and remittances	53,448	Employees on the coast	170,517
Other debtors	8822	Various creditors	716,876
Rotterdamsche Handels-Vereeniging	35,521	Balance due to credit paper	2,226,330
Debitors on the coast	178,381	Current money in transfer	2,467,253
Goods—imports	319,883	Kerdijk & Pincoffs	881,439
Goods—exports	328,987		
Goods—consignation	60,000		
Goods—total	708,870		
Deficit	9,501,007		
Total	16,911,108		16,911,108

Source: *Vermeulen, De Afrikaansche Handels-Vereeniging, 31.* Note: *Numbers rounded to full numbers*

not reach its intended effect, it did offer a glimpse into the changing rules of the game that the 1880s would present. A complex balancing act between states, entrepreneurs and other private actors such as missionaries and explorers ensued in the decade to come.

3.4 Dutch Entrepreneurship in West (Central) Africa 1830s–1870s

The story of the Rotterdam entrepreneurs in the 1845 to 1879 period points to a mixed record. Returning to our conceptualisation in the introduction on entrepreneurship, it is clear that the Rotterdam entrepreneurs did identify an opportunity that others mostly perceived as risk, and turned this into an opportunity for profit. They valued the opportunity more or less rightly, and allocated substantial resources to execute the strategy, with mixed success: *Van Rijckevorsel & Zoonen* for example soon lost profitability, whereas *Muller & Co* remained largely profitable in the 1860s and 1870s after the move to Liberia. The AHV of course went bankrupt, but this may have had to do mostly with Pincoffs' leadership skills, as well as the associated choices he made concerning the structure of the firm, and an unlucky timing as the 1860s witnessed a palm oil price slump. The

Rotterdam entrepreneurs largely legitimised novelty by being the first Dutchmen to move 'beyond Elmina', even if they largely followed British entrepreneurs already operating in West Africa in their strategies. British traders were already based in various places in West and West Central Africa (including in the Congo basin), and so were German entrepreneurs from Hamburg, the French slave trading firm *Régis* and various Portuguese firms operating out of northern Angola.[202]

The main focus was on palm oil, which was in high demand across Europe. Dutch palm oil imports quickly rose between 1847 (the first date the import of palm oil was recorded in the statistics) and 1876, as the data below show. While these data should be treated with substantial caution, they give a decent idea of the growing relative importance of palm oil to the Netherlands in the period 1847–1876.[203] The data are to a large extent

[202] Rudin, *Germans in the Cameroon*, 226; Hargreaves, *Prelude*, 110 & 316–317; Reinhard, *Die Unterwerfung der Welt*, 945–948; Burton, *Two Trips*, 17; Baker, *Trade Winds on the Niger*, 89; Newbury, 'On the Margins of Empire', 51; Daumalin, 'Commercial Presence', 211; Fieldhouse, *Economics and Empire*, 140–141; Marchal, *L'État Libre*, 234–235; Newbury & Kanya-Forster, 'French Policy', 254; Law, 'The Historiography'; 'Stokes, 'Late Nineteenth-Century Colonial Expansion'.

[203] Data based on: S.A., *Jaarcijfers uitgegeven door de Centrale Commissie voor de Statistiek. Koloniën 1887–1916* (34 Vols.) (The Hague 1889–1922); *Jaarcijfers uitgegeven door de Centrale Commissie voor de Statistiek. Rijk in Europa 1887–1916* (34 Vols.) (The Hague 1889–1922); S.A., *Jaaroverzichten van den handel in koloniale producten 1891–1914* (24 Vols.) (Amsterdam 1892–1915); S.A., *Statistiek van den handel en de scheepvaart in het Koningrijk der Nederlanden over het jaar 1847–1876* (30 Vols.) (The Hague 1848–1877); S.A., *Statistiek van den in-, uit- en doorvoer over het jaar 1877–1916* (40 Vols.) (The Hague 1878–1917). See for problems with these data the methodological paper accompanying: Dreijer, 'Dutch-African Trade Data'. These statistics may, for example, not be particularly reliable as they were often compiled by simply asking brokers in Amsterdam or Rotterdam how much was imported or exported of a certain quantity. Only after roughly 1900 did the statistics become more reliable, as modern statistical methods were introduced. As a result, the statistics presented here have to be interpreted with caution: they don't offer definitive results, but rather depict general trends. Moreover, for the pre-1875 period, significant gaps remain, for example as for palm oil im- and exports are missing intermittently between 1847 and 1866. For the earlier years of the series, only averages for ten-year periods are available. Moreover, Dutch import statistics only locate 'West Africa' as the area where commodities came from: the statistics indicate that before 1857, only the 'coast of Guinea' is meant by this, but nothing indicates which other areas were included after 1857. As this was the year that Pincoffs and Kerdijk moved into the Congo Basin area under the name *Pincoffs & Kerdijk*, we might assume with some certainty that this included the Congo Basin area, although we of course cannot be totally sure of this fact. Moreover, the statistics thus make no distinction between West and West Central Africa and simply lump everything together under "West Africa".

Table 3.6 Palm oil imports and exports in the Netherlands (1847–1876), ten-year averages, x1000kg; 50 guilders per 100 kg

Years	*Imports*	*Exports*	*Balance*
1847–1856	181	164	17
1857–1866	2171	1207	964
1867–1876	6767	2161	4606

Source: *Jaarcijfers van het Koninkrijk der Nederlanden. Rijk in Europa (1882–1884)*

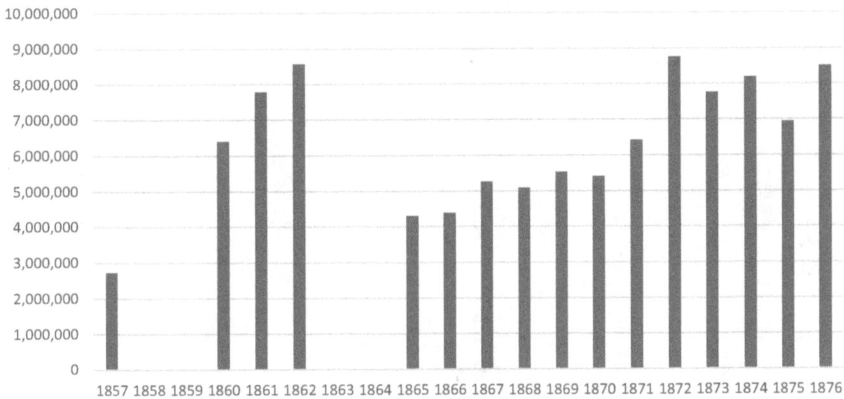

Graph 3.7 Total imports of palm oil into the Netherlands (1857–1876), in guilders (1858–1859 & 1863–1864 Missing). (Source: *Statistiek van den handel en de scheepvaart (1847–1877)*)

congruent with what we know from the literature, as lots of palm oil was re-exported to Britain, explaining the substantial share of exports as well(Table 3.6 and Graphs 3.7 and 3.8).[204]

Moreover, as Graph 3.9 shows, trade data concerning imports and exports from and to West Africa show that in particular the imports in the 1870s were fairly substantial, reaching almost five million guilders in 1879, of which probably half was palm oil. In 1877, imports from West Africa contributed nearly one-fourth of the total palm imports in the Netherlands. Table 3.7 shows the percentages of palm oil imports from West Africa as a total of the Dutch palm oil imports for the 1857–1879 period, showing that for the post-1865 period, the percentage hovered between 12 and

[204] Oosterwijk, *Ik verlang geen dank.*

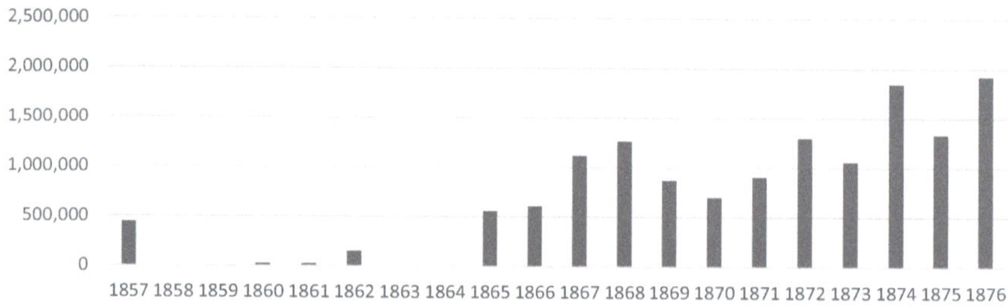

Graph 3.8 Palm oil imports from West Africa into the Netherlands (1857–1876), in guilders (1858–1859 and 1863–1864 missing). (Source: *Statistiek van den handel en de scheepvaart (1847–1877)*)

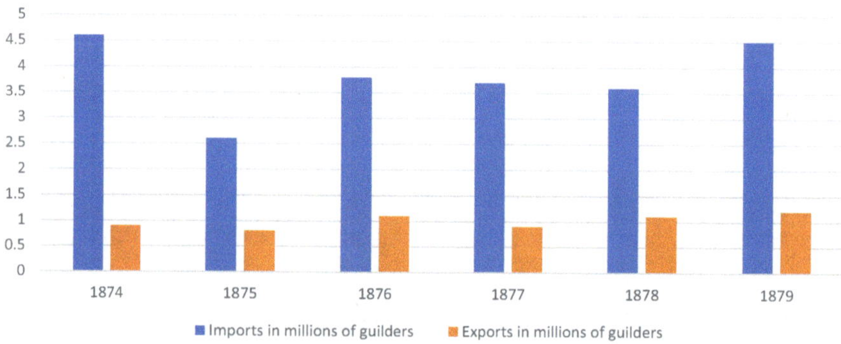

Graph 3.9 Dutch-West (Central) Africa trade, imports and exports (1874–1879), in millions of guilders. (Source: Jaarcijfers *van het Koninkrijk der Nederlanden. Rijk in Europa (1882–1884)*)

25%. While the imports from the Dutch East Indies were certainly more numerous and voluminous, the value of imports from West (Central) Africa was not insubstantial either, at least after 1865.

One intriguing potential explanation for the Rotterdam entrepreneurs' decision to move into West Central Africa, rather than to opt to try to break the NHM's Amsterdam-dominated monopoly in the Dutch East Indies, has been suggested by Paul van de Laar. He argued that the (anticipated) opening of the Suez Canal, in 1869, also played a role in the decision of Rotterdam entrepreneurs to move into Africa.[205] Judging that the

[205] Van de Laar, *Stad van formaat*, 67 & 156; Private Communication with Paul van de Laar, August 2022; see also De Kok, 'De koloniale connectie', 63–68.

Table 3.7 West African palm oil imports as share of total palm oil imports into the Netherlands, 1857–1879 (1858–1859 & 1863–1864 missing), in guilders

Year	*West African palm oil imports*	*Total palm oil imports*	*West African percentage*
1857	442,670	2,718,357	16.28%
1858	NB	NB	NB
1859	NB	NB	NB
1860	23,972	6,393,688	0.37%
1861	20,872	7,774,681	0.27%
1862	150,716	8,569,494	1.76%
1863	NB	NB	NB
1864	NB	NB	NB
1865	554,765	4,295,027	12.92%
1866	605,813	4,383,692	13.82%
1867	1,117,000	5,248,000	21.28%
1868	1,261,000	5,085,000	24.80%
1869	866,800	5,524,000	15.69%
1870	698,499	5,396,372	12.94%
1871	903,297	6,413,035	14.09%
1872	1,298,766	8,747,924	14.85%
1873	1,059,485	7,741,657	13.69%
1874	1,844,546	8,174,494	22.56%
1875	1,332,321	6,915,990	19.26%
1876	1,921,333	8,490,283	22.63%
1877	1,985,295	8,265,094	24.02%
1878	1,198,134	7,167,097	16.72%
1879	1,903,355	9,129,678	20.85%

Source: *Jaarcijfers van het Koninkrijk der Nederlanden. Rijk in Europa (1882–1884) & Statistiek van den handel en de scheepvaart (1847–1877)*

Suez Canal would substantially decrease transport costs for many entrepreneurs operating from Asia, one way to outcompete the imports from the Dutch East Indies on costs was to move closer to home, in this case Asia.[206] This explanation may hold partially true as this allowed Rotterdam entrepreneurs to compete with palm oil from the Dutch East Indies (imported by Amsterdam entrepreneurs) on price; it does not fully explain the timing of the Rotterdam entrepreneurs in the late 1850s and 1860s to move elsewhere across Africa, as the Suez Canal had not yet opened and its impact was moreover still unclear.

[206] Muller, *Muller*, 117–193; De Kok, 'De koloniale connectie', 63–68.

The opening of the Suez Canal may indeed have strengthened the case of the Rotterdam entrepreneurs to double down on their African bet, but their reason to operate in Liberia and the Congo Basin should certainly also be seen in the light of the Dutch neglect of its colony on the Gold Coast, the (lack of) quality of palm oil on the Gold Coast, the need for an outlet of capital from Rotterdam and above all the monopolisation by the Amsterdam-dominated NHM of the trade in raw commodities to and from the Dutch East Indies. That the economic rationale was thus complex was admitted by Muller Szn. and Pincoffs themselves as well. In the so-called *Scheepvaartsenquête* ('Shipping Survey') of 1877, a committee of the Dutch Lower House of Parliament inquired why the share of Dutch shipping had declined after roughly 1850.[207] Much of the *Scheepvaartsenquête* focused on trade with the Dutch East Indies, but some of the main players in the Rotterdam-Africa trade were also interviewed by the committee.[208] The committee noted that the NHM had a negative impact on Dutch shipping due to its monopoly position, but noted the African trade as a small positive point in all the negativity that surrounded the *Scheepvaartsenquête*, a sentiment echoed by most of the people appearing before the committee. The committee for example noted that whilst in 1851 Dutch-West Africa trade only numbered 457 tonnages, in 1872 this had already gone up to 6108 tonnages.[209] Only two years before Pincoffs' fall, the committee highlighted the African trade as one of the few success stories.

As Liberals, both Muller Szn. and Pincoffs forcefully argued for free trade in West Africa and the Dutch East Indies. Both men complained about various aspects of government policy that, in their view, did not

[207] See for context: F.S. Gaastra, 'Vragen over de koopvaardij. De 'Enquête omtrent den toestand van de Nederlandsche koopvaardijvloot' uit 1874 en de achteruitgang van de handelsvloot', Inaugural Lecture Leiden University (Leiden 2004), available at https://scholarlypublications.universiteitleiden.nl/handle/1887/4519 [Retrieved 31/05/2022]. For the *verbatim* transcription: S.A., *Enquête omtrent den toestand van de Nederlandschen koopvaardijvloot: verslag der commissie* (The Hague 1875). I like to thank Gerhard de Kok for pointing out the existence of this source to me, and sharing his thoughts on this matter with me.

[208] Ibidem.

[209] Tweede Kamer (hereafter NL-TK), Stuk 52, 22-09-1873, available at https://zoek.officielebekendmakingen.nl/resultaten?q=(c.product-area==%22sgd%22)and(w.vergaderjaar==%221873-1874%22)and(cql.textAndIndexes=%2252%22)%20AND%20w.dossiernummer==%2252%22&zv=52&pg=10&col=Alle&hist=1&sf=dn%7c52 [Retrieved 12/09/2022].

sufficiently support entrepreneurs. Pincoffs for example complained about the high fees Dutch consuls levied;[210] both Pincoffs and Muller Szn. complained about the high costs to insure ships, arguing this was much cheaper in London;[211] and Muller Szn. complained about the state of the port of Rotterdam and the way that Elmina had been transferred to British sovereignty (although not the fact itself, he claimed, which he had vehemently opposed at the time).[212] Muller Szn. argued that the retraction of the Dutch state from Elmina had hurt his business.[213] Whilst supporting free trade when it suited them, both Pincoffs and Muller looked to the government for all sorts of direct and indirect support to aid them in trading.

3.5 Conclusion

Dutch dispersion across the African continent followed the retreat of the Dutch state from the Gold Coast (part of which remained until 1872 *de jure* under Dutch rule) after the abolition of the slave trade. Firms from both Amsterdam and Rotterdam tried at various points to revive trade from Elmina, but with limited success, as palm oil was expensive and often of poor quality. Huibert van Rijckevorsel, with the help of the Dutch colonial state in the form of Governor Anthony van der Eb, achieved some success, but also ran into trouble in the 1850s and 1860s. Other entrepreneurs from Rotterdam, faced with British competition and the limited prospects on the Dutch Gold Coast, started looking for other places where palm oil was produced. They found these opportunities in Liberia, Angola and other places in the Congo Basin area. During this 'prelude' to the Partition of Africa, places that were (largely) outside of European state offered the best chances for Dutch entrepreneurs to operate without steady and consistent Dutch state support.

Profiting from their (kinship and financial) links with Manchester, both Muller Szn. and Pincoffs established factories across West and West Central Africa. Other factors may also have played a role in the efforts of the Dutch entrepreneurs to move 'beyond Elmina', like the opening of the Suez Canal and the protectionist market in the Dutch East Indies. The move to other places beyond the Gold Coast was, however, not necessarily

[210] S.A. *Enquête*, 170.
[211] Ibidem, 171 & 277.
[212] Ibidem, 278--282.
[213] Ibidem, 282.

easy either. A slump in the prices of palm oil ate into profit margins from the 1860s onwards. *Muller & Co*, which primarily operated in Liberia, largely remained profitable between 1863 and 1879. The AHV had a harder time, due to a complex set of problems, including the price slump, its legal status, and its director Pincoffs' management skills. A last-minute effort to save the AHV by cosying up to Leopold II, the Belgian King who showed an interest in setting up a colony in the Congo basin, went nowhere, as Pincoffs' fraud came to light before the firm could be saved. The AHV went bankrupt after some twenty difficult years in 1879, after Pincoffs was ousted by Marten Mees, the main financier of the AHV.

This may have been the end of the Dutch entrepreneurial activities in West and West Central Africa, but nothing like that turned out to be the case. As Chap. 4 will show, the reincarnated NAHV quickly picked up the thread and under Muller's leadership re-established itself as one of the largest firms in the Congo basin. Even if the foundations of the AHV were shaky, there was apparently a solid entrepreneurial case to be made.

CHAPTER 4

Dutch Entrepreneurs in the Partition of Africa (1880s–1890s)

4.1 Introduction

With the bankruptcy of the AHV in 1879, the first phase of Dutch involvement in the Scramble for Africa ended. Crucially, 1879 also marked the year when the Belgian king Leopold II set his eyes firmly on establishing a colony in the Congo basin, in effect inaugurating the *Partition of* Africa in the lead-up to the 1884–1885 Berlin Conference. This chapter looks at the Dutch entrepreneurs in this period between 1879, when the AHV was re-established as the NAHV and Leopold set up the *Association Internationale du Congo* (AIC), and 1899, just after the Fashoda incident, often seen as the apex and climax of the Partition of Africa. This was a time of fast-paced change and marks the transition from small-scale family firms to large-scale capitalist enterprise in a period just short of twenty years for the Dutch firms operating across West and West Central Africa. Moreover, it covers the expansion of both the Dutch entrepreneurial reach in West Central Africa, as well as the expansion of various empires, primarily the Congo Free State, the French Congo and Portuguese Angola. In 1879, only Portuguese Angola (nominally) existed: in 1899, the three empires exercised sovereignty over large swathes of territory, necessitating a new approach for the Dutch entrepreneurs to deal with colonial administrations that did not necessarily favour secure property rights or foreign investment.

G. Dreijer, *Private Entrepreneurship and European Imperialism*,
Palgrave Studies in Economic History,
https://doi.org/10.1007/978-3-032-01086-5_4

Whereas the AHV and *Muller & Co* were by 1879 basically still family firms operating as early modern merchants bartering on the coast, the new circumstances also challenged their entrepreneurial basis. Interestingly, the trajectories of the two firms differed markedly, which was largely the result of the context and circumstances in which the firms had to operate. Whereas *Muller & Co* (after 1893 part of the *Oost-Afrikaansche Compagnie*) remained operative largely as before, the NAHV transitioned to become one of West Central Africa's largest businesses, run more like a managerial firm than an early modern family firm. One result of the transition was that the original group of entrepreneurs was gradually replaced by new names: in 1879, after Pincoffs' fall, Muller Szn. became *the* central figure in the Dutch trade with West and West Central Africa, and much attention will be paid to his entrepreneurship during the 1880s.[1] Yet, during the 1890s, when Muller Szn. faded into the background, a new generation took over within the NAHV, also changing the personal dynamics of the Dutch-African trade. This transition, of course, also necessitated a new approach to the entrepreneurial processes.

4.2 *Muller & Co* and the OAC in West Africa

As shown in the previous chapter, *Muller & Co* was fairly profitable in its early years, with the exception of the year 1879 when its trade was hit by the Pincoffs affair. Muller Szn.'s attention, up to this point, had mostly been on running his family firm. This changed in the 1880s: Muller Szn., who had been an investor in the AHV, put himself forward to take over the NAHV, and in 1883 also rescued the ailing *Handels-Compagnie Mozambique* (HCM), restructuring it to become the *Oost-Afrikaansche Compagnie* (OAC). This meant that in the space of four years, Muller Szn. had become (co-)director of three firms rather than one. Muller therefore established himself as an invaluable and crucial player in the Dutch-African trade, but this did on the other hand also stretch his abilities to run those firms. Muller moreover opted to keep the three firms as separate, rather than integrating them into one firm (mergers would eventually follow in 1893 between *Muller & Co* and the OAC and, eventually, in 1921 between the OAC and NAHV): the archival documents do not indicate that this has ever been a serious proposal, even if this may have made sense from the present-day perspective.

[1] Muller, *Muller*, 350.

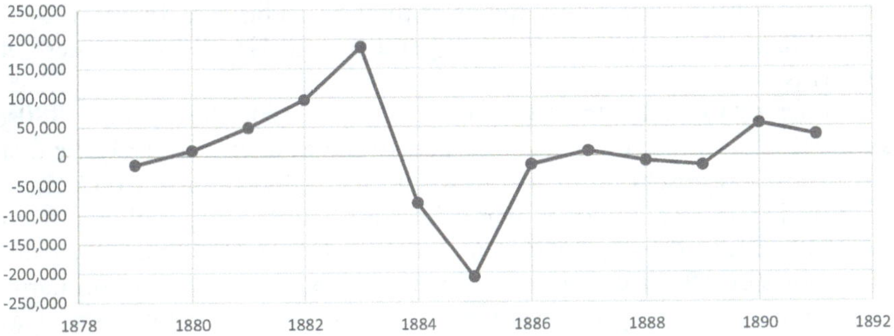

Graph 4.1 Profits and losses on the Guinea Coast trade of Muller & Co, 1879–1891, in guilders. (Source: *NL-SAR, Archief Muller, inv. 41, nr. 168.* Note: *Profits in black, losses in red*)

Table 4.1 Profits and losses of Muller & Co, 1863–1900

Years	Profit/Loss in guilders
1863–1883	551,200
1884–1900	521,400

Source: Muller, *Muller*, 351. Note: *Profits in black, losses in red*

One practical consequence of the matter was that Muller Szn.'s attention was mostly on the NAHV, and less so on *Muller & Co* in Liberia. Moreover, the economic situation in Liberia did not improve for *Muller & Co*, largely as a result of increasing competition both on the market in Africa and in Europe. *Muller & Co* lost money in 1879 following Pincoffs' fraudulent activities, but restored profitability in the first years of the 1880s (see Graph 4.1). From 1884 onwards, however, losses often prevailed over profits and even in the years that profits were made (like 1887). Although the profits outweighed the losses by 90,000 guilders over the period 1879–1891, it is also clear from Table 4.1 that there was a loss of overall profitability after 1884, which Muller Szn.'s biographer calls a 'crisis year' for the firm.[2] Competition increased markedly in the 1880s all over Africa, and the fact that *Muller & Co* still used sailing ships rather than steamers meant that the firm faced a substantial cost disadvantage.[3] Muller Szn. himself still lent his name to the firm, but in the early 1880s

[2] Ibidem, 351.

[3] See Dreijer, 'Handel en scheepvaart', 48.

transferred day-to-day management of the firm to his son Abram Muller. Muller Szn. thus freed up time to spend on the NAHV, the largest of the firms.

Muller & Co still retained some ties with Elmina during the 1880s, although this was only a very minor part of the business: in 1884, the first year where a distinction is made between Liberia and Elmina, for example imported 105,392 guilders from Liberia against 764 guilders from Elmina.[4] Liberia thus by far remained the most important place for palm oil imports by *Muller & Co* into the Netherlands, but as prices of primarily palm oil dropped and production in Liberia and adjacent countries such as Sierra Leone rose, competition also increased, diminishing the profitability of the firm. In Liberia, *Muller & Co* owned at least five factories (in Monrovia, Robertsport, Buchanan, Edina and Greenville), even if it probably owned more around 1885.[5] According to the Swiss Johann Büttikofer, who travelled Liberia and published a lengthy two-volume travelogue of his journey in 1885, *Muller & Co* was among the largest and well-established foreign firms in Liberia, next to the German Woermann firm from Hamburg.[6] The other activities of *Muller & Co*, such as the trade in the Dutch East Indies, were too insignificant, loss-making, or a combination of both, to make up for the increasing problems that the firm faced after 1884.[7]

Parts of the business empire of Muller Szn., initially successful after restructuring the NAHV and OAC, largely faltered in the late 1880s and early 1890s.[8] In the years before, Muller Szn. had agreed to take on a task of the Dutch government to recruit soldiers in Liberia and across West Africa more broadly for service in the Dutch East Indies, where the Dutch colonial government needed a constant flow of soldiers to fulfil its imperial ambitions.[9] West Africa had long been a recruiting ground for (black) soldiers (the so-called *Belanda Hitam*, see previous chapter) in the Dutch East Indies, already starting with Daendels, although this had more often

[4] NL-SAR, Archief Muller, nr. 167, Profits and Losses 1863–1887.

[5] Muller, *Muller*, 348; J. Büttikofer, *Reisebilder aus Liberia* (2 Vols.) (Leiden 1890), in particular the first volume.

[6] Büttikofer, *Reisebilder* (Vol. 2), 98 & 108.

[7] NL-SAR, Archief Muller, nr. 164, Balances, Profits and Losses 1863–1901.

[8] Ibidem, 348–351.

[9] NL-SAR, Archief Chabot, nr. 1202, Announcement of the OAC, Claim Hendrik Muller, 1892; NL-HaNA, Archief NAHV, nr. 772, Note Regarding Recruitment of Black Soldiers.

than not a problem for the Dutch.[10] In this sense, Muller Szn. stood in a long tradition of Dutch recruitment of soldiers across West Africa, despite the limited success of this process. In late 1889, Muller Szn. agreed to start the process all over again, and in October 1890 even went to Liberia himself to set up the recruitment process. This was the first time Muller Szn. set foot in Africa. Having agreed upon set numbers every year, Muller Szn. was unable to fulfil his quotum for 1890. Moreover, the Dutch government was unhappy with the quality of the soldiers, arguing they were not fit to fight upon arrival in Batavia (present-day Jakarta).[11] The Dutch government subsequently declined to pay Muller Szn., although some soldiers were sent to the Dutch East Indies and did actually fight there. Muller Szn. launched an arbitration case against the Dutch government, which grinded on for some years.[12]

Increasingly, Muller Szn. came under pressure from his sons Hendrik P.N. and Abram Muller to hand over his firm, and in 1889 Muller Szn. agreed to do so in the near future (in 1888, he also stepped down as director of the NAHV, aged almost seventy at that point).[13] In 1891, with the support and help of Marten Mees, he drew up new statutes for the firm to turn it into a so-called *Commanditaire Vennootschap* (CV), a structure we already encountered before with the AHV.[14] Moreover, a public request for loans to the firm was done in Amsterdam and Rotterdam to finance potential new operations in Liberia.[15] Once this was done, the directorship of the firm was handed over to Abram Muller. He decided that the OAC and *Muller & Co* would profit from a merger, and quickly moved to do so. On 1 January 1892, the Mozambique-based OAC took over the assets of *Muller & Co* in Liberia, continuing the palm oil trade there. Abram Muller became director of the OAC and thus guaranteed continuity. Moreover, the OAC took over two of *Muller & Co*'s ships, the *Elise Susanne* and *Aethiopia*.[16]

By incorporating the assets of *Muller & Co* into the OAC, Abraham Muller also inherited the dispute with the Dutch government over the soldiers' contractual obligations. As arbitration failed, the OAC soon

[10] Van Kessel, *Zwarte Hollanders*; Van der Meer, 'De Goudkust', 37–43.

[11] NL-HaNA, Archief NAHV, nr. 772, Note Regarding Recruitment of Black Soldiers.

[12] Ibidem.

[13] Idem, nr. 171, Written Agreement H. Muller Szn. with his sons.

[14] Idem, nr. 172, Concept Statutes for CV.

[15] Muller, *Muller*, 349.

[16] Ibidem, 350.

afterwards launched proceedings against Muller Szn. as a private person, alleging that the losses for the soldiers' contract were his fault.[17] The OAC won this case before the Dutch court, afterwards retracting the arbitration case against the Dutch government. Mutually, the Dutch government and the OAC decided that the contract would be declared null and void, allowing the OAC to free itself from the contractual obligation that it inherited from *Muller & Co*'s incorporation.[18]

In 1893, immediately upon the merger, Abram Muller allowed Wigbold Bakker, who had acted as one of its chief agents in Liberia for a while, to trade on behalf of the OAC in Liberia, indicating the firm wanted to remain engaged in Liberia.[19] In 1893, Liberia ratified the Acts of the Brussels Anti-Slavery Conference, which also included new tariffs on arms and alcohol, the main import products that the OAC brought into Liberia (similar to Mozambique and the Lower Congo region).[20] In Mozambique, similar tariffs came into existence, as Portugal ratified the Acts as well. The profits of the OAC thus further diminished, and the longed-for synergy between the Liberian and Mozambiquan parts of the business never really materialised.[21]

The merger did not mean, however, that *Muller & Co* disappeared for good: some trade in the Dutch East Indies and the imports from Elmina remained under the control of *Muller & Co* until 1900, although the administration was done by the OAC.[22] In 1898, a notarial deed concluded between Muller Szn. and Abram Muller gave the latter full control over the firm, after his brother Hendrik P.N. Muller had fallen out with the rest of the family.[23] Soon after, Muller Szn. passed away on 15 August 1898.[24] After some more difficult years, the OAC left Mozambique and focused fully on Liberia after 1905 (see next chapter), essentially returning

[17] NL-SAR, Archief Chabot, nr. 1202, Announcement of the OAC, 1893.

[18] Ibidem.

[19] Büttikotter, *Reisebilder aus Liberia*, 421.

[20] NL-HaNA, Ministerie van Buitenlandse Zaken A-Dossiers, nr. 359, Correspondentie Oost-Afrika 1893–1906, Ratification Liberia, 1893.

[21] NL-HaNA, Archief NAHV, nr. 565, Overige Stukken OAC, Authorisation Muller for Bakker, 27-12-1893.

[22] NL-SAR, Archief Muller, nr. 174, Public Announcements on Termination OAC; Muller, *Muller*, 351.

[23] Idem, nr. 391, Letters H.P.N. Muller on Directorship.

[24] Muller, *Muller*, 387–392.

to its roots as a West African firm, albeit under the confusing name of the East African Company.

4.3 Rising from the Ashes: The NAHV, 1879–1898

As we have seen in the previous chapter, in May 1879 the AHV ran into financial trouble and had to declare bankruptcy. Many investors, including Mees and Muller, lost significant sums of money. In a pamphlet, Muller Szn. complained about the role of the oversight board (headed by Marten Mees) in the execution of the company following the bankruptcy proceedings.[25] Muller Szn. wrote positively about Henry Kerdijk, who he argued was not to blame for the bankruptcy: in contrast, Mees and his firm *Mees & Zoonen* were accused of bad management in the AHV case by Muller Szn. Muller Szn. argued that *Mees & Zoonen* lent significant sums to the AHV without the need for collateral, creating the wrong incentives for Pincoffs.[26] Moreover, Muller Szn. alleged, Mees had even sent more money than the AHV had requested in loans, suggesting nepotism. Mees himself was acquitted before the Dutch *Hoge Raad* (High Council) of mismanagement in the AHV affair, but Mees was replaced as president of the oversight board of the newly established NAHV.[27] Similar accusations were commonplace in Rotterdam: anonymous pamphlets were for example launched at Rotterdam Liberal politicians by those from a more catholic bend, accusing the various Liberals in the West African trade to be perfidious in their business dealings, and by extension also being unreliable as politicians.[28] Moreover, Pincoffs' Jewish background was often hinted at in these writings as proof that he was never to be trusted, a common antisemitic trope.[29]

The impact of the AHV's liquidation, while a shock to Rotterdam's entrepreneurial community, was diminished by Dutch financial institutions, in particular DNB or the Dutch Central Bank.[30] The fall-out of the AHV's bankruptcy sent shockwaves through Rotterdam and, to a lesser extent, Amsterdam, making it necessary for the DNB to step in with credit

[25] Muller, *Over de liquidatie*.

[26] Ibidem, 1–2.

[27] Muller, *Muller*, 328–330.

[28] See e.g. B. Oldenkott, *Potloodstreepjes van Redivivus* (8 Vols.) (Leiden 1879–1880).

[29] As was indeed common, as Oldenkott often hinted at the Jewish background of Pincoffs. See also: Oosterwijk, *Ik verlang geen dank*.

[30] NL-HaNA, Archief De Nederlandsche Bank NV, nr. 16212, Missive 14-05-1879.

lines. Already on 14 May 1879, DNB's Rotterdam office received news of the coming financial mayhem, allowing the DNB to move quickly. Various firms, such as the shipping line *Stoomvaart op Amerika* (American Steamline Service), had intimate financial ties to the AHV and needed emergency loans to survive.[31] The DNB provided some of those, although it stopped doing so already in July as it reckoned the worst was over.[32] The RHV, the other Pincoffs' vehicle to develop Rotterdam's port infrastructure, nevertheless remained in deep trouble.

In June 1879, a meeting of the AHV shareholders took place in Rotterdam, where Muller Szn. was appointed as the chief curator, alongside Willem C. Schalkwijk and J.C. Reepmaker.[33] Their first task, judging from the notes drawn from the first meeting after the shareholder meeting, was to make sure that the company could make a successful restart. This, however, did take a while: only in July 1880, after almost a year of work, the three curators for example released guidance on how shareholders could exchange their AHV shares for new NAHV ones, and organised a new shareholder meeting. Before the meeting, however, a public relations battle was waged in the Dutch media, as for example the prominent Rotterdam ship-owner Willem Ruys publicly argued that the fraud was widely known and should have had more legal consequences for people like Mees.[34] Muller Szn. defended Mees and the other commissioners in an open letter, claiming only Pincoffs and one or two clerks in the Rotterdam office of the AHV had been knowledgeable about the fraud.[35] Muller Szn., in letters to his friend James Hutton, complained about the many problems that he faced, particularly regarding the creditors of the AHV, but in public always defended his actions.[36] Hutton, himself a shareholder of the AHV, was afraid that his money would be lost as a result of speculation with AHV shares, fears that Muller Szn. was able to soothe.[37]

Despite the earlier harsh critical assessment of Mees by Muller Szn., Mees was also invited to the shareholder meeting by means of a private letter, indicating the animosity between the two had in the meantime

[31] Ibidem.
[32] Ibidem, Missive 23-07-1879.
[33] NL-SAR, Familie Mees privé, nr. 2382, Notes of AHV Oversight Board Meetings.
[34] Idem, Archief Muller, nr. 209, Newspaper Reports on RHV Shareholder Meeting.
[35] Ibidem, Open Letter Muller.
[36] Idem, nr. 217, Letter Muller to Hutton, 17-05-1880.
[37] Ibidem.

diminished.[38] The assets of the AHV were, with the agreement of the shareholders, transferred to the new NAHV, which would thus continue the trade in palm oil and other commodities. The RHV, Pincoffs' other vehicle to develop Rotterdam's maritime infrastructure, was saved thanks to the financial support of the Rotterdam municipality and a loan from the NHM, as well as emergency loans from DNB.[39] In 1882, however, the RHV was liquidated by Muller Szn., who was also its curator, as Muller Szn. argued that the creditors were not flexible enough to keep the RHV going.[40]

The NAHV was able to continue with the assets of the AHV. It offered older shareholders new shares for a discounted price, diminishing the losses for the firm: despite the AHV affair, most shareholders gruntingly accepted this, indicating that most shareholders blamed Pincoffs rather than underlying structural factors.[41] The shareholders agreed that Muller Szn. would become the new director, particularly considering his experience with his *Muller & Co* firm in Liberia: next to Muller Szn., his co-curator Schalkwijk also became a director (Image 4.1 and 4.2).

The repercussions were not limited to Rotterdam only, as the investments in Leopold's CEHC had inevitably given the Pincoffs affair an international dimension as well. In November 1890, Leopold himself looked back at the episode in a letter to Joseph Wolseley Garnet, a British army general. Citing 'consistent misunderstandings' around the Pincoffs affair, Leopold set out his views in a document that was apparently dictated to a clerk.[42] In this remarkable document, Leopold claimed that the AHV stopped paying their bills in April/May 1879, in particular the 145,000 guilders they had promised to the CEHC. This meant that the CEHC faced a significant deficit, which according to Leopold led to the Committee ceasing its activities.[43] In May 1880, the re-established NAHV declined to contribute the aforementioned 145,000 guilders, leading Leopold to comment that the CEHC *de facto* had paid to re-establish the

[38] Idem, Familie Mees privé, nr. 2724, Public Announcement Muller.

[39] NL-HaNA, De Nederlandsche Bank NV, nr. 16213 & 16214.

[40] Ibidem.

[41] NL-SAR, Familie Mees privé, nr. 2724, Public Announcement Muller.

[42] Archief van het Koninklijk Paleis Brussel (hereafter BE-KPB), Archives relatives au développement extérieur de la Belgique sous le règne de Léopold II, 1865–1909, inv. 543–158, nr. 377, piece nr. 11, Letter Leopold to Wolseley, 26-11-1890.

[43] Ibidem.

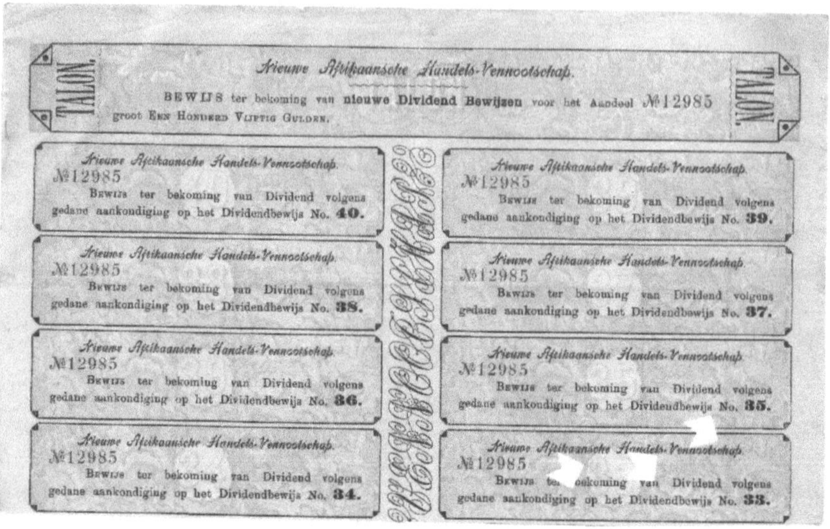

Image 4.1 Proof of dividend of the NAHV, 1880. (Source: Francoisdjvr via Wikimedia Commons, available at https://commons.wikimedia.org/wiki/File:NAHV_Dividend.tif [Retrieved 10/04/2025])

failed AHV: adding insult to injury, Leopold complained that the AHV had consistently paid high dividends between 1863 and 1877.[44]

The re-establishment of the NAHV furthermore meant that, for the first time, people outside of the original network of families moved into positions of power in the Dutch-West (Central) Africa trade. In Rotterdam, two other people were of key importance during the NAHV years. These were Schalkwijk, who alongside Muller Szn. restructured the AHV after the bankruptcy of 1879 and subsequently became one of the directors,[45]

[44] Ibidem; see for the dividends Vermeulen, *De Afrikaansche handels-vereeniging*, 22–35.

[45] Schalkwijk was a prolific pamphletist, see e.g.: W.C. Schalkwijk, *De Anti-Slavernij-Conferentie en invoerrechten in den Congo-Staat* (Rotterdam 1890); Idem, *De Kongo-Vrijstaat en de handel: antwoord op de brochure « La Conférence de Bruxelles et les Pays-Bas » par « un Ami de la vérite »* (Rotterdam 1890); Idem, *De Congo-Staat en zijn Pleitbezorger: antwoord op de brochure « L'État Indépendant du Congo et la Compagnie de Rotterdam » par « un Ami de la Vérité » (Antwerpen bij Max Ruef)* (Rotterdam 1890). For his role in the liquidation of the AHV, see: Muller, *Over de liquidatie*.

Image 4.2 Stock certificate of the NAHV, 1880. (Source: Francoisdjvr via Wikimedia Commons, available at https://commons.wikimedia.org/wiki/File:NAHV_Stock_Certificate_(front).tif [Retrieved 10/04/2025])

and Georges Philippi, another director from the late 1880s onwards.[46] Philippi was particularly instrumental in using his German heritage for political and financial support.[47] These men thus were not part of the 'original' network of Rotterdam-based African traders, but they only joined once the NAHV was established. Contrary to the elder group of entrepreneurs, who never set a foot in the areas where they held so many trading interests (Pincoffs for example never traveled to Africa), this newer group often climbed the ladder by first acting as agents in Africa or at least visiting Africa a number of times before being promoted at the head offices of the firm in Rotterdam.

Similarly, in the Congo basin, a new group of men acquired importance. The best example was Anton Greshoff (1855–1905), who acted as the main agent for the NAHV on the ground from its inception, but

[46] Philippi was also co-director, alongside De Bloeme, of some of the concession companies in which the NAHV participated. See: Coquery-Vidrovitch, *Le Congo*, 60–61.
[47] See e.g. NL-HaNA, Archief NAHV, nr. 694.

already worked for the AHV before that time.[48] Greshoff was on friendly terms with Stanley.[49] Besides Anton, other family members also were engaged in the African trade: his brother Maurits Greshoff for example lived for some fifty years in Angola.[50] Anton Greshoff remained in the Congo Basin area until 1904/1905, shortly before he passed away in the Netherlands after a prolonged illness. Greshoff was a prolific letter writer, and therefore a significant deal of his thoughts can be traced through the thousands of letters sent to and from Greshoff. Greshoff was a somewhat difficult man, who for example often publicly attacked the Belgian king and sovereign of the Congo Free State Leopold II, attracting the latter's ire.

In 1892, his diplomatic credentials were for example retracted by Leopold in the Congo Free State, forcing Greshoff to seek exile in the French Congo. Greshoff also was key in sending objects to newly established museums in the Netherlands, which also shows he was active as collector besides a trading agent.[51] Greshoff was a family member of Andries de Bloeme, who acted as agent for the NAHV in Africa, and later as director and main concessionaire on behalf of the NAHV in the French concession companies, and also was present at the Berlin Conference in 1884–1885.[52] Other agents of importance were Oscar Fontaine de la Verwey, who was the chief agent for the AHV at its main factories in Banana (at the mouth of the Congo River), as well as Leendert Van der Most, who acted as chief agent in Banana in the 1880s and 1890s.[53]

[48] This section is primarily based on: Wesseling, 'De Greshoffs en Afrika', *Nieuw Letterkundig Magazijn*, 26, 2 (2008), 51–59. Wesseling draws in this article on: J. Greshoff, *Catrijntje Afrika* (The Hague 1944); Idem, *Afscheid van Europa: leven tegen het leven* (The Hague 1969).

[49] As is clear from the many letters they wrote: see BE-AMT, Stanley Archives, nrs. 42, 44, 76, 80, 641, 866, 1057–1103, 1326, 3739, 4355, 4366, 4437, 5216–5218, 5993–5995 & 6842.

[50] Greshoff, *Afscheid van Europe*, 60.

[51] See e.g. J. Wijs, 'De collectie Hanken: een bewogen geschiedenis', *Object en verzamelaar*, 3 (2014), 7–30; In general see J. Willink, *De bewogen verzamelgeschiedenis van de West-Centraal-Afrikaanse collecties in Nederland (1856–1889)* (Ridderkerk 2006), available at https://scholarlypublications.universiteitleiden.nl/access/item%3A2899672/view [Retrieved 05/08/2021].

[52] Wesseling, 'Nederland en de Conferentie van Berlijn', 570; Greshoff, *Afscheid van Europa*, 35.

[53] See e.g NL-HaNA, Archief Buitenlandse Zaken B-Dossiers, nr. 1494, Stukken betreffende Consulaire vertegenwoordiging Congo. See also: W. Bouwman, 'Handelaar en verzamelaar: Biografisch dossier van de NAHV-agenten J.C.W.J. Cremer F. de la Fontaine Verweij

In the Congo basin area itself, not much changed on the ground between May 1879 and the summer of 1881. The news of the AHV bankruptcy only reached the agents of the AHV later, as the AHV agent Zwier van Sandinck recounted:[54] trade continued as before whilst the agents waited for more news, which only came once the AHV was restructured as the NAHV. Bartering, after all, remained possible with the commodities that had arrived just before the financial troubles came to light in the Netherlands, although in 1880 and 1881 only a couple of ships arrived in the Congo Basin. The data for imports and exports from and to West Africa also show a significant drop in 1880 and 1881, indicating a short blip that followed the AHV bankruptcy.[55] Nevertheless, trade largely recovered after 1882, and the NAHV essentially quickly recovered its market share in palm oil, ivory and other African commodities. With the same agents, but new management in Rotterdam, the NAHV performed better than the AHV, indicating that the entrepreneurial behaviour of Pincoffs, consisting of speculation on financial assets, had been at the root of the problem.[56]

The early 1880s witnessed a number of developments that threatened the NAHV's business, but also offered potential new opportunities. This included the establishment of the Congo Free State in 1885, but also the unpredictable policy of the Dutch state concerning Africa. Notwithstanding the general Dutch policy of staying out of Africa, the 1880s witnessed a few incidents in which the Dutch state allowed navy ships on their way to or from the Dutch East Indies to check in on the coast of West Central Africa. The first action of its kind was to send the *Tromp* on its return voyage from the Dutch East Indies in March 1884 to check in on Maculla (near Ambrisette in northern Angola), where a Dutch factory had (reportedly) been attacked by the local population.[57] In a letter to the Ministry of Marine, the Dutch Minister of Foreign Affairs noted that 'dreadful violent actions' had been perpetrated by the local population against the Dutch

L.M. Van der Most J.W. Regeer', Unpublished Internship Report Leiden University & Museum Volkenkunde 2013 (Leiden 2013), 21–26.

[54] Zwier van Sandinck, *Herinneringen*, 114.

[55] See Sect. 4.4.

[56] Oosterwijk, *Ik verlang geen dank*, 151–158.

[57] NL-HaNA, Ministerie van Marine, Scheepsjournalen 1813–1995, inv. 2.12.03, nr. 4507, Logs 25-03-1884, 26-03-1884 & 27-03-1884; Idem, Ministerie van Marine: Openbaar Verbaal, 1813–1900 (1963), inv. 2.12.01, nr. 2589.

factory in Maculla in January 1884, and the *Tromp* was set to execute a punitive expedition in Maculla.[58]

On 22 February 1884, the Dutch government therefore telegraphed to the British, Portuguese and French navies that the *Tromp* would soon sail to Maculla to 'show the Dutch flag' in retaliation for the attack.[59] The situation was, however, more complex than the Dutch Ministry of the Navy proclaimed it was the case: in an accompanying letter, it was made clear that the attack on the Dutch factory in Maculla had been repelled with the help of the Portuguese navy ship *Reinha de Portugal*.[60] A letter from Gericke, the Dutch envoy based in Lisbon, poured more cold water on the assumption that the 'locals' attacked the Dutch factory without an excuse.[61] Even if Gericke noted that various stories did the rounds about the attacks, he noted that some hundred *krumanos* (enslaved Africans) working at the Dutch factory in Maculla had been ordered to attack the local king of Maculla, as he had not responded to an ultimatum for better trade circumstances for the Dutch, who felt they were put at a disadvantage against the British and French firms in Maculla.[62] This directly contradicted the 'Dutch' story pushed by the NAHV, as the initiative for the attack had come from the Dutch rather than the local population. By sending a hundred *krumanos* and ten European soldiers (led by a Portuguese soldier) to attack the local sovereign, the Dutch made matters worse: Gericke noted that they accidently hit a nearby factory of the French *Daumas Béraud & Cie* firm, where gunpowder was kept, leading to an explosion and the burning of that factory.[63]

In retaliation, the king of Maculla ordered a counterattack against the Dutch, in which he was supported by the French and the British, who were quite annoyed by the Dutch attack.[64] Eventually, even if the *Tromp* was sent to check in on the situation in Maculla, the ship appears to have

[58] Idem, Ministerie van Marine: Openbaar Verbaal, nr. 2589, decision nr. 37, 28-01-1884, there letter 23-01-1884 Ministry of Foreign Affairs to Ministry of the Navy: "vrij ernstige vijandelijkheden door de negers gepleegd op de Hollandsche factorij te Maculla". See also: Idem, Ministerie van Marine, Scheepsjournalen 1813–1995, nr. 4507, Logs 26-03-1884 & 27-03-1884.

[59] Idem, nr. 2590, decision nr. 28, 22-02-1884.

[60] Ibidem, Letter Ministry of Foreign Affairs to Ministry of the Navy, 22-02-1884.

[61] Ibidem, Letter Gericke to Ministry of Foreign Affairs, 18-02-1884.

[62] Ibidem.

[63] Ibidem.

[64] Ibidem.

sailed on to the Netherlands fairly quickly, perhaps indicating that the Portuguese, French and British, as well as the king of Maculla, did not appreciate further Dutch escalation.[65] Using 'attacks' by locals as an excuse to send by a navy ship seemed to be a common strategy for the Dutch to exercise a show of force, even if this mostly had adverse consequences. In April 1884, Gericke wrote about threats to the Nokki factory in Angola, even if nothing happened this time.[66] Just over a year earlier, Muller Szn. had felt compelled to dispel myths to the Dutch Ministry of Foreign Affairs about the rumours that Dutch factories were attacked regularly, indicating these were exceptions rather than the rule even in time of fast-changing geopolitical turmoil: Muller Szn. referred to a conflict at Quisembo in Angola in late 1882, where a German and English factory had been attacked (even if the Dutch one was spared).[67] He referred to a French warship waiting before the coast, threatening the Portuguese, even if no action was eventually taken by th French.[68]

Another example occurred during the Berlin Conference, when the NAHV sought support of the Dutch government after the firm's factory in Futila, just north of Cabinda, was attacked.[69] The attack was supposedly orchestrated by frustrated locals, who wanted to protest against Western presence in the area. The Portuguese NAHV agent in charge of the factory was killed in the attack, although we do not know how reliable the reports of the NAHV were, in particular if we regard the actions in Maculla just a year earlier.[70] The attack had likely happened a couple of years before the arrival of the *Atjeh*, a Dutch naval ship, making the action probably a convenient yet false excuse for the retaliatory action, not unlike the situation in Maculla.

The Dutch government was persuaded by the NAHV to send the navy ship *Atjeh* to the coast of Futila to punish the perceived rebels, writing in

[65] Idem, Ministerie van Marine, Scheepsjournalen, nr. 4507, Logs 25-03-1884, 26-03-1884 & 27-03-1884.

[66] Idem, Ministerie van Marine, Proces Verbaal, nr. 2592, decision 64, 03-04-1884.

[67] Idem, Ministerie van Buitenlandse Zaken A-Dossiers, nr. 203, Letter Muller to Ministry of Foreign Affairs, 26-02-1883.

[68] Ibidem.

[69] S.J. De Groot, 'Het geheim van Futila: imperialistisch optreden van de Koninklijke Marine langs de Congo-rivier in 1885', *Mars et Historia*, 31, 1 (1997), 3–7, there 3–4; Wijs, 'De Collectie Hanken', 12; J.W.A. Naber, *Samuel Pierre l'Honoré Naber. Schout bij nacht t.t. naar de correspondentie met zijn ouders, loopende 1880–1913* (s.l. 1939), 40–46.

[70] Ibidem.

the logbook that they had '*getuchtigd*' (chastened) the locals after they killed the NAHV agent.[71] Samuel Pierre Naber d'Honoré, who was on board of the *Atjeh*, also described the massacre in his unpublished diary of the trip, describing it as a retaliatory measure for the killing.[72] To the outside world, the Futila expedition was presented as an act to combat the slave trade, in order to create goodwill for the Dutch: at the Berlin Conference, a message from the *Atjeh* commander was presented accompanied by (forced) statements of local chiefs agreeing that Dutch intervention was necessary, as a thanks allowing the NAHV to take more territory in the area.[73] Yet in truth, it appears that an old attack which had gone unpunished at the time was now used to strengthen Dutch arguments at the Berlin Conference.

Relations with Portugal were tense around the time of the Berlin Conference as well. As Gericke, the Dutch representative in Lisbon, wrote on 19 February 1885, the Portuguese concluded treaties with local sovereigns in the area around Banana to further their claims, against the wishes of most European firms operating there.[74] Later that month a NAHV factory in Angola, near Ambrisette, was set on fire in mysterious circumstances: the Dutch warship *Atjeh* arrived too late to save the Dutch factory (even if it did subsequently reach Futila near Cabinda two weeks later).[75] In August 1885, another factory in Angola was set on fire. Oscar Fontaine de la Verwey, the Dutch consul in the area, complained in a letter to the Minister of Foreign Affairs that the Portuguese entrepreneur J.L. Da Rosa was responsible, in order to hurt the NAHV and favour his *Companhia Portugueze do Zaïre*.[76] Although Portuguese media claimed that the attacks were perpetrated by local disgruntled people, this appears to have been a way to turn the public opinion in their favour. Eventually, Da Rosa

[71] NL-HaNA, Ministerie van Marine: Scheepsjournalen 1813–1995, nr. 271, *Atjeh* 1884–1886, Log 13-02-1885; NL-HaNA, Ministerie van Buitenlandse Zaken A-Dossiers, nr. 206, Congo-aangelegenheden 1885–1894, Letter Muller to Minister of Foreign Affairs, 28-03-1885.

[72] Naber, 'Schout bij nacht', 40–46.

[73] NL-HaNA, Ministerie van Buitenlandse Zaken A-Dossiers, nr. 206, Congo-aangelegenheden 1885–1894, Statement Ministry of Foreign Affairs, 17-02-1885.

[74] Idem, Legatie Portugal, nr. 90, Letters on Portugal at the Berlin Conference, Letter Gericke van Herwijnen to Minister of Foreign Affairs, 19-02-1885.

[75] Idem, Ministerie van Marine: Scheepsjournalen, nr. 271, *Atjeh* 1884–1886, Log 29-01-1885.

[76] Idem, Legatie Portugal 1823–1898, nr. 90, Letters NAHV in Portuguese Territories, Nr. 91. Letter NAHV to Ministry of Foreign Affairs, 15-11-1885.

was declared *persona non grata* in Angola in February 1886, ending the problems the NAHV had with the Portuguese for the moment.[77] Other points of tense negotiations included new tariffs proposed on the import of weapons, which was dropped in late 1885 to appease foreign firms in Angola.

All this did not help the case of the NAHV to persuade the parties attending the Berlin Conference to give in to their demands, even as the NAHV was at this point the largest European firm active in the Lower Congo. Despite Dutch opposition and the efforts of Muller Szn., who was present in Berlin,[78] the Congo Free State was established with Leopold being allowed to administer the area under the dual conditions of guaranteeing free trade and shipping. On 19 August 1885, the NAHV applied to take a place in the commission regulating the free access to the Congo river, but was denied so by Leopold.[79] In November 1885, Leopold established higher import tariffs, in particular on imported weapons.[80] Despite the prohibitions formally in place, Leopold circumvented this agreement by establishing tariffs on transit goods to the French Congo or Angola. Already in late 1885, Gericke van Herwijnen warned the Dutch government extensively that Leopold violated many of the agreements regarding the tariffs and the free trade in the Congo basin area, but the Dutch government preferred good relations with the Congo Free State at this point.[81]

In 1886, the problem of the tariffs however became more pressing. Leopold proposed higher tariffs on firms, prompting the NAHV to assemble a coalition of firms to oppose this.[82] While Van Eetvelde, Leopold's appointed head of the Congo Free State, was broadly in favour of the firms, Leopold proposed tariffs as high as 10–11% to be established on firms operating in the Congo Free State. Still retaining broad political support, De Bloeme, the NAHV head agent in Banana, wrote a letter and had it signed by Mac Creadie (*Hatton & Cookson*), Lasthou (*Daumas Béraud & Cie*), Frazer (*British Congo Company*), d'Oliveira, de Ribeiro, Abseio

[77] Ibidem, Letter Jung to Ministry of Foreign Affairs, 05-02-1886.

[78] Muller, *Muller*, 371–376.

[79] NL-HaNA, Ministerie van Buitenlandse Zaken A-Dossiers, nr. 218, Nieuwe Afrikaansche Handels-Vennoots chap 1884–1887, Application NAHV 19-08-1885.

[80] Idem, Announcement Leopold II, 01-11-1885.

[81] NL-HaNA, Ministerie van Buitenlandse Zaken A-Dossiers, nr. 206, Congo-aangelegenheden 1885–1894, Letters Gericke van Herwijnen to Minister of Foreign Affairs, November-December 1885.

[82] Ibidem.

(*Companhia Portugueze do Zaïre*) and the Portuguese merchants De Souza, Lopo, Borges, Valle et Azevede, Ferreira d'Acosta, Real, De Freitas et Da Sylva.[83] In the letter, De Bloeme agreed to the necessity to pay some taxes, but argued that the tariffs proposed should be levied according to prices in the Congo Basin, rather than European prices.[84] On 30 June, the firms succeeded in having the tariffs (which were supposed to be established on 1 July) postponed for half a year.[85]

The fact that De Bloeme wrote this letter, rather than his boss in Banana Anton Greshoff, might be considered a strategic ploy not to antagonise Leopold: Greshoff was famously blunt and outspoken and often clashed with Leopold publicly.[86] In December 1887, for example, Gericke van Herwijnen had to apologise to Leopold after Greshoff had written negatively about Leopold in the Dutch press, accusing him of continuing the slave trade in the Congo Free State.[87] In retaliation, Leopold in 1887 ordered the NAHV to fly the flag of the Congo Free State, rather than the Dutch flag. Several steamers of the NAHV were as a result of this rule not allowed to enter Banana, leading to another diplomatic incidence (the so-called 'flag incident'), which flared up at times of the years, for example in 1891 and 1893, when new rules were established regarding the flag-flying of foreign-owned ships, each time leading to conflict between NAHV and the Congo Free State.[88]

Stanley remained, at this point, one of the many supporters of the Congo Free State, and in a letter chastised Greshoff: "unfortunately, and it is owing to the prefect transparency of your sympathies or thoughts which appear in such grotesque contrast to the beautiful charming positiveness of your letters, that have been the means of thwarting my intentions to act now [...]. Your words state smoothly [...] that you are friendly to the New State [...], but your sympathies are evidently quite the

[83] Ibidem. For the letter, see: BE-BZ, Archives Africaines, CP, nr. 2571, Document nr. 11, Letter De Bloeme to Congo Free State, 10-06-1886.

[84] Ibidem.

[85] BE-BZ, Archives Africaines, CP, nr. 2571, Document nr. 22, Letter Congo Free State to Foreign Firms, 01-07-1886.

[86] Marchal, *L'État Libre* (Vol. 1), 116–131.

[87] NL-HaNA, Ministerie van Buitenlandse Zaken A-Dossiers, nr. 206, Congo-aangelegenheden 1885–1894, Letter Gericke van Herwijnen to Congo Free State, 12-12-1887.

[88] Ibidem.

reverse."[89] In response to Leopold's unfriendly environment, the NAHV opened an office in Brazzaville (French Congo, just across the river) in 1888.[90] This was however not the end of Leopold's campaign against the NAHV, as in 1889 he would go one step further.

Having committed to combat the slave trade, Leopold had increasingly clashed with Tippu Tip, his erstwhile governor of the Eastern Congo Free State.[91] This dispute revolved around the slave trade, but also very much around ivory: Tippu Tip and the 'Arabs' largely controlled this trade in the inner regions of the Congo Free State.[92] The NAHV spotted an entrepreneurial opportunity and allied with Tippu Tip, particularly as control by the Congo Free State in the Eastern Congo was weak.[93] In particular, Greshoff was active in courting Tippu Tip. As a result, the NAHV became a major player in the area's ivory trade, in turn increasing Leopold's frustration with the firm. The NAHV in this period branched out to more remote corners of the Congo Free State, away from the coast.[94] The NAHV did so in the quest for ivory, which at this point superseded commodities like palm oil in importance. Entrepreneurially speaking, the NAHV thus diversified its commodities in this period, but this also came with significant risks as Leopold also had set his sights on the lucrative ivory trade.[95] The ivory trade was mostly run through small networks of brokers in Central Africa's interior, and subsequently transported either through East Africa (where the 'Arabs' mostly ruled) or the Western coast of the continent. The NAHV, through its network of factories, hosted many of the brokers in the ivory trade and also, crucially, facilitated riverine transport of ivory, thereby holding a substantial entrepreneurial advantage through the specialisation in transportation over other firms and the Congo Free State itself.[96]

The ivory trade thus became one of the main focus points of the negotiations between the NAHV as well as other private firms and the Congo

[89] BE-AMT, Stanley Archives, Nr. 76, Letter Book Stanley August 1884-August 1888, Letter Stanley to Greshoff, 04-11-1885.

[90] Van der Laan, 'Trading in the Congo' 241–242.

[91] Harms, *Land of Tears*, 320–321.

[92] See Wilkinson, *The Arabs and the Scramble for Africa*, for context.

[93] Ceulemans, *La question arabe*, 169–170; Harms, *Land of Tears*, 320–321; Marchal, *L'État libre* (Vol. 1), 129–131; Renault, *Tippo Tip*, 195–196; Wilkinson, *The Arabs*, 311.

[94] Harms, 'The World ABIR Made', 126.

[95] Vangroenweghe, *Voor rubber en ivoor*, 33–80.

[96] Ceulemans, *La question arabe*, 169–170; Harms, *Land of Tears*, 320–321; Marchal, *L'État libre* (Vol. 1), 129–131; Renault, *Tippo Tip*, 195–196; Wilkinson, *The Arabs*, 311.

Free State.[97] Leopold, in 1888 and 1889, aimed to strengthen control over the flow of ivory coming from the interior to Banana, from where it was shipped to Europe. Leopold proclaimed the state to be the monopolist on the export of ivory, thus putting the foreign firms in a bind: although they could sell the ivory to the state, this had to be done at a below-market price, enabling the Congo Free State to make a substantial profit. For private firms, the problem was that the ivory could only be shipped out via Banana or had to be smuggled over the border to Angola, which was rather costly. Purportedly to combat the illegal ivory trade, Leopold proclaimed harsh sanctions against smuggling of ivory and established the monopoly, in an attempt to strengthen his grip.[98] In response to the new rules, Oscar Fontaine de la Verwey, the Dutch consul in Banana and NAHV agent, wrote on 5 September 1889 that civil servants of the Congo Free State expropriated ivory from coastal factories of the NAHV.[99]

However, the Dutch firm was not the only one, as the French firm *Daumas Béraud & Cie* also complained about this on 28 September.[100] Van Eetvelde subsequently wrote to the Dutch ambassador Gericke van Herwijnen that this was a new rule to combat smuggling of ivory.[101] On 9 November 1889, De Bloeme wrote that no NAHV ships were allowed to leave Banana, as there was a dispute about the ivory on board of some of the small ships leaving for Angola.[102] Leopold, keenly aware of the tricky position, then called for the Brussels Anti-Slavery Conference to shore up support for his policies, but with an eye to consolidate control over the ivory trade.[103]

The Dutch government was more assertive at the Brussels Anti-Slavery Conference than in Berlin. According to Wesseling, 1889 was the year the Dutch Parliament started showing some interest in the Congo Question, having largely neglected the Congo area before.[104] The fact that the Congo

[97] Ibidem; Vellut, 'L'État independant du Congo dans l'histoire des géopolitiques du centre de l'Afrique', in: Vellut (ed.), *Congo: Ambitions et désenchantements 1880–1960* (Paris 2017), 21–59, there 52.

[98] Vellut, 'L'État Indépendant du Congo', 55–56.

[99] NL-HaNA, Ministerie van Buitenlandse Zaken A-Dossiers, nr. 213, Handelsbelangen in de Congo-staat (I), Letter Fontaine de la Verwey to Minister of Foreign Affairs, 05-09-1889.

[100] Ibidem, Letter *Daumas Béraud & Cie* to NAHV, 28-09-1889.

[101] Ibidem, Letter Van Eetvelde to Gericke van Herwijnen, 18-10-1889.

[102] Ibidem, Letters De Bloeme to Van Eetvelde, 05-07-1889 & 24-10-1889.

[103] Vangroenweghe, *Voor rubber en ivoor*, 33–80; Vellut, 'L'État Indépendant du Congo', 55–56.

[104] Wesseling, 'The Netherlands and the Partition', 507.

Question became more prevalent in the Netherlands, however, also meant that opinions became more divided: some argued for a hard line against the Congo Free State, whereas others advocated a more compliant line. Gericke van Herwijnen, with the support of the NAHV, for example devised a plan to make Banana a free port to make sure the *ad valorem* tax on trade was circumvented, but he was soon ordered to retract the plan.[105] Gericke van Herwijnen, with some justification, argued that the NAHV was so large that the Congo Free State had more to lose than the NAHV would, and thus advocated a reasonably hard line. Gericke van Herwijnen found some support with other firms that were allied with the NAHV, including SAB, a Belgian firm, as well as *Daumas Béraud & Cie*:[106] however, both the Portuguese and French governments were also looking to raise tariffs on foreign firms, and thus supported Leopold.[107] The NAHV director Schalkwijk travelled to London to drum up support, but despite a last-minute PR offensive by Hutton, the anti-slavery cause in Britain had become more important in public opinion than commercial interests.[108]

Dutch public opinion surrounding the Brussels Anti-Slavery Conference was largely in favour of the NAHV, as various Dutch authors railed in pamphlets against the role that the Congo Free State played at the Brussels Anti-Slavery Conference.[109] Most Dutch authors argued against the new tariffs proposed by pointing to the agreements of the Berlin Conference, which by and large prohibited these tariffs. In response, various anonymous Belgian authors argued that the interests to combat the slave trade were more important than the agreements made in Berlin, and moreover that the Acts of the Berlin Conference did not necessarily prohibit such necessary tariffs.[110] Some Dutch authors, such as Joan Bohl, taking a less

[105] NL-HaNA, Ministerie van Buitenlandse Zaken A-Dossiers, nr. 213, Handelsbelangen in de Congo-staat (I), Proposal Gericke van Herwijnen, 24-05-1890.

[106] Idem, nr. 214, Handelsbelangen in de Congo-staat (II), Letter NAHV to French Ministry of Foreign Affairs, 12-08-1890 & Letter SAB to NAHV, 16-10-1890.

[107] Ibidem, Letter Gericke van Herwijnen to Ministry of Foreign Affairs, 22-08-1890.

[108] Ibidem, Letter Schalkwijk to NAHV, 05-11-1890.

[109] Chatelet, 'Het humanitaire optreden', 20–31; Vellut, '*The Congo Mirror* (River Congo, No. 1, 22 April 1891): Glimpses at the Entry of Congo on a Global Scene', in: Van Schuylenbergh & Leduc-Grimaldi (eds.), *The Congo Free State*, 337–356, there 343–438.

[110] Ibidem. See e.g.: F. De Bas, *Een onpartijdig advies in het Congo-vraagstuk* (Schiedam 1890); Schalkwijk, *De Anti-Slavernij-Conferentie*; Idem, *De Kongo-Vrijstaat*; Idem, *De Congo-Staat en zijn Pleitbezorger*. Pamphlets from Belgium were: S.A., *L'État indépendant du Congo et la compagnie du Rotterdam, par un ami de la vérité* (Antwerp 1890); S.A., *La conférence de Bruxelles et les Pays-Bas par un ami de la vérité* (Antwerp 1890).

economic perspective and a more Christian-humanitarian paternalistic view, argued that the Dutch would have to contribute to this 'civilising mission' and thus had to accept the demands of the Congo Free State.[111] Bohl publicly argued Leopold was driven by humanitarian motives.[112] This pamphlet war appeared to fire up the Dutch government to move into action, but otherwise did not make a significant impression on the international stage.

The Dutch government ordered, on the request of the NAHV, that the *Sommelsdijk* navy ship would be sent to Banana in November 1890, as Fontaine de la Verwey had lobbied the Dutch government to send support to the NAHV in what he called the 'war of extermination' by the Congo Free State against the NAHV and other firms.[113] In February 1891, however, the Congo Free State topped this bluff by sending away all NAHV ships in the area (in this case the *Holland* and the *Frederik*, even shooting at the latter ship upon leaving); soon after, Greshoff was declared *persona non grata* and had his diplomatic credentials retracted.[114] Greshoff had publicly shamed Leopold multiple times for his continued tolerance of slavery and the slave trade, which Stanley had argued did Greshoff and the NAHV no good.[115] Following Greshoff's forced exile, the NAHV subsequently decided to move most of its operation and staff to Cabinda in 1891, which was close to Banana but under Portuguese control, still allowing the NAHV to get their hands on most of the main commodities, such as palm oil and ivory.[116] The NAHV kept some operations running in the Congo Free State, including in the Kasaï, albeit only intermittently and

[111] J. Bohl, *Nederlands Congo-belang* (Amsterdam 1890); see also S.A., *Bedenkingen tegen Nederland's verzet in de Congo-kwestie* (Amsterdam 1890).

[112] Bohl, *Nederlands Congo-belang*, 22–23.

[113] Vellut, 'The Congo Mirror', 348; NL-HaNA, Ministerie van Buitenlandse Zaken A-Dossiers, nr. 214, Handelsbelangen in de Congo-staat (II), Letter NAHV to Ministry of Foreign Affairs, 03-07-1890.

[114] Idem, nr. 215, Handelsbelangen in de Congostaat 1890–1894, Letter Gericke van Herwijnen to Ministry of Foreign Affairs, 09-02-1891 & Letter De Bloeme to Congo Free State 28-02-1891.

[115] Marchal, *L'État Libre* (Vol. 1), 116–131.

[116] NL-HaNA, Ministerie van Buitenlandse Zaken A-Dossiers, nr. 215, Handelsbelangen in de Congostaat 1890–1894, Annual Reports 1891–1892; BE-AMT, Stanley Archives, Nr. 1064, Letter Greshoff to Stanley, 20-08-1891.

not without its problems. In 1892, the headquarters were formally moved to Cabinda (the Angolan enclave north of the Congo river), and in 1893 to Brazzaville.[117]

The NAHV thus lost the dispute with the Congo Free State, and was only allowed to keep a few factories in the southern area (the Kasaï area). The factory Vista, near Banana, for example was simply expropriated by Leopold and used as an operating base to control the ivory trade, particularly after victory in the Congo-Arab War. Moreover, as much of the arms and alcohol trade was heavily taxed at the Brussels Anti-Slavery Conference, the profitability of the NAHV came under substantial pressure. As a result of these problems, the NAHV directors started to look towards other colonies to pursue business opportunities. The adjacent colonies of Portuguese Angola and the French Congo were a logical option, but both also presented upfront problems and challenges of their own: in Angola, the NAHV was largely pushed out in the late 1870s due to high import duties (although the firm retained some factories there, for example in Luanda).[118] A certain distrust between the Portuguese colonial officials and the Dutch still persisted. The French were relatively protectionist and thus also restricted access to the market in French Congo for fear of being outcompeted, particularly by British capital; therefore, they often requested that French capital would be involved, or requested the registration of a French subsidiary.[119] Yet as the NAHV moved its African headquarters to Brazzaville in 1893, this created the necessity to establish a working relationship with the French colonial authorities.[120]

The NAHV again sought the help of the Dutch government, in particular its Ministry of Foreign Affairs, to negotiate the tricky issue of the import tariffs. As a result of the agreements concluded at the Brussels Anti-Slavery Conference, various countries argued they could raise import duties to combat the slave trade, following the example of the Congo Free State. The Ministry of Foreign Affairs negotiated with all relevant parties after signing the Acts of the Brussels Anti-Slavery Conference, including the Congo Free State, French Congo and Angola. Having agreed to the levying of import tariffs, the Ministry clearly saw it as its task to diminish the impact of tariffs for the NAHV, thus walking a rather fine line. In

[117] Van der Laan, 'Trading in the Congo', 242.
[118] See Chap. 3.
[119] See Chap. 5.
[120] Van der Laan, 'Trading in the Congo', 241–242.

1892, the NAHV bombarded the Ministry with requests to sort out questions of import tariffs in the Congo basin area.[121] On 10 March 1892, the directors Schalkwijk and De Bloeme reached out to the Ministry to complain about the lack of progress in negotiations with the French about import tariffs in the French Congo.[122] It remained unclear which documents the French wanted, and in any case, the bureaucracy proved overwhelming to even enter the market in the French Congo, according to the two directors.[123] Long talks with the French followed, as well as with the French firm *Daumas Béraud & Cie*, to see whether a joint venture was also a possibility for the two firms to work around the bureaucratic obstacles.[124] In the end, however, the NAHV was able to enter the market on its own in 1893, as lengthy negotiations between the Ministry, the NAHV directors, Greshoff and the French colonial authorities led to an agreement on the tariffs.

Portuguese Angola was, after the Brussels Anti-Slavery Conference, the main destination for many 'foreign' (i.e. non-Belgian) firms. Already in March 1891, the Dutch representative Baron Gericke van Herwijnen stated in a letter to the Congo Free State (and seconded to the Ministry of Foreign Affairs) that most firms had already left or made plans to leave the Congo Free State, citing the high tax and tariff burden.[125] A month later, he warned the Congo Free State that the NAHV would indeed move the significant majority of its factories and personnel south of the border, citing both the high import duties and the fact that the Portuguese steamers would not call anymore at Banana, where the main factories of the European firms were still located.[126] Gericke van Herwijnen characterised this as a deliberate attempt by the Portuguese to poke traffic from the Congo Free State, which was to a large extent dependent on the Portuguese steamers for support.[127] In October 1891, a report stated that the NAHV had now moved most of its personnel to Angola. In October 1892, for

[121] NL-HaNA, Archief NAHV, nr. 364, Various Files, Letter Gericke van Herwijnen to NAHV, 14-11-1891.

[122] Idem, Ministerie van Buitenlandse Zaken A-Dossiers, nr. 358, Correspondentie Oost-Afrika 1891–1892, Letter NAHV to Ministry of Foreign Affairs, 10-03-1892.

[123] Ibidem.

[124] Ibidem, Letter Gericke van Herwijnen to Ministry of Foreign Aiffairs, 18-04-1892.

[125] Idem, Nr. 207, Congo-aangelegenheden I en II, Letter Gericke van Herwijnen to Ministry of Foreign Affairs, 03-03-1891.

[126] Ibidem, Letter Gericke van Herwijnen to Ministry of Foreign Affairs, 10-04-1891.

[127] Ibidem.

example, the Dutch representative in Lisbon wrote that he would start negotiations over a potential concession for the NAHV in northern Angola.[128] He however also indicated that, given the protectionist instincts of the Portuguese, this was still rather uncertain.

In the meantime, relations with the Congo Free State had reached a low point, both in public and in private. Yet behind the scenes, negotiations between the Dutch and the Congo Free State continued. In 1891, the NAHV offered to transport the body of a Belgian general killed in battle, which helped to improve the relationship.[129] Following the Acts of the Brussels Anti-Slavery Conference, new import tariffs still had to be negotiated between the main colonial powers, which also took a while: in the meantime, the NAHV had to deal with significant uncertainty over the outcome. The French Parliament for example blocked proposals in June 1891 for fear of losing control over the import tariffs, and once this was smoothed out, the Portuguese held up ratification of the Acts over fears of losing revenues in early 1892.[130] In April 1892, the Congo Free State published plans for new import tariffs, which were again opposed by the NAHV: on 18 April, Gericke van Herwijnen wrote that *Daumas Béraud & Cie* had been taken over by a Belgian firm (SAB) to avoid the tariffs.[131] In the same month, the Congo Free State and the French Congo came to an agreement for cross-border trade, setting foreign firms at a disadvantage.[132] Still, this did not end the uncertainty, as the NAHV for example complained in October 1892 about the lack of clarity about which commodities were included in the agreement, and against which tariff.[133]

Once the uncertainty was finally solved after lengthy negotiations in 1892, the years 1893 to 1898 were years of rebuilding and reforming for the NAHV.[134] Greshoff, newly settled in Brazzaville, could not resist a further public fight with Leopold and wrote some heated pamphlets and

[128] Idem, Nr. 215, Handelsbelangen in de Congostaat 1890–1894, Letter Gericke van Herwijnen to Ministry of Foreign Affairs, 19-10-1892.

[129] Idem, Nr. 206, Congo-aangelegenheden 1885–1894, Letter NAHV to Congo Free State, 11-06-1891 & Letter NAHV to Ministry of Foreign Affairs, 12-06-1891.

[130] Idem, nr. 358, Correspondentie Oost-Afrika 1891–1892, Letter Gericke van Herwijnen to Ministry of Foreign Affairs, 12-11-1891 & Letter NAHV to Gericke van Herwijnen, 10-03-1892.

[131] Ibidem, Letters Gericke van Herwijnen to Ministry of Foreign Affairs, 13-04-1892 & 18-04-1892.

[132] Ibidem.

[133] Ibidem, Letter Minister of Foreign Affairs to NAHV & OAC, 22-10-1892.

[134] Van der Laan, 'Trading in the Congo', 241–242.

letters in 1893 against Leopold for his failure to combat the slave trade. Despite this public spat, the NAHV was allowed, after a confidential letter dated 31 January 1893, to remain in the Congo Free State after an agreement had been reached.[135] Through the agreement, the NAHV was circumscribed in where it could trade, as Leopold declared several territories (such as the Crown Domain) off-limits for private firms. This led to new disputes over the property rights of the NAHV, as well as the question where the NAHV was allowed to set up new factories.[136] This problem would dominate relations between the NAHV and the state for the years to come: in 1895, for example, Greshoff wrote that he wanted to expand NAHV's presence in the Kasaï area, but this was not allowed by the state's administration.[137] To push the NAHV into submission, the Congo Free State played up a new dispute over the flag of the NAHV's steamers: Greshoff wrote on 30 October 1893 that he was saddened to see that such would arise a question again.[138] The issue was eventually resolved in 1894.

In 1894, the NAHV was finally allowed to set up a factory in the Luebo in the Kasaï in 1894.[139] In the same year, the Dutch navy ship *Wilhelmina* was allowed to dock in the port of Banana, indicating better relations. Moreover, Greshoff was allowed again to enter the Congo Free State, and his diplomatic credentials were restored that year (Greshoff nevertheless remained based in Brazzaville). Privately, Greshoff continued to rail against Leopold: in letters to Stanley, he argued that the Belgians had made a basic mistake by allying in the first place with the Arabs, who would always turn against them.[140] This was, of course, also a deliberate ploy by Greshoff, as the NAHV sought the help of the Arabs to get their hands on ivory at this point as well.[141] In 1895, the battle over control of

[135] NL-HaNA, Archief NAHV, nr. 364, Various Files, Letter Congo Free State to NAHV, 31-01-1893.

[136] De Roo, 'The Trouble with Tariffs', 10–14.

[137] NL-HaNA, Archief NAHV, nr. 664, Concessions/Terrains 1894/1901, Letters Greshoff to Congo Free State, 09-10-1895.

[138] NL-HaNA, Ministerie van Buitenlandse Zaken A-Dossiers, nr. 206, Congo-aangelegenheden 1885–1894, Letter Greshoff to Ministry of Foreign Affairs, 30-10-1893: "tot mijn leedwezen zie ik mij genoodzaakt mij tot uwe excellentie te wenden, wegens eene nieuwe vlaggen-kwestie met de ambtenaren van den Congo-Staat."

[139] Martens, 'A History', 112.

[140] BE-AMT, Stanley Archives, nrs. 1070–1073, Letters Greshoff to Stanley, 25-10-1893, 16-06-1894, 09-07-1894, 06-08-1894 & 06-08-1894.

[141] Vangroenweghe, *Voor rubber en ivoor*, 33–80.

Table 4.2 Exports of ivory and rubber from the Congo Free State, 1892–1900

	Ivory		*Rubber*	
Year	*Kilograms*	*Value in francs*	*Tons*	*Value in francs*
1892	186,521	3,730,420	156.34	625,356
1893	185,933	3,718,660	241.15	964,612
1894	252,083	5,041,660	338.19	1,472,944
1895	292,232	5,844,640	576.52	2,882,585
1896	191,316	3,826,320	1317.35	6,586,730
1897	245,824	4,916,480	1662.38	8,311,900
1898	215,963	4,319,260	2113.46	15,850,987
1899	291,731	5,834,620	3746.79	28,100,917
1900	262,665	5,253,300	5316.53	39,874,005

Source: Marechal, *De Arabische Campagne*, 282, based on Waltz, *Das Konzessionswesen*, 8–9

ivory came to a head with the Stokes Affair.[142] Unsurprisingly, Greshoff also used the Stokes Affair as evidence of Leopold's bad character, particularly as the NAHV continued to have problems with establishing new factories in the Kasaï.[143] 1895 saw various other developments, including the Belgian loan to the Congo Free State and start of large-scale rubber exports.[144]

The battle for control over ivory, particularly from the inner eastern regions of the Congo Free State, thus remained a major point of contention.[145] As Tables 4.2 and 4.3 show, the Congo Free State, following the conclusion of the Congo-Arab War, was able to consolidate state control over ivory and rubber, and crucially its taxation. To add to the misery of the NAHV, the Congo Free State had temporarily confiscated several of the NAHV's smaller steamers as well for use in the Congo-Arab War against Tippo Tip.[146] In this way, the NAHV did not only exploit the

[142] Ibidem, 149–268.

[143] BE-AMT, Stanley Archives, nr. 1077 & 1078, Letters Greshoff to Stanley, 02-08-1895 & 03-08-1895.

[144] Vanthemsche, *Belgian and the Congo*, 188; A-J. Wauters, *L'État indépendant du Congo* (Brussels 1899), 391–396.

[145] Ceulemans, *La question arabe*, 169–170; Harms, *Land of Tears*, 320–321; Marchal, *L'État libre* (Vol. 1), 129–131; Renault, *Tippo Tip*, 195–196; Wilkinson, *The Arabs*, 311.

[146] Marchal, *L'État libre* (Vol. 1), 277 & 296. I thank an anonymous peer reviewer for pointing this out.

Table 4.3 Congo Free State income from ivory and rubber taxation, 1892–1900

Year	*Income in francs*
1892	4,355,776
1893	4,683,272
1894	6,514,604
1895	8,727,225
1896	10,413,050
1897	13,228,380
1898	20,170,247
1899	33,935,537
1900	45,127,305

Source: Marechal, *De Arabische Campagne*, 284

empire of others, but its assets were also used to aid the conquest of the remainder of the Congo Free State.

The only way for the NAHV to retain relevancy in the Congo Free State was trade in the Kasaï. In 1896, supported by SAB, the NAHV won a legal victory against the Congo Free State and thus was allowed free trade access to the Kasaï region.[147] The SAB and NAHV promised to work together, a solution blessed by the NAHV directors and Leopold but opposed by Greshoff, who hardened in his opposition to Leopold.[148] Immediately, the NAHV was granted several concessions close to Leopoldville (present-day Kinshasa), such as Kisende and Ibanche.[149] The NAHV paid 5000 francs to the Congo Free State for the lease of those territories, to gain a so-called *droit de licence*. By allying with SAB and creating a joint venture, a legal fiction was created that guaranteed at least half of the shares were 'Belgian', but was (in reality) run by the NAHV with some profits flowing to the SAB. More good news followed, as the NAHV won a major contract with the French colonial administration in

[147] Vos, 'The Economics of the Kwango Rubber Trade, c. 1900', in: Heintze & A. Von Oppen (eds.), *Angola on the Move: Transport Routes, Communications and History* (Frankfurt am Main 2008), 85–98, there 90.

[148] NL-HaNA, Archief NAHV, nr. 664, Concessions/Terrains 1894/1901, Letters Congo Free State to De Bloeme, 29-02-1896 & 06-03-1896.

[149] Ibidem, Agreement between Congo Free State and NAHV, *sine dato*; Letter Thys & Van Eetvelde to NAHV, 21-02-1896.

Loango, in the French Congo, for transport of commodities to Brazzaville.[150]

One problem the NAHV encountered was a public fight with Stanley, who wrote a piece in *The Times* defending Leopold and allegedly attacking Greshoff. Both Greshoff and De Bloeme wrote angry letters to Stanley. De Bloeme for example wrote that "While advocating the Belgians was it necessary to blame the Dutch? I fancy to believe it was not at all. [...] As to the hostile feelings towards the State, which you ascribe us, I must positively deny their existence. On the contrary, our Company is on the most friendly footing with the State, since a long time already."[151] In the end, Stanley apologised for any misunderstanding to the NAHV. In January 1897, even Greshoff called Leopold a friend in a letter to Stanley, indicating that the relationship was back on track.[152]

Being on good terms with the Congo Free State, as well as the French and Portuguese administrations, opened up new opportunities for the NAHV. In April 1898, a new conference on tariffs was convened by Leopold, who only invited the major colonial powers holding territory in Africa, annoying the excluded Dutch and Italians: after some considerations, the Dutch were allowed to send two experts and a diplomat (De Pestel) to observe the conference.[153] Next to a reform of the import tariffs, a more major reform took place after 1898: the restructuring of most colonial economies from a relatively free trade area to a system of monopolistic concessions. With the Congo Free State having such companies since 1892, the years 1898 and 1899 marked the years the system was more widely applied there, as well as in the French Congo.[154] For the NAHV, this would usher in another phase of entrepreneurial challenges.

[150] Idem, Nr. 660, Correspondence about Loango Transport, 1896.

[151] BE-AMT, Stanley Archives, nr. 1103, Correspondence Stanley with De Bloeme, September-October 1896, Letter De Bloeme to Stanley, 10-10-1896.

[152] Idem, Letter Greshoff to Stanley, 22-01-1897.

[153] NL-HaNA, Ministerie van Buitenlandse Zaken A-Dossiers, nr. 359, Correspondentie Oost-Afrika 1893–1906, Letter Ministry of Foreign Affairs to Leopold II, 01-03-1898.

[154] Idem, Letter Jonkheer de Pestel to Ministry of Foreign Affairs, 14-07-1898.

4.4 Dutch Entrepreneurship in West (Central) Africa, 1880–1898

Bearing in mind the same reservations expressed previously about the reliability of the data assembled, the numbers for the 1880s and 1890s are both slightly more reliable and, crucially, more complete than in the previous chapter. Graph 4.2 shows an overview of the general imports and exports between the Netherlands and 'West Africa' (which included West Central Africa), indicating that the Netherlands always had a substantial trading deficit with Africa over the period 1879–1898. Exported commodities from the Dutch side were primarily alcohol, with cotton manufactures also playing an important role. Most other export commodities were rather insignificant in terms of its value.

When looking at the imports, it is clear that palm oil remained a major commodity of African export commodities. However, as Graph 4.3 shows, both peanuts and palm nut kernels also became more important as the 1880s progressed. Except for a short-term revival of palm oil imports in 1896, both commodities eventually became more important when looked at by value in guilders, surpassing palm oil around 1891–1892. As the statistics lump together West and West Central Africa, it is impossible to judge how much came from the Congo Basin area and how much from Liberia and Elmina, although it is likely on the basis of the qualitative

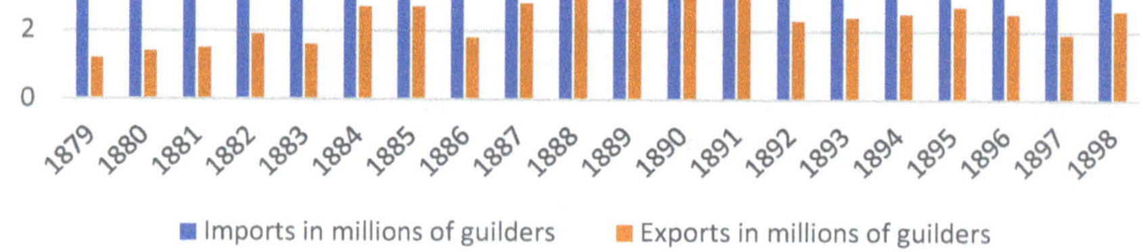

Graph 4.2 Imports and exports from and to West Africa, 1879–1898, in millions of guilders. (Source: *Jaarcijfers van het Koninkrijk der Nederlanden. Rijk in Europa* (1882–1899))

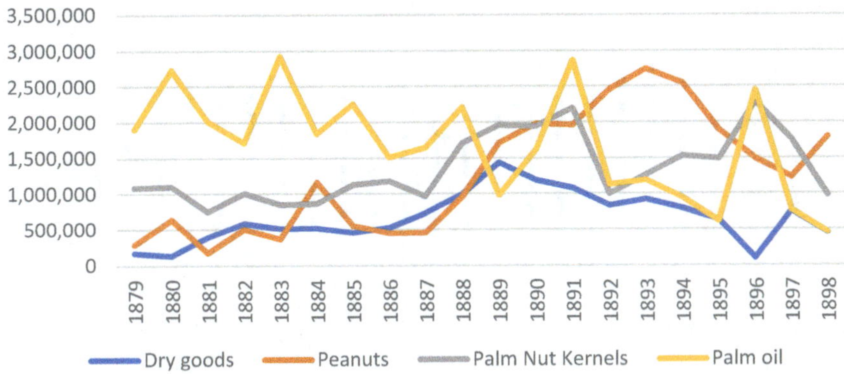

Graph 4.3 Major commodities imported from West Africa, 1879–1898, in guilders. (Source: *Statistiek van den handel en de scheepvaart* (1847–1918), later *Statistiek van den in- uit- en doorvoer)*

evidence presented in the previous pages that it concerns mostly commodities from the Congo Basin.

Graphs 4.4, 4.5 and 4.6 show the total imports of palm oil, peanuts and palm nut kernels into the Netherlands and the share of West Africa in the total. Like the diminishing importance of palm oil as a commodity bought in West Africa, the share of palm oil from West Africa as a percentage also dropped significantly in these decades: in 1891, some 40% of palm oil imports still came from West Africa; by 1898, this had dropped to only 5%. Palm oil plantations in the Dutch East Indies were developing quickly in the 1890s, replacing West Africa as a main source (for the production) of palm oil. Given its importance as both a lubricant and in powering machines in early industrialisation, demand may have outstripped supply, leading to a search for new sites of production. This was found across the Dutch East Indies as the Dutch imperial state actively incorporated new territories across the area. Many of the newly incorporated islands allowed the Dutch to develop palm oil plantations.[155]

West Africa in this period turned into the main area where the Dutch obtained peanuts. By 1891, 80% of peanut imports came from West Africa, steadily rising throughout the previous decade and remaining some 70–80% of the source for imports. Palm nut kernels, the original

[155] Lindblad, 'Economische aspecten', 242.

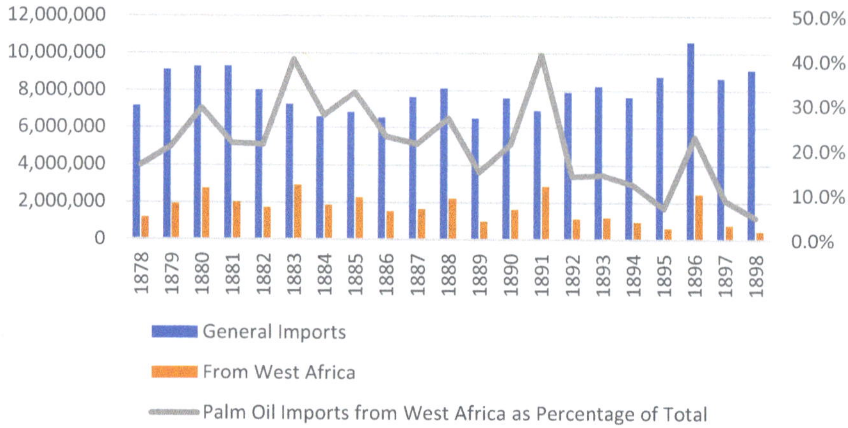

Graph 4.4 Palm oil imports into the Netherlands 1878–1898, in guilders. (Source: *Statistiek van den handel en de scheepvaart* (1847–1918), later *Statistiek van den in- uit- en doorvoer*)

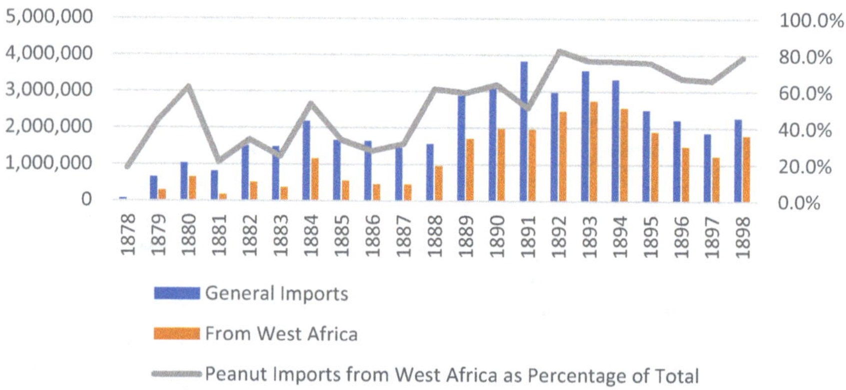

Graph 4.5 Peanut imports into the Netherlands 1878–1898, in guilders. (Source: *Statistiek van den handel en de scheepvaart* (1847–1918), later *Statistiek van den in- uit- en doorvoer*)

commodity of palm oil, saw an absolute rise in imports but a relative decline, suffering from the same logic as palm oil. Having said that, West Africa remained an import supplier for roughly 40% of the total imports across the 1880s and 1890s, suggesting that whilst palm oil production

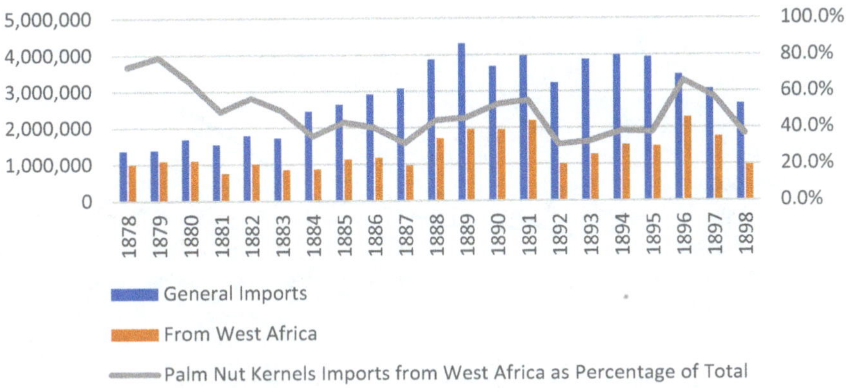

Graph 4.6 Palm nut kernel imports into the Netherlands 1878–1898, in guilders. (Source: *Statistiek van den handel en de scheepvaart* (1847–1918), later *Statistiek van den in- uit- en doorvoer*)

became less important in West Africa (as other areas, for example the Dutch East Indies, outcompeted West Africa for palm oil production), the agricultural production of palm nuts remained competitive enough, allowing actual refining in Europe or for it to be used for different purposes.

Graph 4.7 shows exports from the Congo Free State for the limited years 1888–1897, statistics drawn up by Wauters in his book on the origins of the Congo Free State. Given Wauters' reputation for defending Leopold II brutal regime in the Congo Free State,[156] these statistics should be treated with even more care than the previous graphs. However, it interestingly shows that exports to the Netherlands were significantly larger than all the other export directions combined, including Belgium or Britain up to 1891. This indicates that the NAHV was the major player in the Congo Free State, even as Leopold II increasingly started to make life difficult for firms like the NAHV. Only after the Brussels Anti-Slavery Conference of 1891, when Leopold was allowed to establish export tariffs to (purportedly) combat the slave trade, the share of exports to the Netherlands dropped in favour of exports to Belgium, as Belgian firms were made more competitive by (indirect) state support in the forms of tariffs on firms importing and exporting not to or from Belgium.[157]

[156] Wauters, *L'État Indépendant*; De Roo, 'De Onafhankelijke Congostaat', 32.
[157] De Roo, 'The Trouble with Tariffs', 10–14.

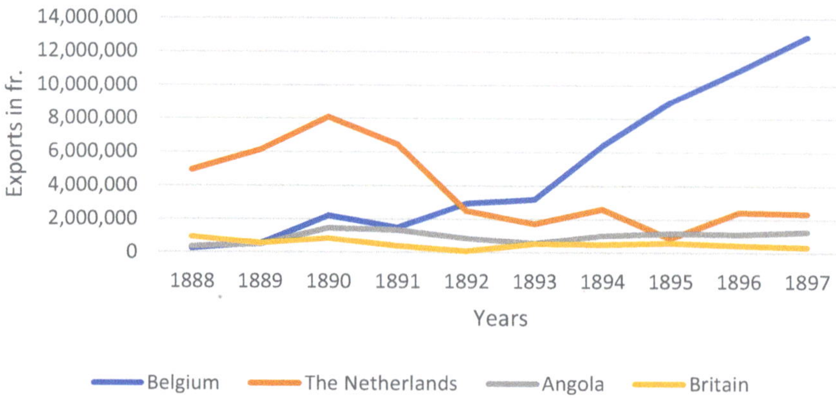

Graph 4.7 Exports from the Congo Free State (in fr.), 1888–1897. (Source: Wauters, *L'État Indépendant du Congo*, 484)

Table 4,4 Import of gum into Rotterdam, 1889–1894, in kilograms

Product	*1889*	*1890*	*1891*	*1892*	*1893*	*1894*
Congothimbles	485,000	425,000	375,000	330,000	320,000	
Congothimbles (black)	20,000	14,000	17,500	13,000	7,000	
Congo balls	43,500	55,000	57,500	54,000	40,000	
Congo [...]	0	0	0	0	8,000	
Benguela [...]	55,000	35,500	46,500	52,000	42,000	
Loanda [...]	33,500	1,500	4,500	20,000	9,000	
Mozambique ballen	26,700	5,800	17,500	13,500	4,500	1,800
Mozambique spoeltjes	16,300	4,200	13,500	6,500	6,500	1,800
Total	680,000	541,000	532,000	489,000	437,000	3,600

Source: *Jaaroverzichten van den handel in koloniale producten 1891–1895*

Finally, Table 4.4 shows the import of gum into Rotterdam, which was made possible by go-betweens in Rotterdam's port estimating imports.[158] It shows that after 1894, when the NAHV left the Congo Free State, the import of gum from the area fell sharply, although a clear downward trend is already visible after 1889. This corroborates the evidence shown in

[158] In the original source, offensive language is used. I have used [...] where the n-word is explicitly used in the source to indicate a certain type of rubber.

Graph 4.7, showing a similar downward trend of imports from the Congo Free State, but also a downward trend of Angolan gum.

Seen in the light of the three entrepreneurial processes (first, envisioning and valuing opportunities; second, allocating and reconfiguring resources; and third, legitimising novelty), the Dutch entrepreneurs were able to envision new opportunities (and to an extent value them) when they hit roadblocks, as for example happened in the Congo Free State between 1885 and 1892. Faced with an increasingly difficult and hostile imperial state, the Dutch entrepreneurs looked elsewhere for new opportunities. This was a mixed bag: in Angola, the old problems with the imperial authorities remained present (primarily over tariffs, not unlike the Congo Free State) and hampered the ability to operate a profitable and substantial business.

In the French Congo, in contrast, the Dutch entrepreneurs slowly but steadily built on their previous presence and managed a working relationship with the French imperial authorities. The fact that the NAHV was Dutch, and therefore *not* British or German, helped in neutralising a potential bad attitude on behalf of the French. As the next chapter shows, the broad geographical reach of NAHV factories in the French Congo and the relatively good relationships made it possible for the Dutch entrepreneurs to bid for concessions, something that could have been possible only if the blueprints had been laid in the 1880s and 1890s. The French imperial authorities, in notable contrast to Leopold's Congo Free State, were more reliable regarding the safeguarding of property rights and sticking to their word, even if the French also raised import tariffs during the 1890s. For the Dutch entrepreneurs, the opportunity in the French Congo was seen and valued. Moreover, the Dutch entrepreneurs acted on this by shifting resources (in particular, their high-performing agents as well as Greshoff) to the French Congo. Yet, the 'pivot' to the French Congo was never complete. The Dutch entrepreneurs never left the Congo Free State and, perhaps against their better judgement, remained operative in the parts of the Congo Free State that were not closed off to private entrepreneurs. Their bet on allying with Tippu Tip was initially successful as the military power combined with the NAHV's entrepreneurial reach in the Eastern Congo Free State worked well from the perspective of trade. However, after the defeat in the Congo-Arab War of 1892–1894, the Congo Free State's army gradually started to get a grip on the more remote regions of the state, and the state was able to tax the ivory trade more effectively, diminishing the profitability and grip of the Dutch entrepreneurs.

Regarding the first two processes, the Dutch entrepreneurs may thus have been moderately successful—but with important caveats, in particular concerning their ongoing attempts to remain relevant in the Congo Free State, and their inability to create a lasting, profitable trade in Angola. The Dutch entrepreneurs may have misjudged the political challenges that became associated with operating in a colonial environment and in the 'empire of others', even if they appeared to learn from their mistakes in the Congo Free State (and Angola) to build a better relationship with the French imperial authorities. The challenges and opportunities for the NAHV also needed to be reflected in both the make-up of the directors, and in the type of firm it was. In the 1880s, after the NAHV was resurrected after Pincoffs' fraud, a new group of entrepreneurs entered the story, who did not come from the small Rotterdam inner circle that had dominated the Rotterdam-Africa trade since the 1850s. Most of these men worked their way up from agent in Africa, as was the case for Andries de Bloeme. In 1888, Muller Szn. retired as NAHV director, citing disagreements with his co-directors De Bloeme and Schalkwijk, indicating that the baton was passed to a new generation at this time.[159] After all, Muller Szn. had been at the apex of power in 1883, when he was simultaneously director of *Muller & Co*, the NAHV and the OAC. Slowly but gradually, the older Muller was pushed aside by his sons or by a new generation of former agents. The 1880s were thus crucial in the transition from a family firm, based on a number of close-knit families of entrepreneurs from Rotterdam, to a new situation in which experience became more crucial.

These developments also had a crucial impact on the legal and financial basis of the firms. The NAHV moved from a small-scale family firm as the AHV to a firm drawing outside investment, and having a merit-based system of promotion. Moreover, it became a major diplomatic and political actor as well, in the wake of the many proposals of the Congo Free State to hike import tariffs: in 1886 De Bloeme, later director of the NAHV in Rotterdam, assembled a 'coalition of the willing' to oppose the proposed import tariffs as chief agent in Banana, and Greshoff established himself as one of the crucial Europeans in the Congo basin, even if his operations could not necessarily be considered tactful. In contrast to the NAHV, *Muller & Co* in Liberia essentially remained operative in the 1880s and 1890s as it did before, as a small-scale family firm with a number of agents

[159] Muller, *Muller*, 387.

and only five or six factories in the coastal areas. The circumstances in and context of Liberia, one of the few places not colonised by Europeans, did apparently not necessitate the envisioning of new opportunities, or the reallocation of resources in any substantial way. This lack of innovation, eventually, came to haunt *Muller & Co*, as it became loss-making by the 1890s when faced with lower prices and greater competition on the world market.

For both *Muller & Co* and the NAHV, the third element of the entrepreneurial processes, the legitimising of novelty, was the least successful part. *Muller & Co* essentially continued as it did in the palm oil trade, and a diversification into rubber was short-lived and unsuccessful. The NAHV tried to diversify in other ways—by seeking new markets, by trying to integrate backwards and to increasingly control production in the inner parts of the Congo basin, but never was a leader in terms of 'legitimising novelty'. Even if the NAHV was an early participant in the rubber trade from Angola and the Kasaï, it did not do much to market its applications in Europe. In this sense, as had been the case for the AHV, the NAHV did mostly follow trends on the world market, rather than making those trends.

4.5 Conclusion

The 1880s and 1890s were a time of significant change in Africa, partly as a consequence of well-known events like the Partition of Africa that had a major impact on Africa's economic, political and social trajectory. However, European imperialism also changed the game for European entrepreneurs who had already been established in Africa for some time, as was the case for the Dutch entrepreneurs: the last two decades of the nineteenth century forced them to reckon with unprecedented changes, and in the case of the NAHV this meant that the firm was, by 1899, basically unrecognisable to the agents who had been employed by the AHV when it went bankrupt in 1879. The small-scale family firm, run by a small circle of families and entrepreneurs, was gone: the NAHV was by 1899 one of West Central Africa's largest firms, professionally run by a number of experienced agents in Rotterdam, a relatively well-run transport line from and to Europe, and experienced in dealing with various colonial administrations. These changes in a timespan of twenty years were impressive, but largely the consequence of the circumstances, as *Muller & Co* for example remained largely the same firm it was in 1899 as it was in 1879, even if its name changed in 1893.

The 1880s and 1890s necessitated the Dutch entrepreneurs to learn how to operate in the 'empire of others': as these empires were colonising and learning to govern a colonial population at the same time, reliable institutions and secure property rights could not be counted upon. Next to pure 'economic' challenges for the Dutch entrepreneurs, the political and diplomatic challenges may therefore have been even greater. The Dutch entrepreneurs navigated this with mixed success, and were frequently outmanoeuvred by imperial authorities, in particular in the Congo Free State. Yet their decision to remain in the Congo Free State also meant the Dutch entrepreneurs assumed a degree of *complicity* in the establishment, maintenance and expansion of the empire. The expansion of the Dutch entrepreneurs across West and West Central Africa helped them in eventually diversifying their business model, but also made them vulnerable to co-optation by the empires to further their goals. The gradual closing of the gap between the *political* and *economic* interests also facilitated the rise of larger, capitalistic firms. The NAHV, in this sense, adapted to these circumstances quite well and was therefore well prepared for the system of the concession companies that would be developed in the early decades of the twentieth century. Chapter 5 turns to this era of the concession companies and analyses the role Dutch entrepreneurs played in this system of 'colonial capitalism'.

CHAPTER 5

Dutch Entrepreneurship in the Era of the Concession Companies (1899–1921)

5.1 Introduction

The era of the concession companies presented a new saga in European imperialism in Africa. As argued in Chap. 2, the era of the concession companies should be considered as the moment when the *political* interests of the Partition and the *economic* interests of the Scramble joined forced, to develop a repressive, monopolistic and capitalist system that Hopkins termed 'colonial capitalism'.[1] Whereas most studies of the concession companies focus on specific concessions in specific territories, this chapter emphasises the importance of cross-imperial ties, as made evident by the role that Dutch entrepreneurs played. The chapter demonstrates how the Dutch entrepreneurs adapted to the new demands of the system through trial and error, eventually contributing to a highly repressive and extractive system. Moreover, it shows the strong international and cross-imperial dimension of Dutch capital investments across Africa, as the Dutch entrepreneurs invested across five different imperial entities in West and West Central Africa in the period between 1899 and 1914 (Liberia, Portuguese Angola, Congo Free State/Belgian Congo, French Congo and later also German Cameroon).

Similar to the previous chapter, the focus is mostly on the activities of the NAHV, the (by far) largest Dutch firm operating on the West coast of

[1] Hopkins, *Capitalism in the Colonies.*

G. Dreijer, *Private Entrepreneurship and European Imperialism*, Palgrave Studies in Economic History,
https://doi.org/10.1007/978-3-032-01086-5_5

the African continent. However, the operations of the *Oost-Afrikaansche Compagnie* (OAC) in Liberia were still also part and parcel of the Dutch investments in the region, in particular as the firm left Mozambique in 1905 after having failed to obtain a concession there, and the firm decided to focus solely on Liberia.[2] Following the pivot away from the Congo Free State after 1892, the NAHV focused primarily on the French Congo. Until 1910, the NAHV retained some trading interest in Angola, where protectionism prevented the NAHV from gaining a concession. In the French Congo, the NAHV (co-)participated in various concession companies, sometimes on its own and sometimes in a consortium with French investors, to safeguard their investments and property rights after the experiences the firm had in the Congo Free State.

Meanwhile, the NAHV was unwilling to leave the Congo Free State for good, and remained operative in the Kasaï region, where free trade was allowed until the end of the nineteenth century. Breaking promises to protect free trade (again), Leopold II forced the NAHV (alongside other firms) to take part in the so-called *Compagnie du Kasaï* (CdK) in 1900–1901, against the wishes of most of these private investors.[3] However, this was the sole opportunity for the Dutch entrepreneurs to remain active in the Congo Free State. Next to the activities in the CdK, the NAHV was able to invest as a minor, often silent partner in a number of (largely unsuccessful) ventures across the Congo Free State. Since the sources for the NAHV's participation in the CdK are (comparatively) plentiful, this story is told in a separate Chap. 6: the other investments in the Congo Free State are analysed in this chapter.

5.2 The OAC in Liberia (1899–1921)

The OAC did reap some results from the merger with *Muller & Co* after 1892–1893. Profits rose in conjunction with the recovery of the world market after the price crisis for agricultural commodities in the 1880s, but soon fell back. After this short-lived efflorescence, profits dropped again, and in 1905, the OAC finally decided to leave Mozambique and focus solely on Liberia.[4] Ironically, the firm kept its name (East Africa Company) while trading in Liberia and, in the 1910s, also in Nigeria, although it

[2] Van den Berg, 'Hendrik Pieter Nicolaas Muller', 83.

[3] Martens, 'A History', 233–302.

[4] Muller, *Muller*, 353.

appears that some products were exported under the name of the firm *Muller & Co*, which only existed in name after the passing of Muller Szn.[5] According to documents from 1914 and 1915 (among the few left for the years after 1905), the OAC still made a reasonable profit despite the outbreak of the First World War and the sinking of a ship.[6] Moreover, despite their promise to leave Mozambique, it still kept a number of buildings it rented out to Dutchmen operating in Mozambique.[7] In 1921, the OAC would eventually merge with the NAHV to create one large Dutch firm operating across West and West Central Africa.[8]

In a sense, the OAC after 1905 essentially went back to its core function by trading in agricultural commodities like palm oil and, increasingly, rubber, from its base in Liberia. In marked contrast to the NAHV, the firm appears to have stuck to its core as a trading firm in agricultural commodities. Part of this was the result of its geographical focus, as Liberia as one of the few independent African states did not develop as a colonial state with repressive, large-scale 'colonial capitalism': its economy remained dependent on small-scale agricultural production, much like many of Africa's economies before the advent of European imperialism.[9] Whereas in Mozambique the firm tried to obtain various concessions, it lacked the capital requirements, political contacts and/or support, and the importance to be considered to administer large swathes of land. In Liberia, this large-scale capitalist competition was lacking, as most Europeans opted to focus elsewhere.[10]

In terms of its organisational structure, its relatively small-scale trade in agricultural commodities meant that no significant changes were necessary over the years. In its transition from *Muller & Co* to the OAC, the firm essentially remained a private family firm controlled by a small number of shareholders and financiers. Even if the *volume* of trade appears to have risen, the firm retained its core characteristics and strategies, including sailing ships, limited capital investments in Africa itself and a small number of

[5] Van den Berg, 'Hendrik Pieter Nicolaas Muller', 83; Muller, *Muller*, 353.

[6] NL-SAR, Archief Chabot, nr. 1199, Stukken betreffende de Oost-Afrikaansche Compagnie, Report OAC over 1914, p. 3.

[7] Ibidem, p. 7. In 1914, the OAC still had properties worth 114.392 guilders in Mozambique.

[8] Muller, *Muller*, 354; Van der Laan, 'Trading in the Congo'.

[9] Gardner, *Sovereignty without Power*, 20–29.

[10] Ibidem.

agents on the ground in Liberia.[11] This marks an interesting contrast with the NAHV, which transitioned due to the changing circumstances on the ground from a similar small-scale family firm to a large-scale capitalist investor in some twenty to twenty-five years. Dutch entrepreneurship in Liberia therefore did not change much in fifty years of presence.

5.3 The NAHV in Angola: Minor Activities in Plantation Economy (1899–1910)

In a sense, the operations in terms of scope or scale of the NAHV in Angola were comparable to those of the OAC in Liberia. Angola had long been dependent on the slave trade and slave labour and therefore did not have a very diversified economy. Once it finally diversified as a result of the transition to the legitimate commerce, the 1880s and 1890s in northern Angola were characterised by a rubber boom. Rubber production in Angola preceded the boom in the Congo Free State and French Congo by some thirty years, with the first production known in 1867 in the Kongo Kingdom.[12] The peak of rubber exports from Angola can be situated in 1898–1899, with a steady decline afterwards.[13] In contrast to many other regions in Africa, no particularly exploitative institutions were developed to extract rubber: under the Umbundu king Ekwikwi, a system of relatively free production existed, with much of the rubber also transported to the northern part of the Congo river.[14] Therefore, the regime of property rights also differed, as much of the production was in the hands of Africans, in contrast to the forced labour production, and later the plantations, that would boom in the Congo Free State and French Congo under the concession system. Leopold argued that the so-called *capitas* were illegal traders who crossed the Angolan-Congo Free State border with rubber, but in fact, they acted as they always did, having long served as important brokers and middlemen in the area.[15]

As the rubber boom faded, the Angolese colonial authorities sought new ways to provide revenue. In contrast to Mozambique, as the previous

[11] Muller, *Muller*, 340–354.

[12] Vos, 'The Economics', 86.

[13] J. Ball, 'A "Time of Clothes": The Angolan Rubber Boom, 1886–1902, *Ufahumu: A Journal of African Studies*, 28, 1 (2000), 25–42, https://doi.org/10.5070/F7281016584, there 36.

[14] Ibidem, 25.

[15] Vos, 'The Economics', 95.

section indicated, Angola however started allowing concessions only by the late 1910s, particularly in mining. Da Silva and Neves argued that the settler-capitalist nature of Angola did not particularly induce agricultural development on a large scale, thus favouring other investments like infrastructure.[16] Foreign investment did flow in, particularly in building the Benguela railway, which was largely financed by British and Belgian capital provided by the Belgian investor Albert Thys.[17] With better transport connections, the northern Angolan frontier area became more integrated into the regional economy, diminishing smuggling.[18] Despite better integration into the world economy, the colonial authorities (particularly after the Portuguese took possession of São Salvador in 1888) remained largely dependent on high tariffs and taxes on commerce for their revenues, driving away most foreign firms, including (eventually) the NAHV.[19] Moreover, the continuing use of forced labour following slavery's abolition did not help in attracting British and Dutch firms to the area.[20]

The NAHV during the late nineteenth century and early twentieth century made modest inroads into Angola. The NAHV for example had opened a factory in Ango-Ango in 1885 following the one in Luanda in 1879, in addition to the coastal factories it already owned since the late 1850s and early 1860s.[21] From the start, problems surrounding tariffs plagued Dutch investments in Angola, and this continued in the twentieth century. In January 1903, the head agent of the firm in Luanda, Van der Most, for example wrote to the Portuguese Governor in Angola to request a partial return of the taxes the NAHV had paid.[22] The NAHV moreover requested to set up large-scale plantations in Angola, even submitting maps with detailed plans for the plantations.[23] This plan however appears to have never been approved by the colonial authorities. Otherwise, almost

[16] Da Silva & Neves, 'The Paradox of Nationality', 1630–1631.

[17] Pirio, 'Commerce, Industry, and Empire', 92–93 & 109–115. See for Thys; Vellut, 'Réseaux transnationaux dans l'économie politique du Congo Léopoldien, c. 1885–1910', in: L. Marfaing & B. Reinwald (eds.), *Afrikanische Beziehungen, Netzwerke und Räume* (Münster 2001), 131–146.

[18] Pirio, 'Commerce, Industry, and Empire', 160.

[19] Vos, *Kongo in the Age of Empire*, 51–52.

[20] NL-HaNA, Archief Buitenlandse Zaken A-Dossiers, nr. 361, Letter van der Staal to Minister of Foreign Affairs, 24-07-1909 & Various Documents 1912–1913.

[21] Vos, *Kongo in the Age of Empire*, 51–52.

[22] NL-HaNA, Archief NAHV, nr. 629, Letter Van der Most to Portuguese Governor-General 20-01-1893.

[23] Ibidem.

no archival evidence on the activities of the NAHV in Angola has survived after roughly 1900, indicating the NAHV focused primarily on the French Congo and the Congo Free State.

Later in 1903, the NAHV appears to have sought help from a man only named in the archives as Queriol. Queriol (full name Nuno de Freitas Queriol) had between 1893 and 1895 and briefly again in 1896 been Portugal's Governor in 'the Congo district', *in casu* the region north of the Congo river that Portugal formally claimed sovereignty over but was not acknowledged by other countries.[24] With the help of an agent called Francisco Ribeiro de Carvalho, the NAHV tried to persuade Queriol to help them to a concession, even if Queriol by this point had taken up a position in Mozambique under the Portuguese administration. In the letters, Queriol appeared to be willing to help, as long as the firm was incorporated in Portugal and its main investors were (at least on paper) Portuguese.[25] Although Queriol and NAHV director De Bloeme did sign a memorandum of understanding for a concession, it appears that eventually something held up the actual implementation of the agreement. It is likely that Queriol did not have the powers to push through such wide-ranging measures in Angola anymore, having moved to Mozambique, and the NAHV eventually never operated a proper concession in Angola. In 1910, the NAHV eventually quit Angola for good, citing the burden of taxes and tariffs.[26] The trading operations in Angola had steadily decreased in terms of value after 1903, and the remaining factories were sold to local firms.

In Angola, the NAHV retained a small-scale operation based on the trade in agricultural commodities. Whereas the NAHV made the transition in the Congo Free State and French Congo to a large-scale investor with various trade and transport operations on the side, this transition did not materialise in Angola. Without investments in large-scale infrastructural projects such as the Benguela railway and the opportunity to participate in concessions, and with Angola remaining a colony dependent on relatively small-scale agriculture, the NAHV in Angola remained in 1910 largely the firm it was when it first set up business in 1857–1858: a

[24] Idem, nr. 676, Letter Francisco Ribeiro de Carvalho to Van der Most, 11-11-1903. I thank Cátia Antunes for helping me to track Queriol in Portuguese documents. For Queriol, see: L. Ferin, 'Clima do Congo', *Revista portugueza: colonial e maritima*, 1, 2 (1897–1898), 665–672, there 671.

[25] Ibidem.

[26] Vos, *Kongo in the Age of Empire*, 59.

small-scale firm focused on the barter trade in agricultural commodities. In this regard, it was more similar to the OAC in Liberia than the NAHV in the Congo Free State and the French Congo after 1899.

5.4 The NAHV in the Congo Free State in the Era of Concessionary Companies

The situation in the Congo Free State was rather different. Partly due to the long entanglement with Leopold's administration and the central importance of the NAHV in the 1880s and 1890s, the situation in the Congo Free State played out in a very different way. The Congo Free State had been a pioneer in the concession system in 1892 with the establishment of the Crown Domain.[27] Soon after, one of the concession regions in the north was given to ABIR; in 1897, the region given in concession to *Anversoise* was also closed off to free enterprise. Leopold opted to use concession companies to promote economic 'development', and also used those companies to further strategic goals, such as to occupy the Katanga region through the *Comité Special du Katanga* public-private partnership, as a way to steep off Rhodes and the British.[28] The Congo Free State held substantial shares in all these companies.

The NAHV was in a difficult position to profit from these developments, or perhaps had put itself in a difficult position to do so. All of the concessionaires were vetted by the Congo Free State's administration, and judged on whether they were able to act in the best interests of the state. This was evidently not true for the NAHV. Even if the NAHV indicated interest in obtaining concessions in the north of the Congo Free State, it appears that the state's administration quickly made clear the Dutch entrepreneurs would not be considered.[29] The few options remaining for the NAHV were therefore minor and less profitable options in the Congo Free State (see Image 5.1 for an example of a factory kept). This primarily concerned the Kasaï, which remained one of the few free trading zones after 1892, even if by 1900 the Congo Free State's administration also *de facto* closed off this region as well with the establishment of the CdK.

[27] Vangroenweghe, *Leopold II en Kongo: het evenaarsdistrict en het Kroondomein, 1885–1908* (Bruges 1985).

[28] Ibidem; Idem, *Rood rubber*; Marchal, *L'État libre* (Vol. 1), 202–203.

[29] Marchal, *L'État libre* (Vol. 1), 202–203.

Image 5.1 NAHV factory in Coquilhatville (Mbandaka), Congo Free State, 1910–1925. (Source: Collectie Wereldmuseum, inv. Nr. TM 60032119, available via https://commons.wikimedia.org/wiki/File:COLLECTIE_TROPENMUSEUM_Een_kleine_groep_mannen_gezeten_voor_het_gebouw_van_de_Nieuwe_Afrikaansche_Handels_Vereeniging_TMnr_60032119_(corrected).jpg [Retrieved 10/04/2025])

Despite all the difficulties associated with operating in the Congo Free State, the NAHV managed to invest in two more firms active in the Congo Free State after 1900. First, it invested in 1904 in the *Société Générale de Procédes d'Extraction du Caoutchouc*, but this was mentioned only for this year, indicating it was a rather short-lived experiment.[30] Second, and more importantly, the NAHV set up a collaboration with the *Compagnie du Bruxelles pour le commerce du Haut Congo*, whose name was often shortened to *La Bruxelloise. La Bruxelloise* was not a concession company, but rather one of the firms operating in the small 'free' trading zone left in the Congo Free State, located mostly in the region running from the coast and the mouth of the Congo river to the hinterland between the Crown Domain and the ABIR concession. Not much is known about the firm, which was formed on 24 December 1900 and was, as its name implies, headquartered in Brussels.[31] *La Bruxelloise* sought to establish private rubber plantations, something proposed by Greshoff, who apparently kept good relations with the agents of *La Bruxelloise.* Although evidence is lacking, it may well have been possible that *La Bruxelloise* was set up with the NAHV's tacit (financial) backing to circumvent restrictions and pushback.

In July 1901, Greshoff proposed to the director of *La Bruxelloise* that the firm could use the Dutch factories in Muene-Kundi and Muene-Sita to set up a plantation there for rubber harvesting, arguing that formal Belgian ownership would help them circumvent the applicable rules. Just before this offer, the NAHV had received news that the Congo Free State's administration was planning to fine the NAHV for having established the two factories without permission, even if they had been the NAHV's property for at least twenty years at this point. This indeed happened later in 1902, as the state announced it would levy a high tariff on the trade from the factories, and also requested a share of the rubber produced there on the plantations as taxation *in natura*.[32] *La Bruxelloise* had bought four factories in the 'free trading area' from the NAHV earlier that year (Umangi, Krenghi, Muene-Kundi and Lulanga), and protested that the factories were not Dutch property any more (even if Dutch agents were still employed there). This was to no avail, and the fines remained in place. The fact that Dutch agents were employed does add to the suspicion that

[30] NL-HaNA, Archief NAHV, nr. 174, Annual Report NAHV 1902–1903.

[31] Idem, nr. 669, Draft Agreement *La Bruxelloise*, 20-11-1900.

[32] Ibidem, Letters Congo Free State to NAHV, 12-03-1902 & 21-03-1902.

La Bruxelloise was essentially a front for the NAHV to operate out of sight of the colonial administration.

In 1903, the cooperation between the two firms would go even further. According to an agreement signed in September 1903, the NAHV would invest 61,900 Belgian francs in *La Bruxelloise*, in return receiving the right to sell the commodities of *La Bruxelloise* on the wider European market, as well as a 10% ownership stake in the firm (consisting of 2000 shares).[33] De Bloeme and Philippi, the NAHV's two main directors at this point, signed the agreement on behalf of the NAHV: a Belgian named Marten Roos did so on behalf of *La Bruxelloise*. This agreement followed the gradual building of ties between the two firms, as the NAHV had already invested almost 57,230 francs into *La Bruxelloise* in November 1901. The NAHV negotiated an annual 4% dividend payment on the profits that *La Bruxelloise* would make. Later, the NAHV would buy an additional 1500 capital shares and 2500 dividend shares in *La Bruxelloise*. In the annual report for 1903–1904, the shares in *La Bruxelloise* are named, but were not allocated a value.[34] In 1911, the directors wrote in the annual report that they had sold their remaining shares in *La Bruxelloise*, indicating that the adventure had never been particularly successful. Not once did the value of the shares or a mention of dividend payment on profits by *La Bruxelloise* make the annual shareholder reports. The solution to set up a joint venture with a Belgian-owned firm may have allowed the NAHV to keep operating in the Congo Free State, yet *La Bruxelloise* turned out to be too small to make a substantial profit.

5.5 The NAHV in the French Congo: Chasing Natural Resources

The NAHV almost naturally got involved in the French concession system following its pivot towards the French Congo after 1892. Being Dutch was an advantage, as Belgian and Dutch capital interests were seen as less threatening than British or German capital interests: in short, in the French Congo, there was no 'liability of foreigness', but rather an advantage by coming from a state that harboured no imperial ambitions in

[33] Ibidem, Agreement NAHV & *La Bruxelloise*, 17-09-1903.
[34] Ibidem, nr. 174, Annual Report over 1903–1904.

Africa.[35] The NAHV directors, recognising this, thus sought connections with French capitalists, as one of the applicable rules for the concession system was that a concession company would have its legal seat and headquarters in France. The NAHV therefore set up a holding company headquartered in Paris, named *La Brazzaville*, to seek cooperation with French investors, allowing the holding company to bid for some of the forty-two French concessions that were announced and set up in 1899.[36]

The move by the Dutch entrepreneurs into the French Congo after 1892 did not come out of the blue. The NAHV already owned a number of factories across the area that would later become French Equatorial Africa (for an example see Image 5.2), with factories in the present-day Central African Republic, Gabon, Congo-Brazzaville and even Cameroon.[37] This wide geographical scope made the NAHV an attractive partner for the French colonial authorities, something the NAHV skilfully exploited. As its main agent in the French Congo, the NAHV appointed Victor Flachon, a Frenchman with extensive experience in Africa, and with good contacts with the French colonial authorities. Flachon did most of the lobbying in Paris to allow access for the NAHV in the French Congo, for which director Philippi promised a substantial renumeration as this was rather successful.[38] Moreover, being headquartered in Brazzaville after 1893, as well as the relatively good contacts Greshoff kept with the French Governor in the city (in notable opposition to his relationship with Leopold), allowed the NAHV to relatively safely invest in the French Congo without having to fear for sudden expropriation or other problems arising like had been the case in the Congo Free State.[39]

In general, foreign investment in the French concession companies was quite limited, as the significant majority of capital was invested by French banks (who, of course, may well have had foreign capital sources).[40] According to Coquery-Vidrovitch, De Brazza, the sometime 'explorer' and, by 1899, governor of the French Congo, established the concession system, recognised the value of having foreign investors on board,

[35] See e.g. Lubinski, 'Liability of Foreignness in Historical Context: German Business in Preindependence India (1880–1940)', *Enterprise & Society*, 15, 4 (2015), 722–758, https://doi.org/10.1093/es/khu045.

[36] See Coquery-Vidrovitch, *Le Congo*; Idem, 'Les idées économiques'.

[37] NL-HaNA, Archief NAHV, nr. 668, Letter Philippi to Flachon, 17-12-1899.

[38] Ibidem, Letter Philippi to Flachon, 17-11-1899.

[39] Van der Laan, 'Trading in the Congo', 247–248.

[40] Marseille, *Empire colonial*, 150.

Image 5.2 Building of the NAHV, 1910–1925. (Source: Collectie Wereldmuseum, inv. Nr. TM 60032123, available via https://commons.wikimedia.org/wiki/File:COLLECTIE_TROPENMUSEUM_Het_gebouw_van_de_Nieuw_Afrikaansche_Handelsvereeniging_TMnr_60032123.jpg [Retrieved 10/04/2025])

particularly as he feared French capital investment would be low.[41] Moreover, many of the steamers transporting commodities to and from the French Congo were insured in Amsterdam, making good relations with the Dutch state and its entrepreneurs a near-necessity.[42] As a result, the NAHV was allowed to partner with French investors to offer capital, as was the Belgian SAB.[43] As Coquery-Vidrovitch noted, the total share of foreign investment was relatively small, but in some individual concession companies the share of foreign investment was quite large.[44] British

[41] Coquery-Vidrovitch, 'Les idées économiques de Brazza', 80.
[42] Idem, *Le Congo*, 59–61.
[43] Coquery-Vidrovitch, *Le Congo*, 41–42 & 234–235.
[44] Ibidem.

investors, in contrast to the Dutch and Belgians, were not welcomed by De Brazza and thus kept out, although they may have invested silently through Parisian banks [45].

The NAHV set up *La Brazzaville* (full name *La Brazzaville Compagnie française d'exploitation*) to bid for concessions.[46] The NAHV invested 300,000 francs in *La Brazzaville*, alongside French investors who offered the remaining 200,000 francs.[47] As the primary *publiciste*, the person listed as main owner of the company was Flachon. Together with Dupuy-Dutemps (no first name is known), Arthur Guinard, Louis Mainard, Paul Cabaret and Flament (no first name is known either), he bid for concessions on behalf of *La Brazzaville*. The directorship of *La Brazzaville* consisted of Flachon, Guinard, Mainard, Cabaret, as well as Philippi and De Bloeme, the two NAHV directors.[48]

Through *La Brazzaville*, the NAHV bid for two concessions that would later become the *Compagnie Commerciale de Colonisation du Congo français* (CCCCF or 4CF, indicated under number 21 on Image 5.3) and the *Compagnie de L'Ouhamé et Nana* (*Ouhamé-Nana*, indicated as number 37 on Image 5.3). Most of these men also subsequently became administrators of the CCCCF and *Ouhamé-Nana*.[49] Anton Greshoff became the executive director 'on the ground' of both the subsidiary holding company and the two concession companies. *La Brazzaville* was thus a subsidiary to fulfil the criteria set out by Brazza to participate in the concession system.[50] *Mees & Zoonen* offered part of the capital for the NAHV to invest in the French subsidiaries, again showing how interlinked the Rotterdam entrepreneurial elite was.[51] The French authorities indicated that they even welcomed Mees' investment.[52] In a sense, the use of holding companies was not unlike the operations of many American firms operating abroad in this period [53] (Graph 5.1)

[45] Ibidem.

[46] Amin & Coquery-Vidrovitch, *Histoire économique*, 44.

[47] NL-HaNA, Archief NAHV, nr. 174, Balance 31-10-1904.

[48] Coquery-Vidrovitch, *Le Congo*, 60–61.

[49] Ibidem.

[50] Idem, 'Les idées économiques de Brazza', 80.

[51] Idem, *Le Congo*, 60–61 *n*2.

[52] NL-HaNA, Archief NAHV, nr. 671, Letter French Ministry of Foreign Affairs to Philippi, 04-12-1899 & Letter Etienne Watel to Philippi, 01-12-1900.

[53] See e.g. Wilkins, *The Emergence*.

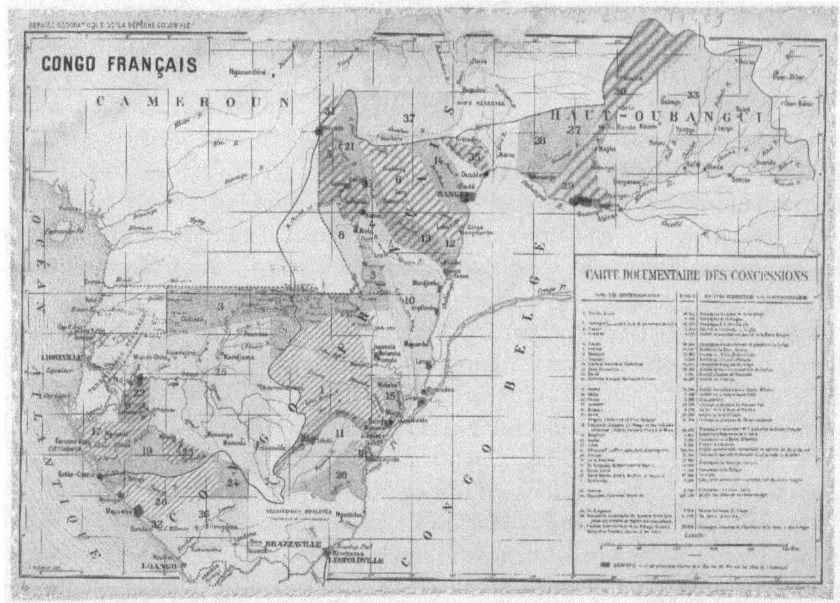

Image 5.3 Concession companies in the French Congo. (Source: Bibliothèque nationale de France, Public domain, via Wikimedia Commons, Available at https://commons.wikimedia.org/wiki/File:Congo_fran%C3%A7ais._Carte_documentaire_des_concessions._L._Robelin_del_-_Service_g%C3%A9ographique_de_%22La_Dep%C3%AAche_coloniale%22_-_btv1b532042215.jpg [Retrieved 19/11/2024])

The start of *La Brazzaville* was not necessarily successful. *La Brazzaville* worked together with the so-called *Sultanate du Haut Oubangui* for transport purposes, and even discussed insuring transport facilities together.[54] Moreover, it bought commodities like ivory and rubber from the concession company *La Haute Sangha*, although *La Haute Sangha* also requested transport levies when commodities were transported through its concession territory, leading to a dispute.[55] In 1904, the balance of *La Brazzaville* showed a significant loss of 96,744 francs, with a significant amount of the money going to salaries and depreciations in the French

[54] Ibidem, Letters Watel to Philippi, 10-11-1900 & 16-11-1900.
[55] Ibidem, Letter Durand to Philippi, 7-11-1902 & 8-11-1902.

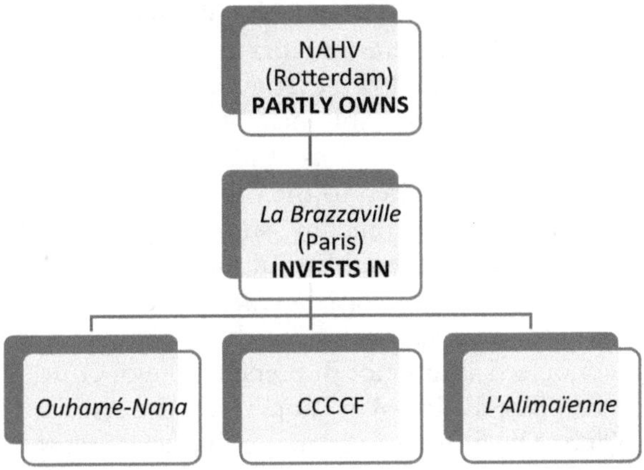

Graph 5.1 Simplified NAHV investment structure in the French Congo

Congo, according to the NAHV directors aligned with setting up factories in the colony and preparing to exploit Arabic gum on its plantations there.[56]

In the balance of the NAHV of 31 October 1904, it is shown that 1,357,334 guilders out of a total balance of 3,630,175 guilders were allocated to the Belgian and French concession companies.[57] Thanks to the 'normal' trade of the NAHV in the French Congo that was still going on as well, a profit of 241,261 guilders was recorded by the NAHV for that year. Over 1904–1905, the NAHV reported higher profits for all concession companies, partly due to higher prices on the world market for rubber.[58] *La Brazzaville* reported a profit of 38,200 francs; a year later, it recorded a profit of 26,398 francs.[59] Over 1907–1908, it even recorded a 84,204 francs profit.[60] In 1909–1910, it recorded a profit of roughly 99,000 francs.[61] In 1910–1911, however, the profit fell to under 10,000 francs, indicating the vulnerability of its operations.[62] By 1911, *La Brazzaville* appeared however to have solved the issue of the levies by

[56] Idem, nr. 174, Balance *La Brazzaville* 31-10-1904.

[57] Ibidem, Balance NAHV 31-10-1904.

[58] Idem, nr. 679, Annual Report NAHV 1904–1905.

[59] Ibidem, Annual Report *La Brazzaville* 1904–1905; nr. 682, Annual Report *La Brazzaville* 1905–1906.

[60] Idem, nr. 711, Annual Report *La Brazzaville*, 1907–1908.

[61] Idem, nr. 688, Annual Report *La Brazzaville* 1909–1910.

[62] Ibidem, Annual Report *La Brazzaville* 1910–1911.

sourcing commodities from elsewhere, as their agent Lefèbvre acted as a buyer on behalf of *La Brazzaville* for ivory and rubber.[63] The NAHV itself wrote in its annual report for 1912 that general circumstances were challenging, but that *La Brazzaville* still made it a profit.[64]

The *Compagnie Commerciale de Colonisation du Congo français* (CCCCF or 4CF) was, compared to the other French concession companies, a mid-sized concession company, with an initial capitalisation of 1 million francs. The NAHV offered half of the capital (500,000 francs out of the total million) via the *La Brazzaville* subsidiary.[65] Flachon was the main concessionaire, and also acted as the main director of the firm: Greshoff was appointed as director in French Congo. Officially, the seat of the CCCCF was at Rue d'Alger 3 in Paris, as was the case for *La Brazzaville* & *Ouhamé-Nana*. The firm owned various ships, according to the balance of 31 October 1901, for a value of 212,000 francs. Most likely, these ships were already in possession of the NAHV before, and simply 'taken over' by the CCCCF. Ivory and rubber were the main export commodities of the CCCCF, which was given the demands of the time (this was the time of the rubber boom and the accompanying red rubber scandals across the Lower Congo region), not particularly surprising. In the annual reports, not much is specified about how the rubber was produced in the area, although the NAHV mentioned their involvement in the so-called *Société Générale de Procédés d'Extraction du Caoutchouc* in 1906.[66]

Greshoff already in February 1900 lobbied for lower import duties in the French Congo, essentially continuing to push for favourable rules for the NAHV-owned concessions as he had done in the Congo Free State in the previous decade.[67] Flachon acted as the intermediary between the French governmental authorities, Greshoff and the NAHV directors back in Rotterdam. The CCCCF got off to a fairly promising start when it obtained the concession to transport the postal letters on behalf of *Messageries Fluviales du Congo* in 1900.[68] Similar to *La Brazzaville*, however, the CCCCF soon became embroiled in a power struggle with *La*

[63] Idem, nr. 671, Order 7-08-1911.

[64] Idem, nr. 688, Annual Report NAHV 1910–1911.

[65] A.Y. Leger, 'Compagnie Commerciale de Colonisation du Congo français (4CF)', 3, available at https://www.entreprises-coloniales.fr/afrique-equatoriale/CCCCF.pdf [Retrieved 09/05/2023].

[66] NL-HaNA, Archief NAHV, nr. 679, Annual Report NAHV 1906.

[67] Idem, nr. 665, Letter Philippi & De Bloeme to Greshoff, 12-02-1900.

[68] Idem, nr. 671, Letter *Messageries Fluviales du Congo* to CCCCF, 25-08-1900.

Haute Sangha about transport levies, which cost the CCCCF a significant amount of money.[69] Thus, costs for the NAHV and its concessions of transporting commodities or letters quickly were raised by concession companies establishing high transport levies in their areas of control. Over 1904–1905, the CCCCF however reported a profit of roughly 383,630 francs; the next year, 211,684 francs.[70]

The CCCCF was thus initially profitable, and in the years after remained largely so. In 1909–1910, for example, CCCCF, recorded a 554,933 francs profit; in 1910–1911, a 608,205 francs profit, with substantial profits coming from the sale of rubber and ivory in France.[71] Moreover, it started to become involved in mining operations.[72] Despite the general profitability, threats on the horizons were present, including lower prices on the world market for commodities like palm oil and rubber. In 1912, the CCCCF was even taken by one of its own former agents for negligible behaviour, as the said agent (Laguesse) had become so ill when working in the area that he was unable to work anymore.[73]

Similar to the CCCF, the *Compagnie du Ouhamé-Nana* (*Ouhamé-Nana*) was seated at Rue d'Alger 3 in Paris, and had the same directors, including Greshoff as executive director on the ground.[74] In 1897, a consortium of French investors including Flachon already presented its interest to the French colonial authorities, although it would take until 21 February 1901 until the concession was actually granted to the group of concessionaires. The capitalisation of *Ouhamé-Nana* was 2 million francs (thus double that of CCCCF), with the NAHV investing half of the capital again. In 1917, the capital of the firm was lowered to 1.2 million francs, probably as the First World War made the company less profitable and less active, making the need for capital less. Compared with many of the other concessions, *Ouhamé-Nana* existed until after the Second World War, with the NAHV participating until roughly 1926 (Image 5.4).

Similar to the CCCCF, *Ouhamé-Nana* traded largely in ivory, rubber and palm oil, and missed the rise of Arabic gum and copal in the early 1900s. Although some profits were recorded in the annual reports over

[69] Ibidem, Letter Durand to NAHV, 22-05-1903.

[70] Idem, nr. 679, Annual Report CCCCF 1904–1905; Idem, nr. 682, Annual Report NAHV 1905–1906.

[71] Idem, nr. 688, Annual Reports CCCCF 1909–1910 & 1910–1911.

[72] Ibidem.

[73] Ibidem, Letter Laguesse to CCCCF, 25-05-1912.

[74] Coquery-Vidrovitch, *Le Congo*, 60–61.

Image 5.4 Share of the *Compagnie française de l'Ouhamé et de la Nana*, 1900. (Source: https://www.entreprises-coloniales.fr/afrique-equatoriale/Ouhame_et_Nana.pdf [Retrieved 25/04/2023])

for example 1902–1903 (194,782 francs), 1903–1904 (221,838 francs), 1904–1905 (222,000 francs) and 1905–1906 (194,568 guilders), in 1906–1907 *Ouhamé-Nana* recorded substantial losses.[75] Part of this had to do with the significant costs it had to incur to build more ships to transport commodities to and from the French Congo.[76] The firm recovered in 1907–1908 with a 182,349 francs profit,[77] but in 1908–1909, 1909–1910, 1910–111 and 1911–1912 recorded 283,420, 609,848, 367,039 and 345,790 francs losses, in particular due to losses on the ivory trade.[78] Philippi and De Bloeme remained co-directors of *Ouhamé-Nana* until the end of the First World War, giving the NAHV a significant role in *Ouhamé-Nana*.

Flachon appeared to have been less involved in *Ouhamé-Nana* than in CCCCF, as he was not mentioned as one of the concessionaires. Guinard, one of the investors-cum-directors in both firms, was likely the more active director in this company, essentially playing the role of a French intermediary between the NAHV and the French colonial authorities. Guinard himself was a weapons trader, who through *Ouhamé-Nana* also delivered weapons to the French state in Congo.[79] Flachon remained instrumental in the background as intermediary in France to obtain fresh capital, as was for example the case in 1910–1911 when he was tasked with raising new capital on the Parisian market.[80] Moreover, he allowed the NAHV to remain operative in the neutral zone by securing access for *Ouhamé-Nana* as well.[81] The new capital was probably necessary as the firm partly 'moved' to *Neukamerun*: in 1911, following the French-Germany Treaty (see below), *Ouhamé-Nana* published new statutes with diminished French capital participation.[82] Despite the difficulties, *Ouhamé-Nana* still

[75] NL-HaNA, Archief NAHV, nr. 679, Annual Report NAHV 1904–1905; Idem, nr. 682, Annual Report NAHV 1905–1906; Idem, nr. 711, Annual Reports *Ouhamé-Nana* 1902–1903, 1903–1904 & 1906–1907.

[76] Idem, nr. 671, Letter De la Brosse & Touché to Direction *Ouhamé-Nana*, 7-03-1906.

[77] Idem, nr. 714, Annual Report *Ouhamé-Nana* 1907–1908.

[78] Idem, nr. 688, Annual Report *Ouhamé-Nana* 1910–1911; Idem, nr. 714, Annual Reports *Ouhamé-Nana* 1908–1909, 1909–1910 & 1911–1912.

[79] Idem, nr. 671, Letter Guinard to Philippi, 29-01-1904.

[80] Idem, nr. 655, Map 9.

[81] Ibidem, Map 9, Letter H. Bobichon to V. Flachon, 18-07-1907.

[82] Idem, nr. 666, *Journal Officiel de L'Afrique Équatoriale Français*, Statutes of *Compagnie Française de l'Ouhamé et de la Nana*, 15-11-1911.

recorded a healthy profit of 295,750 francs over 1912–1913, indicating that the firm could despite the uncertainty still trade in the area.[83]

After 1910, the investments of the NAHV in the French Congo were again subject to significant changes. One was the redistricting of the concession companies, whereby the concessions were redistributed and French capital was given preferential treatment over the others. Although the NAHV remained involved in the three companies (*La Brazzaville*, CCCCF & *Ouhamé-Nana*), the NAHV's ownerships were diminished as a result of new rules requiring the majority of capital shares to be in French hands.[84] As a result, the NAHV brought back its participation in the three concession companies, although it may well have kept some shares via strawmen. More consequential, perhaps, was the Franco-German Treaty of 1911–1912, which transferred parts of the territory of the French Congo to German sovereignty. This Treaty was signed in the wake of the Agadir Crisis of 1911 when the Germans blockaded the Moroccan port of Agadir. The Germans would call this territory *Neukamerun*, indicating a new territory adjacent to German Cameroon.[85] For Germany, the main advantage was that it gained better access to waterways, in this case the area between the Logone and Chari rivers.

For the NAHV, the main problem was that this was exactly the area where the full concessionary area of the CCCCF was located, as well as parts of the *Ouhamé-Nana* concession. Although Germany gave some signals that it would respect the rights of the foreign concessions to remain operative in the area, this change introduced significant uncertainty for the NAHV, as well as the other investors in those concession companies.[86] In the annual report for 1912–1913, the NAHV directors wrote that it was still unclear how the Germans would proceed in the matter: the Germans had taken control over the area, but due to the relatively short timeframe in which the diplomatic solution had been agreed upon, there were no preparations for the take-over of a colonial territory from another country.[87] Notwithstanding the uncertainty, the NAHV directors quickly

[83] Idem, nr. 717, Annual Report *Ouhamé-Nana* 1912–1913.

[84] Coquery-Vidrovitch, *Le Congo*, 257–262.

[85] Conrad, *German Colonialism*, 45–46; Rudin, *Germans in the Cameroons*, 295–296.

[86] See J. Ballhaus, 'Die Landkonzessionsgesellschaften', in: H. Stoecker (ed.), *Kamerun unter deutscher Kolonialherrschaft* (Vol. 2) (Berlin 1968), 99–179, there 105 & 128. The NAHV had owned a separate factory in the region, but had sold this to a German firm already in 1899 (p. 128).

[87] NL-HaNA, Archief NAHV, nr. 691, Annual Report 1912–1913.

diverted their attention to the German colonial authorities in Cameroon and Berlin to save as much as they could. In the archives of the NAHV, one can find extensive German newspapers from the period (such as the *Ambtsblatt*, the newspaper for colonial civil servants).[88] To counter the (at that point potential) take-over by Germany of the area, the NAHV by 1910 already paid publicists to publish positive pieces about *Ouhamé-Nana*.[89]

Philippi, one of the NAHV's directors, in 1913 went to Hamburg and Berlin to negotiate quietly with the German government. It appears from confidential documents that Philippi was seen as the ideal go-between, as a Dutchman with German roots who could negotiate on behalf of two majority French-owned firms without arousing too much suspicion. Philippi even opened an office in Hamburg in June 1914, where he sought contacts and support of the German entrepreneurs active in West Africa.[90] Eventually, the negotiations yielded mixed results for the French concession companies: the CCCCF had to give back its monopolistic concession and open up its concessionary area for German entrepreneurs, whereas *Ouhamé-Nana* was allowed to retain its concession, as only a fraction of its concession area was located in *Neukamerun*. The German colonial authorities were thus willing to guarantee property rights for other European firms to an extent, but also made sure German colonial firms would be able to profit. The NAHV therefore had to deal with a fourth colonial administration, after those of Portuguese Angola, the Congo Free State and the French Congo. Philippi also got in touch with people in the German Colonial Movement, who however often wrote scathingly about the concession companies as firms without much value for the German colonial project.[91]

Philippi officially opened a CCCCF office on 11 June 1914 in Berlin, the second office to exist in Germany after the office in Hamburg. Only a month prior, the agreements between the CCCCF and *Ouhamé-Nana* on the one hand, and the German authorities responsible for the management of *Neukamerun*, had been concluded.[92] Philippi could thus reasonably conclude that he had saved the investments of the NAHV in the

[88] Idem, nr. 692.

[89] Idem, nr. 671, Agreement between Delhom de Frédeville & Lombard, 07-07-1910.

[90] Idem nr. 694, Letter Philippi to Willy Sick, 27-03-1914 & Letter Von der Heydt & Co to Philipi, 18-06-1914; see also Todzi, *Unternehmen Weltaneignung*.

[91] See e.g. Ibidem, Copy of Letter to Philippi (Anonymous), *sine dato*.

[92] As described in Ibidem, Letter Philippi to Ministry of Colonies (Berlin), 18-06-1914.

former areas of the French Congo, by negotiating continued market access for the CCCCF and the continued monopoly for *Ouhamé-Nana*. Indeed, through the firm *Von der Heydt & Co*, the NAHV was even able to sell its commodities on the German market, indicating a general positive attitude by the Germans towards the NAHV.[93]

Just over a month after Philippi opened the Berlin office, the First World War broke out. The conflict quickly became a global one, and the African continent was no exception: soon, the battle for the colonial territories was in full swing. *Neukamerun* was attacked by French forces and eventually reconquered by the French in 1916: after the First World War, German Cameroon, alongside the other German colonies in Africa, were divided between the allied powers. The NAHV at this point remained a presence in the French Congo, although the involvement in the concession companies dwindled: CCCCF was liquidated shortly after the war, *La Brazzaville* already during the war. The NAHV was thus left with *Ouhamé-Nana* as its sole investment in the French Congo after the end of the First World War, leaving it with substantial losses from the war.[94]

Next to the investments in the concession companies, the NAHV also employed several other activities in the French Congo.[95] Two of them were of some importance, and therefore worth mentioning: first, the trading operations of *La Brazzaville* itself, and second, the *Compagnie Agricole du Kouilou*, an agricultural company set up for plantations. *La Brazzaville*, besides being a subsidiary, also unfolded operations in two ways on its own: first, it offered riverine transport in various parts of the French Congo to other concession companies, in which the NAHV was specialised.[96] Second, the firm traded in commodities in the French Congo, taking over the pre-existing factories the company owned in what was now the French Congo.[97] Against the wishes of the French colonial authorities,

[93] Ibidem, Letter Von der Heydt to Philippi, 6-07-1914.

[94] Van der Laan, 'Trading in the Congo', 247–248.

[95] Next to what follows, it may have been the case that the NAHV invested in the *Compagnie du Lobaye*, as Alfons Vermeulen (see Chap. 6) was sent to work for the company between 1904 and 1907. However, no information on this can be found in the NAHV archives or the secondary literature. See: Van Walraven, 'European Memoirs', 2. In general for the *Compagnie du Lobaye*: Coquery-Vidrovitch, *Le Congo*, 183–185 & 264–289; R. Jeaugeon, 'Les sociétés d'exploitation au Congo et l'opinion française de 1890 à 1906', *Revue française d'histoire d'outre-mer*, 48, 172–173 (1961), 353–437, there 424.

[96] NL-HaNA, Archief NAHV, nr. 671, Letter Guinard to Philippi, 15-11-1903.

[97] For example Ibidem, Letter Ministry of Colonies to La Brazzaville, 02-10-1902, Berauld to La Brazzaville, 12-06-1906 & Letter Gheluwe to Philippi, 07-11-1911.

the NAHV moreover had concluded multiple agreements with local chiefs for preferential trade, in particular in the Haut-Oubangui area.[98] Yet in 1898, the French colonial authorities allowed the NAHV to keep operating in the areas where it had operated before for at least thirty years, under the condition that this was done through *La Brazzaville*.[99]

Once the concession system was set up, this nevertheless posed a problem of property rights, as the NAHV did have legally valid contracts with the local chiefs. Moreover, the chiefs protested against the (in their view illegal) factories that French concession companies established in their territories, which the French eventually bought off. Negotiations took rather long, as the question of the NAHV's presence in other concessionary areas was only solved in 1906. Flachon offered to act as an intermediate. Eventually, he suggested that the NAHV would allow to keep its factories, but abandon the lucrative ivory and rubber trade in concession areas, instead focusing on palm oil, tobacco and fruits.[100] Moreover, Flachon negotiated a small neutral zone between the concessions of the *Compagnie Française du Haut-Congo*, the *Société de l'Alimaïenne* and the *Société du Haut-Ogooué*, where *La Brazzaville* could still trade without being threatened by the larger concession companies. This agreement was ratified by the French colonial authorities in August 1906, and a couple of factories were exchanged between *La Brazzaville* and the *Compagnie Française du Haut-Congo*.[101] In March 1907, *l'Alimaïenne* took over some of the NAHV's factories outside of the neutral zone, in return for *La Brazzaville* gaining 280 shares of 500 francs in *l'Alimaïenne*.[102] In December 1907 and January 1908, *La Brazzaville* moreover agreed *l'Alimaïenne* to use some of its factories in the neutral zone for their trading purposes, in essence cementing cooperation.[103]

The second way in which *La Brazzaville* actively profited from its activities in French Congo was through offering riverine shipping transport services. Through *La Brazzaville*, the NAHV was for example contracted to provide transport for the aforementioned *Société l'Alimaïenne*

[98] Coquery-Vidrovitch, *Le Congo*, 243–244.

[99] NL-HaNA, Archief NAHV, nr. 665, Draft Agreement French Ministry of Colonies with NAHV, *sine dato*, 1898.

[100] Coquery-Vidrovitch, *Le Congo*, 245.

[101] Ibidem, 248.

[102] Leger, 'Alimaïenne (L')', 10–12, available at https://www.entreprises-coloniales.fr/afrique-equatoriale/L_Alimaienne.pdf [Retrieved 09/05/2023].

[103] Ibidem.

(established 1899). As the NAHV possessed a large riverine fleet, they were well-suited for these types of transport contracts. At least in 1906, 1907 and 1908, the NAHV was responsible for the transport of commodities harvested by *l'Alimaïenne* to the coast of West Central Africa, perhaps because the *l'Alimaïenne*'s director was a Dutchman named M. Elso Dusseljé.[104] In the archives of the NAHV, only a couple of receipts have been left for 1906–1908, indicating this was either not a major pursuit of the NAHV or a short-lived contract. Another contract from 1913, this time with the French colonial authorities in Bangui (present-day Central African Republic), also proved short-lived as the NAHV hoped that transport would allow the firm to be excluded from new export tariffs, but the French colonial authorities declined to give in on the matter.[105] In the case of *La Brazzaville*, the value of commodities traded and services provided was essentially too small, particularly as it was not allowed to participate in the ivory and rubber trade.[106] In 1910–1911, when the company had obtained the transport contract for *l'Alimaïenne*, the firm was much more profitable and remained so until the First World War.[107]

Somewhat more substantial (though short-lived) was the participation in the *Compagnie Agricole du Kouilou* (CAK). The CAK was established in June 1900 in Paris, gaining a concession on the Kwilu river (*Kouilou-Niari* in French). The CAK gained ownership over a number of plantations previously under the administrative capacity of the French colonial authorities in the area, but also took over both the existing factories and terrains of the NAHV, as well as their rights to all concessions that the NAHV gained before the set-up of the concession system 'proper'. Part of these concessions were in present-day Gabon, in the coastal area where the NAHV also held various concessions. The NAHV owned twelve factories between the port cities of Loango (Congo-Brazzaville, just north of Pointe Noire) and Mayumba (Gabon) since 1888, which were taken over by the CAK in 1900.[108] The CAK made various bids for the factories in 1900, prompting NAHV director De Bloeme to sell the factories for a

[104] Ibidem, 27; see also https://groningersindecongo.jouwweb.nl/elso-dusselje [Retrieved 09/05/2023].

[105] NL-HaNA, Archief NAHV, nr. 718, Letter Leenart to Philippi, 18-12-1913.

[106] Idem, nr. 682, Annual Report NAHV 1905–1906.

[107] Idem, nr. 688, Annual Report NAHV 1910–1911.

[108] It concerned factories in 1) Pointe Noire 2) Calle-Bicalzle 3) Chillala 4) Chabi 5) Massabe 6) Tchicambo 7) Fouta 8) Bambala 9) Kulla Mandou (rive gauche) 10) Kulla Mandou (rive droite) 11) Cayo 12) Sanza. See: Idem, nr. 667, Ownership Proofs of French Factories.

decent price.[109] However, the CAK was slow in acquiring the factories, prompting De Bloeme to ask the agents on the ground to push for action. In November 1902, the remaining six factories and three concession territories were sold to the CAK, although in 1905 the head agent of the NAHV in the area, Cooper, wrote that there were still some administrative problems around the registration of the sale of land.[110]

The CAK only existed until December 1905, as the firm was unable to make a profit from the plantations it owned, particularly in palm oil. As De Bloeme had already indicated upon the sale of the factories to the CAK, the NAHV also had trouble turning a profit in this area. Once the CAK was liquidated, the NAHV nevertheless bought back the factories and corresponding concessions, albeit at a lower price. Another concession company, *Haut-Ogoué*, however claimed that one of the factories was located in their concessionary area, leading to a lengthy legal dispute that the NAHV eventually won, based on an 1888 agreement with the French colonial authorities. In 1907–1908, the NAHV bought additional land in the present-day Congo-Brazzaville/Gabon border region, after lengthy negotiations with the French colonial authorities, including a second factory in Loango bought from a Portuguese firm.[111] Unfortunately, the annual balances of the NAHV do not specifically note the profits made in the French Congo outside of the concession companies, making it difficult to gauge the impact of these minor investments on the overall performance of the NAHV.

5.6 Dutch Entrepreneurship in West (Central Africa), 1899–1921

This chapter has so far told the story of the entrepreneurial activities of the Dutch entrepreneurs in five countries and/or empires: Liberia, Portuguese Angola, the Congo Free State, the French Congo and German Cameroon. Due to the different circumstances in the various empires, the picture of the entrepreneurial activities of the Dutch is therefore also varied: in Liberia (under the OAC) and Angola (under the NAHV), the Dutch entrepreneurs mostly operated as commodity traders in the coastal areas,

[109] Idem, nr. 670, Letters CAK to Philippi, 05-03-1900, 05-06-1900, 07-06-1900, 21-06-1900, 02-11-1900 & 05-11-1900.

[110] Ibidem, Letter Philippi & De Bloeme to Cooper, 06-03-1905.

[111] Idem, nr. 686, Letter De Bloeme to Lucas, 24-08-1908.

without significant changes in entrepreneurial strategy or organisational structures from its starting point in the 1850s: the commodities were largely brought to them by middlemen in exchange for arms and alcohol, with the agents running factories in the coastal regions of Liberia and Angola. This was primarily the result of the economic structures of both regions.

The story of Dutch entrepreneurial involvement in the Congo Free State and the French Congo was rather different. In business-historical terminology, the NAHV in these places moved to integrate backwards into the production of commodities, mostly through the large-scale concession system that was drawn up by the late nineteenth century in both colonial settings. Not only did the NAHV therefore move from commodity trader to producer of commodities through the concession system, but the structure of the firm also changed significantly, not unlike the American firms so well described by Chandler and Wilkins.[112] In Liberia and Angola, the firm remained essentially a small-scale family firm; in the Congo Free State and the French Congo, the NAHV became a full-fledged capitalist investor-cum-producer, at the same time *financially* investing in resources and setting up production on the ground. They were *investor* and *merchant* at the same time, and the organisational structure of the firm grew to include a larger board of directors, a director 'on the ground' in form of Greshoff and the set-up of subsidiary holding companies in Paris.

The NAHV both diversified in terms of the commodities traded (from palm oil into rubber and ivory, among other commodities), setting up production (often unsuccessfully, it should be noted) and specialisation in riverine transport both in the Congo Free State and the French Congo, a unique selling point the NAHV had inherited from its (relatively) long presence in the region. For the period 1899–1918, the data are (compared to the other periods under study here) relatively complete and reliable, and allow us to analyse the involvement of Dutch entrepreneurship in terms of trade. After 1892, the Dutch Statistics Agency used a new method to count trade data, making the statistics somewhat more reliable.[113]

Graph 5.2 shows imports and exports from and to West Africa, which shows that 1910 creates a huge outlier, as in that year an enormous amount of steel and iron (to a cumulative value of 15,932,031 guilders) was

[112] Wilkins, *The Emergence*; Chandler, *Strategy and Structure*; Idem, *Scale and Scope*.
[113] S.A., *Jaarcijfers van Het Koninkrijk der Nederlanden. Rijk in Europa* (1901), 1–2.

exported to West Africa, although it is unknown why this specifically was the case.[114] This thus distorts the statistics, and I have thus also chosen to present Graph 5.3 which strips out 1910, allowing to show the long-term trends a bit better. It can be seen that both exports and imports rose between 1899 and 1916, showing that exports from the Netherlands after 1910 even outstripped imports from West Africa, in marked contrast to the general trends of the previous fifty years. This was largely the result of the export of cotton manufacturing and alcohol (Graph 5.4), which rose significantly between 1899 and 1916.

When looking at the import patterns from West (Central) Africa, we largely see a similar pattern to that observed in previous chapters. Compared to the early 1860s and 1870s, palm oil became relatively less important as a commodity within the mix of imports from West Africa (Graphs 5.5 and 5.6), as well as when considered as a share of the total palm oil imports (rarely making up more than 10% in this period, see Graph 5.7). In contrast, both peanuts and to a somewhat lesser extent palm nut kernels remained very important, with peanut import in the Netherlands coming for roughly 80% from West (Central) Africa: for palm nut kernels, this was roughly 60% (Graphs 5.8 and 5.9). The triumph of palm oil from the Dutch East Indies thus was almost complete,

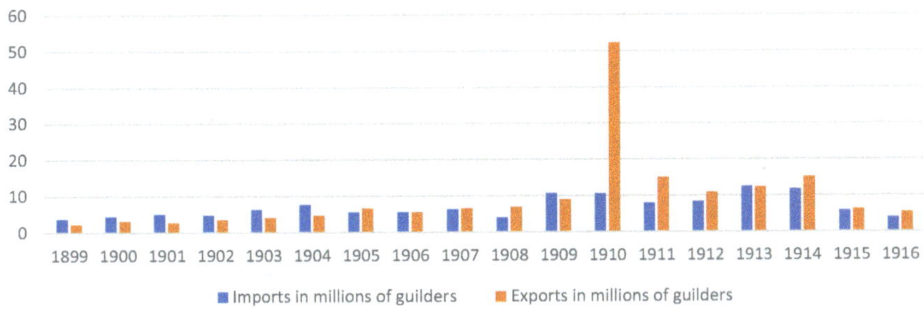

Graph 5.2 Imports and exports from and to West Africa, 1899–1916 (in millions of guilders). (Source: *Jaarcijfers van het Koninkrijk der Nederlanden. Rijk in Europa* (1882–1922))

[114] Of course, it is possible that the Dutch exported iron for railway building, but I have found no evidence of this. For East Africa, this evidence is much more clear, as a Dutch railway company was given the concession to build a railway in the Transvaal to build to Lourenço Marques. See: Van Helten, 'German Capital'.

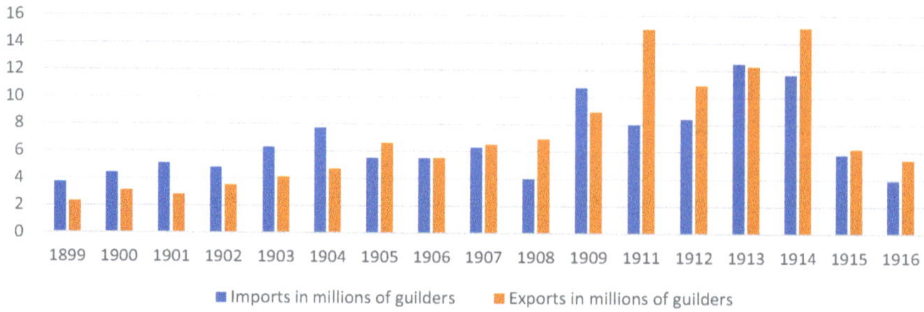

Graph 5.3 Imports and exports to and from West Africa, 1899–1916, 1910 left out (in millions of guilders). (Source: *Jaarcijfers van het Koninkrijk der Nederlanden. Rijk in Europa* (1882–1922))

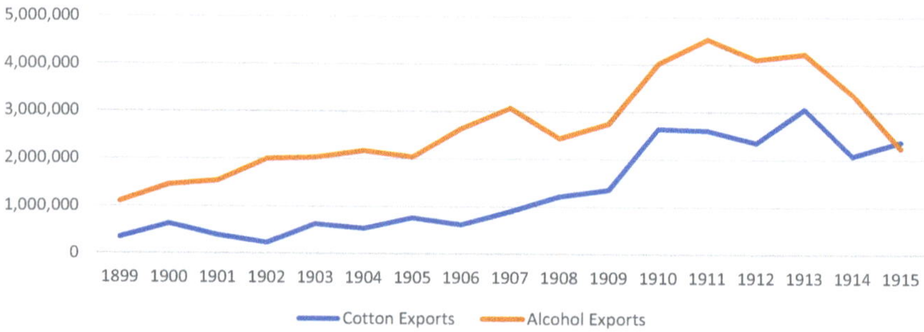

Graph 5.4 Cotton and alcohol exports to West Africa, 1899–1915, in guilders. (Source: *Statistiek van den handel en de scheepvaart* (1847–1918), later *Statistiek van den in- uit- en doorvoer)*

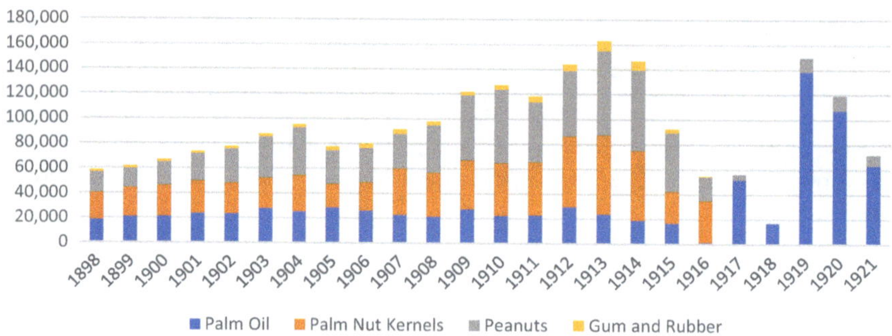

Graph 5.5 Imports of four West African commodities, 1898–1921, in thousands of kilos. Source: *Jaarcijfers van het Koninkrijk der Nederlanden. Rijk in Europa* (1882–1922)

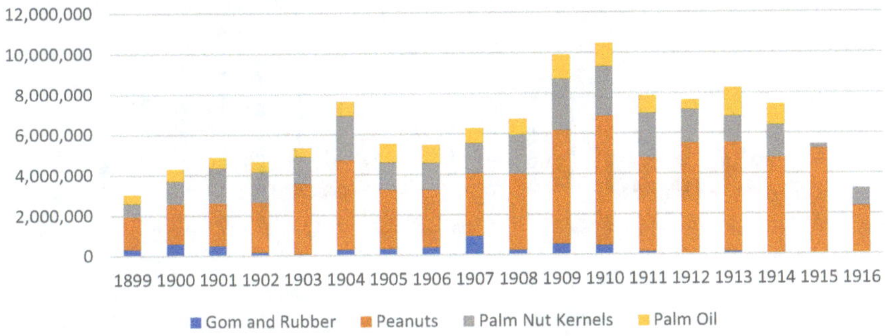

Graph 5.6 Imports of four West African commodities, 1899–1916, in guilders. (Source: *Statistiek van den handel en de scheepvaart* (1847–1918), later *Statistiek van den in- uit- en doorvoer*)

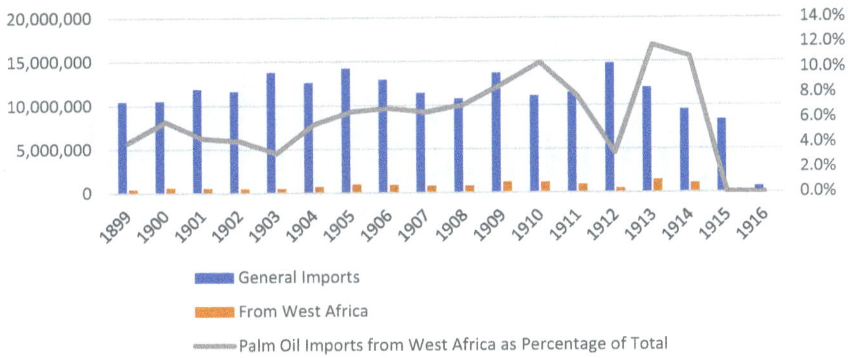

Graph 5.7 Palm oil imports, 1899–1916, in guilders. (Source: *Statistiek van den handel en de scheepvaart* (1847–1918), later *Statistiek van den in- uit- en doorvoer*)

necessitating firms like the NAHV to diversify away from palm oil. The NAHV did so by diversifying into peanuts and palm nut kernels as well as rubber, and to a lesser extent ivory, in a relatively successful way.

Interestingly, some statistics also allow us for some years to specifically show the imports of rubber and gum into the port of Rotterdam, although we should approach these numbers with caution, as these figures were provided by go-betweens who estimated the number of kilos coming into

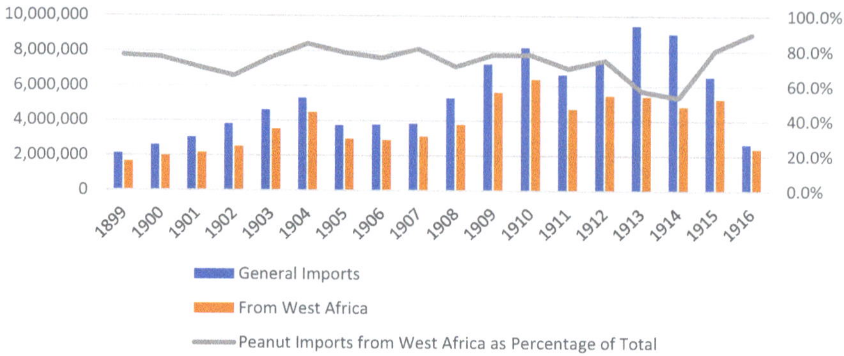

Graph 5.8 Peanut imports, 1899–1916, in guilders. (Source: *Statistiek van den handel en de scheepvaart* (1847–1918), later *Statistiek van den in- uit- en doorvoer*)

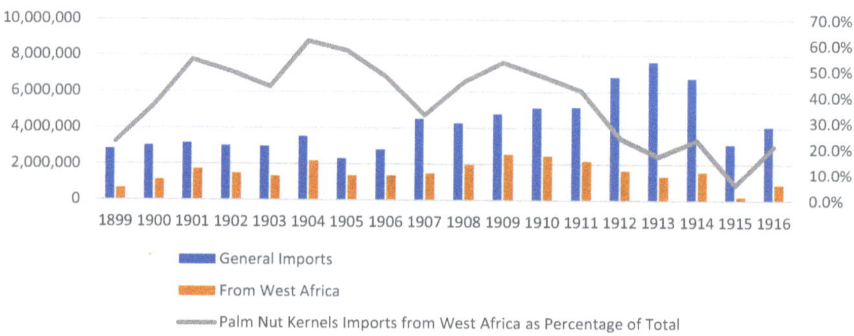

Graph 5.9 Palm nut kernel imports, 1899–1916, in guilders. (Source: *Statistiek van den handel en de scheepvaart* (1847–1918), later *Statistiek van den in- uit- en doorvoer*)

Rotterdam.[115] Table 5.1 shows the import of rubber imported into Rotterdam between 1910 and 1913, divided by region. It shows that while West Africa by far remained the most important territory to source rubber before the First World War, plantations in the Dutch East Indies started producing more than tenfold its original production from 1910 onwards. Table 5.2, finally, shows various ports where rubber was

[115] S.A., *Jaarcijfers van Het Koninkrijk der Nederlanden. Rijk in Europa* (1901), 1–2.

Table 5.1 Import of rubber into Rotterdam, 1910–1913, in kilograms

Region	*1910*	*1911*	*1912*	*1913*
Africa (Congo, Mozambique, Sudan)	763,000	650,000	680,000	1,168,000
Africa (plantation)	0	0	0	7,000
Indonesia (plantation)	65,000	187,000	420,000	826,000
Indonesia (forest)	190,000	238,000	75,000	9,000
Borneo	18,000	26,000	120,000	66,000
South America	102,000	98,000	80,000	25,000
Total	1,138,000	1,199,000	1,375,000	2,101,000

Source: *Jaaroverzichten van den handel in koloniale producten 1891–1914*

imported: Rotterdam only joined this fray in 1910, and remained a small-sized destination for rubber imports before the First World War, on par with Bordeaux. However, ports in the United States, the United Kingdom, Belgium, Portugal, Germany and France were much bigger destinations, showing that while Rotterdam was unable to catch up with those parts before the First World War, even if the NAHV quickly ramped up rubber imports from West (Central) Africa, as well as increasing rubber imports sourced from the Dutch East Indies.

How the Dutch entrepreneurs 'exploited the empire of others' differed across time and space, and how successful this was also differed over time. Moreover, there was no clear-cut 'liability of foreignness', or an advantage for Dutch entrepreneurs: in some cases (e.g. in the era of concession companies in the French Congo) there was a clear advantage to being Dutch, in other cases (e.g. the Congo Free State after 1892) there was a clear liability. How well property rights were respected, also significantly differed: in the case of the Kasaï, they were clearly not respected, but in the French and German case they (generally) were. This also links to the measure of 'success' and 'failure' of the Dutch entrepreneurs in the early years of the twentieth century leading up the First World War. Clearly, there were multiple failures, but just as often the Dutch entrepreneurs proved resilient and found new ways to make money in a rapidly changing environment.

Returning to the conceptualisation of the three entrepreneurial processes, ((1) envisioning and valuing opportunities, (2) allocating and reconfiguring resources and (3) legitimising novelty), the Dutch entrepreneurs again did well in particular on the first two counts. Even though many opportunities were closed off (e.g. in the Congo Free State), the

Table 5.2 Imports of rubber into major ports, 1905–1913, in kilograms

Port	*1905*	*1906*	*1907*	*1908*	*1909*	*1910*	*1911*	*1912*	*1913*
United States	28,582,000	29,936,000	29,433,000	29,477,000	31,129,000	32,916,000	35,088,000	30,395,000	
Liverpool	21,907,000	20,876,000	21,627,000	20,602,000	22,436,000	27,601,000	23,474,000	22,221,000	
Hamburg	8,100,000	8,100,000	8,100,000	7,800,000	7,500,000	7,700,000	7,000,000	6,000,000	
Antwerp	5,713,728	5,772,062	5,054,473	5,035,344	4,685,958	4,058,676	4,335,813	4,777,404	
Le Havre	3,291,000	4,392,000	4,464,123	3,498,000	3,781,000	4,458,028	4,008,577	5,662,043	
London	2,278,000	2,743,000	3,685,000	2,998,000	5,435,000	9,127,000	13,368,000	24,014,000	
Bordeaux	1,330,480	1,716,000	1,516,000	1,078,000	1,987,565	2,326,400	1,832,980	1,364,915	
Lisbon	2,475,893	2,334,000	2,628,000	2,441,000	3,063,000	3,424,400	2,739,417	27,295,111	
Rotterdam						1,138,000	1,199,000	1,375,000	2,101,000
Amsterdam						51,900	240,000	497,000	

Source: *Jaaroverzichten van den handel in koloniale producten 1891–1914*

Dutch entrepreneurs constantly found new opportunities to take advantage of, for example through the concession companies in the French Congo. At least in the French Congo, they envisioned and valued these opportunities rightly. After 1892, the Dutch entrepreneurs allocated and reconfigured financial as well as human resources to the French Congo. In the Congo Free State, this process was less successful, as was the case in Angola and to a lesser extent Liberia. Finally, the third aspect of legitimising novelty was less important in the era of the concession companies, as most commodities were by now common ones on the world market. There was therefore less of a need to 'legitimise novelty', and the Dutch entrepreneurs did not make much of an effort to develop new products beyond what they had already done. What was new was the fact that the Dutch entrepreneurs made an effort to move into production from trade, and therefore integrate backwards. This was moderately successful, even if many of the concessions became less profitable over time.

5.7 Conclusion

The first two decades of the twentieth century were the era of the concession companies in Africa. Colonial states gave power to these monopolistic companies to spur economic development as their own efforts faltered. The concession companies, however, were most often fronts for groups of ruthless capitalist investors whose sole goal was to make a substantial profit. Many of the scandals of colonial rule we today associate with the Scramble for Africa (the 'red rubber' scandals, to name the most important one next to the various forced labour ones across Africa) are in fact associated with the concession companies. Most European entrepreneurs operating in Africa invested in these concession companies, and the Dutch were no exception. After having spent the 1890s rebuilding and repositioning themselves across the Lower Congo area, the NAHV initially reaped the benefits of the good contacts with the French and over time participated in several concession areas, including in the *Compagnie du Kasaï*, one of the 'red rubber' companies in the Congo Free State, as well as in CCCCF and *Ouhamé-Nana*, two middle-sized concessions in the French Congo. In contrast, the entrepreneurial situation in Liberia and Angola was less profitable for the Dutch entrepreneurs, because of the small-scale agricultural production still common there.

The concession companies made the NAHV a truly large player in the Lower Congo area. The problems of 'exploiting the empire of others', however, remained: the Franco-German Treaty of 1911–1912 meant that two of its profitable concessions were (partly) moved to German *Neukamerun*, necessitating another colonial power to build ties with. In practice, the NAHV was often left to building ties with foreign colonial authorities to operate. Supposedly strong, 'European' ideas of guaranteed property rights were weak to non-existent in the colony, making the business environment less predictable and full of risks and even uncertainties. The NAHV appears to have been making the same mistake all over again: relying on the support of a foreign state in Africa, only to be set aside after some years of useful empire-building for the colonial authorities. In that sense, rather often the state exploited the entrepreneur more than the entrepreneur exploited the empire of others.

Despite this, the chapter has shown that Dutch entrepreneurship in West and West Central was nevertheless fairly profitable in the era of concession companies, a result of the envisioning of opportunities and the reconfiguration of resources to deal with these changes. The entrepreneurial success, however, also meant increasing repression and violence, and while there is no evidence of the Dutch entrepreneurs perpetrating harsh violence themselves, they certainly participated and actively supported the merger of the political and economic interests that came together in the concession companies. While not responsible, the Dutch entrepreneurs were certainly *complicit* in European imperialism in Africa, by operating across imperial lines and materially and financially profiting from it.

CHAPTER 6

Dutch Entrepreneurs in the *Compagnie du Kasaï*, 1885–1910

6.1 Introduction

This chapter looks at the role of the Dutch entrepreneurs in the *Compagnie du Kasaï* (established 1901). Through a close reading of the (detailed) sources, it elaborates on and illuminates the difficulties and complexities of entrepreneurship in the 'empire of others'. The chapter shows how the Dutch entrepreneurs were largely against their will dragged into the *Compagnie du Kasaï* but, despite mounting evidence of CdK participation in the red rubber scandals, remained a large shareholder until the 1920s. First, the chapter sets the scene by analysing political, economic, social and cultural developments in the Kasaï region between 1875 and 1910, drawing largely on the work of Jan Vansina, Daisy Martens and Jules Marchal, with the latter in particular reckoning with the role of missionaries in the Congo Free State.[1] Second, the chapter moves on to look at the role of the NAHV in the CdK, analysing the ambivalent role played by the Dutch entrepreneurs in the construction and maintenance of the firm. A third part subsequently provides a microhistory of the Ibanche

[1] Vansina, *Being Colonized*; Martens, 'A History'; Marchal, *L'État Libre* (Vol. 1); Idem, *E.D. Morel*; Idem, *Missie en staat in Oud-Kongo, 1880–1914: witte paters, scheutisten en jezuïeten* (2. Vols.) (Brussels 1992); Vangroenweghe, *Rood rubber.*

G. Dreijer, *Private Entrepreneurship and European Imperialism*, Palgrave Studies in Economic History,
https://doi.org/10.1007/978-3-032-01086-5_6

factory, and in particular the NAHV agent Alfons Vermeulen who wrote his memoirs partly based on his time in the Kasaï.[2]

The chapter shows that the NAHV was on the one hand a largely innocent participant in the unfolding drama of the red rubber scandals, but on the other hand also contributed to the rise of African resistance, quietly and indirectly aiding the violent colonisation of the region. Through an analysis of entrepreneurship from the viewpoint of the NAHV as well as through the eyes of Vermeulen, the chapter demonstrates the ambivalent legacies of Dutch entrepreneurship in the Kasaï, and opens up questions around the 'colonial complicity' of the entrepreneurs.

6.2 The Kasaï Region 1885–1900: Entrepreneurs, Missionaries and African Agency

The Kasaï region remained outside of the European grasp for a long time (Image 6.1). It was too distant from the coastal areas where trade was concentrated for the Congo Free State to claim direct control, and too far north-east from the coastal areas in Angola for the Portuguese to exercise direct control. The area was dominated by four main ethnic groups before the advent of colonialism: the Cokwe (also Chokwe), Luba, Lunda and Kuba (Image 6.2).[3] Attitudes towards the outside differed among these ethnic groups: in particular the Kuba were unwilling to engage with outsiders including Europeans, and responded with violence and moves towards autarky.[4] They were strong enough militarily to fend off most outside threats, a result of a militarisation of society that had already begun in the eighteenth century.[5] The Luba, in contrast, were generally open to outside contacts and traded rubber for cloth, arms and alcohol at an early stage.[6] Already in 1874, rubber became the main export product by the Luba, as it was for other ethnic groups like the Lunda and the Cokwe in the region.[7]

[2] Vermeulen, *De pioniersdagen van Chicongo*; Idem, *De ingang der hel*; Idem, *De memoires van Chicongo*.

[3] Ibidem, 39.

[4] Marchal, *De Kongostaat van Leopold II: het verloren paradijs, 1876–1900* (Brussels 1988), 348.

[5] Etambala, *Veroverd, bezet, gekoloniseerd*, 28.

[6] Marchal, *De Kongostaat*, 342.

[7] Martens, 'A History', 51.

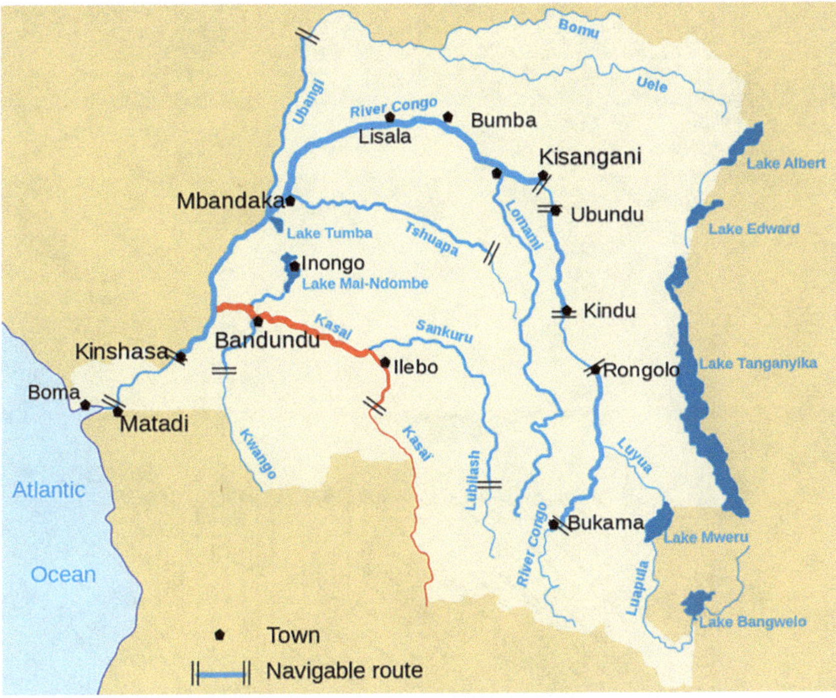

Image 6.1 The Kasaï River (shown in red). (Source: By Kwamikagami–Own work, CC BY-SA 3.0, https://commons.wikimedia.org/w/index.php?curid=15723776 [Retrieved 04/04/2023])

So-called red rubber, named not after the blood as it would become known later but after the red glow of the Kasaï rubber and not be confused with the later scandals, quickly received the reputation to be Africa's best rubber, incorporating the Kasaï into the capitalist world economy within a limited time after 1880.[8] The first European firm to enter the Kasaï was the German Herman von Wissmann, who alongside some local employees arrived in the Kasaï region in 1884, when it set up a trading post in Luluabourg. This in itself indicates that the Kasaï was among those provinces in the Congo basin only explored by the Europeans quite late.[9]

[8] Vansina, *Being Colonized*, 61–62.
[9] Martens, 'A History', 70; Ergo, 'Compagnie du Kasaï', 2; Marchal, *De Kongostaat*, 342.

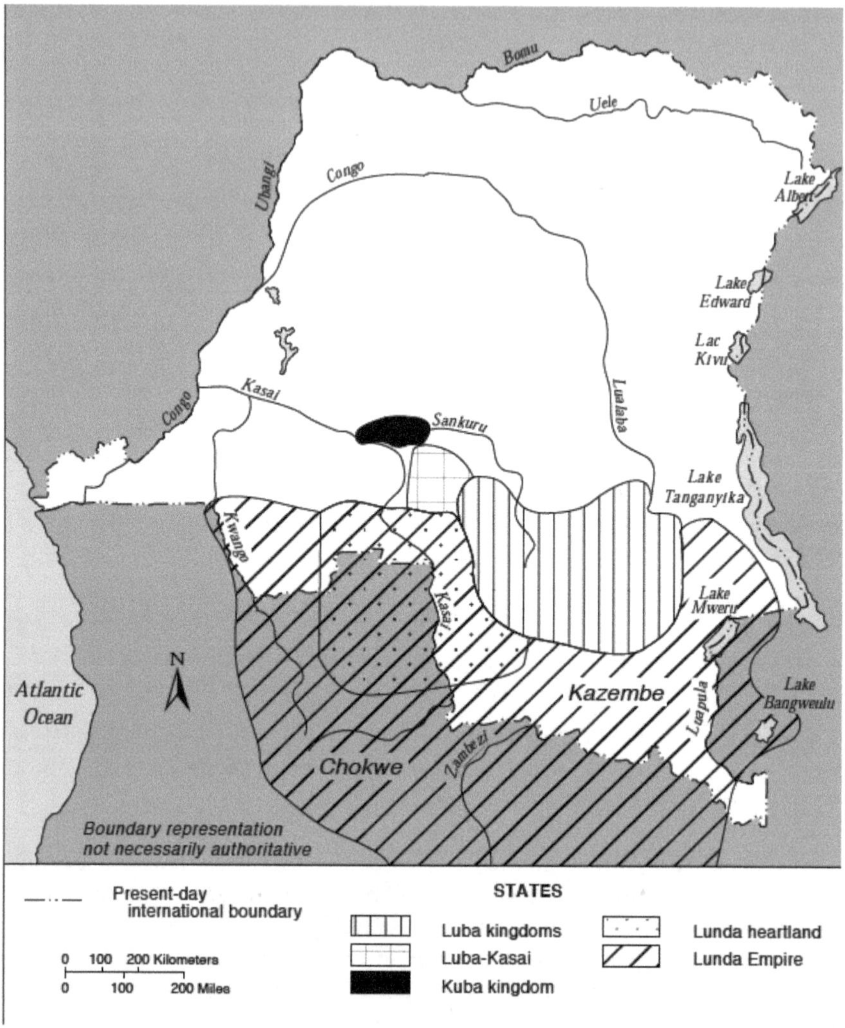

Image 6.2 Kingdoms in the Kasaï area (late nineteenth century). (Source: By Library of Congress–*Zaire: a country study* (1994), Public Domain, https://commons.wikimedia.org/w/index.php?curid=37840534 [Retrieved 06/04/2023])

To obtain rubber, Wissmann cooperated with Luba traders on a relatively egalitarian basis.[10]

Soon afterwards, more Western firms followed, including the American *Sanford Exploring Expedition* (SEE) in 1886, which merged two years later with SAB and thus allowed SAB to gain a head start in the Kasaï.[11] *Daumas Béraud & Cie*, the major French house active in the Congo Free State, chose to participate in the Kasaï rubber trade through the SAB to remain out of Leopold's view, and profit from the SAB's 'home advantage' and the good contacts that Albert Thys held with the King.[12] The Congo Free State also set up state trading posts in the Kasaï, but left the area soon again, indicating a lack of profitable trading opportunities.[13] The NAHV moved into the Kasaï in 1888 by opening a factory in Luebo, after having started negotiations with the Congo Free State over an operating licence in the region in 1886.[14] By 1894, the NAHV had also opened factories at Butala and Zappa Zap.[15] By 1899, it made substantial profits in the Kasaï and held ten factories: Kikongo, Tawamba and Meluna on the Kwilu River; Butala, Bolongola, Bena-Dibele, Ibaka and Lukengo on the Sankuru River; and Luebo and Ibanche on side rivers of the Kasaï (meaning Zappa Zap had been discarded).[16] By the end of the century, fourteen firms were active in the Kasaï.[17] Most were smaller Belgian firms, but the NAHV and SAB remained the most profitable and prominent ones.

Soon after the Western entrepreneurs entered the Kasaï, the Western missionaries followed. From 1892 onwards, missionary organisations started to preach the gospel in the region.[18] Both Protestant and Catholic missionaries spearheaded efforts to move into the Kasaï: the Catholics were based in Luluabourg, the Protestants from 1897 onwards in Ibanche (although they had been in the Kasaï from at least 1892 onwards).[19] The Protestant missionaries were mostly Americans, the Catholic ones were

[10] Marchal, *De Kongostaat*, 342.
[11] Martens, 'A History', 108.
[12] Waltz, *Das Konzessionswesen*, 158.
[13] Ibidem, 83–85.
[14] Ibidem, 112.
[15] Ibidem.
[16] Marchal, *E.D. Morel*, 457.
[17] Buelens, *Congo 1885–1960*, 149.
[18] Marchal, *De Kongostaat*, 346–347.
[19] Ibidem, 560–562.

largely Belgians (so-called *scheutists* after their leader, Scheut).[20] One of the earliest Protestant missionaries, the African-American William Henry Sheppard, in 1892 made a tour to the closed-off Kuba kingdom and after negotiations gained access to the Kuba king Koto Mboke (r. 1890–1896).[21] Although Sheppard did not manage to convert a single Kuba during his trip, he at least managed to create somewhat friendly relations with the Kuba. In 1897–1898, the post in Ibanche was set up as the new Kuba king Mishafe did not allow Sheppard and his colleague, William Morrison, to enter the Kuba kingdom anymore for fear of outside influence.[22] Roughly at the same time, the NAHV bought its factory in Ibanche.

There were substantial differences between the missionaries in their *modus operandi*. The Protestants were largely mobile preachers, but also set up schools for young children with the dual aim of converting and schooling the children. The Catholics in contrast would buy enslaved children to forcefully convert them to the Catholic faith, yet after the example of the Protestants also set up schools.[23] In general, it could be stated that the Protestants were on the side of the local population (although some Protestant missionaries also ran a plantation in Ibanche running on forced labour)[24] and against the atrocities that were committed under the Congo Free State: in 1899–1900, Morrison, one of the two main Protestant protagonists in the Kasaï, for example wrote up allegations against the Congo Free State for mistreating both Kuba and Luba in the region.[25] In contrast, both the Catholic missions under Scheut and later under Cambier essentially acted as handmaidens of the Congo Free State and the *Compagnie du Kasaï*, defending Leopold's regime until 1908.[26] Cambier, Scheut's successor, allegedly even ran transport facilities on behalf of the CdK, as missionaries were exempted from taxation in the Congo Free State, pocketing parts of the profits.[27]

Among the local peoples, the Kuba took centre stage in opposing European imperialism, and therefore some emphasis in the chapter is on them and the actions of (different factions of) their elite. For centuries,

[20] Ibidem, 503–504.
[21] Ibidem, 560–561.
[22] Ibidem, 561–562.
[23] Ibidem, 503–504.
[24] Vansina, *Being Colonized*, 91.
[25] Marchal, *De Kongostaat*, 560–561.
[26] Idem, *Missie en staat in Oud-Kongo* (Vol. 1), 206–207.
[27] Ibidem, 279.

the Kuba had been able to fend off foreign powers, partly as a result as their (relative) military superiority.[28] In this way, the Kuba had been able to fend off most of the pressures of the 'Arab' slave trade as well, even if they actively supplied enslaved people to the Arab slave traders.[29] European colonisation efforts however did trigger tensions within Kuba society, as factions favouring or resisting contact with Europeans increasingly fought against each other.[30] This was best characterised in the 1892 permission of Sheppard by Koto Mboke to make contact with the Kuba, and the subsequent refusal of Koto Mboke's successor Mishafe to allow Sheppard and Morrison to enter Kuba territory.[31]

In 1895–1896, a first uprising by a faction of the Kuba (led by a man named Kalamba) against European encroachment took place, which after several months was with plenty of efforts and trouble put down by the *Force Publique*.[32] From that point on until 1908, uprisings against the colonisation efforts of the Congo Free State by Kuba factions happened at a regular scale.[33] In three successive military campaigns in 1899–1900, most of the Kuba territory was conquered by the *Force Publique*.[34] This was an extremely violent affair: in 1899, a military campaign led by Colonel Scharlaeken against the Kuba for example resulted in 400 deaths.[35] The historian Mathieu Etambala has listed various military campaigns punishing the Kuba just before the *Compagnie du Kasaï* was set up, showing the extent of the violence during the roughly fifteen years that colonisation took place.[36] The Protestant missionary Morrison already made public accusations against the *Force Publique* for their extreme violence immediately afterwards, to no avail.[37]

28 Etambala, *Veroverd, bezet, gekoloniseerd*, 28.

29 Vansina, *Being Colonized*, 24–28.

30 Ibidem.

31 Marchal, *De Kongostaat*, 560–562.

32 Ibidem, 353–354; Martens, 'A History', 89. See also M. Storme, *La mutinerie militaire au Kasai en 1895* (Brussels 1970).

33 Ibidem.

34 Vansina, *Being Colonized*, 69–70.

35 Marchal, *De Kongostaat*, 562–563.

36 Etambala, *Veroverd, bezet, gekoloniseerd*, 63–66.

37 Marchal, *De Kongostaat*, 560–561. See also: Roes, 'Towards'.

6.3 The *Compagnie du Kasaï*, 1900–1910

Leopold, as we have seen in Chap. 5, set up various concession companies in areas north of the Crown Domain, allowing those firms a monopoly on land, labour and exploitation in a certain, demarcated area.[38] The *Compagnie du Kasaï* was a slightly different beast: often seen as one of the concession companies (which it was to a large extent), in fact the CdK was a privileged trading partner for the Congo Free State, holding a monopoly on sales of commodities from the Kasaï to the state.[39] Thus, other firms were allowed to operate in the Kasaï area as well, and as Jean-Luc Vellut has shown, many Portuguese trading houses remained in the Kasaï area to buy ivory and palm oil, which was subsequently smuggled over the porous border with Angola and sold in Luanda.[40] Next to local producers and entrepreneurs, the Kasaï was primarily roamed by Portuguese-speaking middlemen until the late nineteenth century, the so-called *capitas* or *corradores.*

As Daisy Martens has written, the Kasaï offers "a tale of limited and uncertain European penetration, rather than an imperialistic epic".[41] Despite the penetration of entrepreneurs and missionaries from the early 1880s onwards, the majority of the Kasaï region remained off limits to Europeans until the early twentieth century. The Angolan colonial state proclaimed a royal monopoly on ivory in the southern Kasaï, even if smuggling remained rife: neither the Congo Free State nor the Portuguese colonial administration was able to curb the smuggling or enforce the decreed monopolies.[42] Next to ivory, the slave trade, guns, copper and salt were the main commodities produced and traded in the Kasaï before the 1890s.[43] Only with the establishment of the CdK and the simultaneous rubber boom, the Kasaï was also 'discovered' by the Europeans as an excellent space to harvest and extract rubber: of course, the Luba had already been trading rubber for some time.

As noted above, commercial penetration of the Kasaï only started properly after 1885, with SAB and the NAHV emerging by the early 1890s as

[38] Vangroenweghe, *Rood rubber*, 271–304.

[39] Etambala, *Veroverd, gekoloniseerd, bezet*, 37.

[40] Vellut, 'La communauté portugaise du Congo belge. Une minorité ethnique', in: Vellut (ed.), *Congo*, 139–162, there 150–151.

[41] Martens, 'A History', 8.

[42] Vellut, 'La communauté portugaise', 150–151.

[43] Martens, 'A History', 50.

the two main firms.[44] In 1892, soon after the start of the rubber boom, other firms moved in as well, primarily backed by Belgian capital.[45] Competition rapidly improved, lowering prices and profits, although an 1899 decree by the Congo Free State administration aimed to raise production by enforcing the planting of rubber-bearing lianas rather than wild lianas, in order to keep up fast-expanding demand in the world market.[46] This decree largely failed (partly as the plantation grounds were quickly exhausted, and partly because demand was too high to keep up), forcing the administration of the Congo Free State to change tack again.

Despite his previous promise to keep the Kasaï as a free trading zone, Leopold unilaterally broke this promise, as he had done previously with other agreements and promises. Negotiations to establish the CdK took a while, as in particular the NAHV and the SAB were unwilling to give up their position without a fight: within the NAHV, it was Greshoff who in the end pleaded for participation in the CdK, arguing this was the best way to profit from the region's rubber riches.[47] The Congo Free State forced firms operating in the area, including the NAHV and SAB, into the CdK, in which the Congo Free State subsequently took a 50% share to maintain a decisive voice in policy.[48] In total, fourteen firms were incorporated into the CdK after Leopold threatened to retract permission to operate in the Kasaï area for those firms not willing to cooperate.[49] Formally, Leopold lived up to the agreements by keeping the region nominally open for free trade and by making the CdK 'only' a privileged trading partner, even if the property rights of the firms active in the Kasaï were under threat if they would *not* cooperate in the CdK. Eventually, the parties agreed that in the CdK the capital shares of just over one million francs would be equally divided between the Congo Free State (who thus received shares worth 502,500 francs) and the fourteen firms. The NAHV and SAB would become the largest private shareholders (Table 6.1), with both firms

[44] Ibidem, 112.

[45] Ibidem, 106–138.

[46] Ibidem, 115–117.

[47] NL-HaNA, Archief NAHV, nr. 687, Letter Greshoff to NAHV, *sine dato*.

[48] Martens, 'A History', 114; see also Delmotte, *De Belgische koloniale holdings*, 104–105.

[49] Some older literature still portrays the CdK as an economic necessity to limit competition, but this explanation does, I believe, not fully hold in the wake of the evidence of the forceful nature of the establishment of the CdK. Moreover, the larger firms in the Kasaï made a profit before this time. See e.g. Delmotte, *De Belgsiche koloniale holdings*, 104.

Table 6.1 Shares in the *Compagnie du Kasaï* (1901)

Shareholder	*Capital investment in fr.*	*Shares*
Congo Free State	502,500	2010
NAHV	85,000	340
SAB	85,000	340
Société Anonyme des Produits Végétaux	63,750	255
Compagnie Anversoise des Plantations	54,250	217
Plantations Lacourt	51,000	204
La Belgika	49,750	199
Comptoirs Congolais Velde	19,250	77
La Kassainne	18,750	75
La Djuma	18,500	74
L'Est du Kwango	15,500	62
La Loanje	14,500	58
La Centrale Africa Société	13,750	55
Compagnie des Magasins Généraux	7750	31
Le Trafic Congolais	5750	23
Total	1,005,000	4020

Source: Waltz, *Das Konzessionswesen*, 243

holding 340 shares worth 85,000 francs.[50] In practice, this meant that NAHV and SAB combined only held just under 17% of the shares.

The CdK was chartered for thirty years, with its main office in Dima (present-day DRC Congo) and its official headquarter in Brussels.[51] The Congo Free State had the right to appoint representatives on the board of directors and in the upper layers of the management, and always did so to retain decisive influence: after all, no decisions could be forced through without the decisive vote of the state.[52] The CdK would formally take over most facilities of the firms involved, including factories, transport facilities (e.g. steamers) and, importantly, employees. The firms retained the right to run some of their own plantations, although the output had to be sold to the CdK, following the rules of the monopoly established there.

As a result of limited competition, the CdK was initially profitable.[53] The firm established various rubber plantations between 1901 and 1904, and also extracted ivory from the area, which was formally still the

[50] S.A., 'La Compagnie du Kasai'.

[51] Waltz, *Das Konzessionswesen*, 244–248.

[52] Ibidem.

[53] Martens, 'A History', 241–242; Delmotte, *De Belgische koloniale holdings*, 104–105.

monopoly business of the Congo Free State.[54] As the CdK was only a privileged trading partner, soon competitors were established, including the Belgian firm SCMC.[55] This was met with some scepticism by firms incorporated into the CdK, as their preference may well have been to remain independent operators in the CdK. Yet with the sales monopoly in place, the competition had a hard time to make a profit in the Kasaï in the early twentieth century.

As Table 6.1 showed, the NAHV was alongside SAB the largest private shareholder of CdK. After Greshoff had spearheaded extensive efforts to enter the Kasaï in the late 1880s, it would be no surprise to anyone that the NAHV was not looking to be swallowed into a hybrid public-private partnership behemoth, which substantially restricted the influence of the NAHV. Even with the support of SAB, the two firms owned slightly less than 17% of the shares together. The fact that the NAHV eventually agreed to the establishment of the CdK at least appeared to have made Leopold somewhat more favourable towards the NAHV, as the NAHV was allowed to buy a number of factories and adjacent concessions in the Kasaï after 1900.[56] This followed the efforts of Greshoff around 1898, when the NAHV was still blocked from buying new factories on the left bank of the Kasaï river.[57] In 1903, for example, the NAHV was allowed to retain its concession in Luebo, even if this was in the territory of the CdK. In December 1903, the state agreed to allow the NAHV to retain some operations next to the CdK, as long as the core trade of the CdK would not be harmed.[58]

Upon the establishment of the CdK, the NAHV wrote in a letter to the Dutch Ministry of Foreign Affairs that the directors did not resent the establishment of the CdK, but that they did want to have their property rights respected.[59] Eventually, Philippi and De Bloeme, the two NAHV directors, agreed after lengthy negotiations to the establishment of the

[54] Portugal also claimed a royal monopoly over the ivory trade in the southern Kasaï region, but was largely unable to enforce this claimed monopoly.

[55] Waltz, *Das Konzessionswesen*, 244–248.

[56] NL-HaNA, Archief NAHV, nr. 125, Letter Greshoff to Congo Free State, 11-01-1899 & 02-06-1899.

[57] Idem, nr. 664, Letter Greshoff to Congo Free State, 1895.

[58] Idem, nr. 125, Letter NAHV to CdK, 12-12-1903.

[59] Idem, nr. 687, Letter Greshoff to NAHV, *sine dato*: "zich niet verzet tegen den vryen handel en het openstellen der terreinen, maar zy wenscht que les droits acquis soient respectés."

CdK, having been promised a director on the board. The NAHV subsequently appears to have actively tried to contribute as much as possible to make the CdK a success from the start, sharing rather detailed and extensive information with the CdK about their factories, employees and the type of commodities bought and sold in the area.[60] Philippi for example also offered extensive financial reports of all factories in the Kasaï.[61] Moreover, all ships that the NAHV still retained in the Congo Free State were sold to the CdK: the NAHV moreover took on the responsibility to run riverine transports, in which the firm was specialised.[62] Major factories like Luebo and Ibanche would still be run by experienced NAHV managers in the area, guaranteeing continuity.[63] The NAHV also agreed to participate in efforts by the CdK to combat the slave trade, with Philippi noting not enough had been done up to this point by the Congo Free State in this regard.[64]

As the directors tried to make the best of the new set-up, not all NAHV employees were on board with the new situation: some NAHV agents, for example, declined to cooperate with the CdK. At the same time, many of those agents seconded earned much more in the CdK than in the NAHV, without incentives for better performance.[65] Some of the managers declined to offer their ships to the CdK, against the agreements made between the CdK and the NAHV.[66] In a letter dated 23 February 1903, the CdK accused the NAHV of not sharing enough of its profits with the CdK, as had been agreed.[67] Some of the import duties (still) levied by Leopold on the trade of the CdK were, according to the letter of the directors, not paid by the NAHV either.

The CdK did, in contrast to ABIR and *Anversoise*, not hold wide-ranging state-like powers such as jurisdiction and a monopoly on violence (even if in practice this may well have happened). One of the NAHV's agents, only named as Groen, nevertheless was accused of acting as a judge

[60] Idem, nr. 674, Map Factories of NAHV in Kasaï.

[61] Idem, nr. 678, Letter Philippi to Congo Free State, 10-12-1901.

[62] Ibidem, Letter Philippi to Congo Free State, 07-08-1902 & accompanying list of riverine transport. See also: Dreijer, 'Handel en scheepvaart', 50–51.

[63] Ibidem, Letter Cooper to Greshoff, 18-07-1902.

[64] NL-HaNA, Archief Buitenlandse Zaken A-Dossiers, nr. 209, Memorandum Phillipi, 13-08-1903.

[65] NL-HaNA Archief NAHV, nr. 678, Overview Personnel NAHV, 29-11-1901.

[66] See e.g. Ibidem, Note concerning Mr. Groen, *sine dato* (probably 1903).

[67] Ibidem, Letter CdK to NAHV, 23-02-1903.

in a remote factory, for which the CdK reprimanded the NAHV: the NAHV did however not punish Groen for this.[68] Finally, several letters also complained of the fact that some areas of the Kasaï were off-limits to private entrepreneurs, as they were claimed by Leopold for his private use.[69] Protests by the NAHV did not reach the intended effects.[70]

After a promising start, the old mistrust between the Congo Free State and the NAHV soon troubled relations again. Other disagreements followed, for example about prices of commodities, transport facilities offered by the NAHV or the obligatory insurance the state made the NAHV sign in August 1902 for all ships transporting commodities over the rivers to the coastal ports of Boma and Banana.[71] In retaliation for the perceived disobedience of the NAHV, Philippi's and De Bloeme's pick for a commissioner was rejected by the board of directors of the CdK.[72] Philippi, however, was allowed to take the spot himself, promoting himself from director to commissioner within the CdK. Even internally, critical voices about the participation of the NAHV in the CdK were raised: Greshoff (the strongest supporter of participating in the CdK), for example, complained to Cooper about the lack of flexibility the NAHV agents on the ground now had to get their hands on commodities like rubber.[73] In general, the participation of the NAHV in the CdK turned out to be a disappointment for the Dutch entrepreneurs.

As noted previously, some of the region's people, mainly the Cokwe and Kuba, played a crucial role in the developments of the 1900s in the Kasaï. The CdK possessed factories in market towns like Ibanche where threats were limited: around the small market towns, the CdK held small auxiliary posts manned by armed *capitas*, who in essence performed most of the 'primary' safeguarding by performing violence on behalf of the CdK.[74] The *Force Publique*, only a couple of thousand men strong, thus only arrived in case of an emergency or uprising. Violence was common, both by the *Force Publique* as well as by CdK agents: in 1902, the state's chief prosecutor already started investigations into allegations of

[68] Ibidem, Note concerning Mr. Groen, *sine dato* (probably 1903); Letter NAHV to CdK 09-01-1903 & Letter CdK to NAHV, 10-03-1903.

[69] Ibidem, Letters De Bloeme to CdK, 08-11-1902, 11-11-1902 & 20-11-1902.

[70] Ibidem, Letter Congo Free State to NAHV, 23-01-1903.

[71] Ibidem, Letter CdK to Philippi, 01-08-1902.

[72] Ibidem, Letter CdK to NAHV, 11-09-1902.

[73] Ibidem, Letters Greshoff to Cooper, 28-02-1902 & 01-03-1902.

[74] Vansina, *Being Colonized*, 237.

participation in the slave trade, forced labour and violence by CdK agents, but under political pressure this did not lead to much or any persecutions.[75] Moreover, the remoteness of many of the factories and the fact that the CdK had divided the Kasaï into fifteen separate administrative districts meant that many agents possessed substantial leeway to collect rubber as they wished without much oversight.[76]

Soon after its establishment, the CdK came under threat by the Cokwe who had amassed an army in the north-east of the Kasaï, as the Cokwe were strongly opposed to European encroachment.[77] The CdK did not employ much activity in its north-east, and the potential for conflict dissipated quickly. With the Kuba, a different dynamic developed, as in 1904–1905, the Kuba revolted against the CdK, following their uprisings in 1894–1895 and the violent campaigns to conquer Kuba territory around 1899–1900. Although this time the uprising was partly directed against the forced labour practices of the CdK, it was also directed against the missionary encroachment by both Protestants and Catholics on Kuba territory, against their wishes.[78] In this case, the revolt primarily originated in the use of bonded Luba labourers on the Bena Makima plantation near Kuba territory, run by the Catholic missionaries.[79]

The Protestant missionary terrain in Ibanche was the first target (and therefore not the Catholics);[80] in its wake the NAHV factory in Ibanche was also burnt to the ground on 4 November 1904.[81] The *Force Publique* was stretched too thin to intervene, and as a result, the CdK had to deal with the revolt itself. The Congo Free State moreover blamed the CdK for harsh labour practices, including the forced collection of rubber, even if the state itself stimulated the production of more and more rubber for tax purposes.[82] In this case, the *burgerwacht* (civil guard) of the CdK was put in charge of dealing with the revolt.[83] Although the CdK managed to put out the fire of the revolt by a combination of negotiations and violence, it showed that the state was either incapable or unwilling to provide

[75] Ibidem, 342.
[76] Ibidem, 87.
[77] Martens, 'A History', 163.
[78] Etambala, *Veroverd, bezet, gekoloniseerd*, 84.
[79] Ibidem, 82–93.
[80] Ibidem.
[81] Marchal, *E.D. Morel*, 460.
[82] Martens, 'A History', 157–158.
[83] Marchal, *Missie en staat in Oud-Kongo* (Vol. 1), 208.

protection to the concessionary companies. The CdK, in response to the uprising, formed its own army soon after the revolt had ended.[84]

In the *Compagnie du Kasaï*, violence was endemic, although in a slightly different way than in the northern concessions of ABIR and *Anversoise*, as the CdK relied to a greater extent on local chiefs and rulers to exercise control.[85] The CdK exercised a form of indirect colonial control rather than direct colonial control, by collaborating with local political entities and using their political capital to force local populations to work.[86] The CdK collaborated in particular with factions within the Kuba that were less opposed to European colonialism. Within the Kuba, factions slowly gained the upper hand arguing for contact with the colonising entities, in contrast to the factions who had long argued for autarky. The Kuba kings had specialised in the slave trade in the eighteenth century, limiting its outside contact to *corradores* or *capitas* who sold enslaved people the Kuba had captured in wars, including to the Arab slave traders.[87] Moreover, the Kuba kingdom was rich in ivory, which was of course a much sought-after commodity for the Europeans. The slave and ivory trade, coupled with the encroaching imperialism, led to tensions between the Kuba kings, rich and dependent on the slave trade, and their lower officials. Thus, the Kuba factions at times descended into civil war, opting Europeans as allies on both sides of the wars.[88]

The Congo Free State, and by extension the CdK, took the side of the Kuba kings, whereas Portugal often took the side of the lower officials.[89] The Kuba kings therefore became enforcers of the CdK, in particular by forcing their own people to work for the CdK to extract rubber from the rainforest.[90] This both strengthened the position of the monarch: the Kuba king Lukenga was even paid by the CdK to maintain a private army, in order to enforce forced labour for the CdK.[91] The CdK, aided by the *Force Publique*, moreover also organised raids on parts of the Kuba kingdom not under control of the king, in order to gain control over the ivory and rubber in the area. In response, some Bakuba (inhabitants of the Kuba

[84] Martens, 'A History', 279–280.

[85] Gann & Duignan, *The Rulers of Belgian Africa*, 138.

[86] Ibidem; Exenberger & Hartmann, 'Extractive Institutions in the Congo', 25.

[87] Vansina, *Being Colonised*, 35–56.

[88] Ibidem, 58–85.

[89] Ibidem, 86–126.

[90] Exenberger & Hartmann, 'Extractive Institutions in the Congo', 25.

[91] Gann & Duignan, *The Rulers of Belgian Africa*, 138.

Table 6.2 Gross profit margin and depreciations of the *Compagnie du Kasaï*, 1902–1911 (in fr., rounded)

Year	*Gross profit margin*	*Depreciations*
1902	1,465,279	315,108
1903	3,687,161	373,218
1904	5,597,449	1,186,729
1905	7,666,491	1,078,798
1906	8,182,472	557,155
1907	2,159,995	361,654
1908	4,533,045	972,527
1909	6,324,927	620,382
1910	4,926,124	1,485,895
1911	3,413,504	0
Total 1902–1911	47,956,450	6,951,465

Source: Buelens, *Congo 1886–1960*, 152

kingdom) revolted, as had happened in 1904–1905.[92] Other reports about armed expeditions undertaken against the local population, primarily in the Luba and Kuba kingdoms by the *Force Publique*, were later also published by the British.[93]

The CdK thus also was an instrumental player in forcing local populations to work, often working together with local politically powerful players. Moreover, the CdK was allowed to levy (*in natura*) taxes on the local population, which it did with overwhelming 'enthusiasm' and violent force.[94] Thanks to the privileged partnership with the state, the CdK made decent profits during the first years of its existence (Table 6.2).

In the wake of the red rubber scandals that had come to light under two other concession companies, ABIR and *Anversoise*, Morel aimed his guns at the CdK as well.[95] Much has been written about red rubber (see for an overview Chap. 1). What is important is that despite earlier, credible accusations (e.g. by Morisson, as well as by others in the broader Congo Free State about forced labour and other atrocities), it was not until roughly 1905 that the CdK also was included in Morel's purview. Until that time, Morel believed that in contrast to ABIR and *Anversoise* the

[92] Martens, 'A History', 160–166.

[93] Vansina, *Being Colonized*, 91.

[94] Ibidem, 214–216.

[95] For red rubber: Vangroenweghe, *Rood rubber*; Harms, 'The End of Red Rubber'. For the CdK: Martens, 'A History', 355; Marchal, *E.D. Morel*, 460.

rubber companies under the leadership of Albert Thys, like Lomami, SAB and to an extent the CdK, were positive exceptions.[96] Contacts with Sheppard and Morrison, as well as their stories about the Kuba revolt of the previous year, however led Morel in 1906 to write a letter to *The Times* detailing accusations of forced labour and violence against the local population for the first time.[97] Marchal writes that there were rumours before (and indeed public accusations by Morrison)[98] about the CdK, but that they were never substantiated.[99] In a subsequent revised version of his classic *Red Rubber*, Morel named the CdK as one of the 'great red rubber companies', having in the first version published in 1902 largely neglected the firm.[100] Morel furthermore wrote that "they [the Kuba] are now in process of being extirpated and dragged down to the level of the unhappy Mongos, Budjas, A-Babuas and other tribes inhabiting the rubber zone".[101]

Morel's attack contained four elements: first, forced taxation; second, military expeditions and the associated violence; third, forced rubber quotas; and fourth, the effects on the local population.[102] In response to the accusations, the CdK published a document for its shareholders trying to refute the allegations.[103] The CdK wrote that the firm would never use or accept violence, unless its property was attacked.[104] Moreover, the directors wrote that they respected the independence of groups wanting it (*in casu* primarily the Kuba); however, they would try to keep trading with them wherever possible.[105] The CdK argued that military intervention in 1904–1905 had been necessary as their factories had been attacked, but only as a matter of self-defence.[106] Moreover, it argued that rubber was bought for a free and fair price, and that there was thus no pressure on the

[96] Marchal, *E.D. Morel*, 590.

[97] Ibidem, 460.

[98] Idem, *De Kongostaat*, 564–565.

[99] Idem, *E.D. Morel*, 460.

[100] Morel, *Red Rubber* (1906 Version), 130.

[101] Ibidem, 130–131.

[102] Ibidem, 89.

[103] S.A., *Compagnie du Kasaï*.

[104] Ibidem, 35: « La Compagnie du Kasaï n'a jamais été et ne sera jamais partisan de la violence » & 93.

[105] Ibidem, 43: « Certain tribus, certain chefs, refusent toutes avances, tout commerce et, systématiquement, s'opposent à notre pénétration. Nos agents respectent leur indépendance; patiemment ils continuent à insister usant de tous les moyens légaux et bienveillants, et attendent pour s'installer leur assentiment. »

[106] Ibidem, 93.

local population to provide rubber quotas.[107] Moreover, the CdK also emphasised the building of hospitals and schools as evidence of their good intentions, for example the hospital in Dima built by the CdK to benefit the local people.[108] The CdK explicitly tried to distance itself from the atrocities committed by *Anversoise* and ABIR, emphasising its humanitarian actions in the Kasaï, as well as contributions to scientific research. The NAHV, during this time, kept itself in the background, and left the work of protecting the CdK to other directors.

Until 1908, the campaign against the CdK gained limited success, as international attention focused on the Congo Free State and Leopold's rule in general. After the Belgian take-over of 1908, however, Morrison and Sheppard relaunched their efforts to attack the CdK, in concurrence with Morel.[109] Morel received images of the ongoing slave trade from Morrisson and Shephard in the Kasaï region and published these pictures in May 1908.[110] This reinvigorated attention for the CdK case. Although it was not Morrison and Sheppard's goal to necessarily abolish the CdK, Morel went all-in with similar strategies as he had employed in the ABIR and *Anversoise* cases: on the one hand, publish gruelling images and story to capture public attention and on the other hand use the British Empire's machinery and strength to make sure that political consequences followed moral outrage. In the case of ABIR and *Anversoise*, the Casement Report had helped Morel a lot in achieving the second goal: in the CdK case, Morel persuaded the British colonial officials to send Wilfred Thesiger, the British Consul in Boma, to tour the Kasaï region much like Casement had done to write up a report on potential abuses.[111]

In October 1908, Thesiger published (with Morel's help) his report, accusing the CdK of forced labour for rubber production.[112] As Hochschild put it, Thesiger "submitted an excoriating report on starvation and brutality in the Kasai to the British Parliament".[113] Thesiger was particularly critical of armed sentries when locals did not meet their rubber quota, but also of the general system of wild rubber collection.[114] He implicated the

[107] Ibidem, 99.
[108] Ibidem, 28–30 & 78–83.
[109] Martens, 'A History', 355.
[110] Ibidem; Vansina, *Being Colonized*, 108–109.
[111] Etambala, *Veroverd, bezet, gekoloniseerd*, 108.
[112] Ibidem.
[113] Hochschild, *King Leopold's Ghosts*, 262.
[114] Martens, 'A History', 372–373.

capitas in particular, and also gave the example of various *capitas* holding Luba forced labourers at gunpoint to collect wild rubber. The CdK emphatically denied these accusations, but it sounded the alarm across Western Europe, and the CdK was unable to deny many of the accusations subsequently.[115] Soon afterwards, the Belgian state took over the Congo Free State and quickly went after the CdK, afraid to repeat the mistakes Leopold had made: in late 1908, no less than one-third of the CdK agents were under investigation.[116] Morel had again been successful: in 1910, the CdK's monopoly was taken away and forced labour was (at least until World War I) outlawed in the Belgian Congo.[117]

In one final act of resistance in 1908, the CdK filed a case for libel against Morrison and Sheppard at the state's superior court in Boma.[118] As Morel was in London (Morel never visited the Congo region in his lifetime), it was impossible to file a case against the mastermind of the campaign. Thus, the CdK went after the two Protestant missionaries, supported by Cambier's Catholic missionaries.[119] The case itself was postponed, as the Socialist leader (and lawyer by training) in the Belgian Parliament Emile Vandervelde agreed to take on the defence of Morrison and Sheppard in Boma and needed time to travel to Congo.[120] With the Congo Free State abolished and international opinion swayed against the CdK, the firm faced an uphill battle. The court came to the decision that Morrison and Sheppard were to be acquitted of the libel charges, as in their writings or communication with Morel had never explicitly mentioned the name of the CdK (they had only indicated the area).[121] Curiously, however, the CdK was therefore also found not guilty.[122] After this verdict, the CdK realised it would not be able to turn public opinion its way anymore.

The CdK was represented in the Parliamentary commission investigating the potential take-over of the Belgian state by its director J. De

[115] Ibidem, 377.

[116] Ibidem, 402. See for the names and cases: Etambala, *Veroverd, bezet, gekoloniseerd*, 114–116.

[117] Etambala, *Veroverd, bezet, gekoloniseerd*, 127–128.

[118] Hochschild, *King Leopold's Ghosts*, 262–265; Marchal, *E.D. Morel*, 581; Martens, A History', 395.

[119] Marchal, *Missie en staat in Oud-Kongo* (Vol. 1), 206–207.

[120] Hochschild, *King Leopold's Ghosts*, 263–264; Marchal, *E.D. Morel*, 581.

[121] Martens, 'A History', 395.

[122] Ibidem; Hochschild, *King Leopold's Ghosts*, 265.

Hemptinne, but he turned out to be unable to stop the take-over as well.[123] The CdK in the first instance did not agree to the *de facto* privatisation taking effect on 1 July 1910, but under public pressure had to bow and agreed.[124] Although the firm had been more profitable and larger than ABIR and *Anversoise*, its own red rubber scandal meant the end of its monopoly (though not the end of the firm).[125] The underlying profitability of the firm also diminished after the scandals came to light. Net profits started to fall after 1907, partly because of diminishing market circumstances in the world market for rubber. In the annual reports of the NAHV, this was also alluded to, and the NAHV already in the first decade of the 1900s sold some of its shares in the CdK (in particular its priority shares, which paid the biggest dividends) to private investors.[126] The association with Leopold's red rubber scandals also became a risk for the business model of the NAHV, as it also prided itself on its opposition to the slave trade.

Upon taking over the area that constituted the Congo Free State, the Belgian state quickly moved to abolish forced labour in the Kasaï and other areas (although it after the First World War returned to forced labour as a method to make the colony economically viable).[127] Under public pressure of Morel's CRA, the CdK lost its privileged position and on 22 February 1910 the Belgian colonial authorities declared the Kasaï a free trading zone, despite protests by the CdK directors.[128] In 1911, the CdK and the Belgian colonial authorities agreed that the CdK would be 'privatised', taking over all the shares from the state. Difficult years followed, as the CdK was not very well prepared for increased competition.[129] Portuguese traders from Angola outcompeted the CdK on price and quality.[130] The CdK remained a fairly important player in the area in the years to come, trading in rubber: however, it was unable to force the Kuba or Luba to work for them or tax them, which had been their advantage under

123 Vangroenweghe, *Rood rubber*, 306.

124 Buelens, *Congo 1885–1960*, 150–151.

125 Ibidem.

126 Van der Laan, 'Trading in the Congo', 247–248.

127 Seibert, 'More Continuity than Change?', 373–382; Idem, *In die globale Wirtschaft gezwungen*, 161.

128 Martens, 'A History', 299–302.

129 Etambala, *Veroverd, bezet, gekoloniseerd*, 127–128.

130 Vansina, *Being Colonized*, 117; Waltz, *Das Konzessionswesen* (Vol. 1), 250.

their near-monopoly status.[131] One consequence of the take-over of the Belgian Congo of the area was that the Kuba Kingdom lost its independence, and increasingly the Kuba kings started collaborating with the colonisers to retain a degree of agency and independence.[132] Red rubber in the Kasaï thus meant the loss of power of both the CdK and the Kuba kingdom, allowing other to fill the vacuum.

With the rubber boom subsiding as demand slumped, the CdK diversified into palm oil and, only after the First World War, diamond mining. The CdK, over the course of its existence, went through various cycles of boom and bust, as for example the rubber boom came to an end in the late 1900s. The end of the rubber boom increased losses, and despite a short-lived revival during the First World War (turning profits in 1916 and 1917, and breaking even in 1918, after substantial losses at the start of the war), most years in the 1910s witnessed significant losses. The CdK did obtain mining concessions in 1913 for the Kasaï area, but before the 'transition' to mineral extraction had properly taken place sold its mining rights to *Forminière*, a specialised mining firm, by 1919.[133]

The NAHV sold most of its factories in the Kasaï area to other firms over the course of the first ten years as the factories were generally expensive to maintain, for example because they were located rather remotely. By 1910–1911 started gradually divesting from the CdK, roughly at the same time as it started selling its shares in *La Bruxelloise*.[134] Throughout the 1910s, the NAHV thus diminished its active operations in the CdK, but remained a shareholder in the firm, profiting from the short-lived boom during the First World War. After the end of the First World War, the NAHV sold the significant majority of its shares in the CdK: the majority of the shares were already sold in 1918/1919, with further sales following in 1919/1920, 1922/1923 and 1925/1926, after which the NAHV had no shares left in the CdK.[135] Most of the capital (the shares were sold at a profit to the NAHV) was used to try to set up a venture in South Africa after the First World War, where the NAHV nevertheless quickly pulled out.[136] The NAHV remained operative on its own in the Belgian Congo after 1908, when the Belgian colonial authorities allowed

[131] Ibidem, 119.
[132] Ibidem, 125.
[133] Derksen, 'Forminière in the Kasai', 56.
[134] NL-HaNA, Archief NAHV, nr. 688, Annual Report NAHV 1910/1911.
[135] Van der Laan, 'Trading in the Congo', 247–248.
[136] Ibidem.

it to return outside of the framework of the concession companies. Free from the yoke of the concession companies and the unpredictable situation that the Congo Free State created, the NAHV returned to do business on its own in Belgian Congo, eventually divesting from its forced incorporation in the CdK.[137]

6.4 The NAHV and the Ibanche Factory

This section zooms in on one NAHV-owned factory in particular, the Ibanche factory, based on the memoires of Alfons Vermeulen, an NAHV agent seconded to the CdK under the agreement made on its establishment. The story here complements much of what was presented in the previous pages from the viewpoint of Ibanche and Vermeulen, allowing for a more microhistorical approach to the participation of the Dutch entrepreneurs in the CdK. Around 1896–1897, the NAHV started negotiating with the SAB, for example over the sharing of factories, common purchases of rubber and even sharing employees between the two.[138] Ibanche was pinpointed by both firms as a potential place for cooperation as early as 1896–1897, even if at that point was still owned by the state. Ibanche was strategically located between several tributaries of the Kasaï River, and therefore a prized asset for the NAHV and SAB.

Not much can be found on the Ibanche factory in the NAHV archives, except for the documents of sale and lease. On 9 May 1898, General Félix Fuchs, Governor-General in Boma, wrote to Greshoff that the request to buy the Ibanche factory was approved, in response to Greshoff's request to do so on 13 April.[139] Greshoff himself had to confirm the sale in Banana, which he duly did.[140] On 8 August 1898, Fuchs wrote that the NAHV was allowed to start occupying and using the factory from 1 February 1899 onwards.[141] Moreover, the NAHV was exempted from paying the *droit de licence*, a common duty, for operating from the Ibanche factory.[142] Ibanche quickly became one of the NAHV's main outposts in the Kasaï (see Image 6.3).[143] The factory was transferred to the CdK upon its establishment, yet

[137] Ibidem.
[138] NL-HaNA, Archief NAHV, Nr. 664, Map 1896–1897.
[139] Ibidem, Map 1898, Nr. 6, Letter Fuchs to NAHV 09-05-1898.
[140] Ibidem.
[141] Ibidem, Map 1898, Nr. 14, Letter Fuchs to NAHV 08-08-1898.
[142] Ibidem.
[143] Idem, Nr. 674.

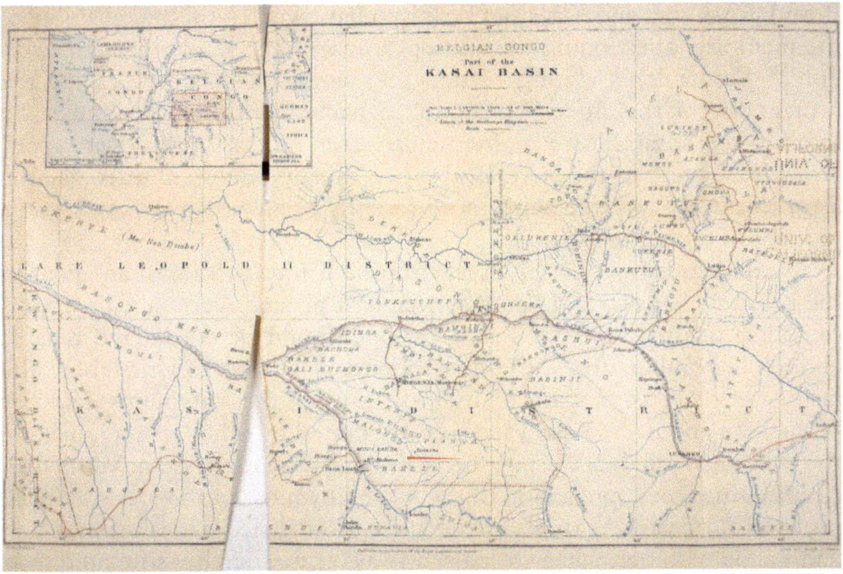

Image 6.3 The Kasaï region (location Ibanche underlined in red). (Source: Land and Peoples of the Kasaï, via Wikimedia Commons, available at https://commons.wikimedia.org/wiki/File:Land_and_peoples_of_the_Kasai;_being_a_narrative_of_a_two_years%27_journey_among_the_cannibals_of_the_equatorial_forest_and_other_savage_tribes_of_the_south-western_Congo_(1911)_(14770273764).jpg [Retrieved 29/10/2024])

still run by NAHV. After the establishment of the CdK, the only mention in the NAHV archives of Ibanche is many accounts from 1903 documenting the delivery of goods, as well as an inventory from 1902 or 1903 of the factory's possessions.[144]

Luckily, we do have the three-volume memoirs of Alfons Vermeulen left. Vermeulen was born on 28 February 1877 and left Rotterdam in October 1899, at the age of 22, as an agent for the NAHV to take service in the Congo Free State.[145] Two of the three volumes were published during Vermeulen's lifetime, but only in 2021 a properly edited edition of all of Vermeulen's writings was published by one of his great-grandsons.[146]

[144] Idem, Nr. 678, Account CdK 17-02-1903 & Inventory [Date Unknown].

[145] Vermeulen, *De memoires*, 400–401.

[146] See the introduction of this chapter.

Both Jan Vansina and Klaas van Walraven have written on the reliability of the memoirs, questioning the 'European gaze' Vermeulen brought with him.[147] Vermeulen's writing borders on memoirs and fiction, calling the protagonist of the story 'Chicongo', a name Vermeulen was given by locals in the Kasaï. However, Vermeulen clearly draws on his own experiences as an agent of the NAHV. The two already-published texts take the form of novels, and the third more recently published text consists of a number of unfinished texts.

As a trilogy, they offer an excellent insight into the life of an agent in the Kasaï. As Vansina and Van Walraven have argued, Vermeulen's work is of course racist by today's standards, but should be considered reliable enough in combination with other sources to be used to write about the history of the Kasaï region.[148] Indeed, many of the statements made by Vermeulen about the Kasaï can be corroborated by other sources, making the work fairly reliable. Despite the racism that is clearly present, Vermeulen clearly gained an appreciation of the life led by most of the locals, criticising the European way of life. Vermeulen also married a local woman and had a child with her: when she passed away, he married her sister and took her to the French Congo with the child. While much of Vermeulen's writing is on local customs, there is also much to be found on how he conducted trade in remote areas of the Kasaï.

Two of Vermeulen's volumes bring forward information on the Kasaï, and Ibanche more in particular.[149] In the third volume, Vermeulen describes how he is sent by the NAHV to work for the *Compagnie du Lobaye* in the French Congo, and will thus not be considered here.[150] Vermeulen arrived in Banana, and was soon transferred to Brazzaville (where he met Greshoff) and subsequently Matadi, a place further upriver on the Congo river. Upon arrival, it became clear to Vermeulen soon that the NAHV was interested primarily in rubber and ivory, and was looking to increase its market share amidst the rubber boom.[151] Vermeulen was sent subsequently to Ibanche, where he would join an NAHV agent only named as Loomans.[152] As Ibanche was close to the Kuba's political centre

[147] Vansina, 'History in Novels'; Van Walraven, 'European Memoirs and Colonialism'.

[148] Vansina, 'History in Novels', 128–129; Van Walraven, 'European Memoirs and Colonialism', 11–12.

[149] Vermeulen, *De pioniersdagen*; Idem, *De memoires.*

[150] Idem, *De ingang der hel.*

[151] Idem, *De pioniersdagen*, 4.

[152] Ibidem, 88.

of power, the Kuba were also the natural trading partners at the factory. Under Loomans, relations were tense in the wake of the 1894–1895 Kuba Revolt. Loomans soon left for one of the main factories in Banana, leaving Vermeulen alone to run the factory after three months.[153]

Vermeulen offers descriptions of the nature of trade and work at the factory. He mentioned that, in practice, he would be the sole judge when disputes broke out on the factory, although this rarely happened.[154] The factory Ibanche had roughly thirty employees, including (Ba)Kuba, Ba-Tétéla and so-called Sappo-Sap: all were, according to Vermeulen, 'sworn enemies' of each other, but he does not mention labour unrest or any violence happening under his watch. Wage labour appeared to have been the norm here, with forced labour not mentioned.[155] The NAHV, however, employed various *capitas* (middlemen), who were armed and in charge of bringing rubber into the factory, by trading with and forcing the local population to work. Vermeulen noted that he had managed to increase rubber production of the Ibanche factory fivefold in two years, by trading the rubber for cotton (and no alcohol, he mentioned specifically).[156] According to Vansina, Vermeulen's descriptions show much agency these *capitas*, mostly Kubas, had in the rubber trade.[157]

Vermeulen does not mention how the *capitas* specifically managed to obtain the rubber: although he did mention that relations with the Kuba improved markedly on his watch. After Loomans had left, Vermeulen invited Kuba representatives to the factory, describing how he negotiated at length with them.[158] Vermeulen subsequently stayed in a Kuba village, ensuring the peace between the Europeans and the Kuba.[159] As a result, less fake rubber was brought as well by the Kuba to the factory, which apparently happened on a regular basis before Vermeulen's arrival.[160] Vermeulen also offered descriptions of the town of Ibanche, which due to the Dutch and missionaries' presence became a regional market town. Vermeulen wrote that there was a lively slave trade at the market, with

[153] Ibidem, 98.
[154] Idem, *De memoires*, 43.
[155] Idem, *De pioniersdagen*, 89.
[156] Ibidem, 124 & 130.
[157] Vansina, *Being Colonized*, 63–64.
[158] Vermeulen, *De pioniersdagen*, 102.
[159] Ibidem.
[160] Idem, *De memoires*, 66–67.

plenty of other goods being traded as well.[161] There is no evidence that Vermeulen bought slaves himself to work on the factory, but the Kuba may have sold Luba or Lunda slaves in Ibanche. Trade was still done via bartering, rather than a monetised system, indicating the legal and practical reach of colonialism was in many ways limited.[162]

After three years at the Ibanche factory, the factory was sold to 'a Belgian firm', *in casu* the CdK.[163] For Vermeulen, not much changed in practice, even if the political situation in the Kasaï did change. Vermeulen was in the summer of 1904 called away from Ibanche, partly because of his proven peace-making ability with the Kuba, to steer factories for the NAHV in the French Congo. Shortly before leaving, an armed conflict between Kuba and Cokwe broke out in the area, whereby the Cokwe slaughtered and burned down a Kuba village near Ibanche.[164] Vermeulen claimed to have acted as an intermediary and peacemaker between the two groups, eventually leading to an armistice in Ibanche and its surroundings.[165] Soon after, Vermeulen's wife passed away and he left for Banana and subsequently for the French Congo. According to Vermeulen, a Kuba representative even came to Ibanche to thank him upon leaving.[166]

His successor Van Obbergen took over, but the armed clash between Kuba and Cokwe spread across the Kasaï soon after Vermeulen left:[167] Vermeulen wrote ominously that after leaving, "within three months the factory Ibanche was a smoking ruin".[168] As we have noted, Vermeulen's text is the sole mention we have of the Dutch factory at Ibanche being burned: the NAHV archives are silent on the issue. What had happened? After Van Obbergen had passed away in the burning or was killed during the fighting, the NAHV had apparently declined to send a new agent there. Leo Frobenius, a German who travelled the Kasaï in the wake of the Kuba Revolt (arriving in August 1905), wrote that the Belgian Van Lauteren had taken over the Ibanche factory as the main agent, indicating the NAHV had retracted its agents from the area and left Ibanche to be

[161] Ibidem, 23 & 39.

[162] Ibidem, 50.

[163] Idem, *De pioniersdagen*, 183–184.

[164] Idem, *De memoires*, 367–368.

[165] Ibidem.

[166] Ibidem, 20.

[167] Ibidem, 20; Idem, *De pioniersdagen*, 232.

[168] Idem, *De pioniersdagen*, 232: "drie maanden later was de factorij Ibanche een rookende puinhoop."

run by the CdK.[169] The archives of the Prosecutor-General in Brussels indicate that, by 1907, Van Lauteren was still the chef of the factory. In 1908, he was succeeded as the chef by a man named Maurice Charles Kraus, who was subsequently prosecuted in 1909 for arbitrary arrests of a local Kuba chief and the fact that his *capitas* at the factory had harshly treated local labourers.[170] Kraus had resorted to these harsh measures after another Kuba uprising in early 1909, but the new regime in the now-Belgian Congo acted forcefully over reports of violence and harsh behaviour towards Africans, particularly in the 'red rubber' areas like the Kasaï. As a result, Kraus was incarcerated in June 1909 and prosecuted for this role in the new forced labour regime.[171]

The NAHV, meanwhile, appears to have retracted itself from running daily operations in the Kasaï region and within the CdK after the killing of Van Obbergen in 1905: in the files of the Prosecutor-General, no mention is made of any NAHV agent.[172] In the same file on the CdK, all agents of the company were listed, without mention of any (known) Dutch agents. The NAHV, after the largely unmentioned burning of the Ibanche factory, appears to have handed over all of its former factories to the CdK. Philippi remained a commissioner, and until the late 1920s, the NAHV kept shares in the CdK.[173] However, it would be fair to say that the NAHV resorted to a very passive role in the CdK after 1905–1906, when the killing of Van Obbergen by the resistant Kuba offered a reality check to the NAHV.

6.5 Dutch Entrepreneurship in the Kasaï 1900–1921

The question of Dutch participation in the *Compagnie du Kasaï* raises questions regarding the entrepreneurial abilities and judgements of the said entrepreneurs. Analysing this episode through the three entrepreneurial processes as defined by Wadhwani and Lubinski ((1) envisioning and valuing opportunities, (2) allocating and reconfiguring resources and (3) legitimising novelty), the entrepreneurial qualities of the Dutch come

[169] L. Frobenius, *Im Schatten des Kongostaates* (Berlin 1907), 228–229.

[170] BE-AGR2-DJC, Archives Africaines, JUST, nr. 58, Files on *Compagnie du Kasaï*, 1908–1909.

[171] Ibidem.

[172] Ibidem.

[173] Van der Laan, 'Trading in the Congo', 247–248.

into sharper focus. The *initial* stage of the Dutch entrepreneurial activities in the Kasaï did bear hallmarks of executing all three entrepreneurial processes successfully: they were among the first European entrepreneurs to move into the Kasaï (following Wissmann & SEE), therefore envisioning and valuing the opportunity rightly. Rather than look for palm oil in the Kasaï, they quickly switched to rubber as their prime commodity for trade. This turned out to be the right judgement in the entrepreneurial sense of the word, as the rubber boom started in the late 1880s and early 1890s, tragically ending in the 'red rubber' scandals in the Congo Free State.

The Dutch entrepreneurs, at the outset, (re-)allocated and reconfigured its resources successfully, investing capital as well as sending its best agents to man the new factories in the Kasaï: Alfons Vermeulen was sent there, for example, and once he proved to be successful in managing the tricky demands of the Ibanche factory, he was sent to the French Congo to build up its network on the ground there. Greshoff, the NAHV's trusted hand on the ground, also was closely involved in the Kasaï involvements. Third, the entrepreneurs legitimised novelty through the rubber trade, showing that the commodity could successfully be sold on the world market, in particular the Kasaï rubber, which turned out to be of a very high quality.

The decision to participate in the CdK however casts more doubt on the entrepreneurial qualities of the NAHV. If we, for a moment, take Casson's definition of the entrepreneur as a specialist in judging risk, then the conclusion should be that the Dutch entrepreneurs were rather bad at doing their job: despite all the obvious warning signs regarding the behaviour of Leopold and his administration, the Dutch entrepreneurs opted to participate in the *Compagnie du Kasaï* with all the risks involved. The NAHV directors, on the advice of Greshoff, invested a substantial sum of initial capital (85,000 francs) into the CdK, but moreover contributed much *in natura* to the establishment of the CdK, for example by providing knowledge, physical factories and transport facilities, as well as labour through its seconded agents. In return for agreeing to participation, Philippi was granted a position as a director (and later commissioner) in the CdK, but in practice, the NAHV was one of the two largest private shareholders without any real influence (the same went for SAB).

Property rights were not respected in the colonial setting, and the NAHV did not have much leeway to make sure their case was given a fair hearing in these circumstances. The CdK, and in particular the state that was its largest shareholder, profited from the knowledge and investments built up by the Dutch entrepreneurship: in other words, the CdK was an excellent instrument for the Congo Free State to exploit the knowledge, capital and property of private entrepreneurs. Nationality did not really matter here, as Thys' SAB essentially suffered the same fate as the NAHV in the Kasaï region.[174] The NAHV may have recouped its initial 85,000 francs investment over the years through the dividends the CdK paid out (especially in its early years), even if it also incurred substantial losses over time as well. For example, the Ibanche factory was attacked, burned down and subsequently taken over by the CdK, leaving the NAHV with an employee killed and no factory in a crucial area of the Kasaï. In the end, the NAHV quietly sold its shares in the CdK after the First World War.[175] Financially speaking, participation in the CdK may have turned a profit in the end, but the non-financial costs were high.

6.6 Conclusion

The case study of the role of the NAHV in the *Compagnie du Kasaï* has brought into focus many of the issues raised in Chap. 5, regarding the entrepreneurial strategies of the Rotterdam entrepreneurs tied to operating in a violent colonial environment. What the (lack of) sources made difficult in the previous chapter was possible to a larger extent because of the detailed sources that we have for the *Compagnie du Kasaï*: to bring a more microhistorical approach to the front, in particular at the Ibanche factory, which was NAHV property after 1898 but was also used by the CdK for its operations. The sources therefore allowed us to include a greater number of actors beyond the directors of the firms and the people high up in the administration of the Congo Free State: Kuba kings and rebels, Protestant missionaries and Dutch agents on the ground like Vermeulen.

The chapter has shown that the NAHV was simultaneously an active participant and a passive bystander in the process of gradual colonisation of the Kasaï. It was active in dealing with the Kuba around the Ibanche factory. Under Alfons Vermeulen, tensions with the Kuba appear to have been managed reasonably well. Vermeulen apparently did not enforce

[174] M. Vancanneyt, 'Een economische geschiedenis van Albert Thys (1876–1908)', Unpublished MA Thesis Ghent University (Ghent 2008), available at https://lib.ugent.be/catalog/rug01:001290438 [Retrieved 15/09/2024], 70, 85 & 92–93.

[175] Van der Laan, 'Trading in the Congo', 247–248.

unreasonable labour requirements upon Kuba or Luba labourers near the factories and managed to discipline his *capitas*. Under his successor, Van Obbergen, things again started going downhill and the Ibanche factory was burned to the ground, an expression of long-standing antipathy of the Kuba towards European encroachment. Although there is no evidence that the most horrendous red rubber crimes happened under NAHV watch, it is clear that at least part of the Kuba resistance happened because *capitas* at various factories were using methods to force Kuba to work for rubber collection.

At the height of the red rubber scandals, however, the NAHV took a very passive stance in the CdK: and despite the fact that the Ibanche factory was burned down, the Dutch appeared not to aim to change too much of the policy of the CdK. It remained a large shareholder and delivered a director and/or commissioner, but largely bowed out of daily operations of the CdK before the red rubber scandals came to a head under public pressure by Morel, and later by the report of Thesiger. Although the Kuba were eventually unsuccessful in getting out the European colonists, it appeared that the combination of Kuba resistance and the management of the region by the CdK led the NAHV to largely disappear from the Kasaï region after 1905.[176]

[176] Only in the 1920s, the NAHV returned to the Belgian Congo and Kasaï region for substantial investments. See: Van der Laan, 'Trading in the Congo', 242–243.

CHAPTER 7

Conclusion

7.1 Conclusion

The First World War interrupted the business of the Dutch entrepreneurs across Africa once more. The various phases of the Scramble for and Partition of Africa had forced the entrepreneurs to adapt in manifold ways many times, but the war once again requested the utmost of the entrepreneurs to come to terms with the new circumstances. According to trade statistics, trade between the Netherlands and West (Central) Africa almost completely stopped after 1916, with only minor trade flows being recorded for 1914 and 1915.[1] Fighting at sea and in the colonies made trade, even to a neutral country like the Netherlands, near impossible. Efforts to make the Belgian Congo neutral territory never materialised.[2] When the war ended, the situation (as had been the case so often before) changed again: *Neukamerun* had become French again, and in the Belgian Congo forced labour was reintroduced to ramp up production in the wake of the war, also returning the colony to a painful past many had hoped to leave behind.[3]

[1] See Dreijer, 'Dutch-African Trade Database'.
[2] NL-HaNA, Archief Buitenlandse Zaken A-Dossiers, nr. 212, Congo-staat 1903–1917, Map 3.
[3] Seibert, *In die globale Wirtschaft gezwungen*, 94–96.

G. Dreijer, *Private Entrepreneurship and European Imperialism*, Palgrave Studies in Economic History,
https://doi.org/10.1007/978-3-032-01086-5_7

In one sense, then, the situation returned to one familiar to those active in pre-war West and West Central Africa. In another sense, however, as Laurens van der Laan has remarked, the period after the First World War ushered in significant changes in terms of the economic policies and political circumstances, and therefore should be studied as a different era from the pre-First World War world.[4] For the Dutch entrepreneurs, the end of the First World War did indeed usher in a different age, one characterised by consolidation and stagnation. As a result, the First World War allows for a 'natural' end point of the book, allowing to see the developments between the 1830s and the start of the First World War in the framework of various developments that were crucial for Rotterdam and Africa: European imperialism, the transition to legitimate commerce and the development of a globalised world economy in which port cities like Rotterdam played a crucial role.[5]

In 1920–1921, the OAC and the NAHV merged, finally bringing together the firms that Hendrik Muller Szn. took over between 1879 and 1883 together in one large conglomerate.[6] The shares of the OAC could be exchanged by shareholders for a share in the NAHV.[7] In a letter dated 14 July 1921 to the *Twentsche Bank*, Hendrik Mees wrote that measures were necessary to limit competition in Africa and on the Dutch market, in order to compete with the British firms established across Africa.[8] Despite some shareholder protests, the merger was pushed through by the directors and finally took place in late 1921. The reconstituted NAHV (re-) gained a foothold in West Africa (Liberia and present-day Nigeria), alongside continuing to invest in the Congo Free State and the French Congo.

Until the 1950s, the NAHV remained a business behemoth across West and West Central Africa in trade and production of raw commodities.[9] In 1954, the NAHV merged with *Lindeteves N.V.*, a Dutch firm that

[4] Van der Laan, 'Trading in the Congo'; Idem, 'Selling Africa's Tropical Export Crops'.

[5] See also: Coquery-Vidrovitch, 'The Colonial Economy of the Former French, Belgian and Portuguese Zones, 1914–35', in: Boahen (ed.), *General History of Africa. VII*, 351–381.

[6] NL-SAR, Archief Chabot, nr. 2482, Stukken betreffende aandelen in de OAC en de NAHV, 1921.

[7] NL-ABN, Archief Mees en Zoonen, nr. 777, Verwisseling aandelen OAC naar NAHV (1921).

[8] Ibidem.

[9] Van der Laan, 'Trading in the Congo'; Muller, *Muller*, 353; M. Kind, *Van kippenveren tot dieselmotoren: de geschiedenis van de technische handelsmaatschappij Lindeteves NV* (Schoorl 2000), 41 & 51.

originated in the Dutch East Indies in the 1860s, and which in the wake of the Second World War and the Dutch 'loss' of Indonesia in 1949 sought new business opportunities in West Africa.[10] The merger was only moderately successful, and in 1982 the ailing firm was taken over by a Pakistani investment firm.[11] This take-over ended over 125 years of involvement by Dutch entrepreneurs in West and West Central Africa. The entrepreneurs had started out with small-scale family firms operating in the coastal regions of West and West Central Africa, and over the years got swept up in the transition to the legitimate commerce, European imperialism in Africa and beyond, the Partition of the continent and the economic and political developments that eventually came to its apex in the concession companies, as well as the pushback against the excessive violence perpetrated under these companies.

At the start of this book, two questions were introduced that animated the analysis presented: first, *why* did entrepreneurs from Rotterdam move into West (Central) Africa, and second, *how* did they operate there? The first question can be answered by referring to a combination of push and pull factors. On the one hand, the monopolisation of the production and trade of commodities from the Dutch East Indies by the old mercantile elite from Amsterdam pushed the 'new kids on the block' from Rotterdam elsewhere. West Africa, and subsequently West Central Africa, which went through the transition from slave trade to legitimate commerce, almost naturally pulled them from Asia to Africa. The *why* question can therefore be explained by ***internal*** (Dutch, contingent) as well as ***external*** (international, structural) factors.

The *how* question was perhaps the more complicated question, as the book through the chapters has detailed the changing strategies of the Dutch entrepreneurs over a period of some eighty years. To analyse the activities of the Dutch entrepreneurs, the book looked through the conceptual lens of entrepreneurship and, inspired by the work of Wadhwani and Lubinski, at three 'entrepreneurial processes' ((1) envisioning and valuing opportunities, (2) allocating and reconfiguring resources and (3) legitimising novelty).[12] This conceptualisation of entrepreneurial processes, which combined the ideas of authors like Schumpeter and Casson

[10] Kind, *Van kippenveren tot dieselmotoren*, 41–51; J.P.B. Jonker & K.E. Sluyterman, *Thuis op de wereldmarkt: Nederlandse handelshuizen door de eeuwen heen* (The Hague 2000), 154.

[11] Sluyterman & Jonker, *Thuis op de wereldmarkt*, 154.

[12] Wadhwani & Lubinski, 'Reinventing Entrepreneurial History'.

in one overarching model, was combined with the emphasis that theorists like Casson put on the societal embeddedness of the entrepreneur: in short, the acknowledgement that entrepreneurs acted from a moral framework embedded in their time, but in particular from their physical environment.[13] In the case of the Dutch entrepreneurs, this environment was the city of Rotterdam, the Netherlands' rising port city at the time.

These facts determined, to a significant extent, their outlook and their entrepreneurial choices: as the book has made clear, the fact that these entrepreneurs were from *Rotterdam* was crucial for how the story unfolded. Rotterdam became a global port city in the second half of the nineteenth century, and its entrepreneurial inhabitants thus sought ways to participate in the global economy. While unique in the Netherlands, both Rotterdam and its entrepreneurs were comparable to other rising 'second' port cities, like Hamburg in Germany, Marseille in France and Liverpool in Britain. Differences certainly also existed (Hamburg and Marseille, as port cities, were already prominent in the early modern period, for example), but overall, these port cities together largely dictated the flows of nineteenth-century colonial commodity and shipping flows.

Africa's transition to legitimate commerce facilitated the Rotterdam entrepreneurs' interest in West (Central) Africa.[14] The analysis of the entrepreneurial processes in this book has proceeded in three stages roughly corresponding to the pre-Partition period between the 1850s and 1870s, the High Partition of the 1880s–1890s and the concession company era between the late 1890s and the First World War. The various stages involved rather different entrepreneurial challenges and opportunities. In the early stage of the Scramble for Africa, the Rotterdam entrepreneurs clearly envisioned and valued an opportunity in the Congo basin as well as Liberia, where European imperial control was either weak or nonexistent, for commodities like palm oil. They shifted attention, and resources, from Dutch-controlled Elmina to other regions across West and West Central Africa and were largely successful at doing so. While finding a new supply market, they were slightly less successful at the third entrepreneurial process, legitimising novelty, as they essentially followed the lead of British entrepreneurs.

The political Partition of Africa changed the circumstances for the Dutch entrepreneurs after 1880, as they now had to deal with nascent

[13] Casson & Casson, *The Entrepreneur in History*, 120–134.

[14] See Dalrymple-Smith, *Commercial Transitions*.

European empires, the lack of functioning institutions and protection of property rights, and the harsh and sometimes extreme violence that accompanied imperial expansion. Within the limitations set by these empires, in particular the Congo Free State under King Leopold II, the Dutch entrepreneurs acted as well as they could, but were often set back as 'foreign' (i.e. non-Belgian) firms were put at a disadvantage. The political challenges that the Partition brought made the execution of the entrepreneurial processes much more difficult, even if the Dutch entrepreneurs remained (naively, probably) confident for some time that the international community would safeguard the agreements reached in Berlin, and that free trade in the Congo Free State would remain unimpeded.

Reality, however, intervened, and from an entrepreneurial perspective, the Dutch entrepreneurs in the NAHV did not adapt quickly enough to the new political circumstances: in other words, they valued the (lack of) opportunities in the Congo Free State too high, and did not properly see the risks of extractive colonial rule. In the short term, allying with the 'Arab' warlord Tippu Tip allowed the Dutch entrepreneurs some grip on the ivory trade, but in the medium term, this allowed Leopold to crush opposition and consolidate power. In the early twentieth century, the tables turned, as information partly supplied by the NAHV director Anton Greshoff contributed to Leopold's downfall in 1908, when the red rubber scandals came to light. From an *entrepreneurial* viewpoint, however, the early 1890s presented an exceptionally difficult time for the Dutch entrepreneurs across West and West Central Africa, partly for political reasons, but also for economic reasons, as was also clear in the case of the Dutch entrepreneurs in Liberia.[15]

In 1892, the NAHV largely admitted defeat and for the most part left the Congo Free State (with the exception of the Kasaï), pivoting towards the French Congo, where it already had built up a network of factories before the Partition of Africa. In moving there, the Dutch entrepreneurs rekindled their entrepreneurial spirits and successfully seized on the opportunities that presented themselves there. The Dutch bid for a number of concessions and set up subsidiaries in Paris with French capital cooperation to safeguard their investments: in this sense, they had clearly learned from their mistakes in the Congo Free State and made sure to play by the rules. The first two entrepreneurial processes (envisioning and valuing opportunities and allocating and reconfiguring resources) therefore were

[15] Muller, *Muller*, 341–354.

fairly successfully in the French Congo between 1892 and 1910: the legitimising novelty part, as was the case previously, was less clearly pronounced.

The NAHV was forced to participate in the *Compagnie du Kasaï* in 1901, setting up a difficult arrangement to continue the (limited) involvement in the Congo Free State. Here, the Dutch entrepreneurs basically appeared to have fallen into the same trap as before, even if they were able to net passive profits from the CdK until the early 1920s. In the French Congo, the post-1910 period witnessed a similar development, as (part of) the territorial concessions that were transferred to German *Neukamerun* for geopolitical reasons. In conclusion, it would therefore not be unfair to say that the Dutch entrepreneurs may have been decent entrepreneurs, but not very good at the politics of operating in the 'empire of others': as long as their capital or knowledge was useful for the empire they operated in, they were able to operate and make money, but once the political and/or economic interests of the colonial administrations changed, they were discarded just as easily. This mechanism played out over and over again, without the Dutch entrepreneurs managing (at least in West Central Africa) to foresee this process or, even better, preventing it. On the other hand, the Dutch entrepreneurs were certainly *resilient*, opting for new opportunities multiple times. In a way, the study presented here thus not only shows the challenges and opportunities associated with 'exploiting the empire of others', but also of entrepreneurial resilience in a challenging environment.

In recent years, there has been much talk of a 'new Scramble for Africa', in particular as Chinese investment in Africa has surged.[16] *The Economist*, having dubbed Africa 'the hopeless continent' in 2000,[17] even argued in 2019 that the 'new' Scramble could now actually benefit Africans (in implicit contrast to the 'old' Scramble).[18] In particular, Africa's reservoir

[16] See for example *The Africa Brief*, 'Africa's Minerals', 28-03-2023, available at https://theafricabrief.beehiiv.com/p/special-africas-minerals [Retrieved 18/10/2023]. For academic work, see: O.C. Eze & C.A. Anigbo (eds.), *New Scramble for Africa* (Lagos 2010); P.R. Carmody, *The New Scramble for Africa* (Cambridge & Malden MA 2016); J. Ewalefoh, 'The New Scramble for Africa', in: S.O. Oloruntoba & Falola (eds.), *The Palgrave Handbook of Africa and the Changing Global Order* (Cham 2022), 309–322, https://doi.org/10.1007/978-3-030-77481-3_15.

[17] *The Economist*, 13-05-2000, available at https://www.economist.com/weeklyedition/2000-05-13 [Retrieved 18/10/2023].

[18] *The Economist*, 'The New Scramble for Africa', 07-03-2019, available at https://www.economist.com/leaders/2019/03/07/the-new-scramble-for-africa [Retrieved 18-10-2023].

of rare earth minerals (the continent being home to roughly 30% of the world's mineral reserves) is attractive to foreign powers like the United States or China seeking to secure these strategic minerals. Most famously, this is the case with the cobalt mined in the DRC Congo for the mobile phones, leading to forced (child) labour and widespread abuses in the Eastern Congo, bringing back memories of the atrocious 'red rubber' scandals in the very same area under the Congo Free State.[19]

As journalistic and societal hypes go, talk of a 'new Scramble for Africa' may be overblown to an extent, and indeed this idea appears to return in cycles, with every twenty or thirty years proclaimed as a 'new Scramble for Africa'.[20] Most of the works talking of a 'new Scramble' essentially fall into the same traps as many historians have made, by focusing on great power competition and taking the perspective of the nation/country, thereby neglecting the work of private actors, and essentially conflating the Partition and Scramble in present-day terms as well.[21] Moreover, much of this talk also denies Africans their agency in this process, not unlike some of the historical work on the nineteenth-century Scramble.[22] Historians should thus maintain a healthy scepticism towards such claims, but it is undeniable that there is a growing interest in Africa's resources, running the risk that many of the grave mistakes of the late nineteenth century are being made again.[23] Of course, the common story that established 'great powers' like the United States, China, Russia (and to a lesser extent the European Union)[24] vie for power on the African continent is true to an extent, with African elites aiming to extract as much as possible from playing these great powers against each other. However, investments from countries like India, the United Arab Emirates, Indonesia, Thailand and

[19] Indeed, some work on cobalt mining explicitly refers to this, see e.g.: S. Kara, *Cobalt Red: How the Blood of the Congo Powers Our Lives* (New York 2023). For red rubber, see e.g.: Vangroenweghe, *Rood rubber*.

[20] See e.g. E.A. Tarabrin, *The New Scramble for Africa* (Moscow 1974), for just one example.

[21] See e.g. Ewalefoh, 'The New Scramble for Africa'.

[22] See e.g. Pakenham, *The Scramble for Africa*, for an example of Europe-centred work.

[23] See e.g. E. Obadare, 'A "New Scramble for Africa?"', *Council on Foreign Relations*, 02-05-2023, available at https://www.cfr.org/blog/new-scramble-africa 'Retrieved 18/10/2023].

[24] See e.g. for the European Union's infrastructural initiatives in Africa's port regions: Germany Trade & Invest, 'Special: Global Gateway in Afrika', available at https://www.gtai.de/de/trade/afrika/specials/global-gateway-in-afrika-1003740 [Retrieved 30/10/2023].

Turkey for example all increased in the period 2006–2018, based on trade statistics.[25]

What the historical Scramble for Africa and the present-day rush for Africa's mineral resources have in common, this book suggests, is that the underlying story is more complex than a simple story of great power competition. Today, there may be Turkish entrepreneurs building infrastructure or delivering weapons to African states,[26] or Indonesian entrepreneurs aiming to profit from Africa's resources to become a producer of batteries.[27] To tie this back to the story told in this book, this is not dissimilar to entrepreneurs from countries like the Netherlands aiming to extract raw resources from the African continent to fuel Rotterdam's boom to become a major port city, a status it still profits from today.[28] Individually, these entrepreneurs may or may not be consequential in their actions, but the story stands for something bigger by showing that the narrative of great power competition in Africa, and perhaps in continents beyond Africa, is incomplete. Not only 'great powers' participate in the 'scramble' for resources, but many others from purportedly smaller states also participated in the process of extracting and exploiting imperial resources. That is, of course, not to say that great power competition is unimportant (and nor is the historical Partition), but neither does this tell the whole story.

In the historical Scramble, private actors like entrepreneurs, missionaries and explorers played a major role in paving the way for the coming of formal empire, and thereby eventually contributing to the actual Partitioning of Africa in the period between 1875 and 1914. Even if some, including the Dutch entrepreneurs central to this study, *tried* to remain out of the reach of European states by moving their operations to the Congo basin, eventually they had to deal with those very states. In the context of 'colonial capitalism', it proved impossible to operate outside of

[25] *The Economist*, 'Choices on the Continent', 07-03-2019, available at https://www.economist.com/briefing/2019/03/07/africa-is-attracting-ever-more-interest-from-powers-elsewhere [Retrieved 18/10/2023].

[26] See e.g. *The Economist*, 'Turkey is Making a Big Diplomatic and Corporate Push into Africa', 23-04-2022, available at https://www.economist.com/middle-east-and-africa/2022/04/23/turkey-is-making-a-big-diplomatic-and-corporate-push-into-africa [Retrieved 06/09/2024].

[27] See e.g. BNN Bloomberg, 'Indonesia Aims to Sign $3.5 Billion in Deals in Africa Forum', 01-09-2024, available at https://www.bnnbloomberg.ca/business/international/2024/09/02/indonesia-aims-to-sign-35-billion-in-deals-during-africa-forum/ [Retrieved 06/09/2024].

[28] See e.g. Van de Laar, *Stad van formaat*.

the reach of the state. This necessitated a new approach by the entrepreneurs as well, as they essentially operated in an 'early modern' way in the 1850s and 1860s in their business operations: no presumed 'modern' innovations like steamers, limited liability companies and extensive insurance contract were apparently deemed necessary. The transition to 'colonial capitalism' and modern business operations came quickly, in the timeframe of some fifteen to twenty years, and was forced under the pressure of imperial expansion, associated violence and a quick adaption to the rules of the world economy. This is what I call the *colonial complicity* of the Dutch entrepreneurs, as they in the end opted to stay, rather than to seek their fortunes elsewhere.

Reflecting on the historical Scramble and the presumed Scramble today, we can see similarities as well as differences. Obvious similarities include the great power competition, but also the entanglement between firms and states cooperating to exploit Africa's raw resources, for example in the Chinese case. In that sense, the danger of new 'red rubber' scandals is imaginable, and indeed present-day authors explicitly refer to this historical analogy.[29] The role of private actors remains important as well: in the nineteenth century, these concerned entrepreneurs and missionaries, today NGO's and multinational companies populate the continent in a quest for raw resources.[30] And as economic historians like Ewout Frankema and Marlous van Waijenburg have argued, this may eventually contribute to 'Africa rising', borrowing *The Economist*'s famous phrasing.[31]

On the other hand, some of the differences may indicate that some learning from past mistakes has taken place. At least in form, many of the firms now cloud their efforts in a language of cooperation and improvement of living standards across Africa, even if this also makes these firms vulnerable to attacks of hypocrisy, particularly when the firms are Western: moreover, African agency is taken more seriously by public and private

[29] Kara, *Cobalt Red*.

[30] Carmody maintains that among the differences between the 'old' and 'new' Scramble, today's presence of multinational companies is a major difference. See: Carmody, *The New Scramble for Africa*, 23. I would respectfully disagree with this point, given the fact that many firms in the nineteenth-century Scramble were *de facto*, if not *de jure*, multinationals.

[31] Frankema & Van Waijenburg, 'Africa Rising? A Historical Perspective', *African Affairs*, 117, 469 (2018), 543–568, https://doi.org/10.1093/afraf/ady022. *The Economist* itself recently revisited Africa's economic prospects. See: *The Economist*, 'The Africa Gap', available at https://www.economist.com/special-report/2025-01-11, 01-11-2025 [Retrieved 20/01/2025].

actors alike, with African governments also strongly asserting their independence and strength. There may be a new Scramble for Africa, but no new Partitioning of Africa, with most African governments choosing sides in the power struggle between the great powers based on their own interests (even if this is to the disliking of most Western observers). This creates a more complex geopolitical environment, and one in which the risk of 'colonial complicity' remains high for private actors involved, with accusations of 'neocolonialism' around every corner.

The study of the Dutch entrepreneurs in West and West Central Africa shows how difficult it was for private actors to remain out of reach of the great powers involved in the Scramble and Partition of Africa: in a colonial context, politics, empire-building and violence were impossible to escape. Yet the Dutch entrepreneurs also made fateful choices, most importantly to remain in the Congo Free State between 1885 and 1914. Even considering the rapidly changing geopolitical circumstances in Africa between 1875 and 1914, the Dutch entrepreneurs did have agency to make different choices: for example, they could have cooperated with the Liberian government to expand the production of palm oil there, but instead opted to work with the regime of Leopold II, even if they also helped Morel in bringing to light the red rubber scandals. They could have left the Congo Free State after 1890, when Leopold ripped up prior agreements and went ahead with his harsh exploitation of his private colony.

Avoiding any form of complicity in European colonialism may well have been impossible. Yet Africans were, on balance, not helped by the presence of the Dutch entrepreneurs in the Congo basin, whereas it is clear that Rotterdam did substantially profit in its rise as a global port city from the trade in raw commodities by 'exploiting the empire of others'. In the end, the Dutch entrepreneurs were not *responsible* for European imperialism in West and West Central Africa, but they were *complicit* in building, expanding and maintaining European empires, despite their private misgivings about the actions of many of the stately actors. Without the contribution of the private firms, European imperialism in the Congo basin would have faltered. Therein may lie our most important lesson for today's 'new' Scramble for Africa, if there is one.

CHAPTER 8

Epilogue

8.1 Epilogue

In December 2021, the mayor of Rotterdam, Ahmed Aboutaleb, apologised for the role the city played in the Dutch slave trade and slavery.[1] Following Amsterdam, Rotterdam was the second city in The Netherlands to do so, essentially paving the way for a broader (long-awaited) reckoning in Dutch society with the legacies of slavery and colonialism, something that can be attributed mainly to the long-standing activism of the diaspora of Surinamese people in the Netherlands (including in Rotterdam). In 2020, this resulted in three books about the colonial past of the city, its links to slavery and the slave trade and the emergence of Rotterdam as the Netherlands' main postcolonial or 'superdiverse' city.[2] These books established a landmark in how a city like Rotterdam deals with its colonial past.

Although the three books pointed to widespread involvement in all sorts of colonial activities (not only slave trade and slavery but also many instances of other forms of forced labour, violence and ruthless exploitation), public attention quickly narrowed down to Rotterdam's link with

[1] The speech (in Dutch) can be found here: https://www.youtube.com/watch?time_continue=1&v=RyUt7COdang&feature=emb_logo [Retrieved 26/10/2022].

[2] Oostindie (ed.), *Het koloniale verleden van Rotterdam*; Van Stipriaan, *Rotterdam in slaverni*; Guadeloupe, Van de Laar & Van der Linden (eds.), *Rotterdam, een postkoloniale stad in beweging*.

G. Dreijer, *Private Entrepreneurship and European Imperialism*,
Palgrave Studies in Economic History,
https://doi.org/10.1007/978-3-032-01086-5_8

the slave trade and slavery.[3] This also goes for the broader debate on Dutch colonial history: the focus is overwhelmingly on the slave trade and slavery in the Atlantic world, with the Dutch decolonisation war in Indonesia and, more recently, the Dutch slave trade in the Indian Ocean also receiving some attention.[4] Whilst both explainable (many people of Surinamese or Antillean descent live in the Netherlands and in particular its largest cities) and understandable (these groups want the wrongs of the past to be properly acknowledged and dealt with by Dutch society), this narrative also leaves out many of the other colonial involvements of Dutch people and institutions between the late sixteenth century and the late twentieth century. As this book has sought to demonstrate, Rotterdam's main colonial 'responsibility' can probably be pinpointed to the nineteenth century,[5] and had for a significant part to do with the activities its inhabitants employed across Africa, something (with some exceptions) often overlooked in the literature.[6]

Colonial or imperial entrepreneurship is never morally 'clean', and many studies have reaffirmed as much in recent years. The case of Rotterdam however also shows us something that goes beyond the standard stories, and that is that gains made in the 'empire of others' also significantly contributed to the city's rise as a global major port city. Money earned in Africa was reinvested in Rotterdam's port infrastructure by Lodewijk Pincoffs; Pincoffs for example built the *Entrepotgebouw* (Entrepot Building) which he used as the firm's main warehouse for commodities brought from Africa. Today, the *Entrepotgebouw* is part of an apartment and business complex called *De Vijf Werelddelen* (The Five Continents), clearly showing Rotterdam's links to the world, including Africa. Wealth accumulated from the African trade within families like the Van Rijckevorsels and the Mullers was used by their descendants to collect

[3] See e.g. the following, which zooms in solely on the apologies for slavery: https://nos.nl/artikel/2408945-gemeente-rotterdam-biedt-excuses-aan-voor-slavernijverleden [Retrieved 26/10/2022].

[4] See for example the recent issue of the *Low Countries Journal of Social and Economic History*: https://tseg.nl/issue/view/657 [Retrieved 26/10/2022]. Symptomatic is that the second book in the 'trilogy' focused solely on Atlantic slavery, whereas other forms of slavery or forced labour received scant attention.

[5] De Kok, 'De koloniale connectie'. 60–73; Idem, 'De koloniale impact', 118–125 & 131–133.

[6] See e.g. De Kok, 'De koloniale connectie', 60–68 & 70–73; Idem, 'De koloniale impact', 118–125. Other work mostly overlooked the consequences for Africa and Africans, see e.g.: Oosterwijk, *Ik verlang geen dank*.

many of the ethnographic collections that are still shown today in sites like the *Wereldmuseum* (World Museum) in Rotterdam. Moreover, most of them derived social and political status from the African trade, for example by using their influence in the Rotterdam municipal council or the Dutch Senate to push for certain policies (not always successfully, it has to be said).

The gains from the African trade thus were financial, but also much broader than that. With most attention in societal debate and scholarship going to the gains that were 'earned' in the empire of 'one's own', this book has argued for the strong need for a broader view and the incorporation of trans-imperial perspectives on this matter. This is not only of academic interest: after all, as this book has shown, substantial profits have flowed to Rotterdam through the exploitation of other empires and Africa's raw resources, with effects literally visible to this day. While not primarily responsible for European imperialism in Africa, the Dutch entrepreneurs were at times certainly *complicit* in the process of imperial expansion, for example by keeping enslaved people on their factories before 1880, or through the long-standing investments in the *Compagnie du Kasaï* in the early twentieth century, even after news of Leopold's crimes came to light in Europe. On the other hand, operations in Liberia were not necessarily reprehensible or based on inequal relations, and the Dutch entrepreneurs contributed to the eventual fall of Leopold through the red rubber scandals.

As a result, the legacy of the private Dutch entrepreneurs in West and West Central Africa is mixed. This shows the actual reality of colonialism on the ground, which in societal debate and some scholarly work often has been simplified to stories of brutal European violence against African resistance. While this was indeed often true, this book has shown that reality often was more complex, changed over time, and the agency of different actors (European of African) was more real than is often granted in stories of repression and violence. The fact that there was *complicity* rather than *responsibility* should not mean that the repercussions in the present day should be underestimated, denied or downplayed: rather, the aim has been to *complexify* our understanding of complicity and responsibility for the colonial past, and demonstrate that the gains of European imperialism in Africa were more widespread than previously acknowledged in 'nationally' geared histories of empire.[7] Indeed, as the case of Rotterdam's ties to Africa shows, it is hard if not impossible to draw a strict line between private and public involvement, as all entrepreneurs were also actively involved in local or national politics, and reinvested the money earned in the African trade into public-private partnerships that cemented Rotterdam's status as a global, rising port city. Moreover, as this happened outside of the official channels of the Dutch imperial system and under the responsibility of foreign imperial administrations, the question of responsibility must, under close historical scrutiny, therefore be diffused and shared.

This may pose its problems in the present day, with Dutch municipalities like Rotterdam having taken the lead in apologising for and dealing with the colonial past and its repercussions today, primarily so for its role in the (Atlantic) slave trade and slavery, which was to a significant extent linked to the state and its components, and was in the public imagination limited to the Dutch Empire. The story told in this book makes such stories more complex, for reasons sketched above. This book offers no blueprint for politicians and citizens on how to deal with this, but recognises and emphasises the importance of a deeper societal conversation on the responsibility for and complicity in the colonial past and its effects to the present day, that moves beyond a state-centred approach and beyond a focus on the Dutch colonial empire only. Moreover, these questions are not only pertinent to the Netherlands but also applicable across the Western world, where similar debates and conversations are happening. Only the acknowledgement of complexity that flows from detailed academic historical research will allow civil society to see the full picture of European colonialism and imperialism, and the effects it had in the past and has in the present. This book has hopefully contributed meaningfully to this aim.

[7] See for similar arguments for the case of Japanese imperialism in Korea: Jun, *Brokers of Empire*. I am aware of the controversies around this argument, but still would like to point out the similarities of the argumentation.

Bibliography

Unpublished Primary Sources

Koninklijke Bibliotheek Den Haag (NL-KB)

Stukken Robidé van der Aa, inv. KW 128 F 9, 4d, nr. 46.
Brieven aan de familie Van der Aa, inv. KW 132 G 17, nrs. E3 & E4.

UB Leiden, Bijzondere Collecties (NL-UBL-BC)

Brieven aan Willem Geertrudus Cornelis Byvanck, inv. BPL2246a, Brieven L. Pincoffs, 2 stuks (1869–1870) & Brieven A.L. Pincoffs, 4 stuks (1869–1874), hierbij ook brief M.T. Goudsmit, 1 stuk (1869).

Stadsarchief Rotterdam (NL-SAR)

Handschriftenverzameling Gemeente Rotterdam (aanvullingen 1848–1987), inv. 33–01, nrs. 905, 906, 3263 & 4884.
Handschriftenverzameling Gemeente Rotterdam (aanvullingen 1988–1996), inv. 33–02, nrs. 9552 & 9572.
Archief Familie Mees privé, inv. 39, nrs. 1682, 1683, 1685, 1686, 2378, 2381, 2382, 2384, 2722 & 2724.

G. Dreijer, *Private Entrepreneurship and European Imperialism*, Palgrave Studies in Economic History,
https://doi.org/10.1007/978-3-032-01086-5

Archief van de Familie Baelde, inv. 40, nr. 307.
Archief Muller, inv. 41, nrs. 151–161, 164–170, 203, 204, 209, 217, 330 & 422.
Aanvulling Archief Muller, inv. 41a.
Archief Familie van Rijckevorsel, inv. 42, nrs. 106 & 236.
Archief Chabot, kassiers en makelaar in assurantie, inv. 70, nrs. 1195, 1199, 1202, 1307 & 2482.
Archief Advocatenkantoor en familie Sieuwertz van Reesema, inv. 87, nr. 18.
Archief Hudig & Veder, inv. 271–01, nr. 1167.
Archief Mees & Zoonen, inv. 305, nrs. 623–631.
Archief van R.S. Stokvis & Zonen, inv. 355, nrs. 752 & 1884.
Archief Familie Dunlop, inv. 400, nr. 106.

Maritiem Museum Rotterdam (NL-MMR)

Handschriften, nrs. H472, H508 & H753.

Scheepvaartsmuseum Amsterdam (NL-SMA)

Handschriften, nr. I285.

Stadsarchief Amsterdam (NL-SAA)

Archief van de Commissiehandel Kerkhoven & Co, inv. 592, nr. 165.

Internationaal Instituut voor Sociale Geschiedenis, Nederlands Economisch-Historisch Archief (NL-IISG-NEHA)

Collectie Combinatie voor den Handel op de West en/of Zuidwestkust van Afrika, inv. ARCH03684.
Collectie Huibert van Rijckevorsel (Rotterdam), inv. ARCH03896.
Collectie Handelshuis Dunlop & Mees, Rotterdam, inv. ARCH04463.

Archief ABN AMRO, Amstelveen (NL-ABN)

Archief Mees en Zonen, s.l., nrs. 390, 777 & 2284.

Nationaal Archief Den Haag (NL-HaNA)

Archief Nederlandse Bezittingen ter Kuste van Guinea, 1658–1872, inv. 1.05.114, nr. 987.
Archief van de Tweede Kamer der Staten-Generaal, 1815–1945, inv. 2.02.22, nrs. 3273–3277.
Archief Buitenlandse Zaken 1813–1870, inv. 2.05.01, nrs. 2349, 2350, 2358, 2359, 2367.
Archief Buitenlandse Zaken A-Dossiers, inv. 2.05.03, nrs. 141, 203–217 & 356–361.
Archief van het Nederlandse Gezantschap in Portugal (1789) 1823–1889, inv. 2.05.10.12, nrs. 72 & 88–92.
Archief van het Gezantschap Verenigde Staten / Legatie Washington, inv. 2.05.13, nr. 161.
Archief Buitenlandse Zaken B-Dossiers, inv. 2.05.38, nr. 1494.
Archief Hoge Raad der Nederlanden, inv. 2.09.28, nr. 534.
Archief Ministerie van Marine: Openbaar Verbaal, 1813–1900 (1963), inv. 2.12.01, nrs. 2589–2592 & 2596.
Archief Ministerie van Marine, Scheepsjournalen 1813–1995, inv. 2.12.03, nrs. 271 & 2407.
Archief van de NAHV, (1854) 1880–1959 (1981), inv. 2.18.10.09, nrs. 123, 147, 173, 174, 364, 627, 629, 655, 664, 665, 666, 669, 671, 673, 674, 676, 677, 679, 682, 685, 687, 688, 690, 710–713, 715, 717, 769, 770, 772, 781, 782, 793.
Archief De Nederlandsche Bank NV, inv. 2.25.68, nrs. 16212–16217.

Nederlandse Tweede Kamer (NL-TK)

Archief Officiële Bekendmakingen, 1873–1874a, inv. 52, nrs. 1–24, available at https://zoek.officielebekendmakingen.nl/resultaten?q=(c.product-area==%22sgd%22)and(w.vergaderjaar==%221873-1874%22)and(cql.textAndIndexes=%2252%22)%20AND%20w.dossiernummer==%2252%22&zv=52&pg=10&col=Alle&hist=1&sf=dn%7c52 [Retrieved 31/05/2022].
Archief Officiële Bekendmakingen, 1873–1874b, inv. 7, nrs. 1–4, available at https://zoek.officielebekendmakingen.nl/resultaten?q=(c.product-area==%22sgd%22)and(w.vergaderjaar==%221874-1875%22)and(cql.textAndIndexes=%227%22)%20AND%20w.dossiernummer==%227%22&zv=7&pg=10&col=Alle&hist=1&sf=dn%7c7 [Retrieved 31/05/2022].

Archief Buitenlandse Zaken, Brussel (BE-BZ)

Archives Africaines, Classement Provisoire, nr. 2571.

Archief Africamuseum Tervuren (BE-AMT)

Stanley Archives, nrs. 42, 44, 76, 80, 641, 866, 1057–1103, 1326, 3739, 4355, 4366, 4437, 5216–5218, 5993–5995 & 6842.

Algemeen Rijksarchief Brussel, AGR-2, Depot Joseph Cuvelier (BE-AGR2-DJC)

Archives Africaines, JUST, nr. 58.

Archief van het Koninklijk Paleis, Brussel (BE-KPB)

Archives relatives au développement extérieur de la Belgique sous le règne de Léopold II, 1865–1909, inv. 543–158, nr. 377.

Published Primary Sources

De Bas, F., *Een onpartijdig advies in het Congo-vraagstuk* (Schiedam 1890).

Bastian, A., *Die deutsche Expedition an der Loango-Küste, nebst älteren Nachrichten über die die zu erforschende Länder* (2 Vols.) (Jena 1874–1875).

Bentley, W.H., *Pioneering on the Congo* (2 Vols.) (London 1900).

Bohl, J., *Nederlands Congo-belang* (Amsterdam 1890).

Burton, R.F., *Two Trips to Gorillaland and the Cataracts of the Congo* (2 Vols.) (London 1876).

Büttikofer, J., *Reisebilder aus Liberia* (2 Vols.) (Leiden 1890).

Chavanne, J., *Reisen und Forschungen im alten und neuen Kongostaate in den Jarhen 1884 und 1885* (Jena 1887).

Frobenius, L., *Im Schatten des Kongostaates* (Berlin 1907).

Gramberg, J.S.G., *Schetsen van Afrika's Westkust* (Amsterdam 1861).

Van den Hoek, F. (ed.), Vermeulen, A. (author), *De pioniersdagen van Chicongo: een verhaal uit het pioniersleven in den Congo* (Amsterdam 1934 / s.l. 2021a).

Van den Hoek, F. (ed.), Vermeulen, A. (author), *De ingang der hel: episode uit het Afrikaansche pioniersleven* (Amsterdam 1938 / s.l. 2021b).

Van den Hoek, F. (ed.) m.m.v. Vansina, J., Vermeulen, A. (author), *De memoires van Chicongo* (s.l. 2021).

Jeekel, C.A., *Onze bezittingen op de kust van Guinea* (Amsterdam 1869).

Johnston, H.H., *The River Congo from its Mouth to Bolobu* (London 1895).
Kerdijk, H. & Pincoffs, L., *Stenografisch verslag van het getuigenverhoor en de pleidooien, gehouden voor den Hoogen Raad der Nederlanden* (Utrecht 1880).
Koopman, J.F., *Verslag van eene reize naar de westkust van Africa* (s.l. 1861).
Mees, R. (ed.), *Gedenkschrift van de firma R. Mees & Zoonen ter gelegenheid van haar tweehonderd-jarig bestaan, 1720–1920* (Rotterdam 1920).
Monteiro, J.J., *Angola and the River Congo* (London 1875).
Morel, E.D., *King Leopold's Rule in Africa* (London 1904).
Muller, H., *Over de liquidatie der Afrikaansche Handels-Vereeniging* (Rotterdam 1880).
Muller, H., *De afstand der kust van Guinea aan Engeland* (Rotterdam 1871).
Naber, J.W.A. (ed.), *Samuel Pierre l'Honoré Naber. Schout bij nacht t.t. naar de correspondentie met zijn ouders, loopende 1880–1913* (s.l. 1939).
Nagtglas, C.J.M., *Een woord aangaande de vraag: "Wat moet Nederland doen met zijne bezittingen ter kuste van Guinea?"* (The Hague 1863).
Oldenkott, B., *Potloodstreepjes van Redivivus* (8 Vols.) (Leiden 1879–1880).
Pechuel-Loesche, E., *Kongoland* (2 Vols.) (Jena 1887).
Pincoffs, L., *Open brief aan de redactie van "De Maasbode"* (Rotterdam 1871).
Pincoffs, L., *Open brief aan de aandeelhouders der Ned. Ind. Gasmaatschappy* (New York 1879).
Robidé van der Aa, P.J.B.C., *Afrikaansche studiën: koloniaal bezit en partikuliere handel op Afrika's westkust* (The Hague 1871).
S.A., *Enquête omtrent den toestand van de Nederlandschen koopvaardijvloot: verslag der commissie* (The Hague 1875).
S.A., *Bedenkingen tegen Nederland's verzet in de Congo-kwestie* (Amsterdam 1890a).
S.A., *L'État indépendant du Congo et la compagnie du Rotterdam, par un ami de la vérité* (Antwerp 1890b).
S.A., *La conférence de Bruxelles et les Pays-Bas par un ami de la vérité* (Antwerp 1890c).
S.A., *Reply to the Memorandum published by the Nieuwe-Afrikaansche Handels-Vennootschap in August, 1890, upon the Recent Decrees of the Congo Free State, by an African* (London 1890d).
S.A., *Réplique à l'Africain, auteur de la brochure: Réponse au mémorandum* (Rotterdam 1890e).
S.A., *Bedenkingen tegen Nederland's verzet in de Congo-kwestie door een Nederlander* (Amsterdam 1890f).
S.A., *La Compagnie du Kasai à ses actionnaires : réponse à ses détracteurs: la question congolaise* (Brussels 1906).
S.A, *Jaarcijfers uitgegeven door de Centrale Commissie voor de Statistiek. Koloniën 1887–1916* (34 Vols.) (The Hague 1889–1922a).
S.A., *Jaarcijfers uitgegeven door de Centrale Commissie voor de Statistiek. Rijk in Europa 1887–1916* (34 Vols.) (The Hague 1889–1922b).

S.A., *Jaaroverzichten van den handel in koloniale producten 1891–1914* (24 Vols.) (Amsterdam 1892–1915).

S.A., *Statistiek van den handel en de scheepvaart in het Koningrijk der Nederlanden over het jaar 1847–1876* (30 Vols.) (The Hague 1848–1877).

S.A., *Statistiek van den in-, uit- en doorvoer over het jaar 1877–1916* (40 Vols.) (The Hague 1878–1917).

Schalkwijk, W.C., *De Anti-Slavernij-Conferentie en invoerrechten in den Congo-Staat* (Rotterdam 1890a).

Schalkwijk, W.C., *De Kongo-Vrijstaat en de handel: antwoord op de brochure « La Conférence de Bruxelles et les Pays-Bas » par « un Ami de la vérite »* (Rotterdam 1890b).

Schalkwijk, W.C., *De Congo-Staat en zijn Pleitbezorger: antwoord op de brochure « L'État Indépendant du Congo et la Compagnie de Rotterdam » par « un Ami de la Vérité » (Antwerpen bij Max Ruef)* (Rotterdam 1890c).

Schepel, A.F. (ed.), Kerdijk, L. (author), *Reisjournaal van Lodewijk Kerdijk: West-Africa 1857/1858* (Schiedam 1978).

Stanley, H.M., *The Congo and the Founding of its Free State: A Story of Work and Exploration* (New York 1885).

Tengbergen, H.F., *Verhaal van den reistogt en expeditie naar de Nederlandsche bezittingen ter West kust van Afrika* (The Hague 1839).

Twain, M., *King Leopold's Soliloquy: A Satire* (London 1907).

Vermeulen, C.W., *De Afrikaansche handels-vereeniging en haar werkkring: rapport aan den Hogen Raad der Nederlanden* (Rotterdam 1880).

Wauters, A-J., *L'État indépendant du Congo* (Brussels 1899).

Zwier van Sandick, O., *Herinneringen van de Zuid-Westkust van Afrika: eenige bladzijden uit mijn dagboek* (Deventer 1881).

Unpublished Secondary Literature

Alexopoulou, K., 'An Anatomy of Colonial States and Fiscal Regimes in Portuguese Africa: Long-Term Transformations in Angola and Mozambique, 1850s-1970s', Unpublished PhD Dissertation Wageningen University (Wageningen 2018).

Alltmont, R.C., 'Belgian Overseas Expansion during the Nineteenth Century', Unpublished PhD Dissertation University of Delaware (Newark DE 1969).

Van den Berg, G., 'Hendrik Pieter Nicolaas Muller en de Oost-Afrikaansche Compagnie', Unpublished MA Thesis VU Amsterdam (Amsterdam 1986).

Bouwman, W., 'Handelaar en verzamelaar: Biografisch dossier van de NAHV-agenten J.C.W.J. Cremer F. de la Fontaine Verweij L.M. Van der Most J.W. Regeer', Unpublished Internship Report Leiden University & Museum Volkenkunde 2013 (Leiden 2013).

Broeckaert, M., 'Het blank personeel van de Kongo-staat 1885–1908: Recrutering – profiel – carrières?', Unpublished PhD Dissertation Ghent University (Ghent 1988).

Callahan, M., 'The Harbor Barons: Political and Commercial Elites and the Development of the Port of Rotterdam, 1824–1892', Unpublished PhD Dissertation Princeton University (2 Vols.) (Princeton NJ, 1981).

Direito, B.P.T., 'Políticas coloniais de terras em Moçambique: o case de manica e sofala sub a Companhia de Moçambique, 1892–1942', Unpublished PhD Dissertation University of Lisbon (Lisbon 2013).

Gaastra, F.S., 'Vragen over de koopvaardij. De 'Enquête omtrent den toestand van de Nederlandsche koopvaardijvloot' uit 1874 en de achteruitgang van de handelsvloot', Inaugural Lecture Leiden University (Leiden 2004), available at https://scholarlypublications.universiteitleiden.nl/handle/1887/4519 [Retrieved 31/05/2022].

Joosse, N., 'Afrikaanse droom: de handel van Henry P. Kerdijk en Lodewijk Pincoffs in Afrika, 1857–1879', Unpublished MA Thesis Erasmus University Rotterdam (Rotterdam 2016), available at https://thesis.eur.nl/pub/34933 [Retrieved 05/08/2021].

MacMillan, H.W., 'The Origins and Development of the African Lakes Company: 1878–1908', Unpublished PhD Dissertation University of Edinburgh (Edinburgh 1970), available at https://era.ed.ac.uk/bitstream/handle/1842/24105/MacMillanHW_1970redux.pdf?sequence=1&isAllowed=y [Retrieved 21/07/2022].

Martens, D.S., 'A History of European Penetration and African Reaction in the Kasai Region of Zaira, 1880–1908', Unpublished PhD Dissertation Simon Fraser University (Burnaby 1980), available at http://summit.sfu.ca/item/3231 [Retrieved 05/08/2021].

Van der Meer, D., 'De Goudkust na de slavenhandel: plannen om de Nederlandse bezittingen ter Kuste van Guinea rendabel te maken', Unpublished MA thesis Utrecht University (Utrecht 1990), available at https://meergeschiedenis.nl/goudkust/de-goudkust-na-de-slavenhandel.pdf [Retrieved 10/10/2022].

Naranch, B.D., 'Beyond the Fatherland: Colonial Visions, Overseas Expansion, and German Nationalism, 1848–1885', Unpublished PhD Dissertation John Hopkins University (Baltimore MD 2006).

Neil-Tomlinson, B., 'The Mozambique Chartered Company: 1892 to 1910', Unpublished PhD Dissertation The School of Oriental and African Studies University of London (London 1982).

Plasman, P-L., 'L'État independent du Congo et Léopold II (1876–1906): étude sur le paradoxe de la gouvernance léopoldienne', Unpublished PhD Dissertation UC Louvain (Louvain-la-Neuve 2015), available at https://dial.uclouvain.be/pr/boreal/object/boreal:159323 [Retrieved 23/10/2024].

Pirio, G.R., 'Commerce, Industry and Empire: The Making of Modern Portuguese Colonialism in Angola and Mozambique, 1890–1914', Unpublished PhD Dissertation University of California Los Angeles (Los Angeles CA 1982).

Qian, Z., 'The Rise of the Shanxi Merchants: Empire, Institutions, and Social Change in Qing China, 1688–1850', Unpublished PhD Dissertation Stanford University (Stanford CA 2017), available at https://purl.stanford.edu/bg803zm7823 [Retrieved 23/09/2024].

Särkkä, T., 'Hobson's Imperialism: A Study in Late-Victorian Political Thought', Unpublished PhD Dissertation University of Jyväskylä (Jyväskylä 2009).

Vancanneyt, M., 'Een economische geschiedenis van Albert Thys (1876–1908)', Unpublished MA Thesis Ghent University (Ghent 2008), available at https://lib.ugent.be/catalog/rug01:001290438 [Retrieved 15/09/2024].

Vandamme, T., 'Beyond Belgium: The Business Empire of Edouard Empain in the First Global Economy (1880–1914)', Unpublished PhD Dissertation Ghent University (Ghent 2019), available at https://biblio.ugent.be/publication/8640740/file/8643749.pdf [Retrieved 23/10/2024].

Van Walraven, K. 'European Memoirs and Colonialism in Equatorial Africa: Reflections on the Reminiscences of Alfons Vermeulen (1877–1965)', *ASC Working Paper*, nr. 151 (2021), available at https://www.ascleiden.nl/publications/european-memoirs-and-colonialism-equatorial-africa-reflections-reminiscences-alfons [Retrieved 05/08/2021].

Wheeler, D.L., 'Portuguese Expansion in Angola since 1836: A Re-Examination', *The Central Africa Historical Association Local Series*, 20 (1967).

Wiggers, R., 'De "Federation pour la defense des interets belges à l'étranger' en de Congo', Unpublished MA Thesis Katholieke Universiteit Nijmegen (Nijmegen 1986).

Willink, J., *De bewogen verzamelgeschiedenis van de West-Centraal-Afrikaanse collecties in Nederland (1856–1889)* (Ridderkerk 2006), available at https://scholarlypublications.universiteitleiden.nl/access/item%3A2899672/view [Retrieved 05/08/2021].

Published Secondary Literature

Abbeloos, J-A., 'Belgium's Expansionist History between 1870 and 1930: Imperialism and the Globalisation of Belgian Business', in: Lévai, C. (ed.), *Europe and Its Empires* (Pisa 2008), 105–127.

Adele Jinadu, L., 'Conceptual and Theoretical Issues in the Scramble for Africa', in: Eze, O.C. & Anigbo, C.A. (eds.), *New Scramble for Africa* (Lagos 2010), 15–26.

Adelman, J., 'Mimesis and Rivalry: European Empires and Global Regimes', *Journal of Global History*, 10, 1 (2015), 77–98, https://doi.org/10.1017/S1740022814000291.

Akinyoade, A., Dietz, T. & Uche, C., 'Introduction', in: Akinyoade, A., Dietz, T. & Uche, C. (eds.), *Entrepreneurship in Africa* (Leiden & Boston 2017), 1–21.

Aldrich, R. & Stucki, A., *The Colonial World: A History of European Empires, 1780s to the Present* (London 2023).

Alexandrowicz, C.H., *The European-African Confrontation. A Study in Treaty Making* (Leiden 1973).

Allina, E., *Slavery by Any Other Name: African Life under Company Rule in Colonial Mozambique* (Charlottesville VA & London 2012).

Amin, S. & Coquery-Vidrovitch, C., *Histoire économique du Congo 1880–1968: du Congo Français à l'union douanière et économique d'Afrique centrale* (Paris 1969).

Anghie, A., *Imperialism, Sovereignty and the Making of International Law* (Cambridge 2004).

Anstey, R.T., 'British Trade and Policy in West Africa between 1816 and the Early 1880s', *Transactions of the Historical Society of Ghana*, 3, 1 (1957), 47–71.

Anstey, R.T., *Britain and the Congo in the Nineteenth Century* (Oxford 1962a).

Anstey, R.T., *King Leopold's Legacy: The Congo under Belgian Rule 1908–1960* (Oxford, London, New York & Ibadan 1962b).

Anstey, R.T., 'The Congo Rubber Atrocities – A Case Study', *African Historical Studies*, 4, 1 (1971), 59–76.

Antunes, C.A.P., Münch Miranda, S. & Salvado, J.P., 'The Resources of Others: Dutch Exploitation of European Expansion and Empires, 1570–1800', *Tijdschrift voor Geschiedenis*, 131, 3 (2018) 501–521, https://doi.org/10.5117/TVGESCH2018.3.006.ANTU.

Ascherson, N., *The King Incorporated: Leopold II in the Age of Trusts* (London 1963).

Ashby Turner jr., H., 'Bismarck's Imperialist Venture: Anti-British in Origin?', in: Gifford, P. & Roger Louis, W.M. (eds.), *Britain and Germany in Africa: Imperial Rivalry and Colonial Rule* (New Haven & London 1967), 47–82.

Axelson, E., *Portugal and the Scramble for Africa 1875–1891* (Johannesburg 1967).

Baesjou, R. & Emmer, P.C., 'The Dutch in West Africa: Shipping, Factories and Colonisation, 1800–1870', in: Everaert, J. & Parmentier, J. (eds.), *International Conference on Shipping, Factories and Colonization (Brussels, 24–26 November 1994)* (Brussels 1996), 191–213.

Baker, G.L., *Trade Winds on the Niger: The Sage of the Royal Niger Company* (London 1996).

Ball, J., 'A "Time of Clothes": The Angolan Rubber Boom, 1886–1902, *Ufahumu: A Journal of African Studies*, 28, 1 (2000), 25–42, https://doi.org/10.5070/F7281016584.

Ballhaus, J., 'Die Landkonzessionsgesellschaften', in: Stoecker, H. (ed.), *Kamerun unter deutscher Kolonialherrschaft* (Vol. 2) (Berlin 1968), 99–179.

Bandeira Jerónimo, M., *The 'Civilising Mission' of Portuguese Colonialism, 1870–1930* (Basingstoke 2015).

Barth, V. & Cvetkovski, R., 'Introduction – Encounter of Empires: Methodological Approaches', in: Barth, V. & Cvetkovski, R. (eds.), *Imperial Co-Operation and*

Transfer, 1870–1930: Empires and Encounters (London & New York 2015), 3–34.

Bayly, C.A., *The Birth of the Modern World 1780–1914: Global Connections and Comparisons* (Malden MA, Oxford & Victoria 2004).

Belich, J., *Replenishing the Earth: The Settler Revolution and the Rise of the Anglo-World, 1783–1939* (Oxford 2009).

Betts, R.F., *The False Dawn: European Imperialism in the Nineteenth Century* (Minneapolis MN 1975).

Bevernage, B., 'The Making of the Congo Question: Truth-Telling, Denial and "Colonial Science" in King Leopold's Commission of Inquiry on the Rubber Atrocities in the Congo Free State (1904–1905)', *Rethinking History*, 22, 2 (2018), 203–238, https://doi.org/10.1080/13642529.2018.1451078.

Blocher, J. & Gulati, M., 'Transferable Sovereignty: Lessons from the History of the Congo Free State', *Duke Law Journal*, 69, 6 (2020), 1219–1274.

Blocher, J., Gulati, M. & Oosterlinck, K., 'King Leopold's Bonds and the Odious Debt Mystery', *Virginia Journal of International Law*, 60, 3 (2020), 489–530.

Boele, C., 'Een erfenis van Pincoffs: de familie Enthoven en hun actions de jouissance van de N.V. Nederlandsch-Indische Gas-Maatschappij', *Rotterdams Jaarboekje*, 9, 9 (1991), 310–321.

Bontinck, F., 'Les archives de la Nieuwe Afrikaansche Handelsvennootschap conservees a Schaarsbergen (Pays-Bas)', *Bulletin des Seances de l'Academie Royale des Sciences d-Outre-Mer* (1970), 178–194.

Boonstoppel, E., 'Mees, familie', in: Visser, J., Van Jaarsveld, M. & Van de Laar, P. (eds.), *Rotterdamse ondernemers 1850–1950* (Rotterdam 2003), 142–149.

Bosma, U., 'The Economic Historiography of the Dutch Empire', *Tijdschrift voor Sociale en Economische Geschiedenis – Low Countries Journal of Social and Economic History*, 11, 2 (2014), 153–174.

Bouman, P.J., 'Lodewijk Pincoffs: een hoofdstuk uit de geschiedenis van Rotterdam', *Vragen des Tijds*, 53 (1927), 1–18.

Broadberry, S. & Gardner, L., 'Economic Growth in Sub-Saharan Africa, 1885–2008: Evidence from Eight Countries', *Explorations in Economic History*, 83, Article 101424, https://doi.org/10.1016/j.eeh.2021.101424.

Broadhead, S.H., 'Beyond Decline: The Kingdom of the Kingo in the Eighteenth and Nineteenth Centuries', *The International Journal of African Historical Studies*, 12, 4 (1979), 615–650.

Brunschwig, H., *Mythes et réalités de l'impérialisme colonial français 1871–1914* (Paris 1960).

Buelens, F., *Congo 1885–1960: een financieel-economische geschiedenis* (Berchem 2007).

Buelens, F. & Frankema, E., 'Colonial Adventures in Tropical Agriculture: New Estimates of Returns to Investment in The Netherlands Indies, 1919–1938', *Cliometrica*, 10, 2 (2016), 197–224, https://doi.org/10.1007/s11698-015-0128-z.

Buelens, F. & Marysse, S., 'Returns on Investments during the Colonial Era: The Case of the Belgian Congo', *The Economic History Review*, 62, 1 (2009), 135–166.

Burbank, J. & Cooper, F., *Empires in World History: Power and the Politics of Difference* (Princeton NJ 2010).

Burnett, A., *The Dutch Rediscover the Dutch-Africans (1847–1900)* (Leiden & Boston 2022).

Burroughs, R., *African Testimony in the Movement for Congo Reform: The Burden of Proof* (Abingdon 2019).

Cain, P.J., *Economic Foundations of British Overseas Expansion 1815–1914* (London & Basingstoke 1980).

Cain, P.J. 'J.A. Hobson, Financial Capitalism and Imperialism in Late Victorian and Edwardian England', *The Journal of Imperial and Commonwealth History*, 13, 3 (1985), 1–27, https://doi.org/10.1080/03086538508582691.

Cain, P.J., *Hobson and Imperialism: Radicalism, New Liberalism, and Finance 1887–1938* (Oxford 2002).

Cain, P.J. & Hopkins, A.G., 'The Political Economy of British Expansion Overseas, 1750–1914', *The Economic History Review*, 33, 4 (1980), 463–490.

Cain, P.J. & Hopkins, A.G., 'Gentlemanly Capitalism and British Expansion Overseas II: New Imperialism, 1850–1945', *The Economic History Review*, 40, 1 (1987), 1–26.

Cain, P.J. & Hopkins, A.G., *British Imperialism: Innovation and Expansion 1688–1914* (London & New York 1993a).

Cain, P.J. & Hopkins, A.G., *British Imperialism: Crisis and Deconstruction 1914–1990* (London & New York 1993b).

À Campo, J., 'Orde, rust en welvaart. Over de Nederlandse expansie in de Indische archipel omstreeks 1900', *Acta Politica: Tijdschrift voor Politicologie*, 15, 2 (1980), 145–189.

Candido, M.P., 'Merchants and the Business of the Slave Trade at Benguela, 1750–1850', *African Economic History*, 35 (2007), 1–30.

Candido, M.P., *An African Slaving Port and the Atlantic World: Benguela and Its Hinterland* (Cambridge 2013).

Carmody, P.R., *The New Scramble for Africa* (Cambridge & Malden MA 2016).

Ceulemans, R.P., *La question arabe et le Congo (1883–1892)* (Brussels 1959).

Chamberlain, M.E., *The Scramble for Africa* (London 1974).

Chatelet, L., 'Het humanitaire optreden van Leopold II in Kongo-Vrijstaat. De anti-slavernijconferentie van Brussel (1889–1890)', *Afrika Focus*, 4, 1–2 (1988), 5–47.

Clarence-Smith, W.G., 'The Myth of Uneconomic Imperialism: The Portuguese in Angola, 1836–1926', *Journal of Southern African Studies*, 5, 2 (1979), 165–180.

Clarence-Smith, W.G., 'Business Empires in Equatorial Africa', *African Economic History*, 12 (1983a), 3–11.

Clarence-Smith, W.G., 'Les investissements belges en Angola, 1912–1961', in: Coquery-Vidrovitch, C. & Forest, A. (eds.), *Entreprises et entrepreneurs en Afrique (XIXe et XXe siècles* (Vol. 1) (Paris 1983b), 423–442.

Clarence-Smith, W.G., *The Third Portuguese Empire 1825–1975: A Study in Economic Imperialism* (Manchester 1985).

Clarence-Smith, W.G., 'The Portuguese and Spanish Roles in the Scramble for Africa: An Economic Explanation', in: Förster, S., Mommsen, W.J. & Robinson, R. (eds.), *Bismarck, Europe and Africa: The Berlin Africa Conference 1884–1885 and the Onset of Partition* (Oxford 1988), 215–227.

Clement, P., 'The Land Tenure System in the Congo, 1885–1960: Actors, Motivations, and Consequences', in: Frankema, E. & Buelens, F. (eds.), *Colonial Exploitation and Economic Development: The Belgian Congo and the Netherlands Indies compared* (London & New York 2013), 88–108.

Cole, A., 'An Approach to the Study of Entrepreneurship: A Tribute to Edwin Gay', *Journal of Economic History*, 6, S1 (1946), 1–15, https://doi.org/10.1017/S0022050700052876.

Conrad, S., *German Colonialism: A Short History* (Cambridge 2012).

Coombs, D., *The Gold Coast, Britain and The Netherlands 1850–1874* (London 1963).

Cookey, S.J.S., 'The Concession Policy in the French Congo and the British Reaction, 1898–1906', *The Journal of African History*, 7, 2 (1966), 263–278.

Cooper, F., *Colonialism in Question: Theory, Knowledge, History* (Berkeley CA 2005).

Coquery-Vidrovitch, C., 'Les idées économiques de Brazza et les premières tentatives de companies de colonisation au Congo Français, 1885–1898', *Cahiers d'Études Africaines*, 5, 17 (1965), 57–82.

Coquery-Vidrovitch, C., 'French Colonization in Africa to 1920: Administration and Economic Development', in: Gann, L.H. & Duignan, P. (eds.), *Colonialism in Africa 1870–1960. Volume 1: The History and Politics of Colonialism 1870–1914* (Cambridge 1969), 165–198.

Coquery-Vidrovitch, C., *Le Congo au temps des grandes compagnies concessionnaires 1898–1930* (Paris & The Hague 1972).

Coquery-Vidrovitch, C., 'Investissements prives, investissements publics en AEF, 1900–1940', *African Economic History*, 12 (1983), 13–31.

Coquery-Vidrovitch, C., 'The Colonial Economy of the Former French, Belgian and Portuguese Zones, 1914–35', in: Boahen, A.A. (ed.), *General History of Africa. VII: Africa under Colonial Domination 1880–1935* (Paris 1985), 351–381.

Cornelis, S., Creemers-Palmers, M., Goris, J-M., Hambrouck, G., Jespers, P., Luwel, M. & Marechal, P. (eds.), *H.M. Stanley: explorateur au service du Roi* (Tervuren 1991).

Coupland, R., *The Exploitation of East Africa 1856–1890: The Slave Trade and the Scramble* (London 1968).

Crandall, R., *The Research Center in Entrepreneurial History at Harvard University, 1948–1959* (Cambridge MA 1960).

Craven, M., 'Between Law and History: The Berlin Conference of 1884–1884 and the Logic of Free Trade', *London Review of International Law*, 3, 1 (2015), 31–59, https://doi.org/10.1093/lril/lrv002.

Dalrymple-Smith, A.E., *Commercial Transitions and Abolition in West Africa 1630–1860* (Leiden & Boston 2020).

Danker-Hagenaars, D.L.M.T., *Op het spoor van de concessie: Een onderzoek naar het rechtskarakter van de concessie in Nederland en in Frankrijk* (The Hague 2000).

Darwin, J., *After Tamerlane: The Global History of Empire* (London 2007).

Daumalin, X., 'Commercial Presence, Colonial Penetration: Marseille Traders in West Africa in the Nineteenth Century', in: Pétré-Grenouilleau, O. (ed.), *From Slave Trade to Empire: Europe and the Colonization of Black Africa 1750s–1880s* (London 2004), 209–230.

David, L.E. & Huttenback, R.A., *Mammon and the Pursuit of Empire: The Political Economy of British Imperialism, 1860–1912* (Cambridge 1986).

Deaton, A., 'Commodity Prices and Growth in Africa', *Journal of Economic Perspectives*, 13, 3 (1999), 23–40.

Decker, S., *Postcolonial Transition and Global Business History: British Multinational Companies in Ghana and Nigeria* (New York 2022).

Dejung, C., *Commodity Trading, Globalization and the Colonial World: Spinning the Web of the Global Market* (New York & Oxon 2018).

Delmotte, L., *De Belgische koloniale holdings* (Leuven 1946).

Derksen, R., 'Forminiere in the Kasai, 1906–1939', *African Economic History*, 12 (1983), 49–65.

Destrain, E., 'Bassin du Quilou Niadi: Le District de Stéphanieville', *Bulletin de Société Royale belge de Géographie*, 15 (1891), 485–513.

Van den Doel, H.W., *Het Rijk van Insulinde: Opkomst en ondergang van een Nederlandse kolonie* (Amsterdam 1996).

Van den Doel, H.W., *Zo ver de wereld strekt: de geschiedenis van Nederland overzee vanaf 1800* (Amsterdam 2011).

Dolan, L., 'Explaining the Transition from Forced to Free Labour in Colonial Angola's Diamond Mines', *Revista de Historia Industrial-Industrial History Review*, 33, 92 (2024), 161–198, https://doi.org/10.1344/rhiihr.44588.

Dorhout Mees, E., 'Kerdijk, Henri Polak', in: Visser, J., Van Jaarsveld, M. & Van de Laar, P. (eds.), *Rotterdamse ondernemers 1850–1950* (Rotterdam 2003), 119–121.

Dreijer, G.P., 'Nederlandse handel en scheepvaart op West-Afrika 1830–1914', *Tijdschrift voor Zeegeschiedenis*, 43, 1 (2024), 38–55.

Van Driel, H., 'Innovation and Integration in Mineral Bulk Handling in the Port of Rotterdam, 1886–1923', *Business History*, 44, 3 (2002), 63–90.

Dummett, R.E., 'Introduction: Exploring the Cain/Hopkins Paradigm: Issues for Debate; Critique and Topics for New Research', in: Dummett, R.E. (ed.), *Gentlemanly Capitalism and British Imperialism: The New Debate on Empire* (London & New York 1999), 1–43.

Dumoulin, M., *Léopold II un roi genocidaire?* (Brussels 2005).

Eckstein, A.M., 'Is There a "Hobson-Lenin Thesis" on Late Nineteenth-Century Colonial Expansion?', *The Economic History Review*, 44, 2 (1991), 297–318.

Emerson, B., *Leopold II of the Belgians: King of Colonialism* (London 1979).

Emmer, P.C., *Engeland, Nederland, Afrika en de slavenhandel in negentiende eeuw* (Leiden 1974).

Etambala, M.Z., *Veroverd, bezet, gekoloniseerd: Congo 1876–1914* (Gorredijk 2020).

Etherington, N., 'Reconsidering Theories of Imperialism', *History and Theory*, 21, 1 (1982), 1–36.

Exenberger, A. & Hartmann, S., 'Extractive Institutions in the Congo: Checks and Balances in the *longue durée*', in: Frankema, E. & Buelens, F. (eds.), *Colonial Exploitation and Economic Development: The Belgian Congo and the Netherlands Indies compared* (London & New York 2013), 18–40.

Ewalefoh, J., 'The New Scramble for Africa', in: Oloruntoba, S.O. & Falola, T. (eds.), *The Palgrave Handbook of Africa and the Changing Global Order* (Cham 2022), 309–322, https://doi.org/10.1007/978-3-030-77481-3_15.

Ewans, M., *European Atrocity, African Catastrophe: Leopold II, the Congo Free State and its Aftermath* (London & New York 2002).

Falola, T., *A History of West Africa* (London & New York 2024).

Fereirra, R., 'The Conquest of Ambriz: Colonial Expansion and Imperial Competition in Central Africa', *Mulemba*, 5, 9 (2015), 1–16, https://doi.org/10.4000/mulemba.439.

Ferin, L., 'Clima do Congo', *Revista portugueza: colonial e maritima*, 1, 2 (1897–1898), 665–672.

Fieldhouse, D.K., '"Imperialism": An Historiographical Revision', *The Economic History Review*, 14, 2 (1961), 187–209.

Fisch, J., 'Africa as *terra nullius*: The Berlin Conference and International Law', in: Förster, S., Mommsen, W.J. & Robinson, R. (eds.), *Bismarck, Europe and Africa: The Berlin Africa Conference 1884–1885 and the Onset of Partition* (Oxford 1988), 347–375.

Fieldhouse, D.K. *The Theory of Capitalist Imperialism* (Malta 1967).

Fieldhouse, D.K., *Economics and Empire, 1830–1914* (London 1973).

Flint, J., 'Chartered Companies and the Transition from Informal Sway to Colonial Rule in Africa', in: Förster, S., Mommsen, W.J. & Robinson, R. (eds.), *Bismarck, Europe and Africa: The Berlin Africa Conference 1884–1885 and the Onset of Partition* (Oxford 1988), 69–83.

Forbes Munro, J., 'Monopolists and Speculators: British Investment in West African Rubber, 1905–1914', *The Journal of African History*, 22, 2 (1981), 263–278.

Frankel, S.H., *Capital Investment in Africa: Its Course and Effects* (Oxford 1938).

Frankema, E., 'African Economic Development: Growth, Reversals, and Deep Transitions', in: Broadberry, S. & Fukao, K. (eds), *The Cambridge Economic History of the Modern World. Volume II: 1870 to the Present* (Cambridge 276–305, https://doi.org/10.1017/9781316671603.011.

Frankema, E. & Van Waijenburg, M., 'Africa Rising? A Historical Perspective', *African Affairs*, 117, 469 (2018), 543–568, https://doi.org/10.1093/afraf/ady022.

Frankema, E. & Van Waijenburg, M., 'From Coast to Hinterland: Fiscal Capacity Building in British and French West Africa, c. 1880–1960', in: Frankema, E. & Booth, A. (eds.), *Fiscal Capacity and the Colonial State in Asia and Africa, c. 1850–1960* (Cambridge 2019), 161–192.

Frankema, E. & Van Waijenburg, M., 'Bridging the Gap with the "New" Economic History of Africa', *The Journal of African History*, 64, 1 (2023), 38–61, https://doi.org/10.1017/S0021853722000792.

Frankema, E., Williamson, J. & Woltjer, P., 'An Economic Rationale for the West African Scramble? The Commercial Transition and the Commodity Price Boom of 1835–1885', *Journal of Economic History*, 78, 1 (2018a), 231–267, https://doi.org/10.1017/S0022050718000128.

Frankema, E., Woltjer, P., Dalrymple-Smith, A. & Bulambo, L., 'An Introduction to the African Commodity Trade Database, 1730–2010: Social and Economic History', *Research Data Journal for the Humanities and Social Sciences*, 3, 1 (2018b), 1–12, https://doi.org/10.1163/24523666-01000009.

Franssens, K., 'De vestiging van "Kerdijk en Pincoffs" te Banana, 1857–1859', *Mededelingen der zittingen van de Koninklijke Akademie voor Overzeese Wetenschappen*, 22 (1976a), 683–697.

Franssens, K., 'Nederland na de Aardrijkskundige Conferentie van Brussel (1877–1879)', in: Staner, P. & Stengers, J. (eds.), *Bijdragen over de Aardrijkskundige Conferentie van 1876* (Brussels 1976b), 501–516.

Frederick, K., Juif, D. & Meier zu Selhausen, F., 'The Revival of African Economic History in the 21st Century: A Bibliometric Analysis', *Revista de Historia Industrial-Industrial History Review*, 33, 92 (2024), 11–48, https://doi.org/10.1344/rhiihr.47560.

Friedman, K.E., *Catastrophe and Creation: The Transformation of an African Culture* (Chur 1991).

Frost, D., 'British Imperial Trade and West African Kru Seamen', in: Everaert, J. & Parmentier, J. (eds.), *International Conference on Shipping, Factories and Colonization (Brussels, 24–26 November 1994)* (Brussels 1996), 215–219.

Galbraith, J.S., *Crown and Charter: The Early Years of the British South Africa Company* (Berkeley CA 1974).

Gallagher, J. & Robinson, R., 'The Imperialism of Free Trade', *The Economic History Review*, 6, 1 (1953), 1–15.

Gallagher, J. & Robinson, R., *Africa and the Victorians: The Official Mind of Imperialism* (London 1961/1981).

Gann, L.H., 'Belgian Administration in the Congo: An Overview', in: Gann, L.H. & Duignan, P. (eds.), *African Proconsuls: European Governors in Africa* (New York, London & Stanford CA 1978), 367–373.

Gann, L.H. & Duignan, P., *The Rulers of Belgian Africa, 1884–1914* (Princeton NJ 1979).

Gardner, L., 'Fiscal Policy in the Belgian Congo in Comparative Perspective', in: Frankema, E. & Buelens, F. (eds.), *Colonial Exploitation and Economic Development: The Belgian Congo and the Netherlands Indies compared* (London & New York 2013), 130–152.

Gardner, L., 'New Colonies, Old Tools: Building Fiscal Systems in East and Central Africa', in: Frankema, E. & Booth, A. (eds.), *Fiscal Capacity and the Colonial State in Asia and Africa, c. 1850–1960* (Cambridge 2019), 193–229.

Gardner, L., *Sovereignty Without Power: Liberia in the Age of Empires 1822–1980* (Cambridge 2022).

Gardner, L., 'Slavery, Coercion, and Economic Development in Sub-Saharan Africa', *Business History Review*, 97, 3 (2023), 199–223, https://doi.org/10.1017/S0007680523000338.

Gardner, L. & Roy, T., *The Economic History of Colonialism* (Bristol 2020).

Geiss, I., 'Free Trade, Internationalization of the Congo Basin, and the Principle of Effective Occupation', in: Förster, S., Mommsen, W.J. & Robinson, R. (eds.), *Bismarck, Europe and Africa: The Berlin Africa Conference 1884–1885 and the Onset of Partition* (Oxford 1988), 263–280.

Gjersø, J.F., 'The Scramble for East Africa: British Motives Reconsidered, 1884–95', *The Journal of Imperial and Commonwealth History*, 43, 5 (1015), 831–860, https://doi.org/10.1080/03086534.2015.1026131.

Van Goor, J., 'Imperialisme in de marge?', in: Van Goor, J. (ed.), *Imperialisme in de marge: De afronding van Nederlands-Indië* (Utrecht 1986), 9–18.

Van Goor, J., *De Nederlandse koloniën: Geschiedenis van de Nederlandse expansie 1600–1975* (Bilthoven 1997).

Gordon, D.M., 'Precursors to Red Rubber: Violence in the Congo Free State, 1885–1895', *Past and Present*, 236, 3 (2017), 133–168, https://doi.org/10.1093/pastj/gtx018.

De Graaf, T., *Voor handel en maatschappij: geschiedenis van de Nederlandsche Handel-Maatschappij, 1824–1964* (Amsterdam 2012).

Gras, N.S.B., 'Why Study Business History?', *The Canadian Journal of Economics and Political Science*, 4, 3 (1939), 320–340.

Green, T., 'Africa and Capitalism: Repairing a History of Omission', *Capitalism: A Journal of History and Economics*, 3, 2 (2022a), 301–332, https://doi.org/10.1353/cap.2022.0012.
Green, E., *Creating the Cape Colony: The Political Economy of Settler Colonization* (London 2022b).
Greshoff, J., *Catrijntje Afrika* (The Hague 1944).
Greshoff, J., *Afscheid van Europa: leven tegen het leven* (The Hague 1969).
Griffiths, P.J., *A Licence to Trade: The History of English Chartered Companies* (London 1974).
De Groot, S.J., 'Het geheim van Futila: imperialistisch optreden van de Koninklijke Marine langs de Congo-rivier in 1885', *Mars et Historia*, 31, 1 (1997), 3–7.
Gunn, J., *Outsourcing African Labor: Kru Migratory Workers in Global Ports, Estates and Battlefields until the End of the 19th Century* (Berlin & Boston 2021).
Gwaindepi, A. & Siebrits, K., 'How Mineral Discoveries Shaped the Fiscal System of South Africa', in: Frankema, E. & Booth, A. (eds.), *Fiscal Capacity and the Colonial State in Asia and Africa, c. 1850–1960* (Cambridge 2019), 264–298.
Haasnoot, R., *Langzame wals* (Breda 2008).
Hammond, R.J., *Portugal and Africa 1815–1910: A Study in Uneconomic Imperialism* (Stanford CA 1966).
Hargreaves, J.D., 'Towards a History of the Partition of Africa', *The Journal of African History*, 1, 1 (1960), 97–109.
Hargreaves, J.D., *Prelude to the Partition of West Africa* (London 1963).
Harms, R.W., 'The End of Red Rubber: A Reassessment', *The Journal of African History*, 16, 1 (1975), 73–88.
Harms, R.W., 'The World ABIR Made: The Margina-Lopori Basin, 1885–1903', *African Economic History*, 12 (1983), 125–139.
Harms, R.W., 'King Leopold's Bonds', in: Goetzmann, W.N. & Rouwenhorst, G.K. (eds.), *The Origins of Value: The Financial Innovations that Created Modern Capital Markets* (Oxford 2005), 343–357.
Harms, R.W., *Land of Tears: The Exploration and Exploitation of Equatorial Africa* (New York 2019).
Hausen, K., *Deutsche Kolonialherrschaft in Afrika: Wirtschaftsinteressen und Kolonialverwaltung in Kamerun vor 1914* (Freiburg 1970).
Hedinger, D. & Heé, N., 'Transimperial History – Connectivity, Cooperation and Competition', *Journal of Modern European History*, 16, 4 (2018), 429–452.
Heintze, B., *Afrikanische Pioniere: Trägerkarawanen im westlichen Zentralafrika (ca. 1850–1890)* (Frankfürt am Main 2002).
Den Heijer, H.J., *Geschiedenis van de WIC* (Zutphen 2013).
Den Heijer, H.J., 'Rotterdamse ondernemers en bestuurders: een koloniale kruisbestuiving', in: Oostindie, G. (ed.), *Het koloniale verleden van Rotterdam* (Amsterdam 2020), 145–193.

Van Helten, J-J., 'German Capital, the Netherlands Railway Company and the Political Economy of the Transvaal 1886–1900', *The Journal of African History*, 19, 3 (1978), 369–390.

Hennessey, J.L. & Lahti, J., 'Nordics in Motion: Transimperial Mobilities and Global Experiences of Nordic Colonialism', *The Journal of Imperial and Commonwealth History*, 51, 3 (2023), 409–240, https://doi.org/10.1080/03086534.2023.2205699.

Henriet, B., 'Colonial Law in the Making: Sovereignty and Property in the Congo Free State (1876–1908)', *Tijdschrift voor Rechtsgeschiedenis*, 83 (2015), 202–225, https://doi.org/10.1163/15718190-08312p10.

Henriet, B., *Colonial Impotence: Virtue and Violence in a Congolese Concession (1911–1940)* (Berlin & Boston 2021).

Henriet, B., Lauro, A. & Juste, R., 'Archives of Military Courts in Colonial Congo: New Sources for the History of Violence and Agency in Central Africa', *History in Africa*, 50 (2023), 259–274, https://doi.org/10.1017/hia.2023.9.

Van Herwaarden, J., 'Rijckevorsel, Huibert van', in: Visser, J., Van Jaarsveld, M. & Van de Laar, P. (eds.), *Rotterdamse ondernemers 1850–1950* (Rotterdam 2003), 202–207.

Heyse, T. & Leonard, H., *Régime des cessions et concessions de terre et de mines au Congo Belge* (Brussels 1932).

Hilton, A., *The Kingdom of Kongo* (Oxford 1985).

Von Hirschhausen, U., 'Diskussionsforum: A New Imperial History?', *Geschichte und Gesellschaft*, 41 (2015), 718–757.

Von Hirschhausen, U. & Leonhard, J., *Empires: Eine globale Geschichte 1780–1920* (Munich 2023).

Hobsbawm, E.J., *The Age of Empire (1875–1914)* (New York 1989).

Hobson, J.A., *Imperialism: A Study* (Cambridge 1902/2010).

Hochschild, A., *King Leopold's Ghost: A Story of Greed, Terror, and Heroism in Colonial Africa* (New York 1998).

Hofstra, S., 'Eenige gegevens over het schip "Lodewijk en over den handel van Rotterdam op West Afrika in de negentiende eeuw', *Rotterdams Jaarboekje*, 4, 6 (1938), 179–195.

Hoogendijk, D.A., 'Mr. Herman Willem Daendels als Gouverneur ter kuste van Guinea', *Nieuwe West-Indische Gids*, 25, 1 (1943), 257–266 & 289–302.

Hopkins, A.G., 'Economic Imperialism in West Africa: Lagos, 1880–92', *The Economic History Review*, 21, 3 (1968), 580–606.

Hopkins, A.G., *An Economic History of West Africa* (London 1973).

Hopkins, A.G., 'Imperial Business in Africa. Part I: Sources', *The Journal of African History*, 17, 1 (1976a), 29–48.

Hopkins, A.G., 'Imperial Business in Africa. Part II; Interpretation', *The Journal of African History*, 17, 2 (1976b), 267–290.

Hopkins, A.G., 'Big Business in African History', *The Journal of African History*, 28, 1 (1987), 119–140.

Hopkins, A.G., 'Back to the Future: From National History to Imperial History', *Past & Present*, 164, 3 (1999), 198–243.

Hopkins, A.G., 'The "New International Economic Order" in the Nineteenth Century: Britain's First Development Plan for Africa', in: Law, R. (ed.), *From Slave Trade to 'Legitimate' Commerce: The Commercial Transition in Nineteenth-Century West Africa* (Cambridge 2009), 240–264.

Hopkins, A.G., 'Fifty Years of African Economic History', *Economic History of Developing Regions*, 34, 1 (2019), 1–15.

Hopkins, A.G., *Capitalism in the Colonies: African Merchants in Lagos, 1851–1931* (Princeton, NJ 2024).

Howe, S., 'David Fieldhouse and "Imperialism": Some Historiographical Revisions', *The Journal of Imperial and Commonwealth History*, 26, 2 (1998), 213–232, https://doi.org/10.1080/03086539808583033.

Howe, S., 'Introduction: New Imperial Histories' in: Howe, S. (ed.), *The New Imperial Histories Reader* (London & New York 2010), 1–20.

Hudig, J., 'In memoriam L. Pincoffs', *Rotterdams Jaarboekje*, 1, 10 (1912), 175–185.

Van Hulle, I., *Britain and International Law in West Africa: The Practice of Empire* (Oxford 2020).

Van Hulle, I., 'The Blood Brotherhood and Colonial Treaties and Alliances: Between Myth and Reality', *Journal of the History of International Law*, 25 (2023), 471–498.

Ingenbleek, P., 'Muller, Hendrik', in: Visser, J., Van Jaarsveld, M. & Van de Laar, P. (eds.), *Rotterdamse ondernemers 1850–1950* (Rotterdam 2003), 161–164.

Isaacman, A.F. & Isaacman, B., *The Tradition of Resistance in Mozambique: Anti-Colonial Activity in the Zambezi Valley 1850–1921* (London 1976).

Isaacman, A. & Vansina, J., 'African Initiatives and Resistance in Central Africa, 1880–1914', in: Boahen, A.A. (ed.), *General History of Africa. VII: Africa under Colonial Domination 1880–1935* (Paris 1985), 169–193.

Janssen, R., *Grof geld: financiële schandalen en speculatie in Nederland* (Amsterdam 2013).

Jeal, T., *Stanley: The Impossible Life of Africa's Greatest Explorer* (London 2007).

Jeaugeon, R., 'Les sociétés d'exploitation au Congo et l'opinion française de 1890 à 1906', *Revue française d'histoire d'outre-mer*, 48, 172–173 (1961), 353–437.

Jerven, M., Strangio, D. & Weisdorf, 'A Case of Its Own ? A Review of Italy's Colonisation on Eritrea, 1890–1941', *The Journal of European Economic History*, 50, 1 (2021), 99–132.

Jewsiewicki, B., 'Notes sur l'Histoire socio-économique du Congo (1880–1960)', *Etudes d'Histoire Africaine*, 3 (1972), 209–241.

Jewsiewicki, B., 'Zaire Enters the World System: Its Colonial Incorporation as the Belgian Congo, 1885–1960', in: Gran, G. (ed.), *Zaire: The Political Economy of Underdevelopment* (New York 1979).

Jewsiewicki, B., 'Raison d'Etat ou raison du capital: l'accumulation primitive au Congo belge', *African Economic History*, 12 (1983), 157–182.

Jones, C.J., *International Business in the Nineteenth Century: The Rise and Fall of a Cosmpolitan Bourgeoisie* (New York 1987).

Jones, G.G., *Merchants to Multinationals: British Trading Companies in the Nineteenth and Twentieth Centuries* (Oxford 2000).

Jones, G.G., *Multinationals and Global Capitalism: From the Nineteenth to the Twenty-First Century* (Oxford 2005).

Jones, G.G., *Entrepreneurship and Multinationals: Global Business and the Making of the Modern World* (Cheltenham & Northampton MA 2013).

Jonker, J.P.B. & Sluyterman, K.E., *Thuis op de wereldmarkt: Nederlandse handelshuizen door de eeuwen heen* (The Hague 2000).

Jun, U., *Brokers of Empire: Japanese Settler Colonialism in Korea, 1876–1945* (Cambridge MA & London 2011).

Kanya-Forstner, A.S., 'French African Priorities and the Berlin West Africa Conference', in: Förster, S., Mommsen, W.J. & Robinson, R. (eds.), *Bismarck, Europe and Africa: The Berlin Africa Conference 1884–1885 and the Onset of Partition* (Oxford 1988), 171–187.

Kara, S., *Cobalt Red: How the Blood of the Congo Powers Our Lives* (New York 2023).

Katzenellenbogen, S., 'It Didn't Happen at Berlin: Politics, Economics and Ignorance in the Setting of Africa's Colonial Boundaries', in: Nugent, P. & Asiwaju, A.I. (eds.), *African Boundaries: Barriers, Conduits and Opportunities* (London & New York 1996), 21–34.

Van Kessel, I., *Zwarte Hollanders: Afrikaanse soldaten in Nederlands-Indië* (Amsterdam 2005).

Kind, M. *Van kippenveren tot dieselmotoren: de geschiedenis van de technische handelsmaatschappij Lindeteves NV* (Schoorl 2000).

De Kok, G.J., 'De koloniale connectie: geschiedenis van de Rotterdamse koloniale scheepvaart en handel', in: Oostindie, G. (ed.), *Het koloniale verleden van Rotterdam* (Amsterdam 2020a), 35–89.

De Kok, G.J., 'De koloniale impact: industrie en financiële dienstverlening', in: Oostindie, G. (ed.), *Het koloniale verleden van Rotterdam* (Amsterdam 2020b), 91–143.

Koppius, W.J., 'Herman Willem Daendels, Gouv. Gen. Ter kuste van Guinea 1816–1818, *De Indische Gids*, 52, 2 (1930), 892–904 & 979–997.

Koskenniemi, M., *The Gentle Civilizer of Nations: The Rise and Fall of International Law 1870–1960)* (Cambridge 2004).

Kubicek, R.V., *Economic Imperialism in Theory and Practice: The Case of South African Gold Mining Finance 1886–1914* (Durham NC 1979).

Kuitenbrouwer, M., *Nederland en de opkomst van het moderne imperialisme: koloniën en buitenlandse politiek 1870–1902* (Amsterdam & Dieren 1985).

Kuitenbrouwer, M., 'Het imperialisme-debat in de Nederlandse geschiedschrijving', *BMGN-Low Countries Historical Review*, 113, 1 (1998), 56–73.

Van de Laar, P.T., *Stad van formaat: geschiedenis van Rotterdam in de negentiende en twintigste eeuw* (Zwolle 2000).

Van der Laan, L.H., 'Trading in the Congo: The NAHV from 1918 to 1955', *African Economic History*, 12 (1983), 241–259.

Van der Laan, L. 'Selling Tropical Africa's Export Crops: The Experience of the Inter-War Period', in: Dewey, C. (ed.), *The State and the Market: Studies in the Economic and Social History of the Third World* (New Delhi 1987), 238–261.

Landes, D.S., 'Some Thoughts on the Nature of Economic Imperialism', *The Journal of Economic History*, 21, 4 (1961), 496–512.

Lanslot, I., 'Pierre Savorgnan de Brazza, le "Grand Chef Blanc": Le portrait contemporain d'un homme légendaire', in: Comberiati, D., Halen, P. & Iounes-Vona, R. (eds.), *Des Italiens au Congo aux Italiens du Congo: Aspects d'une glocalité* (Paris 2020), 43–54.

Law, R., 'The Historiography of the Commercial Transition in Nineteenth-Century Africa', in: Fayola, T. (ed.), *African Historiography: Essays in Honour of Jacob Ade Ajayi* (Ikeja 1993), 91–115.

Law, R., 'Introduction', in: Law, R. (ed.), *From Slave Trade to 'Legitimate' Commerce: The Commercial Transition in Nineteenth-Century West Africa* (Cambridge 2009), 1–31.

Lenin, V.I., *Imperialism, the Highest Stage of Capitalism: A Popular Outline* (Moscow 1963).

De Leur, W.J. & Schoone, F.A.M. (eds.), *Tentoonstelling: Pincoffs en de Rotterdamse havens* (Rotterdam 1979).

Lindblad, J.T., 'Economische aspecten van de Nederlandse expansie in de Indonesische archipel, 1870–1914', in: Van Goor, J. (ed.), *Imperialisme in de marge: De afronding van Nederlands-Indië* (Utrecht 1986), 227–265.

Van der Linden, M., *The Acquisition of Africa (1870–1914): The Nature of International Law* (Leiden & Boston 2017).

Lindner, U., 'Colonialism as a European Project in Africa before 1914? British and German Concepts of Colonial Rule in Sub-Saharan Africa', *Comparativ*, 19, 1 (2009), 88–106.

Lindner, U., *Koloniale Begegnungen: Deutschland und Grossbritannien als Imperialmächte in Afrika 1880–1914* (Frankfürt am Main & New York 2011).

Linneweh, B., 'Global Trading Companies in the Commodity Chain of Rubber between 1890 and the 1920s', *Business History*, 65, 5 (2023), 863–879, https://doi.org/10.1080/00076791.20.

Lloyd, T., 'Africa and Hobson's Imperialism', *Past & Present*, 55 (1972), 130–153.

Locher-Scholten, E.B., 'Dutch Expansion in the Indonesian Archipelago around 1900 and the Imperialism Debate', *Journal of Southeast Asian Studies*, 25, 1 (1994a), 91–111.

Locher-Scholten, E.B., *Sumatraans Sultanaat en koloniale staat: de relatie Djambi-Batavia (1830–1907) en het Nederlands imperialisme* (Leiden 1994b).

Lovell, R.I., *The Struggle for South Africa 1875–1899: A Study in Economic Imperialism* (New York 1934).

Lowes, S. & Montero, E., 'King Leopold's Ghost: The Legacy of Labour Coercion in the DRC', in: Michalopoulos, S. & Papaioannou, E. (eds.), *The Long Economic and Political Shadows of History – Volume 2: Africa and Asia* (London 2017), 75–86.

Lowes, S. & Montero, E., 'Concessions, Violence, and Indirect Rule: Evidence from the Congo Free State', *The Quarterly Journal of Economics*, 136, 4 (2021), 2047–2091, https://doi.org/10.1093/qje/qjab021.

Lubinski, C., 'Liability of Foreignness in Historical Context: German Business in Preindependence India (1880–1940)', *Enterprise & Society*, 15, 4 (2015), 722–758, https://doi.org/10.1093/es/khu045.

Lukasiewicz, M., *Gold, Finance and Imperialism in South Africa, 1887–1902* (Cham 2024).

Luwel, M., *Otto Lindner 1852–1945: Een weinig bekend medewerker van Leopold II in Afrika* (Brussels 1959).

Lynn, M., 'Change and Continuity in the British Palm Oil Trade with West Africa, 1830–55', *The Journal of African History*, 22, 3 (1981), 331–348.

Lynn, M., 'From Sail to Steam: The Impact of the Steamship Services on the British Palm Oil Trade with West Africa, 1850–1890', *The Journal of African History*, 30, 2 (1989), 227–245.

Lynn, M., *Commerce and Economic Change in West Africa: The Palm Oil Trade in the Nineteenth Century* (Cambridge 1997).

Lynn, M., 'The West African Palm Oil Trade in the Nineteenth Century and the "Crisis of Adaption"', in: Law, R. (ed.), *From Slave Trade to 'Legitimate' Commerce: The Commercial Transition in Nineteenth-Century West Africa* (Cambridge 2009), 57–77.

Macola, G., 'Warlordism in the Congo Basin between the Nineteenth and Twentieth Centuries', *International Journal of African Historical Studies*, 56, 1 (2023), 1–19.

Marchal, J., *E.D. Morel tegen Leopold II en de Kongostaat* (Antwerp 1985).

Marchal, J., *L'État Libre du Congo: paradis perdu: L'Histoire du Congo 1876–1900* (2 Vols.) (Borgloon 1996).

Marechal, P., *De «Arabische» campagne in het Maniema-gebied (1892–1894): situering binnen het kolonisatieproces in de Onafhankelijke Congostaat* (Brussels 1992).

Marseille, J., *Empire colonial et capitalisme français: Histoire d'un divorce* (Paris 1984).

Mathys, G. & Van Beurden, S., 'History by Commission? The Belgian Colonial Past and the Limits of History in the Public Eye', *The Journal of African History*, 64, 3 (2023), 334–343, https://doi.org/10.1017/S0021853723000683.

Mees, P.A.J., 'R. Mees & Zoonen en de Pincoffscrisis', *Rotterdams Jaarboekje*, 9, 9 (1991), 323–330.

Mees, W.C., *Man van de daad: Mr. Marten Mees en de opkomst van Rotterdam* (Rotterdam 1946).

Van der Meulen, D., *Dr. Hendrik Muller: wereldreiziger voor het vaderland (1859–1941)* (Amsterdam 2020).

Miers, S., *Britain and the Ending of the Slave Trade* (Bristol 1975).

Mohun, A.P., *American Imperialist: Cruelty and Consequence in the Scramble for Africa* (Chicago 2023).

Mollan, S., *Imperialism and Economic Development in Sub-Saharan Africa: An Economic and Business History of Sudan* (Cham 2020).

Mollema, A.M.P., 'De afstand der Nederlandse bezittingen ter kuste van Guinea aan Engeland in 1872', in: S.A. (ed.), *Varia Historica: Aangeboden aan Professor Doctor A.W. Byvanck ter gelegenheid van zijn zeventigste verjaardag door de Historische Kring te Leiden* (Assen 1954), 215–242.

Mommsen, W.J., *Imperialismustheorien: Ein Überblick über die neueren Imperialismustheorien* (Göttingen 1977).

Muller, H., Muller: een Rotterdams zeehandelaar Hendrik Muller Szn (1819–1898) (Schiedam 1977).

Neil-Tomlinson, B., 'The Nyassa Chartered Company: 1891–1929', *The Journal of African History*, 18, 1 (1977), 109–128.

Nelson, S.H., *Colonialism in the Congo Basin 1880–1940* (Athens OH 1994).

Newbury, C., 'On the Margins of Empire: The Trade of Western Africa, 1875–1890', in: Förster, S., Mommsen, W.J. & Robinson, R. (eds.), *Bismarck, Europe and Africa: The Berlin Africa Conference 1884–1885 and the Onset of Partition* (Oxford 1988), 35–58.

Newbury, C.W. & Kanya-Forstner, A.S., 'French Policy and the Origins of the Scramble for Africa', *The Journal of African History*, 10, 2 (1969), 253–276.

Newitt, M., *Portugal in Africa: The Last Hundred Years* (London 1981).

Nzemeke, A.D., 'Free Trade and Territorial Partition in Nineteenth-Century West Africa: Course and Outcome', in: Förster, S., Mommsen, W.J. & Robinson, R. (eds.), *Bismarck, Europe and Africa: The Berlin Africa Conference 1884–1885 and the Onset of Partition* (Oxford 1988), 59–68.

Obdeijn, H., 'The New Africa Trading Company and the Struggle for Import Duties in the Congo Free State, 1886–1894', *African Economic History*, 12 (1983), 195–212.

Ochonu, M.E., 'Introduction: Toward African Entrepreneurship and Business History', in: Ochonu, M.E. (ed.), *African Entrepreneurship: A Historical Approach* (Bloomington IN 2018), 1–27.

Oliver, R., 'The Partition of Africa: The European and African Interpretations', in: S.A. (ed.), *Bijdragen over de honderdste verjaring van de Onafhankelijke Kongostaat* (Brussels 1988), 41–50.

Oosterlinck, K., Blocher, J. & Gulati, M., 'Why Did Belgium Pay Leopold's Bonds?', *Law and Contemporary Problems*, 83, 2 (2020), 49–70.

Oosterwijk, B., *Reder in Rotterdam: Willem Ruys (1809–1889)* (Rotterdam 1989).

Oosterwijk, B., *Koning van de koopvaart: Anthony van Hoboken (1756–1850)* (Amsterdam 1996).

Oosterwijk, B., *Ik verlang geen dank: Lodewijk Pincoffs (1827–1911)* (Rotterdam 2011).

Osterhammel, J., *The Transformation of the World: A Global History of the Nineteenth Century* (Princeton NJ & Oxford 2009).

Ottevanger, L., 'Pincoffs, Lodewijk', in: Visser, J., Van Jaarsveld, M. & Van de Laar, P. (eds.), *Rotterdamse ondernemers 1850–1950* (Rotterdam 2003), 185–188.

Pakenham, T., *The Scramble for Africa* (London 1991).

Pateman, J., 'The Centrality of Africa in Lenin's Theory of Imperialism', *Review of African Political Economy*, 49, 172 (2022), 287–302, https://doi.org/10.1080/03056244.2022.2026765.

Pavlakis, D., *British Humanitarianism and the Congo Reform Movement, 1896–1913* (Abingdon 2015).

Pavlakis, D., 'The Crime of the Congo: A Question of Genocide in the Congo Free State, 1885–1908', in: Blackhawk, N., Kiernan, B., Madley, B. & Taylor, R. (eds.), *The Cambridge World History of Genocide* (Vol. 4: Premonitions) (Cambridge 2023), 585–608, https://doi.org/10.1017/9781108765480.025.

Peemans, J-P., 'Capital Accumulation in the Congo under Colonialism: The Role of the State', in: Duignan, P. & Gann, L.H. (eds.), *Colonialism in Africa 1870–1960. Volume 4: The Economics of Colonialism* (Cambridge 1975), 165–212.

Perren, R., *Agriculture in Depression, 1870–1940* (Cambridge 1995).

Phillips, A. & Sharman, J.C., *Outsourcing Empire: How Company-States made the Modern World* (Princeton NJ & Oxford 2020).

Pincoffs, A.L., 'Lodewijk Pincoffs', *Rotterdams Jaarboekje*, 3, 5 (1927), 68–74.

Platt, D.C.M., *Finance, Trade, and Politics in British Foreign Policy 1815–1914* (Oxford 1968).

Platt, D.C.M., 'Further Objections to an "Imperialism of Free Trade", 1830–60', in: Roger Louis, W.M. (ed.), *Imperialism: The Robinson and Gallagher Controversy* (New York & London 1976), 153–161.

Platt, D.C.M., 'Introduction', in: Platt, D.C.M. (ed.), *Business Imperialism 1840–1930: An Inquiry Based on British Experience in Latin America* (Oxford 1977), 1–14.
Porter, A., *Victorian Shipping, Business and Imperial Policy: Donald Currie, the Castle Line and Southern Africa* (Woodbridge 1986).
Porter, A., *Religion versus Empire? British Protestant Missionaries and Overseas Expansion, 1700–1914* (Manchester 2004).
Van der Pot, J.E., 'Abram van Rijckevorsel HZN, 1790–1864', *Rotterdams Jaarboekje*, 5, 1 (1943), 111–152.
Van der Pot, J.E., 'Huibert van Rijckevorsel, 1813–1866', *Rotterdams Jaarboekje*, 5, 2 (1944), 10–24.
Potter, S.J. & Saha, J., 'Global History, Imperial History and Connected Histories of Empire', *Journal of Colonialism and Colonial History*, 16, 1 (2015), https://doi.org/10.1353/cch.2015.0009.
Press, S., *Rogue Empires: Contracts and Conmen in Europe's Scramble for Africa* (Cambridge MA 2017).
Press, S., *Blood and Diamonds: Germany's Imperial Ambitions in Africa* (Cambridge MA 2021).
Press, S., 'Buying Sovereignty: German "Weltpolitik" and Private Enterprise, 1884–1914', *Central European History*, 55, 1 (2022), 15–33, https://doi.org/10.1017/S0008938921001746.
Raben, R., 'A New Dutch Imperial History? Perambulations in a Prospective Field', *BMGN – Low Countries Historical Review*, 128, 1 (2013), 5–30.
Reid, R., 'Africa's Revolutionary Nineteenth Century and the Idea of the "Scramble"', *American Historical Review*, 126, 4 (2021), 1424–1447, https://doi.org/10.1093/ahr/rhab539.
Reid, R., *The African Revolution: A History of the Long Nineteenth Century* (Princeton NJ 2025).
Reinhard, W., *Die Unterwerfung der Welt: Globalgeschichte der europäischen Expansion 1415–2015* (Munich 2016).
Renault, F., *Tippo Tip: un potentat arabe en afrique centrale au XIXème siècle* (Paris 1987).
Van Reybrouck, D., *Congo: een geschiedenis* (Amsterdam 2013).
Reynolds, E., *Trade and Economic Change on the Gold Coast 1807–1874* (London 1974).
Reynolds, E., 'Economic Imperialism: The Case of the Gold Coast', *The Journal of Economic History*, 35, 1 (1975), 94–116.
Van Riel, A., *The Trials of Convergence: Prices, Markets and Industrialization in The Netherlands, 1800–1913* (Leiden & Boston 2021).
Robins, J., 'Primary Commodities and Industrial Consumers: The Case of Palm Oil', in: Curry-Machado, J., Stubbs, J., Clarence-Smith, W.G. & Vos, J. (eds.), *The Oxford Handbook of Commodity History* (Oxford 2024), 287–308, https://doi.org/10.1093/oxfordhb/9780197502679.013.16.

Robinson, R., 'Non-European Foundations of European Imperialism: Sketch for a Theory of Collaboration', in: Roger Louis, W.M. (ed.), *Imperialism: The Robinson and Gallagher Controversy* (New York & London 1976), 128–151.

Robinson, R., 'European Imperialism and Indigenous Reactions in British West Africa, 1880–1914), Wesseling, H.L. & Braudel, F. (eds.), *Expansion and Reaction: Essays on European Expansion and Reaction in Asia and Africa* (Leiden 1978), 141–163.

Robinson, R. & Gallagher, J., 'The Partition of Africa', in: Roger Louis, W.M. (ed.), *Imperialism: The Robinson and Gallagher Controversy* (New York & London 1976), 73–127.

Rodney, W.S., *How Europe Underdeveloped Africa* (London 1972/2011).

Roes, A., 'Towards a History of Mass Violence in the Etat Indépendant du Congo, 1885–1908', *South African Historical Journal*, 62, 4 (2010), 634–670, https://doi.org/10.1080/02582473.2010.519937.

Roger Louis, W.M., 'The Stokes Affair and the Origins of the Anti-Congo Campaign, 1895–1896', *Revue belge de philologie et d'histoire*, 43, 2 (1965), 572–584.

Roger Louis, W.M., 'Great Britain and German Expansion in Africa, 1884–1919', in: Gifford, P. & Roger Louis, W.M. (eds.), *Britain and Germany in Africa: Imperial Rivalry and Colonial Rule* (New Haven & London 1967), 3–46.

Roger Louis, W.M., 'Introduction: Robinson and Gallagher and Their Critics', in: Roger Louis, W.M. (ed.), *Imperialism: The Robinson and Gallagher Controversy* (New York & London 1976), 2–51.

Rönnbäck, K. & Broberg, O., *Capital and Colonialism: The Return on British Investments in Africa 1869–1969* (Cham 2019).

Rönnbäck, K. & Broberg, O., 'From Defensive to Transformative Business Diplomacy: The British South Africa Company and the End of Chartered Company Rule in Rhodesia, 1910–1925', *Business History Review*, 96, 4 (2022), 777–903, https://doi.org/10.1017/S0007680522000022.

De Roo, B., 'The Trouble with Tariffs. Customs Policies and the Shaky Balance between Colonial and Private Interests in the Congo (1886–1914)', *TSEG-Low Countries Journal of Social and Economic History*, 12, 3 (2015), 1–21, https://doi.org/10.5117/TSEG2015.3.DERO.

De Roo, B., 'Taxation in the Congo Free State, an Exceptional Case? (1885–1908)', *Economic History of Developing Regions*, 32, 2 (2017a), 97–126, https://doi.org/10.1080/20780389.2017.1327807.

De Roo, B., 'Colonial Taxation in Africa. A Fiscal History of the Congo through the Lens of Customs (1886–1914)', *Afrika Focus*, 30, 2 (2017b), 61–65.

De Roo, B., 'Customs in the Two Congos: A Connected History of Colonial Taxation in Africa (1885–1914), *Journal of Colonialism and Colonial History*, 19, 1 (2018), https://doi.org/10.1353/cch.2018.0005.

De Roo, B., 'De Onafhankelijke Congostaat: plundermachine in dienst van een meedogenloze Leopold II?', in: Goddeeris, I., Lauro, A. & Vanthemsche, G. (eds.), *Koloniaal Congo: een geschiedenis in vragen* (Kalmthout 2020), 31–46.

Roy, T., 'The Development of the Arid Tropics: Lessons for Economic History', *Economic History of Developing Regions*, Advance Access, https://doi.org/10.1080/20780389.2022.2099371.

Rudin, H.R., *Germans in the Cameroons 1884–1914: A Case Study in Modern Imperialism* (Oxford 1938/1968).

Salmon, P., 'L'État Indépendant du Congo et la question arabe (1885–1892)', in: S.A. (ed.), *Bijdragen over de honderdste verjaring van de Onafhankelijke Kongostaat* (Brussels 1988), 437–460.

Sanderson, G.N., 'The European Partition of Africa: Coincidence or Conjuncture?', *The Journal of Imperial and Commonwealth History*, 3, 1 (1974), 1–54, https://doi.org/10.1080/03086537408582421.

Sanderson, G.N., 'British Informal Empire, Imperial Ambitions, Defensive Strategies, and the Anglo-Portuguese Congo Treaty of February 1884', in: Förster, S., Mommsen, W.J. & Robinson, R. (eds.), *Bismarck, Europe and Africa: The Berlin Africa Conference 1884–1885 and the Onset of Partition* (Oxford 1988), 189–214.

Saul, S.B., *The Myth of the Great Depression, 1873–1896* (London & Basingstoke 1969).

Sassoon, D., *The Anxious Triumph: A Global History of Capitalism, 1860–1914* (London 2020).

Schär, B.C., 'Switzerland, Borneo and the Dutch Indies: Towards a New Imperial History of Europe, c. 1770–1850', *Past and Present*, Advance Articles, https://doi.org/10.1093/pastj/gtab045.

Schepel, A.F., *Polak, Polak Kerdijk, Kerdijk: een familiegeschiedenis sedert 1779* (The Hague 1977).

Schmitz, H., 'Vragen rond Abram van Rijckevorsel (1790–1864)', *Rotterdams Jaarboekje*, 9, 5 (1987), 217–232.

Schumpeter, J.A., 'Capitalism, Socialism, and Democracy: The Process of Creative Destruction', in: Becker, M. (ed.), *Entrepreneurship: Classic Texts by Joseph Schumpeter* (Stanford CA 2011), 313–319.

Seibert, J., 'More Continuity than Change? New Forms of Unfree Labor in the Belgian Congo, 1908–1930', in: Van der Linden, M. (ed.), *Humanitarian Intervention and Changing Labor Relations: The Long-Term Consequences of the Abolition of the Slave Trade* (Leiden & Boston 2010), 369–386, https://doi.org/10.1163/ej.9789004188532.i-556.88.

Seibert, J., *In die globale Wirtschaft gezwungen: Arbeit und kolonialer Kapitalismus im Kongo (1885–1960)* (Frankfürt am Main 2016).

Seleti, Y.N., 'The Development of Dependent Capitalism in Portuguese Africa', in: Konczacki, Z.A., Parpart, J.L. & Shaw, T.M. (eds.), *Studies in the Economic History of Southern Africa. Volume one: The Front-Line States* (London 1990), 30–74.

Sicking, L.H.J., *Frontières d'Outre-Mer: La France et les Pays-Bas dans le monde atlantique au XIXe siècle* (Paris 2006).

Da Silva, A.F. & Neves, P., 'The Paradox of Nationality: Foreign Investment in Portuguese Africa (1890–1974), *Business History*, 64, 9 (2022), 1623–1649, https://doi.org/10.1080/00076791.2020.1797683.

Slinn, P., 'Commercial Concessions and Politics during the Colonial Period: The Role of the British South Africa Company in Northern Rhodesia 1890–1964', *African Affairs*, 70, 281 (1971), 365–384.

Stanard, M.G., *Selling the Congo: A History of European Pro-Empire Propaganda and the Making of Belgian Imperialism* (Lincoln NE 2012).

Stengers, J., 'Leopold II et la rivalité franco-anglaise en Afrique, 1882–1884', *Revue belge de philologie et d'histoire*, 47, 2 (1969a), 425–479.

Stengers, J., 'The Congo Free State and the Belgian Congo before 1914', in: Gann, L.H. & Duignan, P. (eds.), *Colonialism in Africa 1870–1960. Volume 1: The History and Politics of Colonialism 1870–1914* (Cambridge 1969b), 261–292.

Stengers, J., 'Léopold II entre l'Extrême-Orient et l'Afrique (1875–1876)', in: Staner, P. & Stengers, J. (eds.), *Bijdragen over de Aardrijkskundige Conferentie van 1876* (Brussels 1976), 303–374.

Stengers, J., 'Léopold II et le modèle colonial hollandais', *Tijdschrift voor Geschiedenis*, 90 (1977), 46–71.

Stengers, J., 'Leopold II and the Association Internationale du Congo', in: Förster, S., Mommsen, W.J. & Robinson, R. (eds.), *Bismarck, Europe and Africa: The Berlin Africa Conference 1884–1885 and the Onset of Partition* (Oxford 1988a), 229–244.

Stengers, J., 'Léopold II et l'Association Internationale du Congo', in: S.A. (ed.), *Bijdragen over de honderdste verjaring van de Onafhankelijke Kongostaat* (Brussels 1988b), 51–76.

Stengers, J., 'Leopold II et la foundation de l'État Indépendant du Congo', in: Stengers, J., *Congo, mythes et réalités: 100 ans d'histoire* (Paris & Louvain-La-Neuve 1989a), 41–78.

Stengers, J., 'Les cinq legends de l'Acte de Berlin', in: Stengers, J., *Congo, mythes et réalités: 100 ans d'histoire* (Paris & Louvain-La-Neuve 1989b), 79–90.

Stengers, J. & Vansina, J., 'King Leopold's Congo, 1886–1908', in: Oliver, R. & Sanderson, G.N. (eds.), *The Cambridge History of Africa. Volume 6: Western Equatorial Africa* (Cambridge 1985), 315–358, https://doi.org/10.1017/CHOL9780521228039.009.

De St. Moulin, L., 'What is Known of the Demographic History of Zaire Since 1885?', in: Fetter, B. (ed.), *Demography from Scanty Evidence: Central Africa in the Colonial Era* (Boulder CO 1990), 299–326, https://doi.org/10.1515/9781685851521-024.

Stokes, E., 'Late Nineteenth-Century Colonial Expansion and the Attack on the Theory of Economic Imperialism: A Case of Mistaken Identity?', *The Historical Journal*, 12, 2 (1969), 285–301.

Storm, R., '1871: Kust van Guinea verdwijnt van de Nederlandse kaart', in: Heerma van Voss, L., Bouras, N., 't Hart, M., Van der Heijden, M. & Lucassen, L. (eds.), *Nog meer wereldgeschiedenis van Nederland* (Amsterdam 2022), 397–402.

Tarabrin, E.A., *The New Scramble for Africa* (Moscow 1974).

Thomson, R.S., *Fondation de L'état indépendant du Congo: un chapitre de l'histoire du partage de l'Afrique* (Brussels 1933).

Todd, D., *A Velvet Empire: French Informal Imperialism in the Nineteenth Century* (Princeton & Oxford 2021).

Todzi, K.S., *Unternehmen Weltaneignung: Der Woermann-konzern und der deutsche Kolonialismus 1837–1916* (Göttingen 2023).

Todzi, K.S., '"Afrikahaus": Sitz des Woermann-Konzerns', in: Zimmerer, J. & Todzi, K.S. (eds.), *Hamburg: Tor zu kolonialen Welt: Errinerungsorte der (post-) kolonialen Globaliserung* (Göttingen 2021), 83–98.

Vail, L., 'Mozambique's Chartered Companies: The Rule of the Feeble', *Journal of African History*, 17, 3 (1976), 389–416.

Vail, L. & White, L., *Capitalism and Colonialism in Mozambique: A Study of Quelimane District* (London, Nairobi & Ibadan 1980).

Vandermissen, J., *Koningen van de wereld: Leopold II en de aardrijkskundige beweging* (Leuven 2009).

Vangroenweghe, D., *Leopold II en Kongo: het evenaarsdistrict en het Kroondomein, 1885–1908* (Bruges 1985).

Vangroenweghe, D., *Voor rubber en ivoor: Leopold II en de ophanging van Stokes* (Leuven 2005).

Vangroenweghe, D., *Rood rubber: Leopold II en zijn Congo* (Brussels 1986/2010).

Vangroenweghe, D., 'The "Leopold II" Concession System Exported to French Congo with as Example the Mpoko Company', *Journal of Belgian History*, 36 (2006), 323–372.

Vanhee, H. & Vos, J., 'Kongo in the Age of Empire', Cooksey, S., Poynor, R., & Vanhee, H. (eds.), *Kongo across the Waters* (Gainesville FL 2013), 78–87.

Vansina, J., 'Long-Distance Trade-Routes in Central Africa', *Journal of African History*, 3, 3 (1962), 375–390.

Vansina, J., *Kingdoms of the Savanna* (Madison WI, Milwaukee WI & London 1968).

Vansina, J., 'L'Afrique Centrale vers 1875', in: Staner, P. & Stengers, J. (eds.), *Bijdragen over de Aardrijkskundige Conferentie van 1876* (Brussels 1976), 1–32.

Vansina, J., *Paths in the Rainforest: Towards a History of Political Tradition in Equatorial Africa* (Madison WI 1990).

Vansina, J., *Being Colonized: The Kuba Experience in Rural Congo, 1880–1960* (Madison WI 2010).

Vansina, J., 'History in Novels and Memoirs: Alfons Vermeulen on Rural Congo (1899–1904), *History in Africa*, 39 (2012), 123–142, https://doi.org/10.1353/hia.2012.0006.

Vanthemsche, G., *Belgium and the Congo, 1885–1980* (Cambridge 2012).

Vanthemsche, G., 'Free Trade and Fair Justice in the Congo Free State? The Origins of the Rabinek Case (1901)', in: Van Schuylenbergh, P. & Leduc-Grimaldi, M. (eds.), *The Congo Free State: What Could Archives Tell Us? New Lights and Research Perspectives* (Brussels 2022), 291–336.

Da Veiga Pinto, L., *Le Portugal et le Congo au XIXe siècle: étude d'histoire des relations internationals* (Paris 1972).

Vellut, J-L., 'Réseaux transnationaux dans l'économie politique du Congo Léopoldien, c. 1885–1910', in: Marfaing, L. & Reinwald, B (eds.), *Afrikanische Beziehungen, Netzwerke und Räume* (Münster 2001), 131–146.

Vellut, J-L., 'Garenganze/Katanga – Bié – Benguela and Beyond: The Cycle of Rubber and Slaves at the Turn of the 20th Century', *Portuguese Studies Review*, 19, 1–2 (2011), 133–152.

Vellut, J-L., 'L'État independant du Congo dans l'histoire des géopolitiques du centre de l'Afrique', in: Vellut, J-L. (ed.), *Congo: Ambitions et désenchantements 1880–1960* (Paris 2017a), 21–59.

Vellut, J-L., 'La communauté portugaise du Congo belge. Une minorité ethnique', in: Vellut, J-L. (ed.), *Congo: Ambitions et désenchantements 1880–1960* (Paris 2017b), 139–162.

Vellut, J-L., '*The Congo Mirror* (River Congo, No. 1, 22 April 1891): Glimpses at the Entry of Congo on a Global Scene', in: Van Schuylenbergh, P. & Leduc-Grimaldi, M. (eds.), *The Congo Free State: What Could Archives Tell Us? New Lights and Research Perspectives* (Brussels 2022), 337–356.

Vere-Hodge, E.R., *Imperial British East Africa Company* (London 1960).

Verhoef, G., *The History of Business in Africa: Complex Discontinuity to Emerging Markets* (Cham 2017), https://doi.org/10.1007/978-3-319-62566-9.

Verhoef, G., 'Entrepreneurs in Africa – The Agenda for Business History in Africa: Complexity and Continuity', *Zeitschrift für Unternehmensgeschichte*, 69, 2 (2024), 187–211, https://doi.org/10.1515/zug-2023-0033.

Viaene, V., 'King Leopold's Imperialism and the Origins of the Belgian Colonial Party, 1860–1905', *The Journal of Modern History*, 80, 4 (2008), 741–790.

Vink, F., 'Dunlop, familie', in: Visser, J., Van Jaarsveld, M. & Van de Laar, P. (eds.), *Rotterdamse ondernemers 1850–1950* (Rotterdam 2003), 66–71.

Visser, J., 'Ondernemerselite 1850–1950', in: Visser, J., Van Jaarsveld, M. & Van de Laar, P. (eds.), *Rotterdamse ondernemers 1850–1950* (Rotterdam 2003), 10–19.

Vos, J., 'The Economics of the Kwango Rubber Trade, c. 1900', in: Heintze, B. & Von Oppen, A. (eds.), *Angola on the Move: Transport Routes, Communications and History* (Frankfurt am Main 2008), 85–98.

Vos, J., '"Without the Slave Trade, No Recruitment": From Slave Trading to "Migrant Recruitment" in the Lower Congo, 1830–90', in: Lawrance, B.N. & Robert, R.L. (eds.), *Trafficking in Slavery's Wake: Law and the Experience of Women and Children in Africa* (Athens OH 2012), 45–64.

Vos, J., 'Work in Times of Slavery, Colonialism and Civil War: Labor Relations in Angola from 1800 to 2000', *History in Africa*, 41 (2014), 363–385, https://doi.org/10.1017/hia.2014.8.

Vos, J., *Kongo in the Age of Empire, 1860–1913: The Breakdown of a Moral Order* (Madison WI, Milwaukee WI & London 2015).

Wallerstein, I., *The World World-System, Volume IV: Centrist Liberalism Triumphant, 1789–1914* (Oakland CA 2011).

Van Walsum, G.E., 'Abram van Rijckevorsel Hzn., man van de vooruitgang', *Rotterdams Jaarboekje*, 7, 3 (1965), 148–174.

Waltz, H., *Das Konzessionswesen im Belgischen Kongo* (2 Vols.) (Jena 1917).

De Weerd, G., *The Congo Free State: In Search of Historical Truth* (Brussels 2017).

Wesseling, H.L., 'Nederland en de Conferentie van Berlijn, 1884–1885', *Tijdschrift voor Geschiedenis*, 93 (1980), 559–576.

Wesseling, H.L., 'The Netherlands and the Partition of Africa', *The Journal of African History*, 22, 4 (1981), 495–509.

Wesseling, H.L., 'The Giant that was a Dwarf, or the Strange History of Dutch Imperialism', *Journal of Imperial and Commonwealth History*, 16, 3 (1988a), 58–70, https://doi.org/10.1080/03086538808582768.

Wesseling, H.L., 'Les Pays-Bas et la creation du Congo', in: S.A. (ed.), *Bijdragen over de honderdste verjaring van de Onafhankelijke Kongostaat* (Brussels 1988b), 467–476.

Wesseling, H.L., 'The Berlin Conference and the Expansion of Europe: A Conclusion', in: Förster, S., Mommsen, W.J. & Robinson, R. (eds.), *Bismarck, Europe and Africa: The Berlin Africa Conference 1884–1885 and the Onset of Partition* (Oxford 1988c), 527–540.

Wesseling, H.L., 'De Conferentie van Berlijn en de deling van Afrika', in: Wesseling, H.L., *Indië verloren, rampspoed geboren: En andere opstellen over de geschiedenis van de Europese expansie* (Amsterdam 1988d), 116–132.

Wesseling, H.L., 'Nederland als koloniaal model', in: Wesseling, H.L., *Indië verloren, rampspoed geboren: En andere opstellen over de geschiedenis van de Europese expansie* (Amsterdam 1988e), 140–176.

Wesseling, H.L., 'Bestond er een Nederlands imperialisme?', in: Wesseling, H.L., *Indië verloren, rampspoed geboren: En andere opstellen over de geschiedenis van de Europese expansie* (Amsterdam 1988f), 177–194.
Wesseling, H.L., *Verdeel en heers: de deling van Afrika 1880–1914* (Amsterdam 1999).
Wesseling, H.L., *Europa's koloniale eeuw: de koloniale rijken in de negentiende eeuw, 1815–1919* (Amsterdam 2003).
Wesseling, H.L., 'De Greshoffs en Afrika', *Nieuw Letterkundig Magazijn*, 26, 2 (2008), 51–59.
Wesseling, H.L., *De Mullers, Nederland en Afrika* (The Hague 2009).
Wijs, J., 'De collectie Hanken: een bewogen geschiedenis', *Object en verzamelaar*, 3 (2014), 7–30.
Wilkins, M., *The Emergence of Multinational Enterprise: American Business Abroad from the Colonial Era to 1914* (Cambridge MA 1970).
Wilkinson, J.C., *The Arabs and the Scramble for Africa* (Sheffield 2015).
Willequet, J., 'Anglo-German Rivalry in Belgian and Portuguese Africa?', in: Gifford, P. & Roger Louis, W.M. (eds.), *Britain and Germany in Africa: Imperial Rivalry and Colonial Rule* (New Haven & London 1967), 245–274.
Van Winter, P.J., *Onder Krugers Hollanders* (2 Vols.) (Amsterdam 1937–1938).
Wintle, M., *An Economic and Social History of the Netherlands, 1800–1920: Demographic, Economic and Social Transition* (Cambridge 2000).
Yarak, L.W., *Asante and the Dutch 1744–1873* (Oxford 1990).
Van Zanden, J.L. & Van Riel, A., *Nederland 1780–1914: staat, instituties en economische ontwikkeling* (Amsterdam 2000).

Miscellaneous & Internet Sources

The Africa Brief, 'Africa's Minerals', 28-03-2023, available at https://theafricabrief.beehiiv.com/p/special-africas-minerals [Retrieved 18/10/2023].
African Commodity Trade Database, available at https://www.aehnetwork.org/data-research/african-commodity-trade-database/ [Retrieved 25/10/2022].
BNN Bloomberg, 'Indonesia Aims to Sign $3.5 Billion in Deals in Africa Forum', 01-09-2024, available at https://www.bnnbloomberg.ca/business/international/2024/09/02/indonesia-aims-to-sign-35-billion-in-deals-during-africa-forum/ [Retrieved 06/09/2024].
'L. Pincoffs', Parlement.com, available at https://www.parlement.com/id/vg09ll4m0mzy/l_pincoffs [Retrieved 05/08/2021].
'H. Muller Szn.', Parlement.com, available at https://www.parlement.com/id/vg09ll3ijyi4/h_muller [Retrieved 06/01/2022].
'A. (Abram) van Rijckevorsel Hzn.', Parlement.com, available at https://www.parlement.com/id/vg09ll6e63sv/a_abram_van_rijckevorsel [Retrieved 29/04/2022].

'Pincoffs, Lodewijk (1827–1911)', Resources Huygens KNAW, available at http://resources.huygens.knaw.nl/bwn1880-2000/lemmata/bwn1/pincoffs [Retrieved 05/08/2021].

Doortmont, M., 'Gold Coast DataBase: Ghana and the Netherlands: Genealogies, Biographies, Histories', available at https://gcdb.doortmontweb.org/index.php [Retrieved 02/10/2024].

Dreijer, G.P., 'Dutch-African Shipping Dataset (1830–1918)', *DANS Data Station Social Sciences and Humanities*, https://doi.org/10.17026/SS/JFI20J.

Dreijer, G.P. 'Dutch-African Trade Database (1847–1918)', *DANS Data Station Social Sciences and Humanities*, https://doi.org/10.17026/SS/Z84SLW.

The Economist, 'The Hopeless Continent', 13-05-2000, available at https://www.economist.com/weeklyedition/2000-05-13 [Retrieved 18/10/2023].

The Economist, 'The New Scramble for Africa', 07-03-2019, available at https://www.economist.com/leaders/2019/03/07/the-new-scramble-for-africa [Retrieved 18-10-2023].

The Economist, 'Turkey is Making a Big Diplomatic and Corporate Push into Africa', 23-04-2022, available at https://www.economist.com/middle-east-and-africa/2022/04/23/turkey-is-making-a-big-diplomatic-and-corporate-push-into-africa [Retrieved 06/09/2024].

The Economist, 'The Africa Gap', available at https://www.economist.com/special-report/2025-01-11, 01-11-2025 [Retrieved 20/01/2025].

Engelfriet, A., 'Mede dankzij de Rotterdammer Pincoffs kreeg Leopold II zijn privé-kolonie Kongo-Vrijstaat', available at http://www.engelfriet.net/Alie/Hans/congo.htm [Retrieved 09/08/2021].

Ergo, A-B., 'La Compagnie du Kasai', available at http://abergo1.e-monsite.com/medias/files/cie-kasai.pdf [Retrieved 10/08/2021].

Germany Trade & Invest, 'Special: Global Gateway in Afrika', available at https://www.gtai.de/de/trade/afrika/specials/global-gateway-in-afrika-1003740 [Retrieved 30/10/2023].

Groningers in de Congo, available at https://groningersindecongo.jouwweb.nl/elso-dusselje [Retrieved 09/05/2023].

Leger, A.Y., 'Compagnie des caoutchoucs et produits de la Lobay (1899–1910)', available at https://www.entreprises-coloniales.fr/empire/Cie_commerciale_frse.pdf [Retrieved 09/08/2021].

Leger, A.Y., 'Compagnie Agricole du Kouilou (Congo Français) (1900–1905)', available at www.entreprises-coloniales.fr/afrique-equatoriale/Proprietaire_Kouilou-Niari.pdf [Retrieved 11-10-2021].

Leger, A.Y., 'Compagnie Commerciale de Colonisation du Congo français (4CF)', 3, available at https://www.entreprises-coloniales.fr/afrique-equatoriale/CCCCF.pdf [Retrieved 09/05/2023].

Leger, A.Y., Leger, 'Alimaïenne (L')', 10–12, available at https://www.entreprises-coloniales.fr/afrique-equatoriale/L_Alimaienne.pdf [Retrieved 09/05/2023].
Marhisdata, available at https://www.marhisdata.nl/eigenaar&id=31656 [Retrieved 01/01/2024].
Maritiem Museum Rotterdam, available at https://mmr.adlibhosting.com/ais6V50/Details/collect/102359 [Retrieved 10/10/2024].
Mulder, F., 'Holland in de Congo', *HP/De Tijd*, 06-08-2010, available at http://frankmulder.info/2010-08-17/holland-in-de-congo [Retrieved 09/08/2021].
NOS, 'Gemeente Rotterdam biedt excuses aan voor slavernijverleden', https://nos.nl/artikel/2408945-gemeente-rotterdam-biedt-excuses-aan-voor-slavernijverleden [Retrieved 26/10/2022].
De IJzeren eeuw, 'Het geheim van Rotterdam', season 1 episode 6, aired 12-07-2016, available at https://www.npostart.nl/de-ijzeren-eeuw/12-07-2016/VPWON_1262797 [Retrieved 09/08/2021].
Obadare, E., 'A "New Scramble for Africa?"', *Council on Foreign Relations*, 02-05-2023, available at https://www.cfr.org/blog/new-scramble-africa 'Retrieved 18/10/2023].
Petram, L., 'De val van een fraudeur', *Historisch Nieuwsblad*, 4 (2021), 34–40.
Shipafreigt, https://www.shipafreight.com/knowledge-series/largest-ports-in-europe/ [Retrieved 26/10/2022].
Speech Mayor Aboutaleb, available at https://www.youtube.com/watch?time_continue=1&v=RyUt7COdang&feature=emb_logo [Retrieved 26/10/2022].
'Taxonomy of Labour Relations', available at https://datasets.iisg.amsterdam/file.xhtml?fileId=2078&version=2.0 [Retrieved 13/06/2022].
Toen te zien, 'ca. 1880 Kru and "Krumanos"', available at http://www.toen-tezien.nl/musea/ca-1880-kru-and-krumanos/ [Retrieved 09/08/2021].
Toen te zien, '1857–1868 Kerdijk & Pincoffs', available at http://www.toen-tezien.nl/musea/1857-1868-kerdijk-pincoffs/ [Retrieved 09/08/2021].
Quadackers, L., 'Pincoffs: van miljonair tot sigarenboer', *Accountant*, 3 (2015), 40–47, available at https://www.accountant.nl/magazines/accountant-2015-q3/pincoffs-van-miljonair-tot-sigarenboer/# [Retrieved 09/08/2021].
Van Walraven, K., 'Spirits and Love under the Mango Trees: Dutch-Congolese Heritage at a Cemetery in Brazzaville', available at https://www.ascleiden.nl/content/ascl-blogs/klaas-van-walraven/spirits-and-love-under-mango-trees-dutch-congolese-heritage [Retrieved 09/08/2021].
Wilschut, M., 'Het Congo-avontuur van Stanley en Leopold', *Historisch Nieuwsblad*, 1 (2004), 28–32.

Index[1]

A

Aarts, Willem, 124

Afrikaansche Handels-Vereeniging (AHV), 2, 24, 28, 47, 98, 99, 119, 121, 122, 125–131, 128n135, 133–137, 137n192, 139, 141–143, 150–152, 155, 157–160, 162, 163, 186, 187

Alcohol, 40, 68, 110, 123, 127, 156, 173, 180, 216–218, 228, 251

Algeria, 42

Ambrisette, Angola, 163, 166

Ambriz, Angola, 123, 124, 133

Anglo-Belgian Indian Rubber Company (ABIR), 70, 89–91, 197, 199, 238, 241, 242, 244, 246

Anglo-Dutch Gold Coast Treaty (1867), 117

Anglo-Dutch Treaties (1871–1872), 59

Anglo-Portuguese Treaty (1884), 55, 58

Angola, 6, 27, 28, 36, 38, 43, 48, 55, 58, 80, 87, 92–94, 100, 125, 126, 133, 134, 149, 162, 163, 165–167, 170, 173, 174, 185–187, 192, 194–197, 215, 216, 223, 228, 246

Antwerp, 15, 16, 71, 122

Anversoise, 70, 89, 91, 197, 238, 241, 242, 244, 246

Arabs, 41, 41n46, 66, 169, 176, 233, 241, 263

Arms, 68, 110, 127, 156, 173, 216, 228

Asia, 37, 38, 43, 55, 56, 80, 81, 88, 147, 261

Association Internationale Africaine (AIA), 47, 135, 136

Association Internationale du Congo (AIC), 47, 48, 58–61, 136, 151

[1] Note: Page numbers followed by 'n' refer to notes.

G. Dreijer, *Private Entrepreneurship and European Imperialism*, Palgrave Studies in Economic History, https://doi.org/10.1007/978-3-032-01086-5

B
Bakker, Wigbold, 156
Banana, 64, 124, 125, 128–130, 162, 166–168, 170–174, 176, 186, 239, 248, 250–252
Barends, Jan Hendrik, 103
Belgian Congo, 12, 28, 82, 83, 191, 245, 247, 248, 256n176, 259
Belgium, 16, 25, 38, 56, 60, 62, 66, 73, 77, 78, 95, 103, 183, 221
Benguela, 195, 196
Berlin, 50, 53, 54, 56, 57, 60, 61, 65, 66, 71, 91, 95, 167, 170, 171, 211, 263
Berlin Conference (1884–1885), 12, 25, 28, 33, 34, 49–61, 63, 66, 70, 85, 95, 114, 151, 162, 165–167, 171
Black Dutchmen (*Belanda Hitam*), 103
Boma, 44, 63, 64, 69, 71, 239, 244, 245, 248
Bordeaux, 221
Bouman & Van Rijckevorsel, 109
Brazil, 36, 100
Brazzaville, 64, 122, 169, 173, 175, 176, 179, 201, 250
British Congo Company, 167
British South Africa Company (BSAC), 86
Brussels Anti-Slavery Conference (1889–1890), 66, 67, 156, 170, 171, 173–175, 183
Brussels Geographic Conference (1876), 46–48, 135
Business history, 4, 13, 14, 14n45, 19–24

C
Cabaret, Paul, 203
Cabinda, 61, 165, 166, 172, 173
Cabindas, 129, 130
Cameroon, 49, 56, 201, 211
Cape Colony, *see* South Africa
Capital investment, 81, 82, 88, 92, 191, 193, 202
Capitas, 126, 194, 234, 239, 241, 245, 251, 253, 256
Casement, Roger, 72, 244
Chamber of Commerce, Manchester, 55, 135
Chamber of Commerce, Rotterdam, 23, 105
Cheeseman, John, 124
China, 15, 22, 46, 55, 265
Cokwe, 228, 239, 240, 252
Colonial legacy, 2, 8
Comité d'Études du Haut-Congo (CEHC), 44, 47, 136, 159
Comité Special du Katanga, 91, 197
Compagnie Agricole du Kouilou, 212, 214
Compagnie Commerciale de Colonisation du Congo français (CCCCF), 203, 206, 207, 209–212, 223
Compagnie de L'Ouhamé et Nana, 203
Compagnie du Bruxelles pour le commerce du Haut Congo (La Bruxelloise), 199, 200, 247
Compagnie du Kasaï (CdK), 25, 28, 29, 85, 91, 92, 192, 197, 223, 227, 264, 273
Compagnie du Katanga, 91
Compagnie du Lobaye, 212n95, 250
Compagnie du Lomami, 84
Compagnie Française du Haut-Congo, 213
Companhia de Diamantes de Angola (Diamang), 94
Companhia de Moçambique (Mozambique Company), 94
Companhia do Niassa (Nyassa Company), 94

Companhia dos Mercantes del Norte, 125
Companhia Portugueze do Zaïre, 166, 168
Concession companies, 13, 27n106, 28, 70, 71, 77, 79n201, 82, 85–92, 94, 95, 161n46, 162, 188, 191–224, 234, 242, 248, 261, 262
Congo-Arab War (1892–1894), 68, 68n165, 173, 177, 185
Congo Free State, 12, 25, 28, 34, 53, 60–80, 79n201, 82–85, 87, 89–92, 95, 132, 133, 151, 162, 163, 167–179, 183–186, 188, 191, 192, 194, 196–201, 206, 211, 215, 216, 221, 223, 227, 228, 231, 232, 234–242, 244–246, 248, 249, 254, 255, 259, 260, 263–265, 268
Congo Reform Association (CRA), 74, 246
Congo river, 44, 46–48, 55, 58, 60, 64, 68, 119, 122, 125, 129, 130, 133, 136, 162, 167, 173, 194, 196, 199, 250
Corradores, 126, 133, 234, 241
Cotton, 35, 37, 101, 180, 217, 218, 251
Crown Domain, 69, 70, 90, 91, 176, 197, 199, 234
Cultivation System (*Cultuurstelsel*), 46, 46n72, 135
C. Woermann, 154

D
Daendels, Herman Willem, 102, 154
Dahomey, 42
Daumas Béraud & Cie, 125, 164, 167, 170, 171, 174, 175, 231
De Brazza, Pierre Savorgnan, 44–46, 92
De Carvalho, Francisco Ribeiro, 196
De Winton, Francis, 63
De Nederlandsche Bank (DNB), 138, 157–159
Denmark, 56
De Vries & Co, 104
Dupuy-Dutemps (French Investor), 203
Dutch, 1–4, 11–14, 16, 17, 19, 21, 25, 26, 27n108, 32, 33, 35, 41, 58–61, 85, 88, 92, 95, 97–188, 191–224, 227, 259–264, 266–268, 271–274
Dutch East Indies, 10, 12, 16, 17, 37, 59–60, 100–105, 108, 111, 113–116, 119, 132, 146–149, 154–156, 163, 181, 183, 217, 220, 221, 261
Dutch Gold Coast, 59, 97, 100, 102, 103, 107, 108, 117, 118, 149
Dutch imperialism, 10, 12

E
East Africa, 33, 35, 38, 40, 41n46, 44, 48, 169, 217n114
Economic imperialism, 19
Egypt, 7, 42, 48, 50, 56, 57, 82, 101
Elder Dempster, 71
Elmina, 17, 41, 97–104, 107–110, 112, 114, 114n67, 117, 118, 123, 144, 149, 154, 156, 180, 262
Entrepreneurship, 4–14, 19–24, 105, 143–149, 152, 180–187, 191–224, 227, 228, 253–255, 261, 272
Eritrea, 85
Ethiopia, 6, 86

F
Fashoda, South Sudan, 86, 151

Fernado Po, 43
First World War, 12, 27, 28, 33, 34, 39, 78, 82, 193, 207, 209, 212, 214, 220, 221, 245, 247, 255, 259, 260, 262
Flachon, Victor, 201, 203, 206, 207, 209, 213
Flament (French Investor), 203
Fontaine de la Verwey, Oscar, 162, 166, 170, 172
Force Publique, 63, 65, 68, 69, 77, 233, 239–242
Forminière, 91, 247
France, 2, 10, 35, 38, 39, 42, 48, 50, 54–56, 59, 61, 74, 86, 87, 201, 207, 209, 221, 262
Franco-German Treaty (1911–1912), 87n228, 92, 210, 224
Fraud of Lodewijk Pincoffs, 115, 121, 122, 136, 139–141, 150, 186
Free trade, 19, 41, 57–60, 66, 70, 80, 112, 114, 132, 134, 148, 149, 167, 178, 179, 192, 235, 263
French Congo, 27n106, 28, 46, 72, 92, 93, 95, 151, 167, 169, 173–175, 179, 185, 191, 192, 194, 196, 197, 200–216, 221, 223, 250, 252, 254, 260, 263, 264
French West Africa, 86
Fuchs, Félix, 248
Futila, Cabinda, 165, 166

G
Gabon, 46, 56, 201, 214, 215
Genocide, Congo Free State, 78, 79
Genocide, Namibia, 87
Gentlemanly capitalism, 19–24
Gericke van Herwijnen, Baron, 61, 61n135, 167, 168, 170, 171, 174, 175
German East Africa, 56
German South West-Africa, 56
Germany, 2, 16, 32, 41, 44, 48, 54–56, 59, 60, 74, 77, 87, 87n228, 92, 119, 137, 210
Gold Coast, 12, 41, 42, 49, 57, 86, 97–110, 114n67, 117, 118, 131, 132, 148, 149
Great Britain, 38, 39, 56, 81
Greshoff, Anton, 161, 162, 168, 169, 172, 174–179, 185, 186, 199, 201, 203, 206, 207, 216, 235, 237, 239, 248, 250, 254, 263
Groen (NAHV Agent), 238, 239
Guinard, Arthur, 203, 209
Guinea Coast, 108n41, 114n67, 153
Gum, 184, 185, 205, 207, 219
Guns, 40, 69, 234, 242

H
Hamburg, 15, 41, 144, 154, 211, 262
Handels-Compagnie Mozambique (HCM), 27, 152
Hatton & Cookson, 47, 125, 128, 128n135, 131, 135, 167
Herklots & Bouman, 109
Hoboken & Co, 104
Hobson, John A., 7, 19, 32n4
Holland-Amerika Lijn (HAL), 139
Hutton, James, 158, 171

I
Ibanche, Congo, 178, 227, 231, 232, 238–240, 248–256
Imperialism, 3–14, 14n45, 19, 28, 31–39, 32n4, 46, 48, 50, 68, 78, 80, 85, 86, 99, 187, 191, 193, 224, 232, 241, 260, 261, 268, 273, 274
Infrastructure, 2, 16, 18, 23, 33, 38, 80, 85, 101, 102, 105, 119, 120,

140, 141, 158, 159, 195, 266, 272
International law, 53, 54, 57
Italy, 56, 85, 86
Ivory, 65, 68, 69, 91, 104, 124, 126, 163, 169, 170, 172, 173, 176–178, 185, 204, 206, 207, 209, 213, 214, 216, 219, 234, 236, 237n54, 241, 250, 263

J
Janssens, Camille, 63
Japan, 114
Java, 59, 114, 116, 135
Jewish, 119, 121, 123, 157, 157n29
Johannes Boelen & Co, 103

K
Kasaï, 91, 172, 173, 176–178, 187, 192, 197, 221, 227–235, 235n49, 237–240, 237n54, 244, 246–250, 252–256, 256n176, 263
Kasaï river, 229, 237, 248
Katanga, 80, 91, 197
Kerdijk, Henry, 1, 119, 121, 122, 139, 140, 157
Kerdijk, Lodewijk, 122–126, 128–130
Kinsasha, *see* Leopoldville
Kongo Kingdom, 125, 194
Koninklijk Nederlands Indisch Leger (KNIL), 103
Koto Mboke, Kuba King, 232, 233
Kraus, Maurice Charles, 253
Kruboys, 129, 130
Krumanos, 128–130, 164
Kuba, 228, 232, 233, 239–243, 246, 247, 250–253, 255, 256
Kuba Revolt (1904–1905), 240, 243, 252

L
La Brazzaville, 201, 203–206, 210, 212–214
Lado Enclave, 68, 68n166
Lagos, 42, 49
Lake Malawi, 58
Lavigerie, Charles (Cardinal), 65
Legitimate commerce, 5, 27, 34–40, 80, 95, 98, 103, 119, 194, 260–262
Le Havre, 222
Leopold II, King of Belgium, 2, 34, 44, 46, 51, 55, 66, 71–73, 75, 76, 89, 132, 135, 150, 151, 183, 192, 263, 268
Leopoldville, 64, 178
Liberalism, 35
Liberia, 6, 27, 43, 98, 99, 114–118, 114n67, 129, 143, 148–150, 153–156, 159, 180, 186, 187, 191–194, 197, 215, 216, 223, 260, 262, 263, 273
Lindeteves N.V., 260
Lisbon, 25, 94, 135, 164, 166, 175
Liverpool, 15, 41, 121, 128, 262
Livingstone, David, 43, 44
London, 15, 19, 35, 41, 43, 135, 139, 140, 149, 171, 245
Long Depression, 37–39, 37n26
Lothaire, Hubert, 69
Luanda, Angola, 100, 124, 125, 173, 195, 234
Luba, 228, 231, 232, 234, 240, 242, 245, 246, 252, 256
Lunda, 228, 252

M
Macao, 114
Maculla, Angola, 163–165
Mainard, Louis, 203

Manchester, 6n12, 9n25, 15, 41, 119, 122, 123, 128, 135, 149
Marseille, 6n11, 15, 15n48, 262
Mees, Marten, 17, 18n64, 23, 137–139, 137n193, 150, 155, 157, 158, 203
Mees & Zoonen, 18n64, 92n259, 121, 138, 157, 203
Messageries Fluviales du Congo, 206
Meuse River, 120
Mineral, 36, 37, 48, 89, 91, 94, 247, 265, 266
Morel, Edmund Dene, 71, 74, 95, 242–246, 256, 268
Moroccan Crisis, First (1905–1906), 87
Moroccan Crisis, Second (1911), 87
Morocco, 87
Morrison, William, 232, 233, 243–245
Mozambique, 6, 6n12, 27, 43, 48, 55, 58, 80, 92–94, 98n2, 101, 134, 156, 192–194, 196
Muller, Abram, 154–156
Muller & Co, 98, 114–116, 118, 119, 143, 150, 152–157, 159, 186, 187, 192, 193
Muller, H.P.N., 156
Muller Szn., Hendrik, 11, 11n30, 17, 23, 98, 101, 111–116, 118, 119, 148, 149, 152–160, 165, 167, 186, 193
Municipal Council, Rotterdam, 105, 112, 119, 273

N
Naber d'Honoré, Samuel Pierre, 166
Nagtglas, Cornelis, 102
Nederlands Afrikaans Comité, 136
Nederlandse Handel-Maatschappij (NHM), 98, 101, 105, 146, 148, 159
Nederlands-Indische Gasmaatschappij, 119
The Netherlands, 2, 10n29, 15, 18n66, 24, 27n108, 35, 38, 47, 56, 57, 60–61, 66, 97–98, 100, 102, 103, 105, 107, 114, 117n78, 118, 119, 121, 131, 132n163, 134, 135n176, 139, 144–147, 154, 162, 163, 165, 171, 180–183, 217, 259, 262, 266, 271, 272, 274
Neukamerun, 209–211, 224, 259, 264
New Entrepreneurial History, 22, 23
New Scramble for Africa, 264, 265, 268
Niederfüllbacher Stiftung, 77
Nieuwe Afrikaansche Handels-Vennootschap (NAHV), 2, 24, 59, 101, 151, 191, 227, 260, 264
Nieuwe Waterweg, 16
Niger River, 58, 109
North Africa, 42, 48
Nyassa Company, 94

O
Oost-Afrikaansche Compagnie (OAC), 11n30, 27, 152, 186, 192–194, 197, 215, 260
Ottoman Empire, 56, 57

P
Pacific, 56
Padang (Sumatra), 111
Palm nut kernels, 35, 127, 180, 181, 217, 219
Palm oil, 5, 5n10, 6n11, 35–38, 38n31, 40–43, 47, 81, 103–105, 108–110, 115, 119, 124, 126–128, 131, 143–150, 144n203, 154, 155, 159, 163,

169, 172, 180–183, 187, 193, 207, 213, 215–217, 219, 234, 247, 254, 262, 268
Pape, Andries, 133, 134
Paris, 6n12, 13n38, 92, 201, 206, 207, 214, 216, 263
Parliament, Belgium, 62
Parliament, Great Britain, 244
Parliament, The Netherlands, 23, 105, 119, 170
Partition of Africa, 4, 8n22, 10n29, 28, 31, 32, 48, 50, 79, 94, 95, 132n163, 149, 151–188, 259, 262, 263, 268
Peanuts, 35, 124, 127, 180, 181, 217, 219
Philippi, Georges, 161, 161n46, 200, 201, 203, 209, 211, 212, 237–239, 253, 254
Pincoffs & Kerdijk, 11n30, 137, 144n203
Pincoffs, Lodewijk, 1, 3, 11n30, 17, 17n63, 24, 47, 99, 119, 120, 122n97, 140, 141, 272
Port city, 2, 12, 14–19, 120, 262, 266, 268, 272, 274
Porto Novo, Benin, 42, 49
Principle of effective occupation, 57, 60

Q
Queriol, Nuno de Freitas, 196, 196n24
Quisembo, Angola, 124, 165

R
Railways, 16, 27n108, 38, 81, 82, 101, 120, 195, 196, 217n114
Red rubber scandals, 74, 82, 83, 91, 95, 206, 223, 227, 228, 242, 246, 254, 256, 263, 265, 267, 268, 273
Reepmaker, J.C., 158
Régis, 42, 47, 125, 128, 144
Rhodes, Cecil, 19, 80, 82, 86, 91, 197
Rotterdam, 1, 15–19, 41, 98, 155, 203, 249, 260, 271
Rotterdamsche Bank, 139
Rotterdamsche Handels-Vereeniging (RHV), 119–121, 140, 158, 159
Royal Niger Company, 88, 109n50
Rubber, 28, 35, 37, 66, 70, 89, 91, 94, 177, 178, 185n158, 187, 193, 194, 199, 204–207, 213, 214, 216, 219–222, 228, 229, 231, 234–236, 239–241, 243–248, 250, 251, 254, 256
Ruys, Willem, 158

S
Samsom, Leopold, 122–124
Sanford Exploring Expedition (SEE), 231, 254
São Tomé & Principe, 6
Schalkwijk, Willem C., 158–160, 160n45, 171, 172n110, 174, 186
Scheepvaartsenquête (1877), 148
Schut, Albert, 126
Scramble for Africa, 1, 2, 2n2, 4, 6n12, 10, 11, 24, 27, 28, 31–33, 40, 79–85, 94, 95, 97–151, 223, 262, 264–266, 268
Second South African War (1899–1902), 87
Senate, The Netherlands, 105, 118, 119, 273
Senegal, 42, 49, 86
Sheppard, William Henry, 232, 233, 243–245
Shipping lines, 71, 158
Sierra Leone, 49, 129, 154

Slavery, 2, 8, 14n45, 15, 16, 18, 35, 40, 57, 65, 66, 68, 71, 99, 100, 128, 129, 172, 195, 271, 272, 272n4, 274
Slave trade, 5, 5n9, 6n11, 15, 28, 33, 35, 36, 39–41, 57, 65, 66, 68, 71, 80, 95, 97, 100–103, 109, 127–129, 127n132, 132, 149, 166, 168, 169, 171–173, 176, 183, 194, 233, 234, 238, 240, 241, 244, 246, 251, 261, 271, 272, 274
Société Anonyme de Belge (SAB), 85, 92, 171, 171n106, 175, 178, 202, 231, 234–237, 243, 248, 254, 255
Société de l'Alimaïenne, 213
Société du Haut-Ogoou, 213
Société Générale, 94, 199, 206
Société Générale de Procédes d'Extraction du Caoutchouc, 199, 206
Somalia, 86
South Africa, 5, 6n11, 12n34, 13n40, 38, 41, 49, 81, 82, 100, 101, 247
Stamverwantschap, 12
Stanley Falls, 64, 65
Stanley, Henry Morton, 43–47, 44n62, 65, 71, 130, 136, 162, 168, 172, 173n116, 176, 179
Stanley Pool, 64, 65
Steamship, 36, 80
Stokes Affair, 69, 69n172, 71, 177
Stokes, Charles, 69, 144n202
Stoomvaart op Amerika (American Steamline Service), 158
Strauch, Maximilien, 61n135, 62
Sudan, 14n44, 42, 48
Suez Canal, 37, 42, 146–149
Sultanate du Haut Oubangui, 204
Sumatra, 59, 97, 111, 118
Suriname, 2, 16, 101, 108, 118, 271, 272

T

Tariffs, 13n38, 14n44, 19, 38, 39, 61, 63, 68, 108, 125, 131, 134, 156, 167, 168, 171, 173–175, 179, 183, 185, 186, 195, 196, 199, 214
Thesiger, Wilfred, 244, 256
Thys, Albert, 195, 231, 243, 255
Tippu Tip (Hamid bon Mohammed el Moerjebi), 65, 66, 68, 69, 169, 185, 263
Togo, 49, 56
Trakanen & Co, 104
Twain, Mark, 74
Twentsche Bank, 260

U

Union Minière du Haut-Katanga, 91
United States (US), 37, 38, 56, 60, 66, 74, 81, 82, 121, 121n93, 221, 265

V

Van der Eb, Anthony, 102–104, 107–109, 107n34, 107n35, 149
Van der Most, Leendert, 162, 195
Van Eetvelde, Edmond, 62, 167, 170
Van Lauteren (CdK Agent), 252, 253
Van Neuss, Hubert, 62
Van Obbergen (NAHV Agent), 252, 253, 256
Van Rijckevorsel, Abram, 17n61, 23, 105, 107, 111, 112, 115, 119, 132

Van Rijckevorsel & Co (Amsterdam), 110n53, 119
Van Rijckevorsel & Zoonen, 98, 107–109, 111, 112, 114, 115, 119, 121, 123, 143
Van Rijckevorsel, Huibert, 17, 17n61, 24n95, 98, 105–111, 114, 114n67, 272
Van Rijckevorsel, Marie Cornelie, 111
Vandervelde, Emile, 245
Vermeulen, Alfons, 25, 25–26n102, 212n95, 228, 248–252, 254, 255
Vermeulen, Cornelis W., 139, 140
Von Bismarck, Otto, 50, 55, 56
Von der Heydt & Co, 212
Von Wissmann, Herman, 229

W
West Africa, 2, 5, 5n9, 6n11, 11n30, 12n34, 15, 18, 19, 21, 27, 31, 33–36, 39–42, 49, 56, 60, 61, 81, 82, 97–101, 103, 103n17, 105, 107, 109, 110n53, 111, 114, 116, 122, 123, 132, 144–146, 144n203, 148–152, 154, 163, 180–183, 188, 191, 193, 211, 216–218, 220, 260–263, 268, 273
West Central Africa, 2, 15, 18, 19, 21, 27, 31, 34, 35, 81, 82, 97–99, 101, 122, 132, 136, 144, 144n203, 146, 149–152, 163, 180, 187, 188, 191, 193, 214, 260–264, 268, 273

Z
Zambia, 58
Zwier van Sandinck, Otto, 129, 129n138, 163

FSC
www.fsc.org
MIX
Papier | Fördert
gute Waldnutzung
FSC® C083411

Kolibri 360 GmbH
Ferdinand-Jühlke-Straße 7
99095 Erfurt, Deutschland
produktsicherheit@kolibri360.de